HELLENISTIC CULTURE AND SOCIETY

General Editors: Anthony W. Bulloch, Erich S. Gruen,
A. A. Long, and Andrew F. Stewart

I. *Alexander to Actium: The Historical Evolution of the Hellenistic Age*, by Peter Green

II. *Hellenism in the East: The Interaction of Greek and Non-Greek Civilizations from Syria to Central Asia after Alexander*, edited by Amélie Kuhrt and Susan Sherwin-White

III. *The Question of "Eclecticism": Studies in Later Greek Philosophy*, edited by J. M. Dillon and A. A. Long

IV. *Antigonus the One-Eyed and the Creation of the Hellenistic State*, by Richard A. Billows

V. *A History of Macedonia*, by R. Malcolm Errington, translated by Catherine Errington

VI. *Attic Letter-Cutters of 229 to 86 B.C.*, by Stephen V. Tracy

VII. *The Vanished Library: A Wonder of the Ancient World*, by Luciano Canfora

VIII. *Hellenistic Philosophy of Mind*, by Julia Annas

IX. *Hellenistic Culture and History*, edited by Peter Green

X. *The Best of the Argonauts: The Redefinition of the Epic Hero in Book 1 of Apollonius's Argonautica*, by James J. Clauss

XI. *Faces of Power: Alexander's Image and Hellenistic Politics*, by Andrew Stewart

XII. *Images and Ideologies: Self-definition in the Hellenistic World*, edited by A. W. Bulloch, E. S. Gruen, A. A. Long, and A. Stewart

XIII. *From Samarkhand to Sardis: A New Approach to the Seleucid Empire*, by Susan Sherwin-White and Amélie Kuhrt

XIV. *Regionalism and Change in the Economy of Independent Delos, 314–67 B.C.*, by Gary Reger

XV. *Hegemony to Empire: The Development of the Roman Imperium in the East from 148 to 62 B.C.,* by Robert Kallet-Marx

XVI. *Moral Vision in the Histories of Polybius,* by Arthur M. Eckstein

XVII. *The Hellenistic Settlements in Europe, the Islands, and Asia Minor,* by Getzel M. Cohen

XVIII. *Interstate Arbitrations in the Greek World, 337–90 B.C.,* by Sheila L. Ager

XIX. *Theocritus's Urban Mimes: Mobility, Gender, and Patronage,* by Joan B. Burton

XX. *Athenian Democracy in Transition: Attic Letter-Cutters of 340 to 290 B.C.,* by Stephen V. Tracy

XXI. *Pseudo-Hecataeus, On the Jews: Legitimizing the Jewish Diaspora,* by Bezalel Bar-Kochva

XXII. *Asylia: Territorial Inviolability in the Hellenistic Period,* by Kent J. Rigsby

XXIII. *The Cynics: The Cynic Movement in Antiquity and Its Legacy,* R. Bracht Branham and Marie-Odile Goulet-Cazé, editors

XXIV. *The Politics of Plunder: Aitolians and Their* k oinon *in the Early Hellenistic Era, 279–217 B.C.,* by Joseph B. Scholten

XXV. The Argonautika *by Apollonios Rhodios,* translated, with introduction, commentary, and glossary, by Peter Green

XXVI. *Hellenistic Constructs: Culture, History, and Historiography,* edited by Paul Cartledge

XXVII. *Josephus' Interpretation of the Bible,* by Louis H. Feldman

Pseudo-Hecataeus, *On the Jews*

Pseudo-Hecataeus
On the Jews
Legitimizing the Jewish Diaspora

BEZALEL BAR-KOCHVA

University of California Press

BERKELEY   LOS ANGELES   LONDON

University of California Press
Berkeley and Los Angeles, California

University of California Press, Ltd.
London, England

© 1996 by
The Regents of the University of California

Library of Congress Cataloging-in-Publication Data

Bar-Kochva, Bezalel
    Pseudo-Hecataeus, On the Jews : legitimizing the Jewish diaspora /
    Bezalel Bar-Kochva
        p.   cm. — (Hellenistic culture and society : 21)
    Includes bibliographical references and index.
    ISBN 0-520-20059-4 (alk. paper)
        1. Jews—History—to 70 A.D.—Historiography.   2. Greek
    literature—Jewish authors—History and criticism.   3. Josephus,
    Flavius. Contra Apionem.   I. Title. II. Series.
    DS115.5.B36   1996   95-20939
    930'.04924'0072–dc20   CIP

Printed in the United States of America
9 8 7 6 5 4 3 2 1

IN MEMORIAM MATRIS
DINAH FREIDENREICH BAR-KOCHVA (1908–1981)

Contents

Illustrations   ix

Acknowledgments   xi

INTRODUCTION   1

I   HECATAEUS, HIS WORK, AND THE JEWISH
    EXCURSUS   7

    1. The Man, the Ethnographic Genre, and
       Hecataeus's Egyptian Ethnography 7
    2. The Jewish Excursus 18

II THE PASSAGES IN *AGAINST APION*:
    TEXT AND TRANSLATION   44

III THE QUESTION OF AUTHENTICITY   54

    1. Mosollamus the Jew and Bird Omens 57
    2. Ptolemy I and the Jews 71
    3. Hezekiah the High Priest 82
    4. Religious Persecutions and Martyrdom 91
    5. The Destruction of Pagan Temples
       and Altars 97
    6. Jewish Emigration to Phoenicia 101
    7. "Many Fortresses of the Jews" 105
    8. The Geography of Judea and Jerusalem 107
    9. The Annexation of Samaria to Judea by
       Alexander 113

IV DATE OF COMPOSITION 122

1. The Anachronistic References 122
2. *Terminus ante Quem* 137
3. Pseudo-Aristeas and Pseudo-Hecataeus 139

V THE AUTHOR: ORIGIN, EDUCATION, AND
RELIGIOUS GROUP 143

1. Descent and Provenance 143
2. Greek Education 148
3. Jewish Education 159
4. The Religious Division of Egyptian Jewry and
the Author's Affiliation 168

VI THE FRAMEWORK, LITERARY GENRE,
STRUCTURE, AND CONTENTS 182

1. Monograph or Excursus? 182
2. The Title of the Treatise and the Literary
Genre 187
3. The Structure of an Ethnographical Work 191
4. The Structure of *On the Jews*: The Place and
Role of the Hezekiah Story 219

VII THE PURPOSE OF THE BOOK 232

CONCLUSION 249

Appendix A: The Hezekiah Coins, with A. Kindler 255
Appendix B: The Dating of Pseudo-Aristeas 271
Extended Notes 289
Chronological Table 303
Plates 309
Abbreviations 319
References 321
Index of Names and Subjects 363
Index of Greek Terms in Transcription 375
Index Locorum 377

Illustrations

MAPS

1. Phoenicia, the coastal plain, and the regions of
   the interior in the Hellenistic period   102

2. Jerusalem in the period of the Second Temple   111

3. Southern Samaria and the three districts in
   the time of Jonathan   118

4. Jewish fortresses in the time of Simeon   124

5. The Hasmonean expansion   126

PLATES

I. The Hezekiah coins, first group   311

II. The Hezekiah coins, second group   313

III. The Ptolemaic Yehud coins   315

IV. Berenice on the Ptolemaic Yehud coins   317

Acknowledgments

My work on Pseudo-Hecataeus started in the early 1980s as part of a research project on the Jews in Hellenistic literature. The work on the project was facilitated in the years 1981–83 by a fellowship from the Alexander von Humboldt Foundation. Professors Martin Hengel and Wolfgang Schuller, my hosts at the universities of Tübingen and Constance, did everything to provide me with comfortable conditions, and continued to show interest in the progress of my project during the following years. I extend to both my warm thanks. I would also like to thank the Dorot Foundation, New York, and particularly Professor Philip Mayerson of New York University, for financial assistance in the preparation of the manuscript of this book.

Returning to Pseudo-Hecataeus in the last few years, I have incurred pleasant debts to friends and colleagues. I have consulted a number of them about various points: Professors Raphael Freundlich and Ran Zadok of Tel Aviv University; Professor Uriel Rappaport of Haifa University; Professors Adelheid Mette and Bernard Zimmerman of the universities of Münster and Zurich; and especially Professor Louis H. Feldman of Yeshiva University, New York. Mrs. Brigitte Pimpl, of Ratisbonne Institute in Jerusalem, invested much time and effort in editing the bibliography. Professors Doron Mendels and Daniel R. Schwartz of the Hebrew University, Jerusalem, were kind enough to read major parts of the book and comment on them. Dr. Arieh Kindler, director of the Kadman Numismatic Museum in Tel Aviv, is the coauthor of Appendix A. I have benefited from the constructive criticism of Professor Erich S. Gruen, coeditor of the series in which this book appears, and of the anonymous referees for the University of

California Press, who contributed to the improvement of the structure of the book. My thanks go to Mary Lamprech, sponsoring editor for Classics at the University of California Press, and to Paul Psoinos, the copyeditor of this book, for seeing it through to publication with such conscientious devotion and cooperation. I had the good fortune to be able to discuss many a problem with Professor John Glucker of Tel Aviv University, and to gain substantially from his profound, comprehensive knowledge. Finally, my deepest gratitude is due to Mr. Ivor Ludlam of Tel Aviv University, who read thoroughly the whole manuscript more than once and contributed considerably to its improvement.

B.B.
Tel Aviv University
April 1994

Introduction

The subject of this study is the treatise *On the Jews* ascribed to Hecataeus of Abdera, the great ethnographer of the early Hellenistic age. The treatise itself has not survived. All we have are a number of fragments and testimonia in Josephus's celebrated apologetic book *Against Apion* (I.183–204, II.43). All the passages but one appear in the context of Josephus's polemic against anti-Jewish authors of the Roman period, who argued that the Jews were not mentioned by Greek historians and that they were "newcomers" to the society of nations (*Ap.* I.2–5). The material was selected by Josephus to prove, on the contrary, that early Hellenistic authors had in fact referred to and even admired the Jews and their religion. He was also trying to show that the Jewish people had already flourished at least as early as the time of Alexander and the Successors (I.185).

Josephus seems to have believed sincerely that the passages he quotes or summarizes were written by Hecataeus. He repeatedly states that he is citing Hecataeus. In two places he explicitly mentions the latter's book on the Jews (I.183, 205), and once he even advises his readers to consult the book for further information, saying that it is "readily available" (I.205). The existence of the treatise was mentioned by Herennius Philo (Origen, *C. Cels.* I.15), a pagan author of the second century A.D., who seems to have been directly acquainted with it.[1]

The surviving material describes the history and main characteristics of the Jews. The passages open with a report of a voluntary migration to Egypt of many Jews, led by Hezekiah the High Priest (186–89). This

---

1. On this question, see the discussion, p. 185 below.

is followed by passages referring to three subjects—(a) religion: the Jews' loyalty and devotion to their religion, their readiness to sacrifice themselves for their faith, and their intolerance toward pagan cults in their country (190–93); (b) the Jewish land and Jerusalem: demographic, military, political, administrative, and geographic information (194–97); (c) the Temple: its location, defense, and construction, sacred objects, and cult (198–99). Josephus closes the quotations with a poignant anecdote about an Egyptian Jewish soldier named Mosollamus and bird omens, which illustrates Jewish disdain for gentile divination (201–4). There is also an abbreviated sentence from *On the Jews* in Book II of *Against Apion* (II.43) stating that Alexander annexed the region of Samaria to Judea.[2]

An enthusiastic tone permeates almost every paragraph of the excerpts and paraphrases. The individual Jews mentioned are wise and competent in various activities (I.187, 201); the Jews of Judea and Egypt are said to have been greatly favored by Alexander and Ptolemy I, and to have enjoyed special rewards (I.186, 189; II.43); the Jews demonstrated supreme courage, endurance, and loyalty in the face of "tortures and horrible deaths" at the hands of the Persians, who tried to force them to renounce their faith (I.191); their country is beautiful and most fertile (I.195); the city of Jerusalem excels in splendor and is well fortified, large, and populous (I.196–97); the Jewish Temple is without any material representation of the divine or anything that might be interpreted as such (I.199); the priests maintain absolute purity and sobriety (I.199). The author even goes so far as to state that the Jews deserved to be admired for destroying pagan altars and temples (I.193). He further recounts with obvious delight how the clever Jew Mosollamus once made a public mockery of gentile principles and practices of divination (I.200–204). The passages neither criticize nor express reservations about the Jewish way of life and religious convictions. The author is evidently convinced of their superiority and perfection.

The treatise *On the Jews* was not the only monograph on Jewish issues ascribed to Hecataeus of Abdera. Josephus once mentions such a book entitled *On Abraham* (*Ant.* I.159). Several lines preserved from this book (Clement, *Strom.* V.14.113) contain verses pronouncing

---

2. See pp. 114–15 on the origin of this paragraph in the book *On the Jews*.

strong monotheistic and antipagan convictions. The author claims to quote them from Sophocles. They are, of course, nowhere to be found in Sophocles' extant works, and seem typically Jewish. It has therefore been universally accepted that the book *On Abraham* is a Jewish forgery.[3] So in at least one case a Jew evidently tried to promote his ideas and lend them authority and prestige by attributing his work to Hecataeus of Abdera. Hecataeus's reputation and influence, and the famous account of the Jews included in his Egyptian ethnography, could well have tempted Jewish authors to use his name for their pseudonymous compositions.

Hecataeus of Abdera was the leading Alexandrian literary figure at the beginning of the Hellenistic period, and served in the court of Ptolemy I. Of his indisputably authentic writings, we are acquainted only with his monumental ethnography of the Egyptians and the utopian book *On the Hyperboreans*. The first work set an example for later Hellenistic ethnographers. It has been preserved in an abridged paraphrase by Diodorus Siculus in Book I of his *Historical Library*.

Hecataeus incorporated into his Egyptian ethnography an excursus on the Jews. The excursus was recorded in another book of Diodorus's historical work (XL.3.1–8). Diodorus explicitly stated that he had drawn on Hecataeus (3.8), and this has rightly been accepted as true. This version of Jewish history and practices was well known in antiquity, but there is no trace of the treatise *On the Jews* in the gentile literary tradition, except for the reference to it by Philo of Byblos. In the excursus, the attitude toward the Jews is not particularly enthusiastic and even includes one major reservation, characterizing the Jewish way of life as "unsocial to a certain extent, and hostile to strangers" (3.4).[4]

The evident difference in general tone between the excursus and the treatise, as well as the apparent anachronisms in the latter, made the passages in Josephus a bone of contention for many generations of scholars. The authenticity of the treatise had already been challenged in the Roman period by Philo of Byblos (ca. 50–130 A.D.). The discussion was renewed at the beginning of the seventeenth century, and Josef

---

3. See the discussion and bibliography in Holladay (1983) 284–85, 296, 302; Doran (1985) 905–12, 912–13; Goodman in Schürer et al. (1973–86) III.661, 674–75; Sterling (1992) 84–85.

4. On this reservation, see further p. 39 below.

Scaliger, the celebrated Dutch philologist, expressed the view that the treatise was spurious.[5] In 1730 the German scholar Peter Zorn published a comprehensive book on all the surviving material about Jews and Judaism ascribed to Hecataeus, supporting the authenticity of On the Jews.[6] A number of classical scholars and theologians contributed some minor points to the debate from the end of the eighteenth century, being divided over the question of authenticity.[7] The controversy heated up in the late nineteenth century. An important landmark was reached in 1900 with a detailed study by Hugo Willrich, who summarized the previous arguments against authenticity and added a number of his own. The discussion has been carried on into our century, with the weight of scholarly opinion shifting from time to time in either direction.[8]

In 1932 Hans Lewy published a widely acclaimed paper about On the Jews, regarded as a watershed by the advocates of authenticity. His arguments gained support with the discovery in the same year of the first Hezekiah coin.[9] Lewy's article was rediscovered in the late 1950s, and gradually tilted the balance. Increasingly, scholars have come out in favor of authenticity, the opponents being reduced to a small (but prominent) minority.[10] The inherent difficulties appeared to be

5. In his letter to Casaubon of November 1605 (Scaliger [1628] 278–79). But see his uncritical reference to the passages, Scaliger (1598), Fragmenta, Notae, p. xij; id. (1629) Fragmenta, Notae, p. 12. Cf. Zornius (1730) Commentarius, pp. 2–3.

6. Zornius (1730). The book contains no less than 352 pages, comprising an introduction, the Greek texts, a Latin translation, and detailed commentaries. Zorn, who was a professor of Greek and biblical history at the Carolingian gymnasium of Hamburg, concentrates in his commentary on theological questions, also referring to the positive views of former scholars.

7. References in J. G. Müller (1877) 170–71; cf. Schürer (1901–9) III.608.

8. Bibliography in Schürer, ibid.; and M. Stern (1974–84) I.25.

9. For details, see the discussion pp. 85ff. below.

10. See the bibliographical lists in M. Stern, ibid.; Holladay (1983) 298–300; Goodman in Schürer et al. (1973–86) III.676–77; Feldman (1984) 396–99. To these should be added the following entries: Burkert in Hengel (1971) 324; Fraser (1972) II.968 n. 115; Wacholder (1974) 80–82, 85–96; Momigliano (1975) 94; M. Stern (1976) 1105–9; Hengel (1976) 18–20, 31–33, 120ff.; Troiani (1977) 117–20; Millar (1979) 6–9; Conzelmann (1981) 56–58; Attridge (1986) 316; Bickerman (1988) 16–18, 27–28; Gabba (1989) 628–30; Sterling (1992) 78–91; Feldman (1993) 208–9; Pucci Ben Zeev (1993). Among the few scholars

satisfactorily solved: as even the most ardent supporters of authenticity have been puzzled by the contents of one or two sentences in the passages, it has been suggested that Josephus inaccurately paraphrased the material at his disposal or that he used a Jewish version that "slightly" revised the original book by Hecataeus.[11] At the same time, despite this new trend and the multitude of contributions on the subject, several scholars have recently expressed the feeling that research on the question has not produced a definitive solution and is actually at a stalemate, calling for a new breakthrough.[12]

Modern questioning of the passages' authenticity seems to have gained momentum because of its relevance to so-called scholarly anti-Semitism. German scholars and publicists in the past stressed the seemingly unbridgeable gap between Judaism and Greco-Roman culture (the paradigm of the *deutscher Geist*) as evidence of the inadaptability of Jews to European surroundings. The notorious anti-Jewish excursus on the Jews by Tacitus in his *Histories* was frequently quoted to this effect.[13] Jewish scholars, on the other hand, were eager to point out the apparent admiration for Jews and Judaism expressed by Greek authors at the beginning of the Hellenistic period, of which the passages ascribed to Hecataeus could serve as a primary example. It can be said that with few exceptions, as from the late nineteenth century, Jewish scholars tried very hard indeed to verify the passages, while gentiles, especially Germans, endeavored to undermine their authenticity. Only in the last generation has the discussion been freed of bias, as scholars transcended the barriers of religion and nationality in seeking to reach an objective conclusion.[14]

---

who still regard the book as a forgery, noteworthy are Burkert, Feldman, Fraser, Hengel, and Momigliano.

11. This was actually suggested already by Wendland (1900) 1201, (1900a) 2; Schürer (1901–9) III.606. They were followed by M. Stern (1974–84) I.24, (1976) 1104; Gauger (1982); Attridge (1984) 170; Goodman in Schürer et al. (1973–86) III.673; Bickerman (1988) 17–18; Sterling (1992) 91.

12. Schaller (1963) 22; Gager (1969) 131 n. 5; Holladay (1983) 282–83, 288; Attridge (1984) 170, (1986) 316. Cf. Pucci Ben Zeev (1993) 223–24.

13. See, e.g., Treitschke (1879) 663ff. Some material about the use of Tacitus's excursus can be found in Hoffmann (1988).

14. The new tendency started with the important contribution by Gager (1969), which made a number of penetrating observations.

The question of authenticity is invaluable for reconstructing Jewish history at the end of the Persian and the beginning of the Hellenistic period. The available sources on these periods are extremely meager. Consequently they are among the most obscure chapters in ancient Jewish history. If the authenticity of the treatise is verified, we will have a relatively detailed treatment of these two periods, written by a prominent and reliable contemporary Greek historian who claimed even to have witnessed some of the events described. Such a verification would shatter a number of accepted views about the internal development of the Jewish community and religion and the Jews' relations with the major powers of the time, as well as with their pagan neighbors.[15] In addition, much data concerning the beginning of the Jewish Egyptian Diaspora, the High Priesthood, the administration of Judea, and the defense of the country would have to be revised. No less significant are the implications for the evaluation of the attitudes of early Hellenistic intellectuals toward Jews and Judaism and their reception by later authors. If, however, the treatise was a fabrication by an Egyptian Jew, as quite a few scholars maintain, it would provide an insight into some of the basic questions that preoccupied the Jewish Hellenistic Diaspora and expand our acquaintance with its internal division. This would also contribute to our understanding of the major trends and ideologies in Jewish Hellenistic literature.

The discussion of the passages has so far been limited mainly to the historical examination of certain references suspected of being anachronistic. In the present monograph I have tried to combine a historical examination of all the details included in the passages with an analysis of philological, literary, and ideological aspects relevant to the understanding of the original work. A combined study may help to elucidate the question of authorship and the book's political, cultural, and religious background, and its purpose.

15. See the interesting recent reconstruction by Millar (1979) 7ff. So far Millar's paper is the only real attempt at utilizing the information found in the fragments for a revision of Jewish history in these periods.

I Hecataeus, His Work, and the Jewish Excursus

Before turning to examine the treatise *On the Jews*, it would be of advantage to introduce the man Hecataeus, his life and literary work, the genre he specialized in, and, especially, his Jewish excursus. This may help to place the treatise in the right perspective and make it easier to follow arguments and considerations that will be raised in the course of the discussion. The following survey will not try to exhaust all the material and questions involved but will present only information relevant to the subject of this monograph.

1. THE MAN, THE ETHNOGRAPHIC GENRE, AND HECATAEUS'S EGYPTIAN ETHNOGRAPHY

Our knowledge about Hecataeus's life is rather patchy. From the few testimonia, the following résumé can be drawn:[1] Hecataeus was born in Abdera, a prosperous Greek colony on the Thracian coast, around the middle of the fourth century. He reached maturity, and perhaps already had some reputation, by the time of Alexander the Great. In these years he seems to have received good philosophical training. In

---

1. See E. Schwartz (1885); Jacoby, *RE* s.v. "Hekataios (4)", 2750–51; *id.* (1943) 30–34; Guttman (1958–63) I.40–41; Murray (1970) 144–45; Sterling (1992) 59–61, 74. The testimonia are collected in *FGrH* IIIA 264 T 1–9. The most detailed and explicit information is to be found in the introductory notes of Josephus to the quotations from *On the Jews* and in the extracts themselves (*Ap.* I.183, 189, 201). This information is corroborated by circumstantial evidence scattered in other testimonia.

7

the period of the Successors Hecataeus was occupied in the service of Ptolemy I. His precise position in the court was not recorded. It can only be said that he was close to the satrap-king, took part in military expeditions, and went on diplomatic missions abroad.[2] At least one of his works, the Egyptian ethnography, served, in its special way, political goals of Ptolemy I.[3]

The ancient sources describe Hecataeus as a "philosopher" and critical *grammatikos*, and refer to his ethnographical works as "history."[4] Diogenes Laertius, the biographer-compiler of the Greek philosophers, lists Hecataeus among the people who were taught by Pyrrho and includes him among the "Pyrrhoneans" (IX.69). However, it is doubtful whether Hecataeus was indeed Pyrrho's disciple, or that he adhered to his teaching.[5] Another testimonium mentions him as one of the

---

2. The accepted reconstruction of Hecataeus's life was challenged by Diamond (1974) 117, 139–44, who suggests that Hecataeus was a wandering sophist who lived on the Greek mainland. The one argument worthy of attention is that if the treatise *On the Jews* is a forgery, the information provided there on Hecataeus must also be discounted. However, the treatise was written, in any case, in Ptolemaic Egypt. To describe a sophist who resided in Greece as a prominent figure in the Ptolemaic court would have discredited the author at the outset. The biography of the author who wrote the celebrated Egyptian ethnography must have been known to local intellectuals in Ptolemaic Egypt. Moreover, Josephus's introductory biographical notes do not seem to be based on the treatise itself, but on another source. And as was said in the preceding note, the testimonia of *Against Apion* do not stand alone. See also Sterling (1992) 74 n. 81.

3. See pp. 16–17 below.

4. See *FGrH* IIIA 264 T 1, 4, 7, 8.

5. It has been noted that there is no trace of Pyrrhonean or Skeptical thinking in the writing of Hecataeus (von Fritz, *RE* s.v. "Pyrrhon," 92). Prof. John Glucker has drawn my attention to the fact that the statement of Diogenes Laertius that Hecataeus "attended lectures" by Pyrrho or was his pupil (διήχουσε; for its use in this context in the technical sense, cf. Decleva-Caizzi [1981] 197) contradicts other testimonies on Pyrrho's way of life and philosophical activity, and even another statement by Diogenes Laertius himself (IX.63), taken from Antigonus of Carystus (Diog. Laert. IX.62; see Wilamowitz [1881] 35–37). Moreover, the passage IX.69–70, which refers to Hecataeus, is based on a later source, from the generation of Aenesidemus (first century B.C.) or even later. This appears mainly from an analysis of the appellations describing Pyrrho's immediate followers (cf. Decleva-Caizzi [1981] 199; Sedley [1983] 20). In Glucker's view, the passage records the attempts of later Skeptics to fabricate a respectable lineage commencing with

"Abderites," between Democritus and Apollodorus of Cyzicus (Clem. *Strom.* II.130.4), which inspired some speculations about Hecataeus's philosophical conceptions.[6] No name of a philosophical work by him is known, but there is little doubt that he indeed wrote philosophical works.[7] The situation with his contribution as a "grammarian" is not much different: we know that he wrote two books, on Homer and Hesiod (*Suda,* s.v. Ἑκαταῖος), but nothing of them has survived.

Hecataeus's major contribution was his ethnographical work. It was called history because in antiquity there was no generic name for this sort of writing, and it was included in the framework of history.[8] We know of two monographs: an Egyptian ethnography named *On the Egyptians* (Περὶ τῶν Αἰγυπτίων) or *Egyptian Matters* (Αἰγυπτιακά),[9] and another on the legendary Hyperboreans (*On the Hyperboreans*). A review of Hellenistic ethnographical literature indicates that Hecataeus's achievements in his monographs were used as a model for imitation by later ethnographers.[10] This applies also to

---

Pyrrho (see Glucker [1978] 330–79, esp. 347–48 on the "succession literature" and 351–56 on Diog. Laert. IX.115–16; Giannantoni [1981] 15–34; Sedley [1983] 20). They seem to have integrated into the dynasty personalities known to have had some connection with Pyrrho or his thinking. Thus the most one can safely say about Hecataeus is that he was acquainted with or referred in writing to some of Pyrrho's views. The suggestion to read "Hecataeus" instead of the unknown Ascanius in Diog. Laert. IX.61 (Müller, *FHG* II.384) is even more dubious, and philologically does not make sense. See also the objections by Dal Pra (1975) 28–30; Decleva-Caizzi (1981) 135–36.

6. See Reinhardt (1921); Jacoby (1943) 31; Spoerri (1959) 6–30, 164ff.; Cole (1967) 77ff.

7. See Jacoby, *RE* s.v. "Hekataios (4)," 2753–54; *id.* (1943) 32. The testimonia in *FGrH* no. 264, T 3b and 9, could hardly have been taken from Hecataeus's philological or ethnographical works.

8. See Fornara (1983) 1–2.

9. *On the Egyptians* was preferred by Jacoby, *FGrH* IIIA 264, p. 12; *id.* (1943) 75ff.; Murray (1970) 142, 150; Fraser (1972) I.496. Others have suggested *Aegyptiaca*: Wachsmuth (1895) 330; Trüdinger (1918) 50; Burton (1972) 5. Both suggestions are based on known titles of other ethnographic works (and Hecataeus's second book), but direct evidence is lacking. Diod. I.4.6 ("Egyptian Histories") refers also to many other works, all being classified according to their generic name.

10. See Jacoby (1943) 37–38; Murray (1970) 150, 166–69; *id.* (1972) 207; Fraser (1972) I.497.

later ethnographic accounts on the Jews.[11] In order to understand the importance of Hecataeus as an ethnographer, we have to preface here a brief survey of the genre.[12]

Although it did not have a generic name, there is no doubt that Greek ethnographical writing was a genre in its own right, with definite structure, rules, and purposes. Its beginning in the sixth century is connected with Greek colonization and the advance of the Persian empire, which raised the interest of the Hellenes in the surrounding world. Hecataeus of Miletus is regarded as the father of ethnography. His *Periēgēsis*, a geographical tour or survey around the Mediterranean, included a number of geographical accounts of the peoples of these countries. It seems that ethnographical writing at that time was not limited to excursuses in works belonging to other genres. There is some information about monographs by Hellanicus of Lesbos and Charon of Lampsacus that may have been predominantly ethnographic.[13]

The features of the new genre can be defined according to the ethnographical excursuses of Herodotus, especially the comprehensive accounts on the Egyptians and the Scythians. They were composed of the following sections:[14] (a) *origo-archaeologia*, the beginning of the nation; (b) geography; (c) customs; and (d) history. The *origo-archaeologia* described the descent of the people concerned either from their autochthonous beginnings or with their migration, and their early life as a nation. The geography referred to borders, rivers, fertility of soil, flora, and fauna, and elaborated on, among other things, *thaumasia* (marvels and curiosities). The customs section was the most important, and was designed to present the main features of the nation. Attention was given to beliefs and cult, social structure, institutions, and everyday practices. The last section, history, included mainly dynastic records with stories of the major achievements of outstanding rulers, usually concerning monumental buildings and successful military expeditions.

---

11. See below, pp. 211ff.

12. On the ethnographic genre, see Jacoby (1909) 4ff.; Trüdinger (1918); Dihle (1961); K. E. Müller (1972–80); Fornara (1983) 1–15; Sterling (1992) 20–102.

13. See Sterling (1992) 32–33.

14. See the detailed discussion, pp. 192ff. below.

The ethnography of the classical period can be described as nonscientific, resembling Herodotus's historiographical methods: unselective accumulation of material, without an attempt to arrive at the factual truth. There is no causal connection between the various sections of the ethnography or between the details in each section, and there is no reasoning to the mass of material. The sources of information were personal impressions of the author (who in some cases visited the countries described and interviewed local people), together with rumors and hearsay, tourist reports, and references in previous Greek literature. No use was made, directly or indirectly, of the literature or written records of foreign nations.

The first ethnographers did not write their works in the service of rulers or cities. They were, by and large, travelers, amateur geographers, seamen, merchants, or historians who had a keen interest in foreign countries and their inhabitants, and wrote at leisure. Their geographical horizon was limited to neighboring countries and the main divisions of the Persian empire. No clear ideology or pragmatic purpose is visible in these accounts. It can be said that they were basically written to satisfy the curiosity of Greeks who came across foreigners or heard about them. The rise of the genre just at the end of the age of colonization and the rather general character of the accounts rule out the possibility that Greek ethnography was initially meant as a guide to planned colonizations. In the case of excursuses incorporated in works belonging to another genre such as history or geography, the ethnographical accounts were introduced as a necessary preface to historical events or geographical descriptions relating to the nation concerned. They also had a literary role—to diversify the writing and provide some relief in the course of a long and monotonous narrative.

A new impetus in the development of the ethnographical genre naturally arose with the conquests of Alexander and Greco-Macedonian settlement in the newly occupied countries.[15] Interest in foreign nations grew immensely, and increased knowledge carried with it practical implications. The authors were no longer residents of the old Greek world, and in many cases lived in the countries they described. They could, therefore, consult local written sources, thoroughly interview people of

15. See Jacoby (1909) 90–92; Trüdinger (1918) 64ff.; Dihle (1961) 207–39, esp. 207–13; Murray (1972) 207; Sterling (1992) 55ff.; cf. Spoerri (1961) 63ff.; Cole (1967) 25ff.

all ranks of society, and gain firsthand acquaintance and understanding of the subjects referred to. Unlike their predecessors, Hellenistic ethnographers were personally involved with their subject, had definite didactic purposes in presenting their material, and frequently served Greco-Macedonian rulers. Consequently the new writing was no longer a casual accumulation of material arranged into schematized thematic rubrics: its information was carefully selected to fit with Greek literary models, or with premeditated political purposes or philosophical conceptions, or both. The information was not left unprocessed: it received some Greek touches and coloring, and reasoning was provided for the facts. The explanations often disclose the purposes of the writers; in other cases they were just borrowed from Greek tradition. As a result of all these, the final picture may have deviated considerably from the historical truth. By and large, the genre can be described as an *interpretatio Graeca* of the Orient. The more an author adhered to premeditated purposes, the more he departed from the original information. In some cases the outcome was an odd mixture of realism with sheer fantasy.

As far as the structure is concerned, there was no change in the basic scheme of ethnographical works: the same sections appear in Hellenistic ethnographical monographs and excursuses as in their classical counterparts, although in certain cases one or two sections may be missing. However, in contrast to the old ethnography, the various sections did not remain isolated from each other. Authors stress the causal connection between them: customs result from the special circumstances and conditions of the *origo,* or the geography, or both; and history arises from all these. The various subjects in each section are also connected by causal reasoning. As a result, there is more flexibility in the order and sequence of the traditional four sections of the ethnographical work.

The philosophical and political character prevailing in many works of the new ethnography motivated the rise of a subgenre, the utopian ethnography. Utopian features in Greek literature were as old as Homer, and were integrated in various genres.[16] Undertaking to describe remote or legendary peoples, utopian ethnographies were planned and constructed according to the rules of Hellenistic ethnography; but the material was entirely fictitious, designed to illustrate an ideal, nonexistent society. The best-known example is Euhemerus's utopia about the

16. On Greek utopian writing, see Ferguson (1975).

Panchaeans, set on an imaginary island in the Indian Ocean. It included the celebrated Euhemerist religious conception, according to which the gods were actually deified kings and heroes of the past. Less well known is that this idea was expressed earlier by Hecataeus of Abdera with regard to "terrestrial" gods in his Egyptian ethnography (Diod. I.13ff.).[17]

We can now turn again to Hecataeus of Abdera.[18] The general scheme of his works will be discussed below in Chapter VI.3.[19] It will be shown that Hecataeus followed the basic scheme of his Greek predecessors. However, apart from this structural similarity, all other features differed substantially, marking a new phase in the development of the genre. There is an obvious expansion of scope. Hecataeus increased the sources of information, the geographical horizon, and the types of the genre, and expanded its literary framework. He consulted, directly or indirectly, old Egyptian writings (Diod. I.69.7, 96.2) and had access to a variety of oral sources. He wrote two comprehensive monographs, one on the Egyptians, the other on the Hyperboreans. The first described the nation among whom he was residing; the second, legendary people imagined to live on the northern outskirts of the inhabited world. The first work was an idealized version of Egyptian history, institutions, and way of life; the second, an imaginary utopia. In addition to monographs, Hecataeus wrote miniature ethnographies of nations believed to have originated from Egypt. These were incorporated as excursuses in the Egyptian ethnography. The nations described were neighboring peoples such as the Jews, or the Babylonians (whose country was then the center of the rising Seleucid empire), and even Hellenic tribes or cities, such as Athens (Diod. I.28–29).

The great contributions of Hecataeus, however, to the development of the genre were the selection of material according to Greek literary and ideological conceptions, the creation of a causal connection between

17. On the influence of Hecataeus on Euhemerus, and the chronological question, see Jacoby, *RE* s.v. "Hekataios (4)," 2763; Nilsson (1961) II.285–86; Cole (1967) 153–58; Murray (1970) 151; Drews (1973) 206 n. 162; and Oden (1978) 118–19 for further bibliography.

18. On Hecataeus as an ethnographer, see Jacoby, *RE* s.v. "Hekataios (4)," 2755ff.; Guttman (1958–63) I.42ff.; Murray (1970); Fraser (1972) I.496–505; Mendels (1988); Sterling (1992) 61–78.

19. Pp. 192–219 below.

the sections of the work and between the subjects within each section, and the reasoning provided for many statements. Thus, for instance, in the case of an emigrating nation, its experiences in the country of origin and the circumstances of its emigration would influence its everyday life, institutions, language, and attitude toward other nations. The life, history, and character of autochthonous peoples would be dictated, to a great extent, by geography, especially soil, water, climate, and fauna. Cult and beliefs, which were referred to without comment by earlier ethnographers, received rational explanations. Even the notorious Egyptian animal cult was given a detailed rationalization, pointing out the benefits brought by the animals to the Egyptians (Diod. I.86ff.). The like applies to other subjects. The reasoning often drew on Greek experience and thinking. In this respect Hecataeus's ethnography may appear to strive for scientific presentation, but the selection of the material, its coloring, and its reasoning were not necessarily guided by a wish to record absolute historical truth.

This loss to political history and ethnography was a gain for the history of ideas. It would be rather speculative to reconstruct the utopian model envisaged by Hecataeus in his Hyperborean ethnography. The scant surviving material allows only a few conclusions with regard to Hecataeus's religious stance. He seems to have adhered to the traditional cult of classical Greece and was evidently highly tolerant.

The state of preservation of the Egyptian ethnography is much better. Apart from some fragments and testimonia,[20] its contents are to be found in Book I of Diodorus's *Historical Library*, which is devoted to Egyptian ethnography. Following the studies of Eduard Schwartz and Felix Jacoby it has been accepted that Book I of Diodorus (from I.10 onward) is basically an abbreviated paraphrase of Hecataeus's Egyptian ethnography, though it also contains a long section taken from Agatharcides of Cnidus (the description of the Nile, I.32–41) as well as notes and additions by Diodorus himself.[21] This conclusion has been challenged from time to time; arguments have been raised against the attribution of certain passages to Hecataeus, and there have also

20. See *FGrH* IIIA 264 F 1–6.

21. See E. Schwartz (1885) 223–62, following Schneider (1880); Leopoldi (1892); Schwartz, *RE* s.v. "Diodorus," 669–72; Reinhardt (1921); Jacoby, *RE* s.v. "Hekataios (4)," 2759–60; *id.* (1943) 75–76; cf. Fraser (1972) I.497–509, II.1116; J. Hornblower (1981) 23ff.

been those who have tried to minimize Hecataeus's share in Diodorus's version.[22] These attempts have been rightly refuted, and one has to note especially the contribution of Oswyn Murray, who reestablished the old, accepted theory.[23]

The dating of Hecataeus's Egyptian ethnography has been disputed. While some have suggested the early years of Ptolemy's independent satrapy (320–315) others have preferred the first years of his monarchy (306/5–300).[24] The arguments in favor of the first possibility are not decisive. On the other hand the year 306/5 as a *terminus post quem* appears from the introduction to the account of the borders of Egypt (Diod. I.30.1):

> Egypt lies mainly toward the south, and, in natural strength and beauty of land, seems to excel those places that have been separated off [each] into a kingdom.

A comparison is obviously being made with the regions occupied by the other satraps who declared themselves kings after the naval battle of Cyprian Salamis in 306. Given the general context, an account of pharaonic Egypt, the sentence seems to have been written by a contemporary of the Successors, and certainly not by Diodorus, in the days of Augustus. It stands in fact at the head of two definitely Hecataean chapters (30–31.8),[25] and this would appear to clinch the argument. The year 302/1 (not 300) as *terminus ante quem* is suggested by the unbiased attitude toward Jews and Judaism manifested in the Jewish excursus incorporated in the Egyptian ethnography:[26] after the confrontation between Ptolemy I and the Jews in that year, the subsequent harsh treatment of the population, the banishment of scores

---

22. See Spoerri (1959), and esp. Burton (1972) 1–34. Cf. Sacks (1990) 206.

23. See Murray (1970) 145, 148–49, 151–52, 164, 168–70; *id.* (1972) 207ff. Murray's articles actually answer many of the arguments raised by Burton, although Burton's book appeared two years later. Cf. Murray (1975) 287–90; Lloyd (1974) 287–88; Griffiths (1976) 122. See also Gigon (1961) 771ff. on Spoerri's book. See further, on Burton's and Sacks's arguments, Extended Notes, n. 1 p. 289.

24. See M. Stern (1973), Murray (1973), with references there to earlier literature.

25. Diod. I.30–31.8 was taken from Hecataeus; see p. 196 below.

26. See pp. 22, 208–11 below on the original place of the excursus.

of thousands to Egypt, and the sale of many into slavery,[27] a positive account of the Jews without any reference to these developments is hardly to be expected of an author serving in the court.

The very writing of the work and its main message were dictated by the circumstances of the hour: the official end of provincial rule and the establishment of new kingdoms in oriental countries with long monarchic traditions. Ptolemy saw himself as the successor of the pharaohs, a legitimate king of the Egyptians. The predominant feature of the Egyptian ethnography was, therefore, the glorification of Egypt. The country is described as the land of human origins, the cradle of civilization, and of wisdom. Useful inventions such as fire, agriculture, language, and writing, as well as most of the arts, originated on Egyptian soil (I.13ff., 69.5–6). Many nations came from Egypt and were deeply influenced by its culture. The most outstanding of these were the Greeks (including the Athenians) and the Babylonians (I.28–29). Mythical cult figures, lawgivers, poets, and philosophers, such as Orpheus, Musaeus, Solon, Lycurgus, Homer, Protagoras, Democritus, and Plato, visited Egypt, explored its laws and institutions, and drew substantially from them (I.69.3–4, 96ff.). Pharaonic rule appears as a law-abiding monarchy, guided by priests, with the king maintaining virtues like justice, magnanimity, and piety (I.70–71, 73.4). The Egyptian judicial system and its procedures are said to have been planned in a way that facilitated reaching the absolute truth with the utmost objectivity (I.75ff.). Egyptian gods are equated with Greek ones and rationalized: two are explained as representing the great celestial bodies; five others, the basic elements (fire, spirit, etc.); and the rest, renowned mortal heroes and inventors of the past. The rehabilitation of practices deplored by Greeks included not only animal cult (I.86–90) but also incest (I.27.1–2). These were toned down and given rational explanations that made them acceptable to Greek ears.

The tribute paid to the greatness of Egypt was meant to help in establishing the image of the Ptolemaic regime. It raised the prestige of Ptolemy, the new king of this great, old civilization, in the eyes of Greco-Macedonians living under other Hellenistic rulers. This in turn helped to attract to Egypt competent European manpower and the intellectual elite of the Greek world. As for the Greco-Macedonians settled in

---

27. On these events, see pp. 74–77 below.

Egypt, the enthusiastic account of the pharaonic past brought home the royal policy of respecting Egyptian traditions, including superstitions, in order to avoid ugly confrontations with the natives and their strong priesthood.[28] It has been suggested that the work was also intended to flatter the Egyptians themselves. This is quite doubtful: the language barrier was still too high at the end of the fourth century to expect the book to circulate among Egyptians, let alone influence them. Moreover, the glorification of the pharaonic past could have sparked off Egyptian nationalism, and the recurring references to the role of the priests as advisers of the king would only have encouraged the Egyptian priests not to be content with their religious duties. Other suggestions offered for the purpose of the book, such as to establish a general model of government and society for the developing Hellenistic world, or to present an idealized version of the Ptolemaic regime, do not stand up to criticism.[29] The role of the priests is not the only feature refuting these suggestions. Various points in the book have evident didactic purposes, but they do not carry its main message.

It would take us far afield to refer to every thematic aspect of this fascinating ethnography. It is a mine of theological, philosophical, political, and social ideas. I shall restrict myself to noting a number of points that have some relevance to an understanding of the Jewish excursus:

1. The information is based by and large on Egyptian priestly oral and written sources.[30]

2. In certain cases it reflects not historical facts but ideals circulating among those priests.[31]

---

28. For the dangers involved in not respecting Egyptian superstitions like the killing of a cat, see, e.g., the later incident related in Diod. I.83.6–8.

29. For the various suggestions for the point of the work, see E. Schwartz (1885) 233–62; Wendland (1912) 116–19; Jacoby, *RE* s.v. "Hekataios (4)," 2757–63; Meyer (1928) 529ff.; Jaeger (1938) 140, (1938a) 151ff.; Welles (1949) 39–44; Kienitz (1953) 49ff.; Guttman (1958–63) I.45ff.; Murray (1970) 150–69; Fraser (1972) I.497–505; Drews (1973) 126–32, 205 n. 157; Mendels (1988) 15–16; Sterling (1992) 73–75.

30. Diod. I.21.1, 26.1, 43.6, 69.7, 86.2, 96.2; and see Murray (1970) 143 n. 2, 151 n. 1.

31. See Murray (1970) 152–61 with regard to the account of pharaonic kingship. Cf. Burton (1972) 209ff.

3. The interpretation of the facts is Hecataean, and is inspired by Greek tradition and modes of thinking, apart from a few cases where the author explicitly says that an explanation is Egyptian.

4. The interpretation is frequently complimentary, and apologetic in some cases. It includes explicit expressions of praise. The tendency to idealize is evident.

5. The author himself divides the customs recorded in the book into two categories: "extremely strange [*paradoxotata*] customs," and those that might be "most useful" to the reader (I.69.2; cf. 30.4). He introduces customs of the first type in order to provide reasoning for well-known curiosities and to arouse interest in others. The "useful" customs are brought in to serve as models for imitation, to point out their superiority over existing Greek practices, or just for the sake of comparison.[32]

6. Despite his desire to present an appealing, favorable picture of Egyptian life, Hecataeus does not refrain from expressing reservations about Egyptian hostility toward strangers, although he tries to "soften" it (Diod. I.67.10–11, 69.4, 88.5)

2. THE JEWISH EXCURSUS

Hecataeus's Jewish excursus was much discussed in the last century. Being actually the first comprehensive account of Jews and Judaism in Greek literature, it was used by later gentile authors as a basic source of information on the subject. Some features of this account, especially the attribution to Moses of the settlement in Judea and the establishment of basic Jewish institutions and practices, became a vulgate in Greco-Roman literature.[33] In the present monograph, a review of the excursus and its problems is relevant not only to the question of the authenticity of *On the Jews*, but also to the shaping of one of its sections. Be that treatise a forgery or not, its author was certainly acquainted with the excursus.

Like his major works, Hecataeus's original ethnographic account on Jews and Judaism has not been preserved. Diodorus incorporated an abbreviated paraphrase of it in Book XL of the *Historical Library*

---

32. An evident model: Diod. I.73.7–9 (see pp. 37–38 below). Explicit criticism of Greek customs, I.74.6–7, 76; comparisons, I.29.

33. See pp. 211–17 below.

(3.1–8), which is itself now lost, but his version of Hecataeus's Jewish ethnography is preserved by Photius, the Byzantine patriarch of the ninth century. Photius attacks Diodorus for "telling lies" about the Jews. To illustrate this accusation, he cites two extracts. The first is a story about the siege of Jerusalem by Antiochus VII Sidetes (in 134 or 132 B.C.) and the anti-Jewish libels and accusations voiced on that occasion by the king's advisers (cod. 244, 379a–380a = Diod. XXXIV–XXXV.1.1–5). Then comes the Jewish ethnography. The text of Photius runs as follows (cod. 244, 380a–381a):

> From the fortieth book [of Diodorus], about the middle:[34]
> [3.1] Now that we intend to record the war against the Jews, we consider it appropriate to give first an outline [ἐν κεφαλαίοις] of the foundation [ktisis] from its beginning, and of the customs [nomima] practiced among them.
> When in ancient times a pestilence arose in Egypt, the ordinary people ascribed their troubles to the working of a divine power [τὸ δαιμόνιον]; for indeed with many strangers of all sorts dwelling in their midst and practicing different habits of rites and sacrifice, their own traditional observances in honor of the gods had fallen into disuse. [3.2] Hence the natives of the land surmised that unless they removed the foreigners, their troubles would never be resolved. At once, therefore, the aliens were driven from the country, and the most outstanding [ἐπιφανέστατοι] and active among them banded together and, as some say, were cast ashore in Greece and certain other regions; their leaders were notable men, chief among them being Danaus and Cadmus. But the greater number were driven into what is now called Judea, which is not far distant from Egypt and was at that time utterly desolate [παντελῶς δὲ ἔρημον οὖσαν]. [3.3] The colony [apoikia] was headed by a man called Moses, outstanding both for his wisdom and courage. On taking possession of the land, he founded [ἔκτισε], besides other cities, one that is now the most renowned of all, called Jerusalem. In addition he established the temple that they hold in chief veneration, instituted their forms of worship and ritual, drew up the laws relating to their political institutions, and ordered [διέταξε] them. He also divided the people into twelve tribes, since this is regarded as the most perfect number and corresponds to the number of months that make up a year. [3.4] But he had no images whatsoever of the Gods made for them, being of the opinion that God

34. Henceforward (up to 3.8) the extract from Diodorus. The translation: Walton (1967) 279–87 (LCL), with a few necessary emendations. The marking of the paragraphs of the extract is according to the editions of Dindorf (1828–31) and Bekker (1853–54), followed by Walton.

is not in human form [μὴ νομίζειν ἀνθρωπόμορφον]; rather the heaven that encompasses [περιέχοντα] the Earth is alone divine, and rules everything [τῶν ὅλων]. The sacrifices that he established differ from those of other nations, as does their way of living, for as a result of their own expulsion [ξενηλασίαν] from Egypt he introduced a [way of] life which is somewhat unsocial and hostile to strangers [ἀπάνθρωπόν τινα καὶ μισόξενον βίον εἰσηγήσατο]. He picked out the men of most refinement and with the greatest ability to head the entire nation, and appointed them priests; and he ordained that they should occupy themselves with the temple and the honors and sacrifices offered to their God.   [3.5] These same men he appointed to be judges in all major disputes, and entrusted to them the guardianship [φυλακήν] of the laws and customs. For this reason the Jews never [μηδέποτε] have a king, and the leadership [προστασίαν] of the multitude [πλήθους] is regularly vested in whichever priest is regarded as superior to his colleagues in wisdom and virtue. They call this man high priest [ἀρχιερέα], and believe that he acts as a messenger [ἄγγελον] to them of God's commandments.   [3.6] It is he, they say, who in their assemblies and other gatherings announces what is ordained, and the Jews are so docile in such matters that straightway they fall to the ground and do reverence [προσκυνεῖν] to the high priest when he expounds the commandments to them. There is even appended to the laws, at the end, the statement: "These are the words that Moses heard from God and declares unto the Jews." Their lawgiver was careful also to make provision for warfare, and required the young men to cultivate manliness, steadfastness, and, generally, the endurance of every hardship.   [3.7] He led out military expeditions against the neighbouring tribes, and after annexing much land apportioned it out, assigning equal allotments to private citizens and greater ones to the priests in order that they, by virtue of receiving more ample revenues, might be undistracted and apply themselves continually to the worship of God. The common people were forbidden to sell their individual plots [κλήρους], lest there be some who for their own advantage should buy them up, and by oppressing the poorer classes bring on a scarcity of manpower [ὀλιγανδρίαν].   [3.8] He required those who dwelt in the land to rear their children, and since offspring could be cared for at little cost, the Jews were from the start a populous nation. As to marriage and the burial of the dead, he saw to it that their customs should differ widely from those of other men.[35] But later, when they became subject to foreign rule, as a result of their mingling with men of other nations—both under Persian rule and

---

35. This is the end of Hecataeus's excursus. The next sentence is an addition by Diodorus; see p. 24 below.

under that of the Macedonians who overthrew the Persians—many of their traditional practices were disturbed.[36]

So he [Diodorus] says also here about customs and laws common among Jews, and about the departure of those same people from Egypt, and about the holy Moses, telling lies about most things, and going through the [possible] counter arguments, he again distorted the truth, and using cunning devices as a refuge for himself, he attributes to another [author] the abovesaid things which are contrary to history. For he [Diodorus] adds: "As concerns the Jews, this is what Hecataeus of Miletus narrated."[37]

First of all, some comments on the transmission of the text, its preservation, and its original location. Photius explicitly says that the extract was taken from Diodorus's fortieth book. In view of his declared purpose to expose Diodorus's "lies" and considering the typically Diodorean style and turn of phrase, it has rightly been assumed that Photius faithfully transmitted the text of Diodorus.[38] As noted by Diodorus at the head of the extract (3.1), he incorporated the excursus on the Jews at that point to serve as an introduction to his account of the confrontation between the Romans and the Jews, that is, the events surrounding the Roman occupation of Judea in the year 63 B.C. It followed the appeal alleged to have been made by a Jewish delegation to Pompey to dispose of the Hasmonean rulers and restore the Jewish "ancestral constitution" (XL.1a). The extract indeed provides background material for this claim: it elaborates on a Jewish *patrios politeia*, stressing its theocratic character and categorically stating that the Jews "never have a king."[39] The excursus also deals with the military preparation of

36. This is the end of the extract from Diodorus. The following paragraph is a comment by Photius, supplemented by the closing sentence of Diodorus.

37. The sentence closed the original excursus by Diodorus. On the copying mistake "Miletus" instead of "Abdera," see below.

38. See Diamond (1974) 10–12. From codex 238 onward, Photius adheres to his sources, apart from slight and insignificant linguistic improvements. Abbreviations were made only to avoid duplications and stylistic awkwardness, or with regard to redundant details that detract from the main issue. See Palm (1955) 16–26, 29ff., 48ff.; Hägg (1975) 9ff. and 197–203, esp. 201–2. Treadgold (1980) 129 is probably mistaken in assigning Diodorus's excerpts in cod. 244 to what he calls class IIc; it should be class IIIc (see Treadgold's classification on pp. 82–83, 86, 90–91).

39. Cf. Diod. XL.2.2: "their ruler called High Priest, not king." On the contents of the alleged complaint, see Bar-Kochva (1977) 177–81.

the younger generation for war, the motivation of the Jewish farmers to fight, and their abundance of manpower, which obviously are relevant for the coming military confrontation.

Diodorus's extract closes with the statement "this is what Hecataeus of Miletus narrated." "Miletus" instead of "Abdera" is certainly a slip of Photius or a copyist.[40] The original ethnography by Hecataeus was not an independent monograph, but an excursus. It was included in his great ethnographical work on Egypt, most probably as an appendix at the end of the *origo-archaeologia* section, the first of the four sections of the *Aegyptiaca* (Diod. I.28–29).[41] The Jewish excursus was just one of a number of miniature ethnographies of nations, tribes, and cities supposed to have originated from Egypt that were treated in the same context.

Diodorus states in the preface to the excursus that he intends to report on the "founding" (*ktisis*) and "customs" (*nomima*) of the Jews. The excursus indeed contains these two sections; it opens with the founding, namely the *origo*: the expulsion of the Jews together with other aliens (XL.3.1–2), the settlement of the Jews in Judea and Jerusalem under the leadership of Moses (2–3), and the establishment of political and religious institutions (3). Then follows the section on customs: Jewish faith (4), sacrifices (4), attitude toward strangers (4), the duties of the priests (4–5), the role of the High Priest and his authority (5–6), the organization of the army and military expeditions (6–7), the distribution of land (7–8), child rearing and demography (8), marriage and burial (8).

These were also the components of Hecataeus's original excursus. It included only *ktisis* and *nomima*, without geographical and historical sections, which were common in Greek ethnographies. These sections were also absent from the other minor ethnographies in the appendix to the Egyptian *archaeologia-origo*. Hecataeus was primarily concerned in that context to illustrate the origin of certain nations in Egypt, with the evidence of Egyptian influences on their customs to prove it. Geography and history of the new lands would have been quite out of place.[42]

---

40. This has been universally accepted: see, e.g., Reinach (1895) 20; Jacoby (1943) 34, 46; Guttman (1958–63) I.50; Diamond (1974) 128–30; Gabba (1989) 626. The only exception is Dornseiff (1939) 52–65. His arguments do not make sense. How easy it was to mix the two is indicated in a note by Aelian, *NA* 11.1

41. See pp. 208–11 below.

42. See in detail pp. 209–10 below.

At the same time, it is clear that the original content of the *nomima* section was not preserved by Diodorus in its entirety:[43] the account of the daily customs was omitted. This is evident with regard to circumcision (Diod. I.28.2), sacrifice (XL.3.4),[44] and marriage and burial customs (XL.3.8),[45] and may also have happened to explicit references about Jewish exclusiveness (XL.3.4). The first four were omitted because they could not contribute to the aforementioned purposes for which the excursus was incorporated. Illustrations of the Jewish attitude toward strangers were left out, probably because they were very moderate in comparison with the sharp accusations and libels quoted by Diodorus from another source in a previous book (XXXIV–XXXV.1.1–3). Left in the *nomima* section are statements about Jewish institutions and remarks pertaining to Jewish military potential (training, motivation, manpower).[46] The account of Jewish belief was recorded not only because of its uniqueness, but chiefly owing to its relevance for understanding the Jewish theocratical system of government as described by the delegation to Pompey.

Hecataeus's original excursus thus opened with the *origo*, in this case the alleged expulsion of Jews from Egypt. Then came the *nomima* section, which seems to have comprised two main subjects: institutions and provisions made by Moses, and a collection of daily customs. As became customary in the new, Hellenistic, ethnography, the author uses one section to explain another. Here he stresses the influence of the *origo* on the creation and development of Jewish customs. The expulsion explains the "hatred of strangers" (XL.3.4). Daily customs

43. See Jaeger (1938) 150–51; Murray (1970) 144–46, (1973) 168; M. Stern (1974–84) I.34; Diamond (1974) 111–17. The expression ἐν κεφαλαίοις ("summarily") used by Diodorus (para. 1) does not necessarily mean that Diodorus abbreviated Hecataeus's excursus, since it can also be taken as a description of the contents of Hecataeus's excursus itself.

44. Jaeger ([1938] 142ff.) suggested that Hecataeus's account of Jewish sacrifices was preserved by Theophrastus (*ap.* Porph. *Abst.* II.26). This has rightly been rejected on chronological counts; see M. Stern (1973).

45. The abbreviation of the reference to marriage and burial customs, or the omission of the beginning of this new topic, can perhaps further be supported by stylistic observation: the new topic is introduced with the conjunction καί, which has so far only been used to connect ideas within a topic; new topics have regularly been introduced with the particle δέ.

46. On the military implications of the reference to the rearing of children, see pp. 36–38 below.

are compared with those of the Egyptians, with some, like circumcision, being described as originating in Egypt (I.28.3). Others, like marriage and burial customs, were contrasted with those of the Egyptians.[47] Jewish beliefs, governmental institutions, and social provisions were not just listed but were given a causal reasoning.

Apart from the omission of the customs mentioned above, the references to the Jewish *origo* and *nomima* seem to represent the contents of the original text. In three cases there is a striking similarity between the excursus and references to Egyptians and Jews in Hecataeus's *Aegyptiaca*.[48] They indicate that even if some of the statements and explanations were abbreviated by Diodorus, the original meaning was not distorted. Significantly, Diodorus was not tempted by the vicious libels about Jewish origins and attitude toward strangers included elsewhere in his work (XXXIV–XXXV.1.1–4), nor by his own prejudice (XL.2.2, "lawless behavior of the Jews"): the Jews are not described as lepers, and the reason given for their expulsion is not insulting; the reference to Jewish hostility toward strangers expresses just some reservation. These passages certainly reflect the original Hecataean text.

The question whether Diodorus adhered to Hecataeus's vocabulary and syntax is more problematic. It can only be said that there is much of the Diodorean style in the excursus.[49] One sentence, however, is clearly an addition by Diodorus: it is agreed that the statement "but later, when they became subject to foreign rule, . . . many of their traditional practices were disturbed" (XL.3.8) could not have been written by Hecataeus. It records changes in the Hasmonean period and is connected with the alleged complaints of the Jewish notables to Pompey. The reference to the "rule . . . of the Macedonians who overthrew the Persians" indicates that it was written long after the end of Macedonian rule in Judea. A similar note was supplemented by Diodorus at the end of his *epitomē* of Hecataeus's Egyptian ethnography (I.95.6).

---

47. The references to Jewish marriage customs probably stressed Jewish incest prohibitions as opposed to Egyptian permissiveness (mentioned at Diod. I.27.1). An allusion to Jewish rejection of mixed marriages is also possible (cf. the abridged reference to Jewish exclusiveness, para. 4.)

48. See Diod. I.94.2, and pp. 36–38 below on 73.7–9.

49. See the detailed discussion of Diamond (1974) 13ff. Cf. Fraser (1972) II.1116.

The contents of the excursus raise a number of questions that have continually attracted the attention of scholars.[50] Did Hecataeus have real knowledge about Jewish antiquities? What were his sources of information? What were Hecataeus's guidelines in selecting the material? Does the account reflect Jewish life in the period of Hecataeus? To what extent was the account inspired by Greek practices, conceptions, and literary traditions? Does the excursus carry certain messages or didactic purposes? Did Hecataeus intend to idealize the life of the Jewish people or certain customs? How should Hecataeus's note about Jewish separatism and "hatred of strangers" be understood? Is it complimentary, or does it express reservation? And finally: what was, after all, Hecataeus's basic attitude toward Jews and Judaism? All these questions are relevant, in one way or another, to various points in the discussion on the treatise *On the Jews*. However, as they cannot decide the major issues,[51] and the purpose of this chapter is simply to introduce the reader to Hecataeus's work and references to the Jews, I shall refrain from examining in detail the numerous suggestions offered so far concerning these and related questions, and shall not attempt to exhaust all the points involved. The following discussion will try to sort out and define the significant problems, survey the relevant source material, and present what seem to me to be the right solutions. Of most interest to us will be the process by which the excursus was composed, and the considerations behind the selection, arrangement, and shaping of the material.

Do the accounts of the Jewish *origo* and *nomima* accord with Jewish tradition and history? At first sight the answer is firmly negative. Almost every clause, as it stands, can easily be refuted or found inaccurate. This, however, is a hasty conclusion. One has to distinguish

50. See Radin (1915) 92–95; Engers (1923); Jaeger (1938) 144–53, (1938a) 139–41; Dornseiff (1939) 52–66; Jacoby (1943) 39ff. Guttman (1958–63) I.49ff.; Tcherikover (1961) 56–59, 119–25; Murray (1970) 158–59, (1973); Gager (1972) 26–29; M. Stern (1973), (1974–84) I.29–35, (1976) 1105–9; Wacholder (1974) 85–93; Diamond (1974), (1980); Hengel (1973) 564ff.; Lebram (1974a) 244–53; Momigliano (1975) 84–85; Wardy (1979) 638–39; Mendels (1983); Will and Orrieux (1986) 83–92; Bickerman (1988) 16–18; Gabba (1989) 627–29; Mélèze-Modrzejewski (1989); Sterling (1992) 75–78; Feldman (1993) 8–9, 46, 149–50, 234–36.

51. See esp. pp. 55, 99–100 below.

between the facts and their reasoning. The explanations were provided by Hecataeus himself, and are typically Greek. The facts, except one or two, are based on Jewish tradition and history. What is mistaken is the dating and sequence. Hecataeus conflates three periods of Jewish history: (a) the time of the Exodus and the wandering in the desert; (b) the period of the settlement in Canaan; and (c) the Restoration, the Persian rule, and the days of the Diadochs. The three periods are telescoped into one, under the leadership of Moses, the founder. The account fails to distinguish between periods and stages of development, and ignores other long periods. Such telescoping, centering around the personality of the "founder" (*ktistēs, oikistēs*), was quite common in Greek foundation legends and stories relating to the age of colonization, and even to later colonization activities.[52] Events and developments that occurred during long periods, under different individuals, were conflated into one period and attributed to one person, the leader-founder.[53] We shall see later that both the collection and the arrangement of the material were indeed strongly influenced by Greek foundation legends. The Judea portrayed is consequently not historical but mythological. It is difficult to know whether Hecataeus had consciously ignored the real sequence, or whether he had received the information sporadically and unsystematically, and presented it the way Greeks were accustomed to record foundation stories.

Disregarding inaccuracies that result from the conflation and the tendency to attribute everything to Moses, the following data reflect the tradition (as distinct from history) about Moses and his period: the Jews were once aliens in Egypt (Diod. XL.3.2); Moses was their leader and great lawgiver (3); they were divided into twelve tribes (3); their cult avoided images and sculptures (4); they believed in the divine origin of the law (5–6; cf. I.94.2); the High Priest and priests were in charge of

---

52. The influence of foundation stories was first noted by Jaeger (1938) 144–48, although elsewhere he puts it in a somewhat different way: "This sequence is in harmony with the Greek scheme typical for such a historical development: first comes the emigration of the settlers, then the struggle with the people whose land they conquer, then the foundation of a city (πόλις), and finally the legislation. Thus if Hecataeus was told that Moses was the legislator of the Jews, all the other steps had to be put before this final act. He may even have corrected on his own account what the Jewish theologians told him, since this was the normal and natural order" ([1938a] 140).

53. See Virgilio (1972).

sacrifices and cult (XL.3.4), and were appointed to handle major judicial cases (5; cf. Deut. 17.8–12); the Jews reared their children, and therefore were from the beginning a "populous nation" (Diod. XL.3.8; cf. Exod. 1.7, 11). There is even a paraphrased quotation of a formula that recurs in the Pentateuch (Diod. XL.3.6).[54] The second period provided the following data: the Jews settled in their country (3); they went to war against their neighbors and annexed lands (7). The statements that the lots were evenly distributed and were inalienable (7) also have biblical parallels.[55]

Other data and features recall Jewish life and institutions after the Babylonian exile and in the days of Hecataeus:[56] Jews were concentrated in Judea and Jerusalem (3); the Jewish deity was named "Heaven" (4);[57] the High Priest was the leader of the nation (5–6); the priests were, in addition to their cult duties, guides and guardians of the Torah (4–5);[58] there was no king (5); the Temple stood at the center of Jewish life (3, 5–6); the congregation was occasionally assembled in Jerusalem, and the Pentateuch was then publicly read by priests (5–6; cf. Neh. 8.1–8); the kneeling before the High Priest may be an inaccurate reflection of the practice to fall upon the ground and bow before the Lord on such occasions (Neh. 8.6);[59] the belief that the High Priest is a "messenger of

54. Lev. 26.46, 27.34; Num. 36.13; Deut. 28.69, 32.44 (LXX). See Walton (1955); Wacholder (1974) 90 n. 89.

55. Lev. 25.25–34, Num. 26.54, I Kings 21.3–4, and the word גורל ("lot"), which recurs in Joshua. See further Guttman (1958–63) I.56.

56. That the excursus reflects Jewish life in the Persian period was stressed by Radin (1915) 92–95; Tcherikover (1961) 56–59, 119–25; and particularly Mendels (1983). The latter suggests that the reference to the building of the Temple by Moses originates from anti-Samaritan propaganda, that the attribution of Jewish institutions and practices to Moses and the statement that the Jews "never have a king" echoes an attempt by certain priestly circles to erase from memory the period of the kingdom (pp. 100–101), and that the description of Judea as being uninhabited at the time of the settlement applied to the time of the Restoration (p. 99).

57. See Mélèze-Modrzejewski (1989) 6–7, referring to the Cyrus decree, two of the Elephantine documents, and the Books of the Maccabees.

58. Cf. Mal. 2.7; II Chron. 17.8–9, 19.5–10, which reflect the Persian period. See also M. Stern (1974–84) I.31; Will and Orrieux (1986) 85–86. Cf. Deut. 17.8–12.

59. See also Sirach. 50.18, the kneeling of the people at the Temple on the Day of Atonement (noted by Diamond [1980] 88; Will and Orrieux [1986] 85).

God" (Diod. XL.3.5) is identical to a statement by the prophet Malachi, referring to the "priest" (Mal. 2.7);[60] certain priestly families seem to possess great estates, which may account for the statement that the priests were allotted greater lots than common people (Diod. XL.3.7);[61] the stress laid on the inalienability of lands may record a tightening-up of the Torah restrictions on selling lands, a likely feature of Nehemiah's social reform;[62] in addition to the Exodus traditions, the reference to the rearing of children may also record the situation in a Judea small at that time, and apparently overpopulated.[63]

These pieces of information were certainly provided by Egyptian Jews, probably of priestly descent.[64] Given such sources, what is the reason for the absence of any reference to the period of the Israelite and Judean kings (and the statement that "the Jews never have a king," 3.5)? Hecataeus, who served an absolute ruler and illustrated an ideal monarchy in the *Aegyptiaca*, had no motive for concealing that major period of Jewish history. The reason seems to be structural and literary: as was already mentioned, the Jewish excursus, like other miniature ethnographies incorporated in the same context, was planned to include just the *origo* and contemporary customs. It stands to reason that in interviewing his Jewish informants, Hecataeus was interested in collecting material for these sections alone. Consequently he was not informed about (or did not take notes about) matters relating to a historical section. The period of the Israelite and Judean kingdoms, as well as the Babylonian exile, had no place in the excursus. Summing up the implications of the account for the Jewish governmental system, it occurred to Hecataeus that the "Jews never have a king."

In addition to the Jewish informants, the use of Egyptian sources, oral or written, is evident in the statement concerning the expulsion of the Jews from Egypt.[65] Hecataeus seems to have preferred a moderate

60. See Walton (1955) 255; Mendels (1983) 106.

61. See Gager (1972) 33; Mendels (1983) 108–9.

62. Similarly Tcherikover (1961) 122–23.

63. On the overpopulation of Judea proper in the Hellenistic period, see Bar-Kochva (1977) 169–71, (1989) 56–57. Add the data about the mass deportation by Ptolemy I (see pp. 74–75 below).

64. Suggested by Jaeger (1938) 146; Guttman (1958–63) I.51; Murray (1970) 158; Gager (1972) 37; Diamond (1980) 81, 87.

65. So Jaeger (1938) 144, 146; Gager (1972) 28; Diamond (1974) xiv; Will and Orrieux (1986) 83; Bickerman (1988) 17; Gabba (1989) 627. See the

version of the expulsion story,[66] and perhaps even to have "softened" it: to judge from other sources, the Egyptian versions related that the Jews were banished because they suffered from pestilence—leprosy and other diseases—or that they were loathed by the Egyptian gods, or both. In addition, in at least one source the Jews are also accused of impiety.[67] From Hecataeus's version it appears that the whole population in Egypt suffered from the plague, because the Egyptians themselves neglected the worship of their gods. They put the blame on the influence of foreigners who worshipped their own deities, and consequently expelled them. The inclusion of Danaus and Cadmus in the account, which did belong to the original Egyptian story,[68] by itself demanded a "softening" of the original tradition. Another "softening" is evident in the reference to Jewish hatred of strangers ("somewhat," 3.4),[69] which may be based on comments of Egyptians or Greek settlers, but could also reflect Hecataeus's personal impression.

There are, however, other references that could not have been based on Jewish or Egyptian sources, namely the explanations given for Jewish practices. There are also data that do not accord with Jewish traditions known to us: that the Jews settled in an "utterly desolate" land (3.2), that the first priests and all the High Priests were appointed according to merit (4–5), and that Moses made provisions for military training of the younger generation (6). This brings us to the much-discussed question of Greek influence.

It was suggested long ago, and has been repeated since by many scholars, that the excursus is an imaginary account of Jewish history and life based on Greek practices and conceptions. Thus, for instance, it

---

expression ὡς τινές φασιν ("as some say," Diod. XL.3.2). The use of Egyptian sources is explicitly indicated in the collection of minor ethnographies at the end of the *origo-archaeologia* section of the *Aegyptiaca*, the original place of the Jewish ethnographies (Diod. I.28.1–2 *et passim*).

66. The use of more than one source for the expulsion stories is indicated in Diod. I.28.2; see Jaeger (1938) 146; Guttman (1958–63) I.50–51.

67. See the versions of Manetho *ap.* Jos. *Ap.* I.229, 239–40, 248–50 (impiety); Lysimachus, ibid. I.304–9; Posidonius *ap.* Diod. XXXIV–XXXV.1.1–2; Pompeius Trogus *ap.* Justin XXXVI.1.12. The version of Tacitus (*Hist.* V.3.1) ascribes the pestilence to the whole population, and the Jews are portrayed as being hated by the gods.

68. See Bickerman (1988) 17.

69. See p. 39 below.

has been argued that a good number of details actually record Platonic ideals. These statements are too general and sweeping. The whole question of Greek influence requires qualification and more precise definitions. In the great variety of governmental systems, institutions, and political ideas current in Greek civilization, it is not difficult to find a counterpart to almost every clause in Hecataeus's excursus, although these might represent different political models and conceptions. It should be emphasized once more, however, that almost all the data (as distinct from their reasoning) originate in Jewish tradition and history, and that the statements about the dominant role of the priests and High Priests do not accord with Hecataeus's political commitment. The latter references are also specifically Jewish, and the "quotation" from the Pentateuch is the best example for this.

Greek influence can be detected in: (a) the literary structure and sequence; (b) a few details that are absent from or are contradictory to Jewish tradition; (c) the terminology used for the factual material; (d) the explanations provided by the author for Jewish *nomima*. As far as the literary structure is concerned, we have already mentioned the application of the rules of the ethnographical genre: the division of the excursus into a *ktisis* (*origo*) section and a *nomima* section, the causal connection between the two, and the reasoning of the facts. No less important was the structural influence of foundation stories. The conflation of three periods into one and the centering of the major historical developments and institutions around the personality of Moses were explained above by reference to the literary tradition of foundation stories. The influence of this tradition, noticed first by Werner Jaeger,[70] also dictated the selection and arrangement of the material for the two sections of the excursus.

That Hecataeus treated Moses as a *ktistēs* (founder and builder) and Jerusalem as his colony also appears from the terminology: the first section of the excursus is called *ktisis* (3.1), which may record Hecataeus's wording. The verb *ktizein* is explicitly used with regard to the alleged foundation of Jerusalem by Moses (3); Moses is said to have been leading (ἡγεῖτο) the new settlement, called *apoikia* (3). The latter term (literally, "settlement far from home") is usual for a

---

70. Jaeger (1938) 144, 146–47; *id.* (1938a) 140. Cf. esp. Lebram (1974a) 248–49. (The latter, however, thinks that the excursus is a Jewish forgery of the Hasmonean period.)

Greek settlement initiated by a mother city. Hecataeus uses this term even though he describes the Jews in the *ktisis-origo* as foreigners who were expelled from Egypt. Moreover, this is certainly not how Jewish informants would have termed resettlement in the land of the Israelite Patriarchs. Moses is described as a leader who excelled in wisdom and bravery (3), two virtues that are required of and attributed to founders (cf. Dion. Hal. II.7.1). He is not praised for "piety" (*eusebeia*),[71] which Jewish informants might have been expected to stress. Here we have an indication of the selection technique.

Turning to the structure, the similarity with foundation stories is indeed striking. The events and processes recorded in the *ktisis* section (3.1–3) are known from foundation stories and follow their basic sequence:[72] the rise (usually by appointment) of a leader-founder, the emigration, foundation of the city (in foundation stories, building of a wall and then houses), building of a temple, drawing up laws, forming political institutions, and dividing the population into tribes. The *nomima* section opens with three references that deviate from the usual sequence: they relate to everyday customs unique to Jews (faith, sacrifice, and attitude toward strangers). It may well be that these references were originally located by Hecataeus at the end of the excursus, and were brought forward by Diodorus because of some association. These are followed by an elaboration of some of the institutions and laws founded by Moses that were only generally referred to at the end of the *ktisis* section. The sequence again principally follows that of foundation stories: establishment of judiciary and governmental system (3.4–6), preparation of the younger generation for war (6), expansion through military expeditions (7), distribution of agricultural lands and prohibition against selling them (7).[73] Even the final demand to rear children to increase the population (8) has its parallels in traditional foundation stories.[74]

---

71. Noted by Bidez and Cumont (1938) I.241; Jacoby (1943) 51–52; Diamond (1974) 228–29, (1980) 83–84.

72. On the scheme and sequence, see P. B. Schmid (1947) 176–77; Virgilio (1972); Graham (1982) 143ff.; Leschhorn (1984) 85ff., 106ff. Cf. Jaeger and Lebram (n. 70 above).

73. On the equal distribution of lands and the literary tradition concerning their inalienability in Greek colonies, see Graham (1982) 151–52. Cf., for Rome, Dion. Halic. II.7.4.

74. The most detailed is Dion. Halic. II.15.1–3.

The excursus closes with a number of daily customs that are compared with those of the Egyptians (3.8). This may have been the original location of the references to Jewish faith, sacrifices, and attitude toward strangers (4), but they may well have been attached by Hecataeus himself to the *ktisis-origo* by way of association (temple–sacrifice–[dietary laws]–*apanthrōpia* and *misoxenia*). The inclusion of an account of daily customs is not typical of foundation stories, but is an essential component of ethnographies. This indicates that the basic structure of the excursus as a whole is that of a miniature ethnography, not of a *ktisis*. The distinction made by Diodorus between the first section (*ktisis*) and the second (*nomima*) may derive from Hecataeus himself, and reinforces this conclusion.

It must be admitted that the variety of subjects and their sequence in foundation stories were not so rigid as it might appear, and there were local variations according to the circumstances. The main features and basic order, however, are common to many foundation traditions. Naturally, some of them contained subjects not referred to in the Jewish excursus, since this local variation had no place for them. Most conspicuous is the absence of any consultation of an oracle by the founder before embarking on the expedition. Parallel Jewish information drawn from the Book of Exodus was available, but, Hecataeus having chosen the expulsion story, a consultation, which usually centered upon the question whether to emigrate or not, was redundant.

The influence of foundation stories may help to understand the origin of data that contradict or do not appear in Jewish tradition. The statement that Judea was "utterly desolate" (παντελῶς δὲ ἔρημον οὖσαν) at the time of the settlement (3.2) can be explained as a confusion with the information about Moses' long activity in the desert.[75] The conflation of the periods and the concentration of all the information around the personality of Moses seem to have contributed to this confusion. But this explanation cannot stand alone, since Hecataeus's Jewish informants presumably referred in one way or another to the conquest of Canaan. There must be an additional factor that caused the author to forget or disregard this information. I would suggest that it was the influence of foundation stories, mainly those relating to the settlement of "barbaric" nations in the archaic age. Traditions

---

75. This is actually the suggestion of Diamond (1974) 246–49, though her discussion is spoiled by too many wrong assumptions.

concerning the age of colonization mention settlement in both inhabited and uninhabited regions. The latter situation seems to have been the more common, especially in such destinations as the Black Sea area. On some occasions, emigrants were invited by local rulers and did not have to occupy a place by force.[76] However, when referring to barbarian emigrations in the archaic age, Greeks tended to describe them as settling desolate lands.[77]

Another statement, which is not contradictory to but is absent from Jewish tradition, attributes to Moses the making of special provisions for war, especially with regard to the training of the younger generation (3.6). It is followed by the statement that Moses led the nation in wars against neighbors (7), which probably echoes some hazy information about the wars of Joshua. Such wars were frequently mentioned in Greek foundation stories as well. They were preceded by references to intensive military training, especially of the young, as one of the first steps taken in Greek colonies. Having described the Jewish settlement in Judea as a peaceful one, Hecataeus felt it necessary to introduce a stage of military preparations, before the wars of expansion, following the Greek model. We shall see later that Hecataeus also had a special didactic aim in making this point, and that in his Egyptian ethnography he emphasized the need to train the younger generation from childhood (Diod. I.73.9).[78] The requirements from the young, "manliness, steadfastness, ... endurance of every hardship," are typical of the Greek *paideia*.[79]

More problematic is the statement about the appointment of priests and High Priests. Jewish priesthood and High Priesthood were hereditary. Hecataeus seems to be unaware of this fact. He says that the first priests were appointed by Moses on merit (XL.3.4) but does not refer to later generations. With regard to the High Priesthood he states that it is always conferred upon the priest who excels in "wisdom and virtue" (5). It is hardly believable that the Jewish informants

76. See the survey of Graham (1982) 92–143, 155. On the Black Sea: Vinogradov (1981) 11ff.

77. M. Stern (1974–84) I.30 draws attention to Hdt. IV.11.4 (the settlement of the Scythians); Dion. Halic. I.12.1, 13.3 (Italy), and I.22.2 (Sicily). Cf. the place chosen for the foundation of the ideal city in Plato, *Leges* 704b–c.

78. See pp. 36–38.

79. Noted by Jaeger (1938) 152. See, e.g., Plato, *Rep.* 375–90.

deliberately misled Hecataeus on these matters. He may instead have misinterpreted certain complimentary references to the qualities of the priests and the High Priests. In addition, as the position of High Priest was sometimes conferred upon the brother of the legal heir,[80] some process of formal ratification must have existed. This being reported to him, it may have contributed to the misunderstanding. Hecataeus may also have had parallels in Plato's *Laws* (759a–b, 947a–b) at the back of his mind.

The Greek coloring of the facts (as distinct from their explanations) was also achieved by the application of classical political and philosophical terminology to Jewish institutions and practices. We have noted above the terms borrowed from foundation stories. To mention just a few more examples: the Jewish settlements are called *poleis* (Diod. XL.3.3), the position of the High Priest is defined as ἡ τοῦ πλήθους προστασία ("the leadership of the multitude," 5),[81] the priests are described as τῶν ἀνδρῶν χαριέστατοι ("the most refined men," 4),[82] and the High Priest as the one "superior . . . in wisdom and *virtue*" (5).

As far as the explanations provided by Hecataeus are concerned, here the Greek influence is very much in evidence: the nation is divided into twelve tribes "since this is regarded as the most perfect number and corresponds to the number of months" (3.3; cf. Plato, *Laws*, 745b–d; Philo, *De Fug.* 184ff.);[83] the Jews are said to deify "Heaven" because it "encompasses the Earth . . . and rules everything [τῶν ὅλων]" (Diod. XL.3.4),[84] and to have no images because they think that "God is

---

80. See Alon (1957) 72; M. Stern (1974–84) I.31, referring to *Ant.* XI.298 and XII.157, 237–38; II Macc. 4.7ff. On Eliashib, brother (son?) of Yehoyakim, see Cross (1975) 7ff.

81. Cf. τοῦ δήμου προστάτης in Arist. *Ath. Pol.* 2.2, 20.4, 21.1, 28 (cited by Diamond [1980] 94).

82. Arist. *Eth. Nic.* 1095ᵃ19, ᵇ22, 1102ᵃ22; *Pol.* 1267ᵃ40, 1297ᵇ9, 1320ᵇ7 (see Diamond [1980] 94; Feldman [1993] 235).

83. See in detail Guttman (1958–63) I.53–54. More references in M. Stern (1974–84) I.30.

84. The definition of the Jewish God contains several assumptions: that God is material; that the earth as well as heaven is spherical; and that heaven encompasses the earth. For these assumptions, see Arist. *De Caelo* 278ᵇ9–24, 293ᵇ32–294ᵃ1, 297ᵃ8. See also Ps.-Arist. *De Mundo* 391ᵇ19–392ᵃ5, 399ᵃ1–6, which reflect earlier views. For the combination περιέχοντα . . . καὶ τῶν ὅλων κύριον, see Arist. *Phys.* 203ᵇ10. Cf. Hdt. I.131 on the Persian religion. All

not in human form" (4);[85] the priests receive greater lots to provide them enough leisure for performing their public duties (7; cf. Arist. *Pol.* 1269ª35, 1273ª34); the lands are inalienable to avoid the creation of great estates and consequent oppression of the poor classes and scarcity of manpower (Diod. XL.3.7);[86] a community of landowning farmers can easily rear children, and this secures the necessary manpower for the nation (8).[87] The attitude of Jews to strangers is called *apanthrōpia* and *misoxenia* and is explained by their *xenēlasia* from Egypt, which is the term used exclusively for Spartan banishment of strangers.[88] Some inspiration was also drawn from Egyptian tradition to explain Jewish practices: the priests are given greater lots to enable them to be free to perform their public duties (7; cf. I.72.2–3).[89]

It has frequently been argued that the excursus is an idealization of the Jewish people, and was meant to present a model of an ideal society.[90]

---

these have nothing to do with the Jewish God: "heaven," popularly believed to be the residence of the divine, was used by the Jews only as a substitute for the tetragrammaton.

85. See Xenophanes in Diels and Kranz (1935) 21(11) B 23, and the striking similarity with Hdt. I.131 (on Persian religion). Cf. Jaeger (1938) 147–48; Gager (1972) 31–32; Will and Orrieux (1986) 84–85; and esp. Guttman (1958–63) I.58–62. It is still to be proved that this explanation accords with the Jewish conception of the divine at the beginning of the Hellenistic period.

86. Cf. Plato, *Leges* 741b; Arist. *Pol.* 1266ᵇ, 1270ª18ff.; and see Guttman (1958–63) I.56–57; M. Stern (1974–84) I.33.

87. See pp. 36–38 below.

88. See Ginsburg (1934); Guttman (1958–63) I.108–11; Murray (1970) 158–59.

89. Cf. also Euhemerus's utopian treatise on the Panchaeans, where the priests are given, for the same reason, a double share of the produce (Diod. V.45.5).

90. See esp. Jaeger (1938) 149, 151–53; *id.* (1938a) 141; Guttman (1958–63) I.53–65; Murray (1970) 158–59; Hengel (1973) 564ff.; Will and Orrieux (1986) 87–92; Bickerman (1988) 17; Mélèze-Modrzejewski (1989) 12–13. The most outspoken is Joshua Guttman, who describes Hecataeus's version as "a complete and absolute idealization" (p. 63). Guttman says further: "He [Hecataeus] sees the Jewish constitution in the spirit of Platonic doctrine, as blessed in all the advantages of a perfect and exemplary constitution, for it has a divine origin and accords with the rules governing the cosmos. Consequently, the Jewish political system, according to Hecataeus, lacks all the defects that harm the political systems of other nations, and deserves, therefore, to be a model of imitation for all mankind" (p. 66). In contrast to these views, see

The model, however, has been variously described as a "theocracy" or "aristocracy," inspired to a great extent by Plato's *Laws* and *Republic* respectively, a "Spartan oligarchy," and even an "Egyptian Sparta."[91] It has also been suggested that the account describes a "mixed constitution" made of all these. As a matter of fact, none of these conceptions, singly or in combination, perfectly concurs with the contents of the excursus.[92] What should really be asked is whether Hecataeus actually aspired at the outset to idealize the account, and present all of it as a model. The answer must be that he did not. Hecataeus, who served Ptolemy I, would hardly have advocated a society without kings, with the power being entrusted entirely to priests. This also stands in contrast with the government presented in his Egyptian ethnography. It should be reiterated that, by and large, Hecataeus recorded the information provided by his Jewish informants. The interpretation is basically what one would expect to be made of the facts by a Greek intellectual who had a good philosophical education, if he was not himself an original philosopher. The account does not include superlatives or even praises, and it is difficult to see features that could be admired or advocated by Hecataeus, except for those pertaining to military manpower.

The latter features were emphasized, supplemented, and explained with much elaboration, having in mind the Greco-Macedonian reader in Egypt. Much stress was laid on military training of the younger generation, allocation of equal lots, inalienability of land, and the great

---

Jacoby (1943) 48ff.: "es ist ganz deutlich, dass er [Hecataeus] das jüdische wesen nicht als vorbildlich, sondern nur als fremdarting empfunden hat." Cf. Diamond (1980).

91. The expression of Murray, *loc. cit.* (n. 90); cf. Will and Orrieux, *loc. cit.* (n. 90). Noteworthy are the attitude toward strangers, the distribution of equal lots, the inalienability of lands, and the training of the younger generation.

92. Thus, e.g., the encouragement to rear children and increase the population (without setting a limit) does not accord with the ideal of Plato (*Leges* 741d; 928c–930) or Aristotle (*Pol.* 1265^{b}35ff., 1326^{b}4ff., 1355^{b}20ff.), nor with Spartan practice. The same applies to the account about the status of the priests and their allotments, the High Priest, the veneration of the High Priest, and the divine source of all the laws. To equate the priests with Plato's "guardians" or "sages" would not resolve the differences, and would even raise new ones (e.g., the ownership of land).

rate of natural increase that was implicitly praised. A close look at the explanations provided reveals the message: farmers should have viable lots and a sound economic position so that there will be no "scarcity of manpower." The agrarian arrangements are also the way to encourage rearing children. As a result, the Jews are a "populous nation" (3.8). The causal connection in the first point is not made clear, and the advantage of the second is not explained. Hecataeus's original reasoning may well have been cut short by Diodorus. To understand it, we have to turn to the corresponding passages concerning the Egyptian warrior class in Hecataeus's *Aegyptiaca*. The main features and their explanation are actually identical:[93]

> The last part [of the land] is held by the warriors [*machimoi*], who are subject to call for all military duties, the purpose being that those who hazard their life may be loyal to the country because of this allotment of land [*klērouchia*] and may thereby eagerly face the perils of war. For it would be absurd to entrust the safety of the entire nation to these men and yet have them possess in the country no property to fight for valuable enough to arouse their ardour. But the most important consideration is the fact that, if they are well-to-do, they will readily beget children and thus so increase the population that the country will not need to call in any mercenary troops. And since their calling, like that of the priests, is hereditary, the warriors are incited to bravery by the distinguished record of their fathers and, inasmuch as they become zealous [students] of warfare from their boyhood up, they turn out to be invincible by reason of their daring and skill.

The distribution of land and the efforts made for the welfare of the settlers are thus intended to provide them with a good motivation to fight. This is the meaning of the argument of the Jewish excursus that economic hardships "bring on a scarcity of manpower." Even more important is the second purpose: to encourage and enable the settlers to rear children and thus "increase the population." The aim is to secure a situation in which "the country will not need to call in any mercenary troops." Here we find what is missing in the Jewish excursus: rearing many children and becoming a "populous

93. Diod. I.73.7–9. The translation: Oldfather (1933) 253–54 (*LCL*). On the rearing of children in Egypt, see also Diod. I.80.6, where it seems to be factual and free of didactic and military connotations.

nation" confers a military advantage (cf. Polyb. XXXVI.17.5–11). Just as with the Jews in the excursus, the younger generation of Egyptian warriors was trained for war from childhood. The terminology applied in the passage should also be noticed: *machimoi* and *klērouchiai* were the official Hellenistic terms for military settlers of Egyptian descent serving under the Ptolemies, and their settlements, respectively. In the third century, the term *klērouchiai* was also used for settlements of Greco-Macedonian soldiers.[94]

The correspondence of these data and explanations with the situation of the Greco-Macedonian settlers in Ptolemaic Egypt cannot be coincidental. Scarcity of European manpower was the most acute problem facing the young Ptolemaic empire. The Greco-Macedonian conquerors of Egypt were a tiny minority amid the native population, and the possibility of recruiting Greco-Macedonian mercenaries was rather limited, these being divided between the armies of the Successors. In the first generation of the occupation, Ptolemy recruited Egyptians to the army as light troops (e.g., Diod. XIX.80.4), making sure not to provide them with heavy weapons.[95] Hecataeus, who was considering the future of the kingdom, must have realized that even this solution could only be temporary. In the long run, arming and training the natives at all might prove dangerous to the very existence of the Macedonian regime in Egypt. Hecataeus, therefore, suggests measures that will invest in the younger generation of Greco-Macedonian settlers: encouraging the birth and raising of children (contrary to the traditional practice in the motherland), allocating equal and sufficient lots to the settlers to enable each one to raise a large family, prohibiting the sale of lands to secure the continuity of this class of farmer-soldiers, and constantly training the descendants of the first generation of settlers. Ptolemaic military settlement was indeed organized along such lines, but gradually deteriorated, neglecting the preparation of the younger generation for war. As a result, in 217, on the eve of the battle of Raphia, Ptolemy IV was

94. See Lesquier (1911) 5–8, 30ff., 175ff.; Oertel, *RE* s.v. *katoikoi*, 17–18; Holleaux (1938–57) II.37–38; Uebel (1968) 4–11. In the third century B.C. the term *klērouchiai* was applied also to settlements of European settlers, while in second-century Ptolemaic Egypt it was used only for settlements of native soldiers, to distinguish them from *katoikiai*, settlements of Greco-Macedonian soldiers.

95. See Lesquier (1911) 6–7, 19–21; Griffith (1935) 109, 112; Launey (1949–50) I.589; Bar-Kochva (1989) 96 and n. 27.

forced to recruit thousands of Egyptians and to train them as phalanx warriors. The success of these troops in the battle of Raphia raised the self-confidence of the local population and generated a revolt that lasted thirty years, leaving the Ptolemaic kingdom at the mercy of its Seleucid rival.[96]

The assumption that the excursus is a highly idealized account intended to be a model has led a number of scholars to suggest that the reference to the Jewish attitude toward strangers (3.4) was meant to express not reservation but praise.[97] However, in addition to the connotations of *apanthrōpia* and *misoxenia* in Greek culture, which could not be favorable, the qualifier τις ("somewhat," 4), which is certainly original,[98] makes it evident that the sentence was not written as a compliment. Moreover, in his Egyptian ethnography, Hecataeus praises King Psammeticus for his hospitality toward foreigners, in contrast to the hostility of his predecessors (Diod. I.67.8–11; cf. 69.4, 88.5). Hecataeus was then ready to express his negative attitude toward separatism, even in an idealizing context. Praise for hospitality toward Greeks is also voiced in the utopian *On the Hyperboreans* (Diod. II.47.4).

How then should the attitude of Hecataeus toward the Jews be evaluated? Having a basically unbiased attitude, Hecataeus presented the information available to him while interpreting certain features

96. See Milne (1928) 226–34; Griffith (1935) 117, 123, 140; Préaux (1939) I.28–52; Will (1967) II.35–36; Bar-Kochva (1989) 96–98.

97. See Guttman (1958–63) I.63; Lebram (1974a) 274; Diamond (1980) 85–86; Gabba (1989) 629. Cf. the variations of Gager (1972) 35, (1983) 40; Will and Orrieux (1986) 92–93. On the negative character of the sentence, see Reinach (1895) 17, 19; Willrich (1900) 89; Radin (1915) 93–95; Jacoby (1943) 48–49; Tcherikover (1961) 360; Murray (1970) 144; Sevenster (1975) 188–90; Mélèze-Modrzejewski (1989) 11–12; Feldman (1993) 126.

98. Diodorus did not have any reason to introduce this cautious, diminutive expression. Moreover, it does not accord with the material Diodorus had at his disposal on Jewish separatism (Diod. XXXIV–XXXV.1.1–2). The suggestion of Gauger ([1982] 22) that the sentence is an "anti-Semitic" comment by Diodorus cannot, therefore, be accepted. There is also a parallel for the use of τις as a diminutive qualifier in a clause from Hecataeus's Jewish excursus preserved elsewhere (Pseudo-Aristeas 31; see pp. 140–41 below).

according to Greek experience and conceptions. This is just how a Greek author-philosopher would have dealt with the facts; it does not mean that the excursus is an idealization or a "model." The account of the preparation of reliable manpower (including the strict agrarian arrangements) is the only part intended for emulation. However, even this is still not a deliberate idealization: the information given by the Jews is presented in the way Hecataeus, as a Greek, understood it.

One should not exaggerate the significance of the excursus. Hecataeus did not attach so much importance to it as might appear from modern scholarly interpretations. The Jewish excursus was just one of a number of minor ethnographies incorporated into the *Aegyptiaca*. They each presented a different system of government and society. In the way many Greeks viewed most oriental nations at the beginning of the encounter between the two great cultures, so Hecataeus viewed the Jews: he was curious and impartial, attempting to understand the information according to his education and way of thinking. He was indifferent on most topics, but appreciated some features and expressed reservations about others. This discerning evaluation is expressed in a factual style, combined with elaborate reasoning, without explicit compliments, exclamations, or superlatives, and avoiding rhetorical-emotional expressions. Despite the philosophical interpretation of their faith, the Jews are not described as a nation of philosophers, although this appears in contemporary Hellenistic literature.[99] After all, even in referring to Egyptian religion, Hecataeus describes their "first god" as being "the same as the universe [τῷ παντί] . . . invisible and concealed" (Plut. *De Is. et Os.* 354d). The author does not forget to make clear that the Jews are inferior to the immigrants who landed in Greece and Asia Minor (Diod. XL.3.2). Such a comment is not made about the Egyptians, who are constantly praised for their decisive contributions to civilization.

To sum up the discussion: How can the process of composition be imagined? Hecataeus planned an excursus that would include an *origo* section and a *nomima* section, to be incorporated among other

---

99. See Theophrastus *ap.* Porph. *Abst.* II.26; Clearchus of Soli *ap.* Jos. *Ap.* I.179; Megasthenes *ap.* Clem. *Strom.* I.15.

miniature ethnographies put together as an appendix to the Egyptian *origo-archaeologia*. The initial purpose was to show that the Jews, like other nations, originated from Egypt, and that this descent influenced their *nomima*. For this purpose, in interviewing his Jewish informants, he concentrated on the personality of Moses, the settlement in Canaan, and contemporary Jewish institutions and practices. Consequently, the information related to three periods in Jewish history: the Exodus, the settlement, and the time of Hecataeus himself (i.e., the Persian and early Hellenistic periods). However, he disregarded the Jewish Exodus story, perhaps because it appeared to insult the Egyptians whom he praised so much, or because he wanted to equate the background of the Jewish emigration to that of other nations. For the *origo* section Hecataeus consulted, therefore, Egyptian stories circulating in his time, preferring a more moderate one, possibly even "softening" it. In addition he did not refrain from expressing his reservations about Jewish exclusiveness and hatred of strangers.

In composing the excursus, Hecataeus had to sort out, select, and arrange the information into the *origo* and *nomima*, the two planned sections. His basic editorial conception was to follow the accepted model of a foundation story and supplement it with a number of daily customs illustrating the similarities and differences between Jews and Egyptians. The pieces of information selected were mainly those known from foundation stories. They were arranged and conflated according to the accepted sequence and conception of these stories. Moses was described as the founder of the nation as well as of the country, and all Jewish institutions and practices were attributed to him. The historical development was thus distorted, three distinct periods of Jewish history being conflated into one. The foundation story was divided between the *origo* and *nomima*. The *origo* included the story of the expulsion and the headlines of a typical foundation story. The *nomima* comprised two parts: the first elaborated on the institution and the provisions indicated in the *origo*; the second, on a number of everyday customs.

Forming the framework and filling it with information, Hecataeus found it appropriate to complete the picture by adding one or two important statements drawn from foundation traditions, which were not reported by his Jewish informants. Then came the addition of causations and reasoning, according to the rules of the new ethnographical writing. Some customs were explained by the Jewish *origo*, especially the bad memories of the expulsion. Others were interpreted according to the Greek cultural and philosophical heritage. Special emphasis was laid on statements referring to provisions made for securing manpower, by which means Hecataeus tried to indicate how he envisaged the organization of the newly established military settlements in Ptolemaic Egypt, just as he had done in his Egyptian ethnography in the account of the pharaonic warriors.

Finally, it would be helpful to emphasize the points that are directly relevant to various questions concerning the treatise *On the Jews*:

1. An analysis and comparison of the original style and vocabulary of the excursus is precluded by the modifications they have undergone at the hands of Diodorus.

2. The *origo* section opens the excursus, occupies a major role in it, and is used to explain a number of Jewish practices.

3. The excursus is centered around the personality of Moses, with Jewish institutions and practices being attributed exclusively to him.

4. Moses is not only the leader of the emigration, but also the founder of the new settlements.

5. Allowing for inaccuracies resulting from the literary model, it can be said that Hecataeus collected important, reliable information about the life of the Jews in his time. He deleted details that were redundant or did not fit into the framework he had set for himself.

6. Especially important are the references to the High Priest. Hecataeus knew that there was just one High Priest at a time, and was well acquainted with his unique status in the Jewish community.

7. The priests are said to have earned their living from the greater lots granted to them. There is no reference to tithes of agricultural produce.

8. The account sounds unbiased, certainly not enthusiastic, and was not intended to idealize the Jewish people.

9. Hecataeus did not advocate Jewish *misoxenia* and *apanthrōpia*, but expressed his reservation explicitly.

10. Hecataeus's Jewish ethnography was not meant to portray a model society, although one part of it, the provisions for a competent and sufficient source of military manpower, was emphasized in order to serve as an example.

11. The excursus consistently provides causal reasoning as well as social and philosophical explanations for Jewish institutions and practices.

12. As in the Egyptian ethnography, the reasoning in the Jewish excursus is based on Greek tradition, literature, and modes of thinking. As some scholars have put it, the excursus is, by and large, an *interpretatio Graeca* of Jewish history and life.

II   The Passages in *Against Apion*: Text and Translation

The passages containing the fragments of and testimonia to the treatise *On the Jews* appear in Josephus's *Against Apion*. With one exception, they are grouped together in one sequence in Book I of the work. Josephus prefaces the sequence with a statement about his purpose in referring to the treatise and includes biographical notes about Hecataeus, his date, work, and position. Then come a number of passages, separated by conjunctions and words of introduction by Josephus, some of which appear in direct, others in indirect speech.

The Greek text is reproduced from Niese's edition ([1888] V.33–37). The apparatus is based on Niese's, but it is selective and includes only those readings and emendations that may affect the arguments of this book. In several places I have offered supplements to Niese's apparatus. The *sigla* refer to the following manuscripts and testimonia:[*]

> L   Codex Laurentianus (Florence), plut. 69 cod. 22. Eleventh century. This is the archetype of all extant Greek manuscripts.
>
> Eus.   Eusebius, *Praeparatio Evangelica* IX.4.2–9. Eusebius quotes *Ap.* I.197–204. *PE* contains also other extracts from *Against Apion*. Eusebius's readings are often preferable to those of the manuscripts. The most recent critical edition is that of

---

[*] For the evaluation of the manuscripts and the transmission, see further Niese (1888) vol. V, pp. iv ff.; Boysen (1898) p. xxxiv; Thackeray (1926) pp. xvii–xx; Mras (1944) 220ff., (1954–56) vol. VIII, pp. xiii ff., lv ff.; Schreckenberg (1972) 5, 52–53, 79–87; *id.* (1977) 157–69.

Mras (1956), vol. VIII pp. 489–91. Eusebius's text is extant in thirteen manuscripts. The manuscripts mentioned in my apparatus are:

Eusebii cod. G   Laurentianus plut. VI cod. 9. Fourteenth century.

Eusebii cod. I   Venetus gr. 341. Fifteenth century.

Lat.   The Latin translation of *Against Apion*, prepared in the sixth century for Cassiodorus, the minister of Theodoric. Its great contribution consists of the passages II.52–113, which are missing in the Greek manuscripts. There are many mistaken translations, caused by misunderstanding of the Greek text. The translation is extant in three manuscripts. The critical edition used is that of Boysen (1898).

Ed. pr.   *Editio princeps*, the first printed edition of *Against Apion*, in the edition of Josephus by A. P. Arlenius (Basel 1544). It contains readings that may perhaps indicate the use of manuscripts other than L and its apographs.

For the benefit of the reader who cannot consult the Greek text, I endeavored to translate the texts literally, adhering to their verbal contents and syntactical construction rather than to English idiomatic expressions. This may give the reader of the translation some taste of the style of some of the passages (esp. *Ap.* I.202–4a).

Jos. *Ap.* I.183–205

[183] Ἑκαταῖος δὲ ὁ Ἀβδηρίτης, ἀνὴρ φιλόσοφος ἅμα καὶ περὶ τὰς πράξεις ἱκανώτατος, Ἀλεξάνδρῳ τῷ βασιλεῖ συνακμάσας καὶ Πτολεμαίῳ τῷ Λάγου συγγενόμενος, οὐ παρέργως, ἀλλὰ περὶ αὐτῶν Ἰουδαίων συγγέγραφε βιβλίον, ἐξ οὗ βούλομαι κεφαλαιωδῶς ἐπιδραμεῖν ἔνια τῶν εἰρημένων. [184] καὶ πρῶτον ἐπιδείξω τὸν χρόνον· μνημονεύει γὰρ τῆς Πτολεμαίου περὶ Γάζαν πρὸς Δημήτριον μάχης· αὕτη δὲ γέγονεν ἑνδεκάτῳ μὲν ἔτει τῆς Ἀλεξάνδρου τελευτῆς, ἐπὶ δὲ ὀλυμπιάδος ἑβδόμης καὶ δεκάτης καὶ ἑκατοστῆς, ὡς ἱστορεῖ Κάστωρ. [185] προσθεὶς γὰρ ταύτην τὴν ὀλυμπιάδα φησίν· "ἐπὶ ταύτης Πτολεμαῖος ὁ Λάγου ἐνίκα κατὰ Γάζαν μάχῃ Δημήτριον τὸν Ἀντιγόνου τὸν ἐπικληθέντα Πολιορκητήν." Ἀλέξανδρον δὲ τεθνάναι πάντες ὁμολογοῦσιν ἐπὶ τῆς ἑκατοστῆς τεσσαρεσκαιδεκάτης ὀλυμπιάδος. δῆλον οὖν, ὅτι καὶ κατ᾽ ἐκεῖνον καὶ κατὰ Ἀλέξανδρον ἤκμαζεν ἡμῶν τὸ ἔθνος. [186] λέγει τοίνυν ὁ Ἑκαταῖος πάλιν τάδε, ὅτι μετὰ τὴν ἐν Γάζῃ μάχην ὁ Πτολεμαῖος ἐγένετο τῶν περὶ Συρίαν τόπων ἐγκρατής, καὶ πολλοὶ τῶν ἀνθρώπων πυνθανόμενοι τὴν ἠπιότητα καὶ φιλανθρωπίαν τοῦ Πτολεμαίου συναπαίρειν εἰς Αἴγυπτον αὐτῷ καὶ κοινωνεῖν τῶν πραγμάτων ἠβουλήθησαν. [187] "ὧν εἷς ἦν," φησίν, "Ἐζεκίας ἀρχιερεὺς¹ τῶν Ἰουδαίων, ἄνθρωπος τὴν μὲν ἡλικίαν ὡς ἑξήκοντα ἓξ ἐτῶν, τῷ δ᾽ ἀξιώματι τῷ παρὰ τοῖς ὁμοέθνοις μέγας καὶ τὴν ψυχὴν οὐκ² ἀνόητος, ἔτι δὲ καὶ λέγειν δυνατὸς καὶ τοῖς [...] περὶ τῶν πραγμάτων,³ εἴπερ τις ἄλλος, ἔμπειρος." [188] καίτοι, φησίν, "οἱ πάντες ἱερεῖς τῶν Ἰουδαίων οἱ τὴν δεκάτην⁴ τῶν γινομένων λαμβάνοντες καὶ τὰ κοινὰ διοικοῦντες περὶ χιλίους μάλιστα καὶ πεντακοσίους εἰσίν." [189] πάλιν δὲ τοῦ προειρημένου μνημονεύων ἀνδρός, "οὗτος," φησίν, "ὁ ἄνθρωπος τετευχὼς τῆς τιμῆς ταύτης καὶ συνήθης ἡμῖν γενόμενος, παραλαβών τινας τῶν μεθ᾽ ἑαυτοῦ τήν τε⁵ διαφορὰν⁶ ἀνέγνω [...]⁷ πᾶσαν αὐτοῖς· εἶχεν γὰρ τὴν κατοίκησιν αὐτῶν

---

1. ὁ ἀρχιερεὺς ed. pr.

2. οὐκ coni. Hudson (Niese): οὔτ᾽ L.

3. τοῖς περὶ τῶν πραγμάτων L, Niese: τοῖς ... ἔμπειρος indic. lacunam Hudson, Niese: circa causas Lat.

4. τὴν δεκάτην L: decatas Lat.

5. τε om. Lat.

6. διαφορὰν L, Lat: διφθέραν coni. Lewy et Cataudella (p. 221 inf.).

7. διαφορὰν ⟨ἀπέδειξε, καὶ τὴν συγγραφὴν⟩ ἀνέγνω supplevi (pp. 223–24 inf.).

[183] However, Hecataeus of Abdera, a philosopher and at the same time [a man] most competent in practical matters, having flourished at the time of King Alexander and being associated with Ptolemy son of Lagus, [referred to the Jews] not incidentally, but wrote a book about the Jews themselves, from which I want to present the highlights[a] of some of the things said. [184] And first of all I shall establish the date. He mentions the battle of Ptolemy against Demetrius near Gaza. That [battle] took place in the eleventh year after Alexander's death, in the 117th Olympiad, as Castor narrates. [185] For under the head of that Olympiad he says: "In this Olympiad Ptolemy son of Lagus defeated Demetrius son of Antigonus who was called Poliorcetes." And all agree that Alexander died in the 114th Olympiad. It is therefore clear that our nation was flourishing at his [Ptolemy's] time as well as in that of Alexander. [186] Moreover, Hecataeus goes on to say this: "After the battle at Gaza Ptolemy became master of the places near Syria,[b] and many of the men, hearing of his kindness and humanity [*philanthrōpia*] wished to accompany him to Egypt and take part in the affairs [of the kingdom]." [187] "One of them," he [Hecataeus] says, "was Hezekiah, High Priest of the Jews, a man at the age of around sixty-six, highly thought of by his compatriots and not unintelligent in his mind, and, moreover, an able speaker, and in [... and][c] experienced, if indeed anyone was, in the affairs." [188] He also says: "And all the Jewish priests who receive the tithe of the produce and administer public matters number at most about one thousand five hundred." [189] And again, referring to the above-mentioned man: "This man," he says, "having obtained this authority and being well acquainted with us, assembled some of his men and read to them the whole advantage.[d] For he possessed in writing their

---

a. More preferable for κεφαλαιωδῶς than the literal translation "summarily." The latter would hardly be a proper description of the account of the Temple and the Mosollamus episode (paras. 198–204).

b. Possibly also "master of the places in Syria" or "master of Syria."

c. ἔμπειρος can go only with the genitive (or περί + gen.). The τοῖς therefore indicates that an adjectival phrase describing another merit of Hezekiah has disappeared from the text.

d. If my suggestion for the lacuna (n. 7) is to be accepted, the translation of sentence would be: "He assembled some of the men and pointed out to them the advantage and read to them the whole ⟨"decree"? "charter"?⟩. For he possessed. ... "

καὶ τὴν πολιτείαν γεγραμμένην." [190] εἶτα Ἑκαταῖος δηλοῖ πάλιν, πῶς ἔχομεν πρὸς τοὺς νόμους, ὅτι πάντα πάσχειν ὑπὲρ τοῦ μὴ παραβῆναι τούτους προαιρούμεθα καὶ καλὸν εἶναι νομίζομεν. [191] "τοιγαροῦν," φησί, "καὶ κακῶς ἀκούοντες ὑπὸ τῶν ἀστυγειτόνων καὶ τῶν εἰσαφικνουμένων πάντες καὶ προπηλακιζόμενοι πολλάκις ὑπὸ τῶν Περσικῶν βασιλέων καὶ σατραπῶν οὐ δύνανται μεταπεισθῆναι τῇ διανοίᾳ, ἀλλὰ γεγυμνωμένως περὶ τούτων καὶ αἰκίαις καὶ θανάτοις δεινοτάτοις μάλιστα πάντων ἀπαντῶσι μὴ ἀρνούμενοι τὰ πάτρια."⁸ [192] παρέχεται δὲ καὶ τεκμήρια τῆς ἰσχυρογνωμοσύνης τῆς περὶ τῶν νόμων οὐκ ὀλίγα· φησὶ γὰρ Ἀλεξάνδρου ποτὲ ἐν Βαβυλῶνι γενομένου καὶ προελομένου τὸ τοῦ Βήλου πεπτωκὸς ἱερὸν ἀνακαθᾶραι καὶ πᾶσιν αὐτοῦ τοῖς στρατιώταις ὁμοίως φέρειν τὸν χοῦν προστάξαντος, μόνους τοὺς Ἰουδαίους οὐ προσσχεῖν, ἀλλὰ καὶ πολλὰς ὑπομεῖναι πληγὰς καὶ ζημίας ἀποτῖσαι μεγάλας, ἕως αὐτοῖς συγγνόντα τὸν βασιλέα δοῦναι τὴν ἄδειαν. [193] "ἔτι⁹ γε μὴν τῶν εἰς τὴν χώραν," φησί, "πρὸς αὐτοὺς ἀφικνουμένων νεὼς καὶ βωμοὺς κατασκευασάντων ἅπαντα ταῦτα κατέσκαπτον, καὶ τῶν μὲν ζημίαν τοῖς σατράπαις ἐξέτινον, περί τινων δὲ καὶ συγγνώμης μετελάμβανον." καὶ προσεπιτίθησιν, ὅτι δίκαιον ἐπὶ τούτοις¹⁰ αὐτούς ἐστι θαυμάζειν. [194] λέγει δὲ καὶ περὶ τοῦ πολυανθρωπότατον γεγονέναι ἡμῶν τὸ ἔθνος· "πολλὰς μὲν γὰρ ἡμῶν," φησίν, "ἀνασπάστους εἰς Βαβυλῶνα Πέρσαι πρότερον αὐτῶν ἐποίησαν μυριάδας, οὐκ ὀλίγαι δὲ καὶ μετὰ τὸν Ἀλεξάνδρου θάνατον εἰς Αἴγυπτον καὶ Φοινίκην μετέστησαν διὰ τὴν ἐν Συρίᾳ στάσιν." [195] ὁ δὲ αὐτὸς οὗτος ἀνὴρ καὶ τὸ μέγεθος τῆς χώρας ἣν κατοικοῦμεν καὶ τὸ κάλλος ἱστόρηκεν· "τριακοσίας γὰρ μυριάδας ἀρουρῶν σχεδὸν τῆς ἀρίστης καὶ παμφορωτάτης χώρας νέμονται," φησίν· "ἡ γὰρ Ἰουδαία τοσαύτη πλῆθός ἐστιν." [196] ἀλλὰ μὴν ὅτι καὶ τὴν πόλιν αὐτὴν τὰ Ἱεροσόλυμα καλλίστην τε καὶ μεγίστην ἐκ παλαιοτάτου κατοικοῦμεν¹¹ καὶ περὶ πλήθους ἀνδρῶν καὶ περὶ τῆς τοῦ νεὼ κατασκευῆς οὕτως αὐτὸς διηγεῖται· [197] "ἔστι γὰρ τῶν Ἰουδαίων τὰ μὲν πολλὰ ὀχυρώματα κατὰ τὴν χώραν καὶ κῶμαι, μία δὲ πόλις ὀχυρὰ πεντήκοντα μάλιστα σταδίων τὴν περίμετρον, ἣν οἰκοῦσι μὲν ἀνθρώπων περὶ δώδεκα μυριάδες,¹² καλοῦσι δ' αὐτὴν

8. πάτρια coni. Niese: πατρῷα L.
9. ἔτι coni. Niese: ἐπεῖ L et ut vid. Lat.
10. τούτοις ed. pr.: τούτους L.
11. κατοικοῦμεν ed. pr.: inhabitamus Lat.: κατοικουμένην L.
12. δώδεκα μυριάδες L, Eus.: CL milia Lat.

settling and constitution." [190] Then Hecataeus in turn explains how
we regard the laws, that we prefer to suffer everything in order not to
transgress against them and [that] we consider it as virtuous. [191]
"So for example," he says, "all being insulted by their neighbors and
by those who came into [the country], and being frequently abused by
the Persian kings and satraps, they could not be persuaded to change
their way of thinking, but being exposed because of [their adherence
to] them [the laws], they faced tortures and the most horrible deaths
rather than deny their ancestral [laws]." [192] He provided not a few
proofs for the resolute mind with regard to the laws. For he says that
once when Alexander was in Babylon and proposed to clear away [the
rubble of] the ruined temple of Bel, and ordered all the soldiers alike
to carry the earth material, only the Jews did not apply themselves to
[it], but submitted to many floggings and paid heavy penalties, until
the king agreed to grant them indemnity. [193] He says yet further:
"they destroyed all the temples and altars constructed by those coming
to the land against them, for some of which they paid a fine to the
satraps, and for others they obtained forgiveness." And he adds that
it is just to admire them for these [actions]. [194] And he also relates
how our nation became overpopulated. "The Persians," he says, "had
formerly deported many tens of thousands of them to Babylon, and
after Alexander's death, no less immigrated to Egypt and Phoenicia
because of the turbulence in Syria." [195] And this man himself
also recorded the size of the land in which we live and its beauty.
He says: "They possess almost three hundred myriads of [i.e., three
million] *arourae* of the best and most fertile land for all products. Such
is the extent of Judea." [196] Indeed he thus also relates that we
inhabit Jerusalem, that city, the most beautiful and the greatest, from
time immemorial, and the same [man relates] thus about the great
number of people and the building of the temple: [197] "There are
many fortresses of the Jews throughout the country, as well as villages,
but only one fortified city, of about fifty stadia [in] circumference,
which is inhabited by about twelve myriads of [i.e., 120,000] people,

Ἱεροσόλυμα. [198] ἐνταῦθα δ᾽ ἐστὶ κατὰ μέσον μάλιστα τῆς πόλεως περίβολος λίθινος, μῆκος ὡς πεντάπλεθρος, εὖρος δὲ πηχῶν ρ', ἔχων διπλᾶς πύλας, ἐν ᾧ βωμός ἐστι τετράγωνος ἀτμήτων συλλέκτων ἀργῶν λίθων οὕτως συγκείμενος, πλευρὰν μὲν ἑκάστην εἴκοσι πηχῶν, ὕψος δὲ δεκάπηχυ. καὶ παρ᾽ αὐτὸν οἴκημα μέγα, οὗ βωμός ἐστι καὶ λυχνίον¹³ ἀμφότερα χρυσᾶ δύο τάλαντα τὴν ὁλκήν. [199] ἐπὶ τούτων¹⁴ φῶς ἐστιν ἀναπόσβεστον καὶ τὰς νύκτας καὶ τὰς ἡμέρας. ἄγαλμα δὲ οὐκ ἔστιν οὐδὲ ἀνάθημα τὸ παράπαν οὐδὲ φύτευμα παντελῶς οὐδὲν οἷον ἀλσῶδες ἤ τι τοιοῦτον. διατρίβουσι δ᾽ ἐν αὐτῷ καὶ τὰς νύκτας καὶ τὰς ἡμέρας ἱερεῖς ἁγνείας τινὰς ἁγνεύοντες καὶ τὸ παράπαν οἶνον οὐ πίνοντες ἐν τῷ ἱερῷ." [200] ἔτι γε μὴν ὅτι καὶ Ἀλεξάνδρῳ τῷ βασιλεῖ συνεστρατεύσαντο καὶ μετὰ ταῦτα τοῖς διαδόχοις αὐτοῦ μεμαρτύρηκεν. οἷς δ᾽ αὐτὸς παρατυχεῖν φησιν ὑπ᾽ ἀνδρὸς Ἰουδαίου κατὰ τὴν στρατείαν γενομένοις, τοῦτο παραθήσομαι. [201] λέγει δ᾽ οὕτως· "ἐμοῦ γοῦν ἐπὶ τὴν Ἐρυθρὰν θάλασσαν βαδίζοντος συνηκολούθει τις μετὰ τῶν ἄλλων τῶν παραπεμπόντων ἡμᾶς ἱππέων Ἰουδαίων¹⁵ ὄνομα Μοσόλλαμος, ἄνθρωπος ἱκανῶς¹⁶ κατὰ¹⁷ ψυχὴν εὔρωστος καὶ τοξότης δὴ πάντων ὁμολογουμένως¹⁸ καὶ τῶν Ἑλλήνων καὶ τῶν βαρβάρων ἄριστος. [202] οὗτος οὖν ὁ ἄνθρωπος διαβαδιζόντων πολλῶν κατὰ τὴν ὁδὸν καὶ μάντεώς τινος ὀρνιθευομένου καὶ πάντας ἐπισχεῖν ἀξιοῦντος ἠρώτησε, διὰ τί προσμένουσι. [203] δείξαντος δὲ τοῦ μάντεως αὐτῷ τὸν ὄρνιθα καὶ φήσαντος, ἐὰν μὲν αὐτοῦ μένῃ προσμένειν συμφέρειν πᾶσιν, ἂν δ᾽ ἀναστὰς εἰς τοὔμπροσθεν πέτηται προάγειν, ἐὰν δὲ εἰς τοὔπισθεν ἀναχωρεῖν αὖθις, σιωπήσας καὶ παρελκύσας τὸ τόξον

---

13. λυχνία Eusebii cod. G.
14. τούτων: coni. τούτου (inf. p. 163).
15. Ἰουδαίων MSS: Ἰουδαῖος coni. Niese.
16. ἱκανῶς Eusebii cod. I: ἱκανὸς L, Lat., Eusebii cod. G.
17. κατὰ L, Lat: κατὰ τὴν Eusebii cod. I: καὶ coni. Niese.
18. ὁμολογουμένως coni. Niese: ὁμολογούμενος L, Eus.; indubitanter Lat.

and is called by them Jerusalem.   [198] There is there, nearly in the center of the city, a stone wall, five plethra long, and a hundred cubits wide, having double gates, inside which there is a square altar, not of hewn, but of collected, unwrought stones, so constructed: twenty cubits long and ten cubits high, and beside it a great edifice where there is an altar and a lamp stand, both covered with gold and weighing two talents.   [199] Upon these[e] there is a light that is never extinguished night and day. And there are no statues, nor any votive offerings, and absolutely no plants, resembling neither a grove nor anything similar. And the priests pass their time night and day in it purifying themselves by certain [rituals] of purification and entirely abstaining from wine in the temple."   [200] And he further testifies that they served as soldiers under King Alexander, and afterward under his successors. And the [actions] performed by a Jewish man, which he witnessed after he was on an expedition, I shall cite as well.   [201] Now he says thus: "Anyway when I was marching to the Red Sea, a certain Mosollamus was accompanying us, together with the rest of the Jewish[f] cavalrymen who served us as an advance force. [Mosollamus was] a man with a robust mind,[g] and, as agreed by all, the best archer among Greeks and barbarians.   [202] So that man, when many went to and fro along the road, and a certain seer was watching the flight of the birds, and he [the seer] requested all of them to abstain [from all actions], asked why they were halting.   [203] The seer having pointed out the bird to him, and saying that if it [the bird] stays there, it is expedient for all to wait still longer, and if it rises and flies ahead, to advance, but if [it flies] behind, to withdraw at once,

---

e. Possibly "this": see the apparatus and p. 163 below.

f. Niese's emendation, "a certain Jew together with the rest of the cavalrymen," is unnecessary, and was suggested before the discovery of the Elephantine papyri, as well as material testifying to the service of Jewish units (including cavalry) in the Persian and Ptolemaic armies.

g. ἱκανός creates too many difficulties. Niese was probably right in preferring the reading ἱκανῶς, and this has been accepted by later editors (e.g., Thackeray, Reinach, Stern). For an identical manuscript corruption, cf. *Ap.* II.126. A more literal translation would be "a man sufficiently strong in his mind" (or "with a sufficiently powerful mind"), that is, "with a robust mind," "having hard common sense," or the like. For an understatement by the same author with regard to the wisdom of Hezekiah the High Priest, see para. 187. However, some uncertainty about the correct reading still remains.

ἔβαλε καὶ τὸν ὄρνιθα πατάξας ἀπέκτεινεν. [204] ἀγανακτούντων δὲ τοῦ μάντεως καί τινων ἄλλων καὶ καταρωμένων αὐτῷ, 'τί μαίνεσθε,' ἔφη, 'κακοδαίμονες;'[19] εἶτα τὸν ὄρνιθα λαβὼν[20] εἰς τὰς χεῖρας, 'πῶς γάρ,' ἔφη, 'οὗτος τὴν αὑτοῦ[21] σωτηρίαν οὐ προϊδὼν περὶ τῆς ἡμετέρας πορείας ἡμῖν ἄν τι ὑγιὲς ἀπήγγελλεν; εἰ γὰρ ἠδύνατο προγιγνώσκειν τὸ μέλλον, εἰς τὸν τόπον τοῦτον οὐκ ἂν ἦλθε φοβούμενος, μὴ τοξεύσας αὐτὸν ἀποκτείνῃ Μοσόλλαμος ὁ Ἰουδαῖος.'" ἀλλὰ τῶν μὲν Ἑκαταίου μαρτυριῶν ἅλις· [205] τοῖς γὰρ βουλομένοις πλείω μαθεῖν τῷ βιβλίῳ ῥᾴδιόν ἐστιν ἐντυχεῖν.

Jos. *Ap.* II.43

ἐτίμα γὰρ ἡμῶν τὸ ἔθνος, ὡς καὶ φησιν Ἑκαταῖος περὶ ἡμῶν, ὅτι διὰ τὴν ἐπιείκειαν καὶ πίστιν, ἣν αὐτῷ παρέσχον Ἰουδαῖοι, τὴν Σαμαρεῖτιν χώραν προσέθηκεν ἔχειν αὐτοῖς ἀφορολόγητον.

19. κακοδαίμονες; εἶτα τὸν Eus.: κακοδαιμονέστατον L, Lat.
20. λαβὼν Eus.: λαβόντες L, Lat.
21. αὑτοῦ Eus.: αὐτοῦ L, Niese.

he [Mosollamus], after keeping silence and drawing his bow, shot and, hitting the bird, killed [it].   [204] When the seer and some others became irritated and called down curses upon him, he [Mosollamus] said: 'Why are you raving, [you] wretches?'[h] Then, taking the bird in his hands he said: 'How, then, could this [bird], which did not provide for its own safety, say anything sound about our march? For had it been able to know the future, it would not have come to this place, fearing that Mosollamus the Jew would draw his bow and kill it.' "   [205] But this should suffice concerning the evidence of Hecataeus. To those who want to learn more, the book is readily available.

For he [Alexander the Great] honored our nation, as Hecataeus says about us, that because of the fairness and loyalty shown to him by the Jews, he [Alexander] annexed the land of Samaria to them free of tribute.

h. κακοδαίμονες: literally, "possessed by an evil spirit." Given the period, "wretches" is better.

III   The Question of Authenticity

Scholars contesting the authenticity of *On the Jews* have put forward more than a dozen different arguments. Some fail to prove the case. For example, the facts that Hecataeus was credited with the forged book *On Abraham* and that Philo of Byblos had doubted whether Hecataeus wrote the treatise *On the Jews* only illustrate the general problem, but cannot be used as evidence.[1] The enthusiastic description of the Jewish people was, as one might expect, also introduced as an argument against authenticity, but this was rejected in light of certain general parallels to idealized accounts of oriental peoples known from Hellenistic ethnographical literature, and the description of the Jews as "philosophers" by early Hellenistic authors.[2] The evident idealization of Mosaic Judaism in Strabo's ethnographical excursus (XVI.2.36–39) is even more relevant here.[3] Two other arguments, based on a sentence ascribed to Hecataeus by Pseudo-Aristeas (31) and a reference to the Jewish tithes in one of the fragments (Jos. *Ap.* I.188), are by themselves inconclusive and have been rightly rejected.[4] It has also been pointed out that there is no quotation from the book ascribed to Hecataeus in the collection of Hellenistic writings on the Jews compiled by Alexander

1. See Lewy (1932) 118–19; Guttman (1958–63) I.66–67; M. Stern (1974–84) I.23; Holladay (1983) 280–82; Goodman in Schürer et al. (1973–86) III.672–73.

2. See esp. Lewy (1932) 118; Gager (1969) 131–34. On the Jews, see Theophrastus *ap.* Porphyr. *Abst.* II.26; Megasthenes *ap.* Clem. *Strom.* I.15; Clearchus *ap.* Jos. *Ap.* I.179.

3. On this excursus and its origin, see further pp. 212–13 below.

4. See pp. 140ff., 159–60 below.

Polyhistor (first century B.C.), but this argument from silence is even less significant for the debate.[5]

The difference in general tone and attitude toward the Jews between the treatise and Hecataeus's Jewish excursus in the Egyptian ethnography, as well as the contradictory references to the priests' income (Diod. XL.3.7, Jos. *Ap.* I.188), deserves more attention. It has been argued in defense that *On the Jews* was written by Hecataeus at a later date, after he had become better acquainted with Jews and Judaism, or had made a special study in preparation for his treatise on the Jews.[6] Unfortunately these assumptions can be neither proved nor disproved: if *On the Jews* is authentic, it must have been written after the battle of Gaza (312 B.C.), which is explicitly mentioned (*Ap.* I.184, 186), and before the final reconquest of Judea by Ptolemy I (302 B.C.), in which the king treated the Jews harshly and deported many of them to Egypt.[7] As far as Hecataeus's Egyptian ethnography is concerned, it seems to have been written between 305 and 302.[8] There is thus still some room for dating the composition of the Jewish excursus earlier than the Jewish treatise.

The positive evidence brought forward so far to support authenticity is quite meager. It has been argued that the author must have been a gentile, since, while demonstrating an apparently thorough acquaintance with Greek culture, he seems to make a basic mistake concerning the Jewish deportation to Babylonia (*Ap.* I.194). This, however, could well be expected of a Hellenized Jew; we know of such cases in Jewish Hellenistic literature. But, as a matter of fact, the statement about the deportation has already been shown to be reliable,[9] and a close examination of the passages proves that the author had only a partial and inaccurate knowledge of Greek heritage and practices.[10]

On the other hand, a number of arguments against authenticity based on a historical analysis of statements in the fragments themselves still seem in principle to be valid. All of them were mentioned in one way or

5. Contrary to the opinions of Graetz (1876) 344; Willrich (1900) 111; cf. Schaller (1963) 27–28.

6. See esp. M. Stern (1974–84) I.24, and there also other explanations.

7. See the sources and discussion, pp. 71–77 below.

8. See pp. 15–16 above.

9. See pp. 143–44 below.

10. See below, pp. 148–59.

another by Willrich in his *Judaica* (1900), and have since been repeated or elaborated on by other scholars. Nevertheless, the analysis has not always been sufficiently convincing and has also frequently been accompanied, especially in the case of Willrich, by mistaken assumptions and inexactitude. The older arguments, therefore, need far more evidence and elucidation. It is also necessary to scrutinize the counterarguments and solutions offered by the proponents of authenticity.

In discussing the various passages, the following considerations will concern us:

1. Do the views expressed or implied in the passages accord with the conceptions and convictions of Hecataeus?

2. Are the data about Greek practices incorporated in the treatise confirmed by extant knowledge, meaning that they could have been written by Hecataeus?

3. In view of his position in the court, Hecataeus must have been acquainted with, or striven to know, the truth about certain details relating to the Jews (e.g., information having a military significance, Jewish leadership, and the like); can these be verified? We may observe that had Hecataeus not served in the Ptolemaic court, and had he actually resided on the Greek mainland, as one scholar (unjustifiably) maintains,[11] the whole issue of authenticity would have been decided at the outset: Hecataeus's position in the Ptolemaic court is emphasized in the passages (in addition to Josephus's introductory notes).

4. Does the presentation of major events that took place in the time of Hecataeus agree with hard evidence from other sources concerning that time? And if not, could it be that Hecataeus was interested in distorting the real facts?

5. Could all the described historical events and developments relating to Jewish history have taken place before or during the lifetime of Hecataeus?

Unfortunately, a stylistic comparison with Hecataeus's Egyptian ethnography and the Jewish excursus would not be of much help: Diodorus's involvement in shaping the vocabulary and style of the *epitomē* was too great to allow a reliable basis for comparison.[12] One should also be cautious in applying arguments from silence and the like.

11. See p. 8 n. 2 above.
12. See p. 24 and n. 49 above.

Thus the absence from the passages of any reference to Moses as well as of philosophical and social reasonings, which are so predominant in the excursus, may support the claim of forgery, but can be used only as a second line of evidence. On the other hand, caution should also be exercised regarding the detailed and astonishingly accurate knowledge of the Temple and its cult objects demonstrated by the author, which in itself need not necessarily indicate that he was Jewish.

The discussion of this chapter will examine one by one the passages that have appeared suspect to previous scholars, and two additional fragments that have been virtually neglected in the scholarly debate but furnish new evidence. These are *Ap.* I.195–99 and 201–4, containing the geographical account of Judea and Jerusalem, and the Mosollamus story (see sections III.1, 8). We shall keep to the order of the passages as they appear in *Against Apion*, with one exception, the Mosollamus story: though it is the last of the fragments quoted in the first book of *Against Apion* (201–4), it will be placed at the start of the discussion. Being the most complete and comprehensive fragment, it provides a wider range of considerations for evaluating the question of authenticity.

1. MOSOLLAMUS THE JEW AND BIRD OMENS

The author claims to have participated personally in a Ptolemaic military march to the Red Sea, and to be recording an event that took place in the course of the advance. Among the Jewish horsemen who took part in the expedition there was a certain archer, called Mosollamus. He is described as a man with a robust mind and "as agreed by all, the best archer among the Greeks and barbarians" (*Ap.* I.201). At a certain point, the whole force halted because a bird was seen flying about nearby and the seer (*mantis*) wanted to observe its motions. When Mosollamus inquired as to the reason for the halt, the seer pointed to the bird and explained the rules of interpretation (I.203):

> If it [the bird] stays there, it is expedient for all to wait still longer, and if it rises and flies ahead, to advance, but if [it flies] behind, to withdraw at once.

Then Mosollamus, without uttering a word, shot and killed the bird. When the angry seer and certain others cursed him, he took the bird in his hand and retorted (I.204):

How, then, could this [bird], which did not provide for its own safety, say anything sound about our march? For had it been able to know the future, it would not have come to this place, fearing that Mosollamus the Jew would draw his bow and kill it.

The episode already seemed questionable to Philo of Byblos. According to Origen, Philo doubted the authenticity of the book because it stressed the "wisdom" of the Jews (*C. Cels.* I.15). Philo was certainly referring to the Mosollamus story, and most probably also to other pieces of information, which were not preserved by Josephus.[13] The description of the wise Jew who mocks the foolish, superstitious gentiles also convinced some modern scholars that the story was written by a Jew.[14] This, however, is still not enough to establish a forgery.[15]

Other scholars have argued, to the contrary, that the scornful attitude toward omens accords with that of "contemporary educated Greeks" and may therefore represent Hecataeus's own views.[16] The available evidence does not, however, justify such a sweeping statement. To say that educated Greeks had a negative attitude toward omens is an exaggerated generalization, even more so than the rhetorical statement of the supporters of divination in the Ciceronian dialogue that divination had been "the unwavering belief of all ages, the greatest philosophers, the poets, the wisest men, the builders of cities, the founders of republics" (*Div.* I.84; cf. 5, 86).[17] In any case, the main question is not whether an educated Greek would have praised the negative Jewish attitude toward gentile divination and bird omens, but what Hecataeus's personal view was.

---

13. See the discussion, p. 184 below.

14. Geffcken (1907) xv; Jacoby, *RE* s.v. "Hekataios (4)," 2766–67; Reinach (1930) 39; Rappaport (1965) 142–43; Hengel (1971) 303.

15. The only attempt so far to reach a conclusion on the question of authenticity by referring to the details of the story is a short note by W. Burkert in Hengel (1971) 324. However, it could not possibly decide the issue. See the comments in nn. 41 and 50 below.

16. J. G. Müller (1877) 177–78; Lewy (1932) 128–29; Holladay (1983) 333–34 nn. 51–52. See also p. 64 below on the episode in the letter attributed to Diogenes.

17. See the discussions and summaries of Wachsmuth (1860); Bouché-Leclercq (1879–82) I.14ff.; Nilsson (1940) 121–39; Cumont (1960) 57ff.; Flacelière (1961) 103–18; Pease (1963) 75, 206–9, 312; Nock (1972) II.534–50; Pfeffer (1975); Pritchett (1974–91) III.48–49, 141–53.

The tradition about the affiliation of Hecataeus with the disciples and "successors" of Pyrrho (Diog. Laert. IX.69), if accepted, could have provided a clue as to Hecataeus's position: certain contemporary testimonia about Pyrrho indicate at least a tolerant, if not a favorable, attitude toward religious ceremonies and divination.[18] However, this tradition is rather doubtful.[19] Hecataeus's stand with regard to divination should therefore be deduced only from his ethnographical works.

The surviving material does not contain a thematic discussion of the reliability of divination and bird omens. There are, however, quite a number of relevant references. In his Egyptian ethnography, preserved by Diodorus in an abridged version,[20] Hecataeus refers more than a dozen times to Egyptian and Greek divination in a generally positive way. Hecataeus mentions incubation in temples (Diod I.25.3, 53.8), oracles (23.5, 25.7, 66.10; cf. 98.5), inspection of the entrails of sacrifices (53.8, 70.9), dream interpretation (65.5–7), divination in general (73.4), and astrology (73.4, 81.4–6, 98.3–4). One passage reports that hawks and eagles were regarded by the Egyptians as "birds of omen" (87.7–9).[21] Most of the allusions are preceded, as customarily throughout his Egyptian ethnography, by such phrases as "they say" (φασίν), which point to the use of Egyptian and Greek sources. But this does not mean that Hecataeus distances himself from the assertions. He expresses disapproval only once, when referring to the contents

18. The relevant sources: Eus. *PE* XIV.18.26 (Pyrrho preparing a sacrifice for his sister); ibid. 14 (Pyrrho's real or alleged visit to Delphi or Oropus to consult the oracle; see Long [1978] 73–74); Diog. Laert. IX.64 and Hesychius of Miletus *FHG* IV.174 (Pyrrho being appointed high priest). The first two references evidently drew on testimonia from the time of Pyrrho (Antigonus of Carystus and Timon via Aristocles), and the same may be true of the third one (Antigonus of Carystus?). Sext. Emp. *Pyrrh.* I.17 ("to live according to the traditional customs and laws") reflects the later Skeptical tradition.

19. See p. 8 n. 5 above.

20. On Hecataeus and Diodorus's Egyptian ethnography, see in detail pp. 14ff. and esp. Extended Notes, n. 1 p. 289. The narrative material and comments quoted below are definitely Hecataean and not additions by Diodorus (see nn. 21, 22 below).

21. There is no involvement of Diodorus in the contents of the passage, which is part of the rationalization and praise of the Egyptian animal cult; see below p. 99 n. 138 referring to Diod. I.83.8. Porphyry mentions only the hawk as an Egyptian bird of omen (*Abst.* IV.9). He may have drawn on Hecataeus. See further nn. 33 and 53 below.

of an oracle recorded by Herodotus (66.10; cf. Hdt. II.151ff.). His criticism in this case stems not from a rejection in principle of oracles, but from the evident improbability of the story (the circumstances of the rise of Psammeticus to sole rule in Egypt; cf. Diod. I.69.7). On another occasion he even states that the Egyptian sources support their statements with facts, unlike the Greeks, who rely on legends (25.3). There are no reservations with regard to the other references, although Hecataeus does not refrain from criticizing his Egyptian sources when he finds their accounts unreliable (e.g., 23.2; 24.2, 5; 25.2–3). One story recounted by him about divination does not mention sources, and the information given is recorded as objective fact (65.5–7). Above all, Hecataeus precedes three other allusions to divination and astrology (73.4, 81.4–6, 98.3–4) with the statement that he refrained from quoting imaginary tales by Herodotus and other Greek authors, and selected from the records of the Egyptian priests only information "that passed our scrupulous examination" (69.7).[22]

When evaluating this material, it should also be borne in mind that Hecataeus's Egyptian ethnography is, to a great extent, an idealization of Egyptian life and practices.[23] It is therefore hardly credible that the same author would reject or even ridicule pagan divination techniques. The same conclusion is also suggested by Hecataeus's highly tolerant and sympathetic treatment of religious beliefs in the Egyptian ethnography. He even goes so far as to provide explanations for and make favorable comments on the animal cult,[24] which was regarded by the Greeks and Romans as bizarre and contemptible.[25]

Examination of the few fragments of Hecataeus's utopian *On the Hyperboreans* supports this conclusion.[26] The god Apollo plays a central role in the treatise (as in almost all other literary references to

22. The last reference, as well as para. 25.3, mentioned above, which are decisive for the argument, undoubtedly originate in Hecataeus's work. The same applies to the criticism of Herodotus on Egypt. It is agreed that Diodorus did not usually bother to consult more than one source for a single subject, certainly not for minute details, and that he did not indulge in source criticism.

23. See pp. 16–17 above.

24. See pp. 98–99 below.

25. See the sources on p. 98 n. 137 below.

26. On this book as affecting Hecataeus's social, political, and religious ideals, see, e.g., Susemihl (1891) I.314; Jacoby, *RE* s.v. "Hekataios (4)," 2755; *id.* (1943) 52ff.; Guttman (1958–63) I.42–45.

the Hyperboreans).[27] Although the material at our disposal elaborates only on his contribution (and that of his cult) to the musical life of the Hyperboreans (Diod. II.47.6; Aelian, *Nat. Anim.* XI.1), one may assume that Apollo's second main role, as god of divination, was not neglected. Furthermore, Hecataeus enthusiastically describes the regular arrival of "clouds of swans" from afar at the time of the services in the Hyperborean temple. They always join the chorus chanting hymns in honor of Apollo. All is performed in perfect harmony (Ael. *NA* XI.1):[28]

> Never once do they sing a discordant note or out of tune, but as though they had been given the key by the leader they chant in unison with the natives, who are skilled in the sacred melodies.

That nothing in their behavior is accidental attests to divine inspiration. Hecataeus accordingly accepted the belief that swans were Apollo's sacred birds and messengers,[29] and in Greek tradition this also entailed prophetic as well as musical gifts.[30]

This survey of Hecataeus's direct and indirect references to the techniques of ancient mantics, as well as his attitude toward Egyptian cults (including those viewed by the Greeks as superstitious), seems to suggest that Hecataeus could not have written a derogatory story about bird omens. And it cannot be argued that the author merely quotes the view of Mosollamus the Jew. He clearly enjoys telling the story, without reservation, and praises Mosollamus's "robust mind." The story was probably understood in a similar manner by Herennius Philo, who, therefore, suspected the authenticity of the treatise.

Analysis of the various details of the Mosollamus story further shows that it was not written by a knowledgeable Greek, certainly not by an author of the caliber of Hecataeus. The story either lacks or distorts *all* the basic facts about Greek bird divination. And it must be recalled that the author presents himself as an eyewitness (*Ap.* I.200). But before any discussion of the details, an important clarification must be made. It might be argued that the episode is just a joke, and that, consequently, the author was not concerned with accuracy and even deliberately distorted all technical details. This, however, can

27. See Bolton (1962) 22ff., 106ff., *et passim.*
28. The translation: Scholfield (1958–59) II.357–59 (*LCL*).
29. See the sources in Pollard (1977) 145–46 and 195 n. 59.
30. See esp. Plato, *Phaedo* 84b; Arist. *HA* IX.615^{b}2.

be expected of a satire, not of a story—even if it is told as a joke—the whole purpose of which is "to point a moral, or adorn a tale." The last paragraph (204) points the moral. Had the real Hecataeus distorted all the basic facts, he would have spoiled the whole didactic impact of the story. An author who knew his facts would not have done this.[31] Besides, the surviving material of Hecataeus's works (and there is enough of it to judge) does not show any traces of satiric writing.

When we turn to the Mosollamus story, the first conspicuous fact is that the episode does not accord with the Greek theological conception underlying bird omens. Mosollamus says that had the bird indeed been able to "know the future" (προγιγνώσκειν τὸ μέλλον) it would have taken care not to be shot (I.204). But educated Greeks did not believe that a bird could know the future. This was at best a common belief held by ignorant people of the sort found in every society.[32] Xenophon, who in his books frequently described omens and portents, expressed the accepted Greek conception about bird divination in a celebrated passage that refers to the views held by Athenian citizens about various divination techniques (*Mem.* I.1.3–4):

> He [Socrates] was introducing nothing newer than were those believers in divination who rely on bird omens, oracles, coincidences, and sacrifices. For they do not believe that the birds or those met by accident know what will happen to the inquirer, but that the gods indicate what will happen to him through them.

The same explanation for omens, sometimes with specific reference to birds, is known from quite a number of sources.[33] This understanding

---

31. Two stories, which might appear to be similar to the Mosollamus episode, an Aesopean fable (no. 170 ed. Hausrath [Leipzig, 1970]) and a tale about Diogenes of Sinope (*EG*, Diog. no. 38 [p. 253]), ridicule streetcorner soothsayers who were not able to foresee their own troubles. The authors do not record the technicalities of divination, since they were not necessary for the moral. What matters for the present discussion is that they do not distort the basic facts. For the difference in motifs between these two stories and the Mosollamus episode, see pp. 64–65 below.

32. The vulgar opinion is recorded by Philo, *Spec. Leg.* I.60–63, who explicitly relates it to the "mob" (para. 60).

33. Xen. *Hipp.* IX.8–9, *Cyr.* I.6.1; Plut. *Dion* 24; *Sollert. Anim.* 975A–B; Sen. *NQ* II.32.3ff.; Orig. *C. Cels.* IV.88; Amm. Marc. XXI.1.9; cf., e.g., Cic.

gave rise to a number of theological problems. Cicero thus records the deliberations of the Stoics (*Div.* I.118):[34]

> But it seems necessary to determine the way [by which these signs are given]. For the Stoics do not believe that god is involved in every fissure of the liver or in every song of a bird; quite obviously that would be neither seemly nor proper for a god and furthermore would be impossible. But, in the beginning, the world was so created that certain results would be preceded by certain signs, which are given sometimes by entrails and by birds, sometimes by lightning, by portents and by stars, sometimes by dreams, and sometimes by utterances of persons in a frenzy.

The philosophers who rejected belief in omens did not ignore these explanations. Some even tried to refute them point by point. Thus Cicero, in the second book of a long dialogue, examined all aspects of contemporary divination.[35] Others expressed their negative view

---

Div. I.118–19, II.35–39 on the Stoic doctrine of the divination of entrails. Two later sources of the Roman period attribute "understanding" to birds: Pliny states that of all birds, only ravens are able to understand the meaning of the omens they convey (*NH* X.33), while Porphyry attributes this ability to "all mantic birds" (*Abst.* III.5.3). This, however, does not contradict the former sources: certain birds understand the omen themselves, but this does not mean that they know anything beyond the specific event referred to by the omen. The omen in the Mosollamus story applies only to the question of whether or not to continue the march. The relevance of Porphyry, an author of the third century A.D. with strong mystical inclinations, to the accepted view of educated Greeks in the fourth century B.C. is by itself highly doubtful. (One cannot determine the source of his statement, though in the same passage he clearly uses Roman sources.) Pliny for his part stresses that only ravens are gifted with "understanding." It should also be noted that whooper swans, which in addition to being "mantic birds" were believed to know (and sing) when they were about to die (Ael. *NA* V.34, X.36), are an exceptional case described as such. Yet this faculty can be regarded as activated instinctively at the onset of a natural death only, and not by the prospect of an unexpected, sudden death, as in the case of the bird in the Mosollamus story.

34. The translation: Falconer (1923) 351–55 (*LCL*), with a number of changes. Cf. Sen. *NQ* II.32.3–4.

35. See especially the direct philosophical arguments against bird divination in *Div.* II.16, 53, 56–57, 76, 80, 82–83, and, indirectly, 9ff., 18–21, 25. Cf. 30, 36, which actually could also be used against bird omens.

inter alia by short notes, like the rhetorical question of Carneades and Panaetius preserved by Cicero (*Div.* I.12):[36]

> Therefore let Carneades cease to press the question, which Panaetius also used to urge, whether Jupiter had ordered the crow to croak on the left side and the raven on the right.

Even in this rather cynical remark, the question is not whether the bird "knows" or not, but whether the deity reveals his will to mankind in this way.[37] The Mosollamus story, however, does not indicate any familiarity with the accepted Greek conception of bird omens. It has already been explained above why it cannot be argued that Hecataeus simply recorded the Jewish perception.

In this context it would be worth referring to two Greek anecdotes that carry a seemingly similar lesson. Hans Lewy compared the Mosollamus episode with a story in one of the spurious letters attributed to Diogenes of Sinope. The letter relates how, at the time of the Olympic games, Diogenes ridiculed a seer (*mantis*: either an ecstatic prophet or a soothsayer who interprets signs or dreams). Diogenes lifted his stick and asked the man whether he would strike him or not. When the seer answered in the negative, Diogenes, much to the amusement of the bystanders, struck him with his stick.[38] The same motif appears in a fable related by Aesop: a *mantis* who earned his living from prophesying in the market was alarmed by the news that his house had been broken into. A passerby rebuked him, saying: "While announcing that you knew beforehand the affairs of others, you did not predict your own" (no. 170, ed. A. Hausrath [Leipzig, 1970]).

There is, however, an essential difference between the Mosollamus episode and the two anecdotes: Mosollamus ridicules the "foreknowledge" of the bird; that is, he denies the capability of the mantic "instrument" itself to know the future. However, Greeks did not need to challenge this. The two anecdotes, on the other hand, mock the ability of a dilettante to foretell the future or interpret signs. The argument

---

36. See also *Div.* I.85; II.56, 72, 80. For a somewhat similar line of argumentation with regard to another subject, cf. Philo, *De Mutatione Nominum* 61; *Quaest. et Solut. in Genesim* II.79.

37. On the question of Panaetius's attitude toward divination, see the summary and bibliography by Pease (1963) 62–63, and p. 64 on Carneades.

38. Lewy (1932) 129 and n. 4. The letter: *EG*, Diog. no. 38 (p. 253).

is quite different, and was frequently employed against quack prophets, especially streetcorner soothsayers.[39]

No less instructive than the theological conception are both the terminology of the story and the mantic techniques described by the gentile seer himself. The very reliance on bird omens for military purposes is indeed known not only from the history of the Roman army and from other cultures, but is also found in Greek tradition,[40] although it did not take the form of regular, systematic ornithoscopy, but rather of the interpretation of the chance appearance of certain less common birds.[41] Such bird omens were occasionally encountered by armies in the course of their expeditions.[42] So far there is nothing exceptional in the Mosollamus story. However, when the minute technical details are reviewed, one finds it difficult to believe that the story was written

39. See, e.g., Cic. *Div.* II.9ff.; Jos. *Ap.* I.258; Luc. *Deor. Dial.* 16.1 (244). Without referring to the attitude toward divination of Diogenes himself, it is noteworthy that Plutarch, who has a favorable opinion of portents and omens (see, e.g., n. 33 above; cf. Nock [1972] II.538ff.), deplores streetcorner soothsayers (*Pyth. Orac.* 407C, Cic. 17.5, *Lycurg.* 9.5).

40. See the latest collections of material in Pollard (1977) 116–29; Pritchett (1974–91) III.101ff.

41. W. Burkert (in Hengel [1971] 324) argues that the story could not have been written by Hecataeus, since military ornithomantics was not practiced in the Hellenistic period. This is to overlook the fact that the Mosollamus story, whether genuine or not, was in any case composed during the Hellenistic period, indicating that the interpretation of bird omens still was resorted to by armies when a "mantic bird" was observed. Moreover, ornithoscopy was well known and practiced in the Hellenistic period (see some of the sources nn. 48, 49 below), and the disappearance of bird mantics from the Hellenistic battlefields in a period when Greco-Macedonian troops were confronting Roman armies, which adhered so much to their own auguric traditions, is by itself implausible. Polybius's negative attitude toward omens and portents (see esp. VI.56.6–12, IX.19.1, XXXIII.17.2) is chiefly responsible for the absence of references to bird omens in extant accounts of Hellenistic battles, most of which are derived (directly or indirectly) from his version. Burkert seems also to be inaccurate in stating that the inspection of entrails for military purposes was declining. See, e.g., Polyaenus IV.20 and Onasander X.24. Plut. *Aem.* 19.4 and Polyb. V.24.9, XXIII.10.17 may also be taken to indicate sacrifice divination. Be that as it may, bird divination could not have disappeared as early as the beginning of the Hellenistic period.

42. E.g., *Il.* I.168–84, VII.247ff., X.274ff., XII.195–250, XIII.822, XXIV.315; Xen. *Anab.* VI.1.23, 5.2; Plut. *Them.* 12; Cic. *Div.* I.74, 87. Onasander X.26 ("signs of sight and sound") may also hint at bird omens.

by a Greek. Curiously enough, the author does not specify the bird, although the general term *ornis* is repeated four times, and the story is devoted to bird divination.[43] The Greeks regarded some ten or twelve species as birds of omen, but others were excluded.[44] In the words of the poet: "Many birds fly to and fro under the sun's rays, but not all are [birds] of omen" (*Od.* II.181). When it came to military affairs, the usual birds of omen were the eagle, Zeus's sacred bird and "the surest bird of augury" (*Il.* VIII.247),[45] the hawk, consecrated to Apollo (Ael. *NA* VII.9, X.14, XII.4), and occasionally (especially for Athenian troops) the owl.[46] Hecataeus himself elaborates in his Egyptian ethnography on the hawk and eagle as birds of omen (Diod. I.87.7–9). The absence of any specification and the repetition of the word *ornis* indicate, therefore, a lack of exact knowledge about Greek practice. Furthermore, the author does not use the term *oiōnos* even once, although it is the more common designation for a bird of omen.

It may be responded that the author wishes to stress that the sooth-sayer's source of information was just a bird. But one would expect an author—who claims to be an eyewitness—to specify at least once the exact bird he saw; a specific reference to an eagle or a hawk would only have strengthened the didactic effect of the story. Had Mosollamus been able to shoot such a bird, well known for speed, this would have empha-sized the whole point of the story. The author would then still have had a few opportunities to express the idea that the bird was just a bird.

As for the rules of interpretation: like the Roman augurs, Greek diviners also had a *disciplina auguralis*, a set of rules for the interpre-tation of omens, which differed slightly from place to place. It was a rather complicated "science," the rules defining the meaning of a variety

43. The use of just the word *ornis* in incidental or one-time references to birds of omen is not exceptional. See, e.g., *Il.* XIII.821; *Od.* X.242; Hesiod, *Erg.* 828; Aesch. *SCT* 26, *Agam.* 112; Soph. *OT* 52; Eur. *Phoen.* 839; Aristoph. *Birds* 719. However, the only subject of the Mosollamus story is bird omens, and the word is mentioned more than once.

44. See Holliday (1911) 270; Pollard (1977) 120, 126–27.

45. Cf. Cic. *Div.* II.76; Sen. *NQ* II.32.5.

46. See Pritchett (1974–91) III.101ff., 105ff. Add Diod. XXII.3 for owls. The carnivorous bird or raven mentioned in Arr. *Anab.* II.26.4–27 and Curt. IV.6.12 is an exception. The nature of the occurrence (the bird dropped a stone on Alexander's head while he was making a sacrifice) could not but be taken as a warning.

of movements and their combinations. Thus an inscription found in Ephesus, from the time of the Persian Wars, which contains a sacred law code, elaborates on the meaning of bird movements (*SIG*³ 1167):

> [(If) the bird is flying from right to left:] if it disappears—fortunate. But if it raises the left wing: whether it (only) rises or disappears—ill. And (if) it is flying from left to right: if it disappears in a straight (course)—ill, but if after raising the right wing—[fortunate] . . .

These were not all the rules. The code is only partially preserved, and the complete set must have made decision rather difficult. The seer had thus to set in order and balance conflicting signs and rules. The Ephesian code may indeed represent only a local tradition, as some scholars maintain,[47] but there is no doubt that the overall rules applied in the Greek world were quite complicated, as can be deduced from a fair number of sources.[48]

Then again, the very clarification of the basic facts demanded much effort. Even the simplest question, common throughout the Greek world, whether the bird came from the right or the left, was not easy to establish. The flight of an eagle or a hawk near an army usually came as a surprise and happened very quickly. The reports on the direction of the arrival were consequently often contradictory, and whatever evidence there was had to be sorted out and clarified by the seer. In

47. See Wilamowitz (1931) I.145; Pollard (1977) 121; and the opposite view by Holliday (1911) 269 n. 4; Pritchett (1974–91) III.103–4.

48. See Aesch. *PV* 487ff., *SCT* 24ff.; Soph. *Ant.* 953ff.; Eur. *Bacch.* 347; Xen. *Anab.* VI.1.23; Call. *Hymns* V.123–24; Cic. *Div.* I.120–21; Ael. *NA* I.48. Cf. Paus. IX.16.1; Philo, *Spec. Leg.* I.62. The information provided by Michael Psellus, of the tenth century A.D. (see the Herscher edition [1853] p. 167), although contaminated with Roman and later material, is still relevant to ancient Greek and Hellenistic ornithoscopy. Thus Psellus refers to a work by a certain Apollonius of Lacedaemon, said to have elaborated on bird signs. The reference discloses a variety of criteria that were considered by soothsayers before passing judgment. The possibly spurious *Ornithomanteia* attributed to Hesiod (as an appendix to the *Erga*) must also have elaborated on the rules of interpretation. The same applies to the treatise *Peri Palmōn Mantikē* (*palmos* = "twitching") by Melampus (third century B.C.), the *Oiōnoskopika* by Artemidorus of Ephesus (Artemidorus Daldianus; see *Suda* s.v. Ἀρτεμίδωρος), of the second century B.C., *To Palmikon Oiōnisma* by an unknown Posidonius (*Suda* s.v. Ποσειδώνιος), and *Peri Oiōnistikēs* by a certain Telegonus (*Suda* s.v. οἰωνοί). On the empirical basis for the rules, see Cic. *Div.* I.109, 127.

this context there was also the question of defining and determining right and left. If this was to be resolved in relation to the direction faced by the seer himself, the problem arose as to how the latter could be sure of his own exact position at the moment of the bird's arrival. And if it was accepted that the seer always faced the residence of the gods, was that north or east? Or was there perhaps another rule, referring, for instance, to the general direction of the army's advance? The knowledge and experience of a professional seer were thus indispensable.[49] But this was just the beginning. The remaining considerations relating to the bird's overall motions and more particular details could give rise to even greater uncertainties. And there was still the necessity of balancing all the different and complicated instructions.

The seer of the Mosollamus story, however, refers to just three basic positions: flight forward, retreat, and landing. So far as I know, there is no parallel in Greek literature for the application of such rules. These elementary positions could well be regarded as accidental and were therefore discounted as divine signs. Such an interpretation could occur, at most, only to ignorant people unaware of the theological background of bird mantics, not to an official seer, as suggested by the story. In any case, it does not take the expertise of a professional seer to offer this sort of interpretation.[50] On the other hand, there is no reference to the traditional rules accepted by the Greek world, not even to the basic question regarding right and left. We thus see that the author could not have been an eyewitness, nor could he have been a knowledgeable Greek—certainly not one who wanted to win the trust of his Greek readers. Even if one ignores the concluding moral and its necessary effects on the shaping of the story, in order to argue that the intention of the author was to ridicule bird omens at any cost, reference to one

49. Among the relevant sources, see, e.g., *Il.* X.274–77, XII.200ff., 237–40, XIII.821, XXIV.315–20; *Od.* XV.525–26; Plut. *Them.* 12; Xen. *Anab.* VI.1.23; Cic. *Div.* II.80, 82; Ael. *NA* I.48; Michael Psellus (see n. 48), lines 30ff. The main discussions: Bouché-Leclercq (1879–82) I.135–38; Jevons (1896) 22–23; Pollard (1977) 121. For Roman practices, see Pease (1963) 76–77, 482, and further bibliography there.

50. This is what is probably meant by W. Burkert's short, sharp note (without references): "Die Geschichte ... wie der Jude Mosollamus den weissagenden Vogel erschiesst, unterstellt der Vogelschau eine Simplizität, für die es keiner seherischen Kunst bedurft hätte. ... Hier wird, ohne Kenntnis von der Sache, ein Popanz aufgebaut und lächerlich gemacht" (in Hengel [1971] 324).

or two of the real rules (e.g., raising the right or left wing) would have made the episode even more amusing. Thus Philo, wanting to ridicule pagan mantics, refers to reliance on wing motions (*Spec. Leg.* I.62).[51] The same appears from the derisive question of Carneades and Panaetius on croaking from right or left. The author's acquaintance with the practice of interpreting bird omens is, then, superficial and vague indeed.[52]

To conclude the discussion: in view of what appears from his writings, Hecataeus's attitude toward bird omens could not have been negative; the punch line of the story betrays the author's unfamiliarity with the theological doctrine of bird divination; the author neither specifies the bird nor uses the proper term for a bird of omen; and he is ignorant of the rules of interpretation, even of the most basic ones current in the Greek world. All these factors make an attribution of the episode to Hecataeus of Abdera virtually untenable.[53]

51. The passage in paras. 60–62 refers to the vulgar opinion of the mob (cf. n. 32 above).

52. The only typological parallel I can find for gentile mantics does not relate to bird omens. Lucian of Samosata describes the statue of Atargatis in Syrian Hieropolis, which served as an oracle: the statue is carried by the temple priests, and the high priest presents the question. If the statue drives its carriers forward, the sign is positive; if it forces them to retreat, negative (*De Syria Dea* 36–37). A similar oracular technique is known from a later temple in Heliopolis (Macr. *Sat.* I.23.13), and the same may hold for the oracle associated with Alexander's visit to the Ammon temple (Diod. XVII.50–51; see Harmon [1925] IV.392 n.1). The interpretation of such an oracle was based on what were believed to be involuntary movements of the priests, in which a manifest intervention of the deity seemed evident. This was obviously very different from natural, expected, and elementary motions of birds. If this was indeed the former practice in the celebrated Ammon temple, this may suggest a possible source of inspiration for the Mosollamus story. At the same time the "instructions" could also be a product of the author's imagination. After all, it would not take much imagination to invent such an interpretation if the question presented was whether to advance or not.

53. It might be suggested that the author was actually describing an Egyptian, not a Greek, seer. But this still does not resolve the main difficulties. The very possibility that the Ptolemaic army relied on the interpretation of an Egyptian seer in making important military decisions is by itself rather remote, especially at that early stage in the history of the dynasty (despite the number of Egyptian soldiers and service troops; see Diod. XIX.80.4). It is even less plausible in view of the apparently rare resort to bird omens in

In two of the following sections (III.4, 9), I shall refer to explanations offered by the proponents of authenticity for the presence of certain sentences that evidently could not have been written by Hecataeus. These scholars have postulated various ways in which the original text may have subsequently been altered. The validity of the proposed explanations for those passages will be discussed in due course.[54] As far as the Mosollamus story is concerned, they are certainly not applicable. To suggest that the original Hecataean story underwent a "slight" adaptation by an anonymous Jewish author would not resolve the difficulties: a "slight" alteration would not have made all the basic details of the story unreliable. Moreover, Hecataeus had a favorable opinion of Greek mantics; the essence of the story—deriding gentile reliance on omens and divination and praising the wise Jew—could not have been much different in the original. The argument for this interpretation also seems to be supported by the reference of Herennius Philo to Jewish "wisdom." In addition, a Jewish adapter would have had no reason to deviate significantly from the details of the pro-Jewish report; quoting just a few genuine rules of interpretation and specifying the type of bird involved would have been a more effective way of ridiculing gentile divination.

The same arguments also apply against the suggestion that Josephus altered the original text. Furthermore, Josephus twice stresses that he is going to quote Hecataeus (*Ap.* I.200, τοῦτο παραθήσομαι; 201, λέγει δ' οὕτως), and at the end of the episode he refers the reader to further information about the Jews in the book attributed to Hecataeus, saying

---

ancient Egypt. The only extant reference in the plentiful Egyptian texts (and the numerous references to birds) appears in a "civilian" context in one of the el-Amarna letters. (EA 35.26; see Brunner [1977]. Cf. Buchberger [1986] 1047, 1050 n. 23. Brunner's statement that this is the only reference can be trusted, given the encyclopedic knowledge of the Egyptian sources possessed by that prominent Tübingen Egyptologist.) It is surely no accident that this practice does not figure in the numerous Egyptian battle accounts, which contain much information about divination and magic. The references to Egyptian birds of omen by Hecataeus (Diod. I.87.6–9) need not be taken at face value, and may be one of the numerous mistakes and inaccuracies in his Egyptian ethnography, specifically, one of the inaccuracies attributable to (deliberate?) confusion with Greek practices. In any case, Hecataeus does not mention military application. Porphyry (*Abst.* IV.9) may have drawn on Hecataeus, or may reflect Hellenistic influence.

54. See pp. 100–1 and 120–21 below.

that it is easily available (205). It is hardly possible that Josephus would have repeatedly stressed in this way the authenticity of the passage, even exposing it to comparison, while at the same time significantly diverging from the original text. Given the polemic context, this would have undermined his credibility with the readers. It should also be added that the episode is quoted in direct speech; that the author describes his impressions of the expedition in the first person; and that the story forms a complete and independent literary unit. All these further serve to undermine the possibility of a Josephan adaptation of the original story.

Another recurring explanation for the mistakes in the fragments is that Hecataeus had been misled by Hezekiah the High Priest, who figures in Josephus's quotations (*Ap.* I.187–89), or by other Jewish sources. This is equally untenable: the author presents himself as an eyewitness, and, in any case, Hecataeus would not have been misled concerning Greek practices, nor would he have been convinced by such sources to change his mind about Greek divination. The only remaining alternative is that the story in its entirety is a Jewish fabrication.

2. PTOLEMY I AND THE JEWS

Josephus opens the quotations with the celebrated Hezekiah story (*Ap.* I. 186–89). Despite the fragmentary transmission of the text, its basic outline can be determined with a high degree of certainty. The background is the period after the battle of Gaza (312 B.C.) when Ptolemy I became, temporarily, master of Syria. Hezekiah the High Priest and many Jews were so impressed by the "kindliness" and *philanthrōpia* of Ptolemy that they decided to emigrate to Egypt. Their purpose was to "take part in the affairs [of the kingdom]." Upon arriving in Egypt, Hezekiah is said to have kept close connections with the Ptolemaic authority and to have served as the leader of the immigrants.[55]

This ideal picture does not accord with the available information on Ptolemy's treatment of the Jews and other nations and cities in his realm. Consequently a number of scholars have doubted the reliability

---

55. For a more detailed reconstruction of the contents of paras. 188–89 see pp. 221–25 below. See also pp. 225–26 below for the refutation of the hypothesis that the passage records not an emigration but only a trip to Egypt.

of the Hezekiah story and its attribution to Hecataeus.[56]   However, their analyses do not consider all the possibilities, leaving much scope for attempts to harmonize the story with the historical information. In the following pages I shall present the source material and try to clarify the origin of the information, the mutual relationships and reliability of the sources, and the chronology of the events. The conclusions will aid our examination of the story itself.

First, the information about occupied populations in the Ptolemaic realm: according to Diodorus, Ptolemy son of Lagus had in 312 taken severe measures against the native populations in Cyprus and northern Syria. These included the destruction of cities and deportations (Diod. XIX.79.4–6). The inhabitants of Mallus in Cilicia were even sold into slavery, and the region was pillaged (79.6). The concurrent violent struggle in Cyrene (79.1–3) indicates that the occupied population was outraged over its treatment by Ptolemy. As to Coile Syria and Phoenicia, it is reported that immediately after the battle of Gaza Ptolemy won over the Phoenician cities, partly by persuasion, partly by besieging them (85.5). On his retreat a few months later, in 311, he razed the four "most important cities"—Acre, Jaffa, Samaria, and Gaza (93.7). Of the reoccupation of Coile Syria in 302 it is said only that Ptolemy besieged Sidon and that the remaining cities were subjugated, garrisons being stationed in them (XX.113.1–2). In reporting the reoccupation of the cities, Diodorus uses words that imply reluctance, if not resistance, on the part of the local population.

This information can be trusted. It was paraphrased with considerable accuracy by Diodorus from the work of Hieronymus of Cardia.[57] From 317 or 316 on, Hieronymus belonged to the staff of Demetrius,[58] who was operating in Coile Syria and Phoenicia and the surrounding area in 312–311 and reoccupied the region after the withdrawal of Ptolemy. Although at that point Hieronymus served the family of Antigonus, he is known to have been impartial in his writing, and occasionally even criticized Antigonus sharply.[59] The Ptolemaic "satrap

56. E.g., Willrich (1895) 22–33, (1900) 99–100; Jacoby, *RE*. s.v. "Hekataios (4)," 2767.

57. See J. Hornblower (1981) 27–43, 62, and earlier references there. Cf. also Seibert (1983) 2–8.

58. J. Hornblower (1981) 12.

59. Ibid. 107ff.

stele" of 312/11 B.C. indeed confirms the general lines of Ptolemy's policy in the occupied territories as reported by Diodorus-Hieronymus.[60] It records, for example, the deportation of soldiers, men, and women from a place whose name is illegible (lines 5–6).[61] The handling of the population in the region by Ptolemy is correctly summarized in Josephus's *Antiquities* as follows (*Ant.* XII.3):

> The cities suffered ill and lost many of their inhabitants in the struggles, so that Syria at the hands of Ptolemy son of Lagus, then called *Sōtēr* ["Savior"], suffered the opposite of [what is indicated by] his surname.

These statements may be based on the detailed accounts of the period in the books of Hieronymus of Cardia and Agatharcides, which were well known to Josephus (*Ap.* I.205–11, 213–14; *Ant.* XII.5), but the author may also have drawn on an additional source.

Parallel to this explicit information on Ptolemy's harsh treatment of the occupied population, Diodorus provides an especially favorable evaluation of Ptolemy's character, which recalls the enthusiastic account of the Hezekiah story. The term *philanthrōpia* is repeated with some variations. Diodorus praises Ptolemy's treatment of the Greco-Macedonian commanders and captives from other Hellenistic armies (Diod. XIX.55.6, 56.1, 85.3, 86.3). The same applies to the measures taken against the native Egyptians at the beginning of his reign (XVIII.14.1) and the Greco-Macedonian immigrants (XVIII.28.5–6). These references have misled some scholars who utilized them to support the statement in the Hezekiah story about Ptolemy I's *philanthrōpia*.[62] However, the practical and political considerations behind

60. See the text in Brugsch (1871) 1–13, 59–61; Sethe (1904) 11–22; Kamal (1905) I.168–71; Roeder (1959) 100–106; Kaplony-Heckel (1985) 613–19. The better-known translation of Bevan (1927) 29ff. is unreliable.

61. The comprehensive studies of the stele are Wachsmuth (1871), Goedicke (1984), and Winnicki (1991). Preferable to other reconstructions is the suggestion of Wachsmuth and Winnicki that the reference in line 5 is to either Syria or Phoenicia or both. However, Winnicki's hypothesis that line 6 refers to the same region as line 5 is unacceptable, and the identification of the region in line 6 remains anyone's guess. Wachsmuth (1871) 469–70 connects line 5 with Diodorus's report on the destruction of cities in Coile Syria and Phoenicia by Ptolemy I and his transfer of whatever property he could to Egypt (XIX.93.7). This is possible.

62. See, e.g., Lewy (1932) 121; Guttmann (1958–63) I.67; Doran (1985) 916.

this "philanthropy" toward the Greco-Macedonians are quite obvious, and as far as the Egyptian natives were concerned, Ptolemy's attitude changed after he had consolidated his rule.[63] The handling of the occupied populations outside Egypt was from the start quite different. As a matter of fact, it is doubtful whether contemporary sources applied the epithet *philanthrōpos* to Ptolemy I, and it seems to have been supplemented by Diodorus himself.[64] The term was current in Hellenistic Egypt and was one of the main features of ideal monarchy in Hellenistic (and Jewish Hellenistic) literature.[65]

Diodorus does not refer to the policy toward the Jews in the days of Gaza and Ipsus, and Josephus notes in *Against Apion* that Hieronymus of Cardia did not mention the Jews at all in his work (*Ap.* I.213–14). Since in that context Josephus strives to prove that the first Hellenistic authors did mention the Jews and deplores Hieronymus's silence, we may well believe that he took the trouble to read Hieronymus's writings with care.[66] We can therefore accept that Diodorus merely followed Hieronymus in his silence about the relations between Ptolemy I and the Jews.

The fate of the Jews is recorded by a number of other sources. They recount severe treatment of the Jews by Ptolemy I. The sources are gentile, Jewish Hellenistic, and Jewish Palestinian. The most detailed of them, Pseudo-Aristeas, states in brief that the land of the Jews was despoiled (23) and elaborates on the deportation of a hundred thousand Jews from Judea to Egypt, the enslavement of many of these, and the stationing of thirty thousand men in fortresses (12, 22–23, 36–37). The second source is Agatharcides of Cnidus, the celebrated geographer and historian who was employed at the Ptolemaic court in the middle of the second century B.C. In a passage preserved by Josephus (*Ap.* I.205–11) he reports that Ptolemy entered Jerusalem on the seventh

---

63. See Volkmann, *RE* s.v. "Ptolemaios (1)," 1631–35; and also the bibliography and survey in Murray (1972) 141–42; and Seibert (1983) 224–25.

64. On this question, see J. Hornblower (1981) 55, 63. Cf. Sacks (1990) 78–79 *et passim*.

65. On *philanthrōpia* as a Hellenistic ideal, see Rostovtzeff (1940) III.1358 nn. 4–5; Bell (1948) 33–37; Sinclair (1951) 291; Meisner (1970) 145–78; Aalders (1975) 22–23, 90; Préaux (1978) I.207. For sources, see, e.g., Isocr. *Nic.* 15; Polyb. V.11.6; Pseudo-Aristeas 265. Cf. further pp. 152–53 below, and Meisner (1970) 162–78 on its appearance in Jewish Hellenistic literature.

66. It was not that easy to do: see Dion. Halic. *De Comp. Verb.* IV.30.

day, on which the Jews refrained from any work, taking advantage of the failure of the inhabitants to take up arms and defend the city on this day (209–10). Agatharcides concludes by stating: "The ancestral land [of the Jews] was delivered into the hands of a harsh master [δεσπότην πικρόν, 210]." Almost the same had probably been reported in an internal Jewish source, probably Palestinian, used by Josephus (*Ant.* XII.4). This source contains an important addition: Ptolemy cunningly occupied Jerusalem on the Sabbath, pretending that he wanted to make a sacrifice, and for this reason the Jews did not prevent him from entering the city. It may well be that the same source provided Josephus with additional information about the transfer of captives from Samaria and Mount Gerizim to Egypt (*Ant.* XII.7), which is not reported by Pseudo-Aristeas, one of his main sources for the period.[67] The latest source, Appian in his *Syriakē*, says briefly in the context of the occupation of Jerusalem by Pompey in 63 B.C. that Ptolemy destroyed (καθῃρήκει) the city of Jerusalem (Ap. *Syr.* 50 [252]).

A brief look at these sources shows that they are mutually independent.[68] The information is transmitted from the viewpoint of the various parties involved: a Palestinian Jew, a gentile from the Ptolemaic

67. Cf. also the abbreviated version of Josephus in *Ant.* XII.6. On the superiority of the version in *Against Apion*, see M. Stern (1974–84) I.109; Bar-Kochva (1989) 479 and nn. 11, 14. For an interpretation of the sources and the question of defensive war on the Sabbath, see Bar-Kochva (1989) 477–81.

68. Contrary to A. L. Abel (1968) 254 n. 2, 257, who argues that Pseudo-Aristeas's story about the deportation and enslavement originates in Agatharcides. Josephus's quotation, which recounts only Ptolemy's entry into Jerusalem, contains Agatharcides' version in its entirety. Had there been any additional information in Agatharcides, Josephus would certainly have quoted it as well, since he was so interested in proving that the Jewish nation was mature and involved in world events at the beginning of the Hellenistic period. Agatharcides did not refer to this event anywhere else: the episode about the conquest of Jerusalem does not appear in the correct historical sequence but incidentally in the context of third-century Seleucid history. He reports the unfortunate end of Stratonice, the Seleucid princess, caused by her superstitious beliefs, and compares it to the Jewish adherence to the rules of the seventh day, which facilitated the occupation of Jerusalem by Ptolemy I. It stands to reason that had the events also been recorded in the context of the Successors period, the account would have been much more detailed, and Josephus would then have preferred to quote that rather than the short version. See also M. Stern (1974–84) I.104 and n. 3 against the conjecture that Agatharcides was used as an authority on Jewish matters by later writers.

court, and a Jewish Hellenistic author from Egypt. Each recorded the piece of information that concerned him most. Their later date (with the possible exception of the Palestinian Jewish source) does not detract from their general reliability. Although they represent opposing interests and positions, they agree in regard to the essence of the events: Ptolemy I treated the Jews unfairly and cruelly. The story gains special credibility from its recording by Agatharcides: being close to the Ptolemaic court, Agatharcides had access to royal sources. The expression "harsh master" (δεσπότην πικρόν),[69] applied by him to Ptolemy I despite his commitment to the court, further strengthens its reliability. As for Pseudo-Aristeas, despite his exaggerated figures (usual in Hellenistic literature), one cannot imagine that an author who so admired the Ptolemaic dynasty and strove to prove its favorable attitude toward the Jews would have included in his book a story about their deportation and enslavement unless the event was indeed deeply rooted in the memory of his contemporaries. His contrived efforts to excuse Ptolemy's behavior (23) reveal more than anything else how genuine he considered the story to be.

The sources do not date precisely the confrontation between Ptolemy and the Jews. Three invasions of Coile Syria are known, in 320, 312–311, and 302/1. It has been established that the year 320 must be discounted: in that year Ptolemy personally led the naval expedition, while the land invasion was entrusted to his supreme commander, Nicanor (Diod. XVIII.43; Ap. Syr. 52 [264]). However, the various accounts indicate the personal involvement of Ptolemy in the events in Jerusalem (esp. Jos. Ant. XII.4, Ap. I.210).[70] The choice between the invasions of 312–311 and 302/1 is more difficult. In view of the historical circumstances and indications in the sources, the events could have taken place in either invasion. Those who prefer that of 302/1 point out that Jerusalem is not mentioned in the list of cities destroyed by Ptolemy in 312–311 (Diod.

69. There is no reason to doubt the authenticity of this expression. Josephus states that the passage is a quotation from Agatharcides (208–9; in contrast to the anecdote about Stratonice, which is a paraphrase, 206–8), and indeed it appears in direct speech. The abbreviated version in Ant. XII.6 (χαλεπὸν ... δεσπότην) shows that, in any case, this was the essence of Agatharcides' evaluation of Ptolemy's policy toward the Jews.

70. See Willrich (1895) 23; Hadas (1951) 98; Tcherikover (1961) 56–57; as opposed to Droysen (1877–78) II.103; Reinach (1895) 43 n. 1; Lewy (1932) 121 n. 1; Klausner (1950) II.111.

XIX.93.7).[71] The occupation of 302/1 is, on the other hand, only briefly reported (XX.113), which may account for the absence of a reference to the confrontation with the Jews. This argument is not decisive: the destruction of the cities named by Diodorus in 311 was carried out on the eve of Ptolemy's withdrawal from Coile Syria. The events that followed the battle of Gaza, half a year earlier, are, however, recorded only in general terms (an occupation of cities in Phoenicia, XIX.85.5). One may therefore suggest that the capture of Jerusalem took place in the earlier stage of the occupation of 312–311.

Nevertheless, I tend to date the confrontation with the Jews to the year 302/1. What really counts here is the evident absence of any reference to the Jews in the work of Hieronymus of Cardia. Had the event taken place at the time of the battle of Gaza, Hieronymus, who was then nearby at the headquarters of Demetrius, would certainly have mentioned it in one way or another. The drastic measures taken against the Jews by Ptolemy I were no less severe than those taken by him against other natives of the region, actions that were recorded by Hieronymus. The only acceptable explanation for Hieronymus's failure to mention the Jews in the course of his narrative for the years 312 and 311 is that no exceptional events occurred in Jerusalem. However, his silence on such an event in 302/1 is understandable. In that year he was staying with Demetrius in the Aegean and did not return to Coile Syria after its reconquest by Ptolemy I. The account by Diodorus of the occupation of the region in 302 is indeed exceptionally short, probably because he could not find more detailed information in Hieronymus's work,[72] and his text for the year 301 has not been preserved. If the Ptolemaic-Jewish crisis did occur in the days of Ipsus, this would seem to place it rather in the year 302/1, before the decision on the battlefield. After the death of Antigonus at Ipsus and the collapse of his army in 301 there was no point in Jewish opposition to Ptolemy.[73]

71. See Tcherikover (1961) 57; Hengel (1976) 33. For the dating of the event in 312, see Willrich (1895) 23, 26; Meyer (1921) 24; F. M. Abel (1951) 31; Marcus (1943) 5 n. a; Hadas (1951) 98–99.

72. As opposed to A. L. Abel (1968), who draws the conclusion that there was no deportation and enslavement in the time of Ptolemy I. See also M. Stern (1974–84) I.108.

73. I would refrain from seeking support in Agatharcides' statement that the Jews came under "a harsh master" (*Ap.* I.210). This statement does not necessarily indicate a continuous long period of rule and could also have been

Does the last conclusion lend credibility to the information about the cordial relationship between the Jews and Ptolemy in the days of Gaza? Taking a number of considerations into account, the answer is in the negative.[74] The account of the attitude of the occupied populations outside Egypt in 312–311 indicates a generally hard-line policy. Had the Jews been favored vis-à-vis other nations, this would have given them a strong motivation to support Ptolemy in 302/1. I do not see how relations between the two sides could have deteriorated to such an extent in the decade before Ipsus, after the great "philanthropy" attributed to Ptolemy in 312, and the alleged enthusiastic response of the Jews, many of whom are even said to have followed Ptolemy to Egypt in order to assist him in state affairs. It should also be kept in mind that Judea was reoccupied by Antigonus half a year after the battle of Gaza, and consequently in the eleven years preceding the violent events of 302/1 Judea was not under Ptolemaic rule, so that there was no opportunity for a buildup of tension. Ptolemy's hostile measures at the time of Ipsus must have been a natural continuation and result of the relationship between ruler and subjects in the previous periods of Ptolemy's reign in Judea.

No less significant than the evidence for harsh treatment of the Jews by Ptolemy I is the absence of any reference to good relations between Ptolemy I and the Jews in Pseudo-Aristeas. It has already been mentioned that the author admired the Ptolemaic dynasty and strove to demonstrate its favorable attitude toward the Jews. He even tried to excuse Ptolemy's role in their deportation and enslavement. Such an author would not have missed an opportunity to prove his case and put the personality of Ptolemy in a better light if he had been acquainted with the Hezekiah story. The story would even have offered him a most attractive demonstration of Jewish good will toward the dynasty and a flattering explanation for the development of the Jewish community in Egypt: a voluntary immigration headed by the High Priest, aimed

---

applied to a period of a few months, even by an author like Agatharcides, who was celebrated for his accuracy of expression (for details, see Phot. *Bibl.* 213 = *FGrH* IIA p. 260, no. 86 T 2.6). Similarly the use of the attribute *Sōtēr* in Josephus (*Ant.* XII.3) cannot be used to determine the time of the event. On its first application in 305, see Paus. I.8.6, and cf. Diod. XX.100.3, Athen. XV.616; and see Kornemann (1901) 72; Moser (1914) 72.

74. As opposed to Lewy (1932) 121 n. 1; Guttmann (1958–63) I.67; Tcherikover (1961) 56; M. Stern (1974–84) I.40.

at making a contribution to the building of the Ptolemaic kingdom. Would this author, who fabricated the involvement of the Jerusalem High Priest and Ptolemy II in the translation of the Pentateuch into Greek, an entirely internal matter of the Alexandrian community, have passed over such a story? The conclusion from these observations must be that the collective memory and written records of Alexandrian Jewry in the generation of the *Letter of Aristeas* (whatever its exact date may be) did not contain any tradition of friendly relations between Ptolemy I and the Jews, nor of a voluntary immigration in his day.

Another difficulty inherent in the story brings us one step further toward correctly understanding it: Would Hezekiah, who is described as the Jerusalem High Priest, have emigrated to Egypt of his own free will and brought with him many other Jews besides? All this at the age of sixty-six (Jos. *Ap.* I.187), despite the explicit biblical prohibition and warnings not to emigrate to Egypt,[75] and when Judea had come under the control of a ruler said by the author to have demonstrated his good will to the inhabitants? Any migration from the Holy Land to Egypt was usually brought about by some compelling circumstances such as severe drought, deportation, or invasion by a northern enemy.

When this last consideration is combined with the other data that prove Ptolemy I's hard line toward the populations outside Egypt and his maltreatment of the Jews, the only way any historical value may be conceded to the Hezekiah story is to suggest that in reality the move was a forced deportation and not a voluntary emigration. And if this was indeed the case, it should rather be dated to the days of Ipsus. The author, then, transformed an exile into an emigration. Why did he do this? The question will be answered later on, after we have become acquainted with other aspects of his book. But why did he change even the background of the event and date it to the days of Gaza? Presumably he was well aware that because the traumatic experiences of the exile and enslavement in 302/1 B.C. were deeply rooted in the memory of the Jewish community in Egypt, dating his false version of the events to the days of Ipsus would discredit him at the outset.

We thus see that the information attributed to Hecataeus about the relationship between Ptolemy and the Jews in 312–311 B.C. and the voluntary migration of Hezekiah and his people does not stand up to

75. See in detail pp. 234–36 below.

historical criticism: it contradicts information from other sources, as well as historical circumstances and Jewish tradition, and was unknown in Jewish Hellenistic circles in the time of Pseudo-Aristeas. This conclusion does not permit us to believe that the Hezekiah story was recorded by Hecataeus of Abdera.

As Hecataeus was close to the court, it might naturally be suggested that he sought to color events in a positive way. But the drastic measures taken by Ptolemy I against the Jews indicate a particularly virulent animosity between the two sides in his time. Why and for whom, then, should Hecataeus have wished to fabricate such a fanciful story about kind treatment of the Jews by Ptolemy and their enthusiastic response? This was not the practice of Ptolemaic courtiers and court historians in such cases, certainly not of authors of his standing. Even the court chroniclers, who lauded the occupation of Coile Syria in 312–311 and 217 in panegyrical terms, did not fail to emphasize the strong opposition the Ptolemaic rulers had to face from the local population after their victory over their Hellenistic rivals, and the severe retaliatory measures taken by them.[76]

Be that as it may, the absence of any reference to the Hezekiah story in Pseudo-Aristeas comes up here again and decides the issue: the author of Pseudo-Aristeas was well versed in Alexandrian literature and familiar with Hecataeus's works.[77] He even quotes a reference to the Jewish Holy Scriptures from one of them (para. 31),[78] which indicates that he indeed took great interest in Hecataeus's attitude toward the Jews. A monograph on the Jews by Hecataeus, especially one so enthusiastic, would surely have been known to him, and the Hezekiah story would not have escaped his notice.

To close the discussion, a recently suggested interpretation of the Hezekiah story deserves attention. According to this, in the days of Gaza the Jewish community in Judea was divided on the issue of political orientation, and Hezekiah the High Priest supported Ptolemy. When

76. On the "satrap stele" of 312/11 see nn. 63, 64 above. On the Pithom stele, which records the events of the battle of Raphia, see Gauthier and Sottas (1925) 30 line 23; Thissen (1966) 19, 60–63.

77. See E. Schwartz (1885) 258ff.; Wendland (1900a) 2; Hadas (1951) 43–45; Murray (1970) 168–69 and there the parallels to Hecataean Egyptian ethnography.

78. The quotation could not have been taken from the book *On the Jews*. See below, pp. 140–42, esp. p. 141.

the latter withdrew, Hezekiah, fearful of Antigonus's punishment, chose to leave the country with his followers.[79] This reconstruction still assumes a deliberate "inaccuracy" on the part of Hecataeus in describing Ptolemy's general attitude toward the occupied population and the position of the Jewish community as a whole—which, in view of what has been said above on Hecataeus, is a rather remote possibility. It also implies a chronological mistake in the story: the Jewish High Priest and many Jews are said to have migrated to Egypt when "Ptolemy became master of Syria" (*Ap.* I.186), and not at the time of the withdrawal to Egypt. Such a mistake can hardly be attributed to a contemporary author so close to the court. Furthermore, this theory does not provide an explanation for the absence of any mention of the story in Pseudo-Aristeas. In addition, the numismatic material indicates that Hezekiah remained in office in Judea after the Ptolemaic withdrawal, and still held his position close to the time of the Ptolemaic reoccupation on the eve of the battle of Ipsus.[80]

Besides, there is no reference in the sources to a political division in the Jewish community in the period of the Diadochs. The later divisions known from the Ptolemaic and Seleucid periods are no evidence: they developed during generations of daily contact with the Ptolemaic regime and were the result of conflicting personal, economic, cultural, and political interests. But even in those periods, except for the days of the religious persecutions by Antiochus IV, High Priests did not leave the country when the balance of power tilted the other way.[81] Moreover,

79. Hengel (1976) 32; Schäfer (1977) 570; Hengel (1989) 50, 190; Hegermann (1989) 131–32. Cf. Tcherikover (1961) 57; Sterling (1992) 89. The variation by Winnicki (1991) 157 ignores the explicit references to Hezekiah in paras. 187–89.

80. See p. 256ff. below. The identification of Hezekiah as governor and not as High Priest (pp. 89–90 below) does not affect the main arguments given above.

81. The reference in Hieronymus (*In Dan.* XI.14) to an emigration of the "*optimates*" to Egypt after the battle of Panium (200 B.C.), mentioned by some scholars, offers no good parallel. The internal and external circumstances of the Fifth Syrian War were entirely different, and the High Priest was not among the emigrants. The information itself is rather dubious, and was not taken from Porphyry (as M. Stern [1974–84] II.462 and others suggest), at least not in its present form. The "*optimates*" are said to have been taken to Egypt by the returning Scopas, the Ptolemaic general, while another piece of information, which certainly originates in Porphyry, reports that Scopas

the policy of Antigonus toward the local populations in his realm was not of a sort that would have driven an opportunistic High Priest to flee for his life.[82] This policy was well known in Judea in 312 B.C. after three years under Antigonus. The appearance of the name Antigonus in Jewish Orthodox circles already in the third century B.C. (Avot 1.3) indicates at least that Antigonus Monophthalmus did not leave hostile memories in Judea. The strong Jewish opposition to Ptolemy in 302/1 reinforces the impression that Antigonus's policy toward the occupied population, here as elsewhere in his realm, was favorable.

3. HEZEKIAH THE HIGH PRIEST

Hezekiah, the leader of the alleged Jewish migration to Egypt, is described as High Priest (*Ap.* I.187–89). As was pointed out already in the eighteenth century, no High Priest named Hezekiah is known from other sources.[83] He is not mentioned in Josephus's historical account of the period surrounding the battle of Gaza, nor in his narrative of the Persian and Hellenistic periods as a whole.

Josephus records the names Johanan, Iaddous (Jaddua), and Onias as the High Priests in the late Persian age and in the days of Alexander and the Successors (*Ant.* XI.297, 302–3, 347). Quite a number of scholars have tried to disqualify the first two names, claiming that they are just duplicates of the names of two High Priests who served two generations earlier, at the end of the fourth century (Neh. 12.22).[84] However, F. M. Cross, in a celebrated article, has shown the paponymic principle current among the ruling families in Judea and Samaria in the Persian period.[85] The authenticity of the name Johanan in Josephus

---

was trapped in the siege of Sidon and was forced to surrender (Hieron. *In Dan.* XI.15). Gera (1987) suggests that the reference is erroneous, and actually reflects a deportation of pro-Seleucid Jews to Egypt before the battle of Panium.

82. On Antigonus's liberal and conciliatory policy toward the native Asian peoples, see Billows (1990) 305–11.

83. See, e.g., Zornius (1730) 15; Eichorn (1793) 439–41; J. G. Müller (1877) 172; Willrich (1895) 31–32, 107; Reinach (1930) 36; Jacoby (1943) 62.

84. The arguments were summarized by Grabbe (1987) 231–46, together with earlier bibliography.

85. Cross (1975); cf. *id.* (1983) 89–91. The paponymic principle can also be observed in the Zadok family during the Hellenistic period (but see Ackroyd [1984] 159 n. 1).

has recently been decisively established by the coin of Johanan the Priest, which, on clear numismatic grounds, must be dated close to the Macedonian occupation.[86] This also lends credence to the name of Iaddous, described as Johanan's successor, who held office in the time of Alexander's conquest.[87]

The possibility that the name Hezekiah escaped Josephus's notice or was accidentally omitted from the sources at his disposal is highly unlikely. Josephus is proud of his precise rendering of the line of descent (*diadochē*) of the High Priests, and regards it as one of his greatest achievements (*Ant.* XX.261). He testifies to the existence of the pedigrees of the priestly families in the public archives and to their use in practical matters like marriage (*Ap.* I.31–36), and says that he himself used such a pedigree (*Vit.* 6). According to rabbinic sources the pedigree lists of all the priests were kept in a chamber behind the Holy of Holies, and in cases of doubt final decision was passed by the High Court in the Temple.[88]

Furthermore, in Book XX of his *Jewish Antiquities*, Josephus gives the number of High Priests in the various stages of Jewish history up to the destruction of the Second Temple (*Ant.* XX.227ff.). It has been proved that these numbers were based on an authoritative list of the High Priests and not on information scattered in the books of the *Antiquities*.[89] The number quoted for the High Priests from the time of the Restoration until Antiochus Epiphanes (fifteen in all, XX.234)

86. See pp. 263ff. below.

87. The discussion about the paponymic system (and the names Johanan and Jaddua in particular) should be separated from the controversy over the reliability of the stories in *Ant.* XI.302–47. The verification of the two names still does not prove the historicity of the stories. See also D. R. Schwartz (1990). The results of the recent excavations at Mt. Gerizim, which showed that the Samaritan city was built around the year 200 (see Magen [1990] 83, 96; *id.* [1992] 38–40), strengthen the position of the many scholars who rejected them as tendentious legends. This appears also from the remains of the Samaritan temple itself, discovered in 1994 (findings still unpublished).

88. See Middot 5.4; Sifri, Numbers 116; Tosefta, Hagiga 2.9; and Lieberman (1962) 172.

89. Bloch (1879) 147–50; von Destinon (1882) 29–36; Momigliano (1934) 886; Hölscher (1940) 73–75; as opposed to Willrich (1895) 107–15. See more recently D. R. Schwartz (1982) 252–54, with special reference to the section listing the High Priests from the Restoration to Antiochus V.

is identical to that which appears from the chronistic and narrative material in Books XI and XII of the *Antiquities,* thus rendering the inclusion of Hezekiah impossible.[90] Significantly enough, Josephus himself, who not only cited the Hezekiah story in *Against Apion,* but also inserted a sentence based on it in his account of the Ptolemaic era in the *Antiquities* (XII.9),[91] refrained from integrating Hezekiah in the sequence of his account of the historical events and of the chronistic information on the High Priests. Josephus did not usually apply sophisticated critical methods to his sources, and if he chose to ignore the name of Hezekiah in this case, it must have been only because he was convinced of the authoritativeness of the commonly accepted tradition and of the list of the High Priests of the House of Zadok available to him.

A number of scholars have suggested that the High Priest Hezekiah was merely the leading member of a priestly family or an influential priest, as the title is known to have been applied in the later generations of the Second Temple.[92] Other scholars have tried to reinforce this view by arguing that the term appears without the article, which may imply that Hezekiah was only one of the important priests who were active at that time.[93] However, in the Persian and Hellenistic periods, "High Priest" designated only the head of the priestly hierarchy, and there is not a single case in which it was applied to other priests. The loosening of the strict meaning of the term in the Roman period resulted from changes in the appointment procedures and status of the chief priest. The right of just one family to the office was rescinded. High Priests were appointed by Herod, Agrippa I, Agrippa II, and

90. In Book XI of *Antiquities*: Joshua, Joiakim, Eliashib, Jehoyada, Johanan, Jaddua, Onias. In Book XII: Simeon, Eleazar, Menasseh, Onias, Simeon, Onias, Jason, Menelaus. D. R. Schwartz (1982) 254 has cogently argued that the aforementioned list was the basis for Josephus's chronistic information in Books XI and XII of the *Antiquities*. The absence of the names Jaddua and Johanan (the First), the late fourth-century High Priests mentioned in Nehemiah (12.22), from Josephus's account has already been explained by Cross (1975) as caused by haplography in the copy of the list used by Josephus. Unlike these two, there is no textual reason for the omission of the name Hezekiah from that list.

91. See in detail p. 226 below.

92. Schlatter (1893) 340; Büchler (1899) 33; Grintz (1969) 46 n. 23; M. Stern (1974–84) I.40; Schäfer (1977) 570; Rappaport (1981) 15–16; Doran (1985) 915.

93. See Thackeray (1926) 238 n. a; Reinach (1930) 36 n. 1; Gauger (1982) 45–46; cf. Holladay (1983) 326 n. 12.

the Roman governors, and deposed in their lifetimes, the office even being occasionally sold for money. Consequently, deposed High Priests continued to bear their former title, and it was even applied to heads of rich, influential families, whose practical power was frequently equal, if not superior, to that of the officiating High Priest.[94] As for the absence of the article, this also occurs in Pseudo-Aristeas (35, 41) and the Mishna,[95] when referring to the Hasmonean High Priest. The matter is clinched by Hecataeus's Jewish excursus, which describes in detail the qualities and authority of the Jewish High Priest, stating that he was chosen by the people, and designating him without the article (Diod. XL.3.5–6).[96] If Hecataeus had been the author of the Hezekiah story, he would certainly have to be interpreted as saying that Hezekiah was the presiding Jewish High Priest. The flexible use of the title "High Priest" in the Roman period can explain why Josephus, who was acquainted with the lists of the officiating High Priests, did not delete the title attached to Hezekiah.

A new dimension to the question of Hezekiah was introduced by the discovery of the Hezekiah coins. The appearance of Hezekiah's name on those coins encouraged the supporters of the authenticity of the Hezekiah story and brought about a new wave of scholarly contributions in that direction, claiming that the information in Josephus's *Antiquities* was mistaken or incomplete, and that the coins proved that there was indeed a High Priest named Hezekiah at the beginning of the Hellenistic period.[97]

This deduction, however, is unjustified. To show why, the chronological framework of the Hezekiah coins must first be clarified. These coins are divided into two groups, each including a number of variations. The

94. See the survey of the material in Klausner (1950) IV.300–301; Schürer et al. (1973–86) II.227–36, esp. 232–36.

95. Ma'aser Sheni 5.15; Sota 9.10; Yadayim 4.1; cf. Shqalim 6.1.

96. Noted by Tcherikover (1961) 425 n. 46. The explanations of Gauger (1982) 45–46 do violence to the essence of the sentence in Diodorus.

97. See e.g., Sellers (1933) 73; Albright (1934) 20–22; Sukenik (1934) 178–82 (1935) 341–43; Olmstead (1936) 244; Vincent (1949) 281–94; Schalit (1949) 263 n. 22; Avigad (1957) 149; Albright (1957) 29; Tcherikover (1961) 425–26; Aharoni (1962) 56–60; Kanael (1963) 40–41; Gager (1969) 138–39; Kindler (1974) 76; M. Stern (1974–84) I.40; Wacholder (1974) 268; Holladay (1983) 325 n. 11; Meshorer (1982) 33; Goodman in Schürer et al. (1973–86) III.673; Hegermann (1989) 131.

legend on the first group reads יחזקיה הפחה (Hezekiah the *peḥah* [governor]); that on the second, only יחזקיה (Hezekiah). The two groups differ in design, on the obverse as well as on the reverse. Appendix A at the end of this monograph discusses in detail the dating of the two groups.[98] The numismatic analysis shows that the first group of coins was struck in the last years of the Persian period, probably from 340 to 338, and the second in the days of Alexander and under the rule of the Successors. Production of the second group seems to have ceased shortly before the Ptolemaic occupation in 302 B.C., on the eve of the battle of Ipsus.

This dating means that a man named Hezekiah served as the Persian governor in Judea in the late Persian period, and continued as head of the administration of Judea under Alexander and the Successors. This Hezekiah held his leading position in Judea for thirty-six to thirty-eight years. His title in the Persian period was *peḥah*, but under the Macedonian occupation the official oriental title was probably replaced by a Greek one, which does not appear on the coins.

These data not only do not bolster the claim that Hezekiah served as High Priest; they even contribute to its refutation.[99] Hezekiah figures in the first group of coins from the end of the Persian period not as High Priest but as *peḥah*,[100] and it cannot be accepted that he also served concurrently as High Priest.[101] The Persians, who usually appointed Jewish governors, refrained from placing full authority in the hands of one man. The High Priest was in charge of religious matters that, because of the character of Jewish law and tradition, covered many

98. Pp. 256–66.

99. In some discussions of the Hezekiah coins it is argued that the human and zoomorphic images do not permit the identification of Hezekiah as High Priest (e.g., Rappaport [1981] 7, 11). However, images also appear on the coins of Johanan the High Priest (Pl. I no. 7 below) and on a coin of Yaddua, probably a former High Priest of the early fourth century (Spaer [1986/7] 1–3). The prohibition "You shall not make a graven image for yourself nor the likeness of any thing" (Exod. 20.4) was still strictly interpreted in that generation (based on verse 5) as applying to idols alone. See also Hengel (1976) 33; Barag (1986/7) 20. With the influx of Greek art in the Hellenistic period, it became difficult for Jews to distinguish between human and divine images. Hence the new, wider interpretation, prohibiting all representations of the human form.

100. This has rightly been observed by Rahmani (1971) 160; Rappaport (1981) 15–16; Barag (1985) 167.

101. Against Aharoni (1962) 58–59 and others.

areas of life. The Temple treasures also gave him considerable economic power. The rivalry and competition between the Jewish governor and the High Priest saved the Persian authorities from too great an assertion of independence on the part of the *pehah* and facilitated early exposure of such ambitions. In two cases we have evidence of tension and even a rift between these two officials that certainly served the interests of the Persians, and a similar state of affairs is indicated in a third case.[102] Furthermore, we know the names of another seven or eight Jewish governors,[103] not one of whom served as High Priest, and none of them seems to have belonged to the Zadok family. It is difficult to imagine a change in the traditional appointment policy in the fourth century, when the Persians suffered from recurring Egyptian revolts—certainly not just a few years after Tennes's rebellion in Phoenicia (348 B.C.), which spread to Judea as well, and was possibly the cause of the recorded banishment of Jews to Babylonia and Hyrcania.[104]

Direct numismatic evidence can be found in the coin of Johanan the High Priest, mentioned earlier. The numismatic data show clearly that it was struck concurrently with the first group of Hezekiah coins.[105] Hence we may deduce that the office of High Priest was indeed separate from that of governor, at least in the late Persian period, and that accordingly Hezekiah could not have been the High Priest at that time.

But could Hezekiah the Governor have served concurrently as High Priest later, in the Macedonian age, or, as has been suggested,[106] first as governor and later as High Priest? This would have to mean that he belonged to the line of succession of the Zadok family and that during the Persian period, when he was governor, his father or brother

---

102. Zech. 6.13; Neh. 13.7–13, 28; and the absence of Eliashib in chap. 10. See also Cowley (1923) nos. 30–31 lines 1, 17–18; and no. 32.

103. See the list in Avigad (1976) 35; Barag (1986/7) 20. Cf. Aharoni (1962) 56–59.

104. On this revolt and its influence on the Jews see Schürer (1901–9) III.7 n. 11; Klausner (1950) II.13–14; Barag (1966) 6–12; E. Stern (1982) 254–55; M. Stern (1974–84) II.421; Barag (1986/7) 14 n. 58. The arguments of Grintz (1957) 13–15 and Widengren (1977) 501 against the involvement of Palestinian Jews in that revolt do not hold up against the evidence of the sources and the archaeological findings. Cf. pp. 143–44 below on the reference to the deportation of many Jews to Babylonia by the Persians (*Ap.* I.194).

105. See pp. 263–64 below.

106. See Millar (1979) 7–8. Cf. Avigad (1976) 29.

would have served as High Priest. For the reasons given above, such a concentration of power in the hands of one family is extremely unlikely. Moreover, as appears from the numismatic evidence, Hezekiah governed Judea for a long period, about thirty-six years. He must, then, have been an especially dominant figure. If at a certain period he was concurrently (or only) the High Priest, it does not seem credible that he would have disappeared from the authoritative record of the High Priests, and would also be absent from Josephus's *Antiquities* (or rather, from its sources).[107]

Let us turn back now to the main question of our discussion: Can the statement that Hezekiah was High Priest be attributed to Hecataeus of Abdera? Hecataeus knew perfectly well the meaning of the title "High Priest," and elaborated in his Jewish excursus on the preeminence and functions of this position. If he had indeed written a monograph on the Jews, he would have been eager to obtain precise information on the identity of the High Priest of his time. As a prominent figure in the Ptolemaic court he could easily have acquired this information. Is it possible that Hecataeus could have collected so much information about the personality of Hezekiah (character, age, connections with the court, purpose of emigration, influence on the community, and public appearances: *Ap.* I.187–89) but failed to know or to verify the most important point, the exact position and title of the hero of his story? All this, if, as the story has it, Hezekiah kept close connections with the court and settled in Egypt?

For these reasons, the various attempts to explain the statement that Hezekiah was High Priest as merely a "mistake" of Hecataeus do not hold water. Similarly it has been suggested that Hezekiah was a

---

107. Millar (1979) 8 suggests that Hezekiah went to Egypt in 312 for negotiations and came back as High Priest. He further raises the possibility that Hezekiah is absent from the list of High Priests because, having been appointed by Ptolemy, he was not universally recognized by the Jews. For the rejection of Millar's main thesis, see pp. 225–26 below. Notably even notorious High Priests like Jason and Menelaus, who were appointed by gentile rulers and were certainly hated by the majority of the people, appeared on the authoritative list of the fifteen High Priests of the period from the Restoration to the religious persecutions (*Ant.* XX.261; and see p. 83 above). The same is true of High Priests of later periods like Alcimus, and a good number of notorious High Priests of the Roman period.

Samaritan High Priest,[108] or the "High Priest" of the Jews in Egypt.[109] Even less acceptable is the explanation that Hecataeus exaggerated in describing the position of Hezekiah because of the "tendency to idealization" of the treatise, the wish to ascribe great importance to his subject, and his tendency to rely on "priestly traditions."[110] Which "priestly traditions" would have described as High Priest a man who was not? Even from a Greek point of view, how could the Jewish leaders, country, and Temple have been idealized by attributing to the High Priest, whose duty it was to serve in the Jerusalem Temple, initiative for and participation in a migration to Egypt? And would naming Hezekiah as the civil governor of Judea have detracted from the importance of the subject? Finally, how could a Ptolemaic court official attribute to a Jewish secular leader in Egypt a religious position to which he had no claim, with all the implications that that involved for the latter's relations with the authorities?

At the same time, I do not believe that the name Hezekiah in the story is a fabrication by the author of the treatise. As it does not appear among the recurring names of High Priests in the Persian period and is not known even from the biblical name lists of the Zadok family as a whole, the choice of the same name as that of the contemporary governor, who served for such a long period, can hardly be accidental. This suggests that the author was inspired by the name and personality of that governor, but transformed Hezekiah from governor into High Priest, just as he transformed the forced exile to Egypt into a voluntary migration, the harsh treatment of the local population by Ptolemy into "philanthropy," and probably also the time of Ipsus into the time of Gaza. He had good reasons for doing so, and their clarification

108. It should be added that there could not be any real historical connection between the Hezekiah who appears in the medieval Samaritan chronicle as the Samaritan High Priest said to have met Alexander and the Jewish governor Hezekiah. It has already been established that the Samaritan story is only a reversal of Josephus's legend about the meeting between the Jewish High Priest and Alexander or of its later Jewish adaptations. The name Hezekiah may be an invention inspired directly or indirectly by *Against Apion*, but the identity of the names may be also coincidental. On the Samaritan story, see, e.g., Adler and Seligsohn (1902–3); Montgomery (1907) 302; Gaster (1925) 33; Grabbe (1987) 238–40, and further bibliography there.

109. See Zornius (1730) 15.

110. Lewy (1932) 122; Kasher (1985) 40 n. 47.

may help us later to bring to light the purpose of the book. At this stage, suffice it to say that there are quite a few examples of important personalities whom later Jewish and Christian authors turn into High Priests: Moses, Jeremiah, Ezra, Judas Maccabaeus, Eleazar the Martyr, and even Jesus.[111]

Notwithstanding these transformations, the Hezekiah story may contain a kernel of truth. There seems no reason not to accept that Hezekiah, the former governor, was indeed among the people banished to Egypt in the year 302/1. The purpose of the forced exile was to deprive Judea of its political leadership and of its potential military manpower. In view of Hezekiah's personality and former position, it stands to reason that he was soon recognized as the leader of the captives, the new settlers in Egypt. But even if one does not accept this attempt at a historical reconstruction and regards the story as complete fiction, the principal conclusions remain valid: Hezekiah the Governor was transformed into the High Priest; and the forced exile, into a voluntary migration.

Finally, Willrich's interpretation of the Hezekiah story should be mentioned. He suggested that it is just an anachronistic version of the emigration of Onias IV and his followers to Egypt and their settlement in Leontopolis at the time of the religious persecutions by Antiochus IV, and that Hezekiah is only a pseudonym for Onias IV. Willrich even went so far as to suggest that the author was one of the settlers of Leontopolis and the "supporters of the Oniad temple."[112] Despite some resemblance between Hezekiah's deportation, Onias's flight, and their settlement, this hypothesis cannot be accepted as it stands. The arguments considered above against regarding the name of Hezekiah and the entire Hezekiah story as complete fabrications are equally applicable against Willrich's suggestion. Even more telling, though, is the implied criticism voiced by the author against certain practices known to have taken place in the Leontopolis temple (*Ap.* I.199).[113] At the same time it is highly probable that the migration

---

111. See the examples and sources assembled by D. R. Schwartz (1984) 159 and n. 21.

112. Willrich (1895) 32, 80–82; *id.* (1924) 29; cf. Jacoby (1943) 62; Schaller (1963) 27; Denis (1970) 266.

113. See pp. 166, 247 below.

and settlement of Onias had some influence on the shaping of the Hezekiah story.[114]

4. RELIGIOUS PERSECUTIONS AND MARTYRDOM

Turning to Jewish customs, we find, first of all, that the author praises the Jews for their adherence to Jewish laws, saying that they "prefer to suffer everything in order not to transgress against them" (*Ap.* I.190). Illustrating this statement he adds (*Ap.* I.191):

> So for example ... all being insulted by their neighbors and by those who came into [the country], and being frequently abused by the Persian kings and satraps, they could not be persuaded to change their way of thinking [*dianoia*], but being exposed because of [their adherence to] them [the laws], they faced tortures and the most horrible deaths rather than deny their ancestral [laws].

The phrasing of the passage is unequivocal. Its beginning definitely indicates that it applies to Palestinian Jews. They are said to have suffered frequently, not just once, from the "Persian kings and satraps," and not just from a local mob. The suffering is described as "tortures and the most horrible deaths," suggesting recurrent large-scale attempts to force a certain course on the Jews, rather than occasional punishment. The purpose of these measures is indicated by the Jewish readiness to undergo all the sufferings in order not to "deny their ancestral [laws]," and by the failure of the rulers to convince them to "change their way of thinking." These must have been religious persecutions *par excellence*. The Persians accordingly tried in vain to force the Jews to change their religious practices and perhaps also their beliefs. Thus the reference cannot be to retaliatory measures against cultic centers, which in the Persian period were occasionally employed to subdue a revolt or unrest. Nor can the text, as it stands, be interpreted as referring to isolated episodes in which Diaspora Jews in royal service may have been punished for refusing to carry out orders contradicting their laws. Similarly it cannot refer just to possible early cases where Jewish adherence to certain laws, such as the Sabbath (and perhaps also

114. Suggested by Hengel (1971) 303, (1989) 50. See in more detail p. 244 below.

dietary) laws, weakened their defensive capabilities and paved the way for their occupation by an enemy, with all the ensuing sufferings.[115]

The passage does not accord with our knowledge of the Jews in the Persian period. Nor does it coincide with the abundant material about the liberal Achaemenid policy toward local religions in the occupied satrapies.[116] It was therefore suggested long ago that the account is a reflection of the religious persecutions of Antiochus IV.[117] The sentence about the attitude of the neighbors and newcomers should in that case refer to the hostility of the population of the Hellenized oriental cities and the Greco-Macedonian settlers in those days, which is reiterated by the Books of the Maccabees. "Being exposed because of [their adherence to] them [the laws]" may possibly be interpreted as referring to cases where certain Jewish groups refrained from defending themselves on the Sabbath against Seleucid troops trying to force them to violate the holy day (I Macc. 22.29–37).

Scholars urging the authenticity of the passage have, however, argued that there may have been cases of religious persecution under Persian rule. They refer to Josephus's report of the fratricide in the Temple and its punishment by the satrap Bagoses (Bagoas) toward the end of the Persian period (*Ant*. XI.297, 301), the story of Esther, and the narrative section of the Book of Daniel. They also note that the sources for our knowledge of the history of the Jews in the Persian period are too scanty to allow us to eliminate the possibility of more occurrences of religious persecution.[118]

---

115. As opposed to Guttman (1958–63) I.68, Wacholder (1974) 268–69, and Gauger (1982) 44, who quote the refusal of Alexander's Jewish soldiers to help in clearing earth for the rebuilding of the temple of Bel (*Ap*. I.192) and the Jerusalem Jews' failure to protect themselves properly when attacked by Ptolemy I on the Sabbath (see pp. 74–75 above).

116. This evaluation of the Achaemenid policy has been accepted by all prominent Iranologists. See the summaries of the material in Boyce (1984); M. Schwartz (1985); Dandamaev and Lukonin (1989) 320–67. See also Posner (1936) 171ff.; Kienitz (1953) 53–61; Oppenheim (1984); Bresciani (1985) 504–7.

117. Eichorn (1793) 439–40; Willrich (1895) 21, (1900) 92–94, 104; Jacoby (1943) 65, 72, followed by many others. See, e.g., Schaller (1963) 18; Hengel (1971) 302; Walter (1976) 147.

118. J. G. Müller (1877) 173; M. Stern (1974–84) I.42; Holladay (1983) 328 n. 20; Doran (1985) 915; Goodman in Schürer et al. (1973–86) III.673. And see also the references in n. 115 above.

A closer examination of the sources mentioned foils the attempt to trace persecutions and martyrdoms before Antiochus Epiphanes. The Bagoses incident has nothing to do with religious persecution. The Temple is said to have been profaned by the very entrance of the satrap and his men into the holy precinct. Bagoses had done this either to carry out inquiries about the unprecedented murder committed by Johanan the High Priest in the Temple, or to avenge the death of Joshua, his favorite, and prepare punitive measures (*Ant.* XI.298–99). He did not impose any prohibition on the cult or service in the Temple, only a special tax on sacrifices (XI.297), probably for seven years (XI.301). And there is not even an indication that the High Priest was deposed, a fact corroborated by numismatic evidence.[119]

The Book of Esther (regardless of its historicity and time of composition) is also irrelevant to our question: as has been cogently argued by Kaufmann in his monumental *History of the Israelite Religion*,[120] the Jews in the book were not persecuted because of their religion, they were not accused of disparaging the gods of the gentiles, and they were not enjoined to worship other gods. The edict for their annihilation was unconditional: there was no suggestion of pardon for conversion or for adoption of local rites. Moreover, the name of the Jewish God is not mentioned, and there is no explicit reference to the Jews' adherence to His faith, or rejection of pagan cults. The direct cause for the persecution was the struggle for power in the court between an influential Jew and a gentile vizier. The general objection to the Jews arose out of typical xenophobia and ethnic prejudices. The Jews were scattered among the nations and had different customs (esp. Esther 3.8). They were successful and climbed the social and bureaucratic royal ladder. All these factors aroused jealousy and hatred. All in all, the Esther story does not record religious persecution or anything similar to it.

As to the Book of Daniel: the story that may be seen as martyrological is the legend about the three men in the fiery furnace (chap. 3). Its relevance to the passage under discussion depends, first of all, on the solution of the complicated questions that have stood for many years at the center of the study of this book: the unity of the book and its authorship; the connection between its two parts, the narrative section (chaps. 1–6) and the vision section (chaps. 7–12); the dating

119. See pp. 263–65 on the coin of Johanan the High Priest.
120. Kaufmann (1937–56) IV.1.440ff.

of the original composition of the stories, their adaptations, and their redactions; the involvement of the redactor (or author) of the book in the shaping of the stories; and so on. Thus if we accept that the stories as a whole were written by the Hassidic author who (as is universally accepted) composed the vision section, or that they were adapted by him according to a well-calculated plan, this would discount, if not eliminate, the fiery-furnace story as evidence for persecutions in the Persian period. However, as these questions are highly controversial,[121] it is also advisable to isolate the story and examine it on its own merits. Does the story, as it stands, correspond to the statements ascribed to Hecataeus?

The contents of the story differ substantially from the historical indications provided by the passage under discussion. It records what is said to have been an exceptional event and not a recurring one; it refers to a few high-ranking courtiers and not to the Jewish people as a whole;[122] the cause of the confrontation is an arbitrary order by the king that is not directed at the outset against the Jewish people, but is exploited by jealous courtiers against their Jewish rivals; there are no tortures, no Jew actually suffers, and the Jewish courtiers emerge from the fiery furnace unharmed; at the end the king even publicly proclaims the greatness of the Jewish God. The event occurs (and can take place only) in the Diaspora, and not in Judea, where according to the passage Jews were persecuted.[123]

The story in Daniel, an early version of it, or ones based on it could not, therefore, have inspired Hecataeus, directly or indirectly, to write the passage.[124] One may still argue that the story reflects in a legendary, optimistic way events of the Persian period similar to those indicated in the passage. However, what count are the motifs of the legend. Had the fiery-furnace story been a reaction to religious persecution and martyrdom, this would be discernible from its motifs. But the story was

121. For a survey of research on these questions, see Lebram (1974); Koch (1980). For the more recent, see Delcor (1971) 10ff.; Schäfer (1977) 539–41; Hartman and Di Lella (1978) 9ff.; Nickelsburg (1984) 34–35; Collins (1984) 27–39; Goodman in Schürer et al. (1973–86) III.687; Ginsberg (1989).

122. *BT* Sanhedrin 93.1 ("all the people of Israel save Hananiah, Michael, and Azariah bowed to the idol") is just an incorrect interpretation.

123. Cf. the notes of Kaufmann (1937–56) IV.1.420–22, where he rejects for similar reasons the comparison of the Daniel stories with events in the time of Antiochus IV.

124. As opposed to M. Stern (1974–84) I.42.

not designed to tell the reader about martyrdom. After all, there are no real martyrs in it. It was not meant to describe religious persecutions either. The scope of the story is too limited for such a purpose, and the Jewish courtiers are not at the outset persecuted because of their religion: the gentile courtiers only exploit Jewish adherence to certain religious restrictions to get rid of their Jewish competitors.

The story contains three motifs: the natural animosity of gentile courtiers to high-ranking Jewish officials, the dilemma facing Diaspora Jews in royal service with regard to official cults and obligations that stand in contradiction to their faith, and the ordeal by fire by which the truth may be decisively proved.[125] The first motif can be discerned even more clearly in the parallel story about Daniel in the lions' den (Dan. 6): the temporary royal prohibition on making a request to anyone save the king is a result of a cunning plot of the gentile courtiers to impede Daniel (6.6–8), and the king himself deeply regrets it upon discovering its implications for Daniel, his favorite (6.15–16).

The first two motifs do indeed fit into the circumstances of Jewish life in the Persian period: Jews served in the administration and the army, and a few of them (like Nehemiah) even reached high-ranking court positions. These courtiers must have been confronted quite often with the difficulty of reconciling their official commitments with their religious convictions. Outbursts of jealousy by gentile (especially Persian) colleagues would also have been only natural, and differing Jewish religious prohibitions and practices would have been utilized against Jewish courtiers by their rivals. The third motif was borrowed from the Zoroastrian tradition, where tests seem to have been carried out by fire,[126] the symbol of truth; and it may also have been inspired by certain biblical verses (Is. 43.2, Ps. 66.10–12).[127]

Could a courtiers' struggle have developed into official religious persecution sometime in the Persian period, and reached the dimensions indicated in the passage attributed to Hecataeus? This must be ruled out in view of the evidence for the policy of the Achaemenids and their treatment of foreign religions.[128] Furthermore, religious persecutions of the form, scale, and frequency recorded in the passage could not

125. On the last two motifs, see Bickerman (1967) 86–91.
126. For references, see Bickerman (1967) 136 n. 12.
127. See Kuhl (1930) 81; Bentzen (1952) 39.
128. See the references in n. 116 above.

have escaped notice in the historiography and literature of the period, however scantily and fragmentarily it has been preserved. One would expect references to such experiences at least in the oratory of the Maccabean martyrs, or in the battle orations in the Books of the Maccabees, which are replete with allusions to the nation's past. More than that, religious persecutions are bound to provoke extensive literary reactions. The essence of martyrdom (as the word also indicates) is, after all, the desire to leave sound witness for the enlightenment of subsequent generations. The passage attributed to Hecataeus remains the only testimony. This is simply not enough, and casts a heavy shadow of suspicion on the authenticity of the work as a whole.

Other advocates of authenticity have raised the possibility of some mistake by Hecataeus. Thus it has been suggested that Hecataeus confused the Persians with the Babylonians.[129] This is hardly acceptable for a historian who lived at the end of the Persian era; and in any case there were no religious persecutions under the Babylonians, just deportation (which is not mentioned). Another suggestion: since the Jews were described as descendants of the *kalanoi*, the Indian philosophers (so Clearchus of Soli; see *Ap.* I.179), some of their features were also attributed to the Jews.[130] The reference to Jewish martyrology is accordingly only a reflection of the tradition about Calanus, who is said to have preached endurance in the face of death, and even to have burned himself to death. However, neither the passages ascribed to Hecataeus as a whole nor the genuine Hecatean Jewish excursus indicate any connection between the Jews and Indian philosophers, or attribute to the Jews any other "Indian" feature. Of itself, the tradition about Calanus's death has nothing to do with religious persecutions and martyrology. On the contrary, he is said to have received much honor from the rulers. The burning was just an appropriate way he chose to end a happy life, and to set an example of self-control.[131] Furthermore, the explanation does not take into account the abundant data on the identity of the persecutors of the Jews (the Persian kings and satraps; the neighbors; the newcomers to the country), which exclude any such deduction. Besides, Clearchus's reference to the Jews cannot have preceded the

129. Wendland (1900) 1200.

130. Lewy (1932) 124–26; cf. Doran (1985) 914–15.

131. Strabo XV.1.68 (717); Diod. XVII.107; Curt. VIII.9.32; Plut. *Alex.* 69. Cf. Cic. *Div.* I.47, *Tusc.* V.77; Mela III.65.

year 300 B.C.,[132] while if one takes the book *On the Jews* as authentic, it cannot be dated after the year 302.[133] Any influence from Clearchus is, therefore, out of question. Clearchus does indeed put the reference to the Jews in the mouth of Aristotle, but this is certainly apocryphal.[134]

5. THE DESTRUCTION OF PAGAN TEMPLES AND ALTARS

After elaborating on the readiness of the Jews to sacrifice themselves for the preservation of their laws, the author refers to Jewish intolerance toward other religions (*Ap.* I.193):

> They destroyed all the temples and altars constructed by those coming to the land against them, for some of which they paid a fine to the satraps, and for others they obtained forgiveness. And he adds that it is just to admire them for these [actions].

Such acts of violence against foreign cults could not have been perpetrated by the Jewish community in Judea under Persian rule. They are, however, well known from the period of the Hasmonean state. Interestingly, the reference to the rather lenient reaction of the Persian satraps does not accord with the preceding statement about the frequent harsh measures against the Jewish religion by the Persian authorities.

What is even more decisive for evaluating the authenticity of the treatise is the note that the Jews deserve to be admired for these actions.[135] A Greco-Hellenistic writer brought up in a spirit of religious tolerance and on the sacred principle of immunity and asylum for temples and holy precincts would not have praised such barbarous acts of defilement and sacrilege. To counter this argument it has been suggested that admiration for Jewish opposition to polytheism and to material representation of the divine can be expected of a Greek intellectual at the end of the fourth century B.C.[136] However, this would not have been expressed by lauding the violation of the elementary Greek principle of absolute immunity for sacred places. One may doubt

---

132. See M. Stern (1973) 163.
133. See p. 55 above.
134. See M. Stern (1974–84) I.47.
135. See, e.g., Willrich (1895) 21; Hengel (1971) 302; Wacholder (1974) 269.
136. Guttman (1958–63) I.68–69; Holladay (1983) 282.

whether even Xenophanes or Zeno of Citium would have subscribed to such statements.

In any case, this explanation does not agree with what can be deduced about Hecataeus's stance. Hecataeus's interpretation of Egyptian beliefs and cult, being evidently an idealization, is indicative of his attitude toward paganism. In a fragment quoted by Plutarch, Hecataeus says that the Egyptians believe that the "first god" is identical with the universe (τὸ πᾶν) and that it is "invisible and concealed" (*De Is. et Os.* 354d). At the same time Hecataeus describes Egyptian religion as functional: the Egyptians first deified the two great celestial bodies that regulate, generate, and nourish the universe, as well as the five elements (spirit-*pneuma*, fire, dry, wet, and airlike), which are "supplied" by the two celestial bodies (Diod. I.11.5–6). Hecataeus further states that to these were later added kings and heroes of the past who made a significant contribution to the development of civilization (I.13.1ff.).

As for the Egyptian cult, Hecataeus explains the material representation of the celestial gods by their special appearance in nature (11.2, 4; 12.9) and refers without any reservation to the Egyptian traditions about the beginning of the sculpting of the gods and the building of temples (15.3–5, 26.6–7, 45.2–4, 49.5, 56.2). He justifies the deification of rulers (90.2–3; cf. 13.1), and even gives sense to the Egyptian animal cult, which was despised and ridiculed by the Greeks,[137] using expressions of approval and praise (12.9, 89.4, 90.2–4).[138] Hecataeus's

---

137. Hecataeus himself mentions that animal cult was looked upon by most people as "abnormal" (*paradoxon*, Diod. I.83.1). For extremely negative evaluations, see Isocr. *Bus.* 5.10; Strabo XVI.2.36; Plut. *De Is. et Os.* 379E ff. (despite 380F); Ael. *NA* XII.5; Cic. *Nat. Deor.* I.36; Plin. *NH* II.21; Juv. XV.1–13; Sext. Emp. *Pyrrh.* III.219; Celsus *ap.* Orig. *C. Cels.* III.19. Cf. the implied reservation in Hdt. II.65.2. For Jewish contempt and scorn, see Pseudo-Aristeas 138; Sap. Sal. 11.15, 13.14, 15.18–19; Philo, *Deca.* 76–80; *Vit. Mos.* II.161–62, 169, 270; *Contempl.* 8–9; Sibyll. III 75, 79; Jos. *Ap.* I.254, II.81. But see the explanations by Artapanus *ap.* Eus. *PE* IX.27.9, 12; Philo, *Vit. Mos.* I.23. Cf. Orig. *C. Cels.* III.18. The positive approach of Porph. *Abst.* III.16, IV.9–10 stems from his mystical tendencies (cf. p. 63 n. 33 above). The tolerant reference of Theophrastus (*ap.* Porph. *Abst.* II.26) is explained by the context, the Egyptians' abstention from animal flesh, a habit advocated by Theophrastus. On early Christian comments, see Lightfoot (1899) II.2.510ff.; Zimmermann (1912) 87–137.

138. The word "superstition" in Diod. I.83.8 is a comment by Diodorus himself. The passage describes an episode from the time of his visit to Egypt

favorable attitude toward pagan divination, in all its manifestations, was discussed above in detail.[139] Hecataeus's Egyptian ethnography is thus a monument of religious tolerance.

The same religious position appears in the few surviving fragments of his utopia on the legendary Hyperboreans.[140] The Hyperboreans seem to deify the celestial bodies;[141] Apollo, their most respected god, is worshipped in "a magnificent sacred precinct and remarkable temple adorned with many votive offerings" (Diod. II.47.2; cf. Ael. *NA* XI.1),[142] and is evidently anthropomorphic and visible, appearing among his admirers once in nineteen years, dancing and playing the cithara (Diod. II.47.6).[143] In the Egyptian ethnography Hecataeus describes favorably the Egyptian influence on the statue of the Pythian Apollo in Samos (II.98.5–9). We may therefore assume that an author who made such an effort to accommodate popular polytheistic beliefs with the philosophers' conception of the divine, and bothered to justify even cults deplored by the Greeks, would not have "admired" the destruction of temples and cult centers by the Jews.

And finally: in his original, undisputed excursus on the Jews, Hecataeus describes the Jewish way of life as being "somewhat unsocial [ἀπάνθρωπον] and hostile to strangers [μισόξενον]" (Diod. XL.3.4). The expressions *apanthrōpia* and *misoxenia* in a Greek author cannot, under any circumstances, be interpreted as positive or even indifferent.[144] Hecataeus's explicit reservation obviously cannot be reconciled with an enthusiastic justification of the destruction of temples and altars by the Jews.

One may perhaps argue that the praise at the end of *Against Apion* I.193, following the sentence about the destruction of pagan cult centers,

---

(see para. 9). This rules out the possibility that the positive attitude toward animal cult reflects not Hecataeus's view but that of Diodorus himself.

139. See esp. pp. 59–60.

140. Cf. pp. 60–61 and n. 27 above.

141. See Diod. II.47.2 (the spherical shape of Apollo's temple), 47.5 (the reputedly greater size of the moon compared with the earth as seen in the land of the Hyperboreans).

142. The exaltation of Apollo should not mislead us: he is honored more than other gods, but he is not the only divine figure. See, e.g., the references to Leto (Diod. II.47.2) and to Boreas and Chione (Ael. *NH* XI.1).

143. Cf. also *FGrH* IIIA 264 F 10.

144. On the interpretation of the sentence, cf. p. 39 above.

concludes a section that begins at I.190 about the Jews' devotion to their religion. The praise must, however, refer particularly to I.193, which is closest to it. Even if the praise referred just to the Jews' adherence to their laws, Greek authors—certainly Hecataeus—would not have included a reference to the destruction of temples and altars in the context of laudable religious behavior.

Some proponents of authenticity, aware of the inherent difficulties of the statement under discussion, have suggested that Josephus used a Jewish adaptation of Hecataeus's treatise that "slightly altered" the original sentence, or that Josephus himself modified the text.[145]

To attribute the sentence to Josephus would be impossible: he prefaces it with the words "and he [Hecataeus] adds that," and at the end of the quotations he advises readers who want to know more about the subject to consult the book itself, "which is readily available" (*Ap.* I.205). Furthermore, in his *Jewish Antiquities* Josephus omits biblical accounts of violence against pagan cults committed by the Israelites at the time of the conquest of Canaan, and in *Against Apion* he bitterly contests Manetho's allegations about profanation and destruction of Egyptian holy places at the time of the Exodus (I.269–70). He even ascribes to Moses a commandment not to plunder temples and not to insult other gods (*Ant.* IV.207, *Ap.* II.237–46), which contradicts the recurrent imperatives of Deuteronomy.[146]

An adaptation of Hecataeus by a Jewish author is in itself a very remote possibility. There is, indeed, no parallel for an adaptation of a Hellenistic treatise on the Jews by a Jewish author.[147] Before even considering, then, such a remote possibility with regard to the passages quoted by Josephus, one should really have some positive evidence that these passages ultimately originated with Hecataeus or from his period, or were at least written by a gentile. But none is

145. See p. 5 n. 11 above.

146. Cf. Philo, *Spec. Leg.* I.53; *Vit. Mos.* II.205; *Quaest. Ex.* II.5; and LXX to Exod. 22.27. See also Philo, *Hyp. ap.* Eus. *PE* VIII.6.6–7; Artapanus *ap.* Eus. *PE* IX.27.4, 9, 10, 12; and p. 169 below. For Egyptian accusations in Hellenistic literature, see, in addition to Manetho, Lysimachus in Jos. *Ap.* I.310.

147. Strabo's celebrated excursus on Judaism (XVI.2.35–37) was not taken from a Jewish adaptation of Posidonius, as claimed by one or two scholars, but directly from Posidonius's writings. For a detailed discussion, see Bar-Kochva, *Anti-Semitism and Idealization of Judaism,* chap. VI.

available,[148] while too many statements and pieces of information sound anachronistic, or contradict the information at our disposal. In the case of the Mosollamus episode, none of its main details could have been written by Hecataeus. Even to suggest that the story was considerably altered, not just "slightly," would still not help to support the claim for a Hecataean origin.[149]

In practical terms, suggesting that Josephus used a Jewish adaptation of Hecataeus is tantamount to denying the authenticity of the book: an adapter who has gone so far as to have Hecataeus enthusing about Jewish intolerance and ridiculing Greek divination to such an extent may also be suspected of falsifying other reports and statements according to his convictions, purposes, and experiences. The odds are that such an adaptation would have departed considerably from the original. In any case, the passages as they stand are basically a Jewish forgery, and the question whether Hecataeus wrote an account of the Jews in addition to that included in his Egyptian ethnography thus remains one of marginal importance.[150]

6. JEWISH EMIGRATION TO PHOENICIA

Illustrating the overpopulation of the Jews in Judea, the author mentions the deportation of "many tens of thousands" of Jews to Babylonia by the Persians,[151] and adds that after Alexander's death "no fewer emigrated to Egypt and Phoenicia because of the disturbance [*stasis*] in Syria" (*Ap.* I.194). The context obviously allows for many thousands emigrating to Phoenicia alone. The sentence explains that the Jews moved from Judea to Phoenicia because their country was suffering from the recurring wars in the region in the time of the Successors. This means that Phoenicia was not affected by the "disturbance."

---

148. See p. 55 above.

149. See p. 70 above.

150. Cf. Jacoby's comment in a rather similar context: "es ist wirklich sehr gleichgiltig, ob er [the Jewish author] Hekataios nun auch 'benutzt' hat" ([1943] 65).

151. On the possible background and date of this deportation, see pp. 143–44 below.

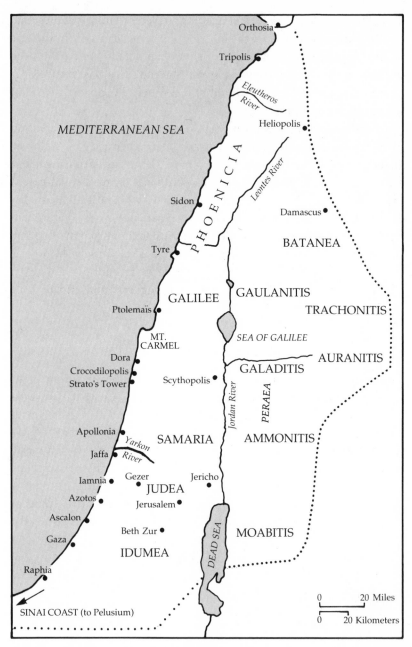

MEDITERRANEAN SEA

Orthosia

Tripolis

Eleutheros River

Heliopolis

PHOENICIA

Sidon

Leontes River

Damascus

BATANEA

Tyre

GALILEE

GAULANITIS

Ptolemaïs

TRACHONITIS

MT. CARMEL

SEA OF GALILEE

AURANITIS

Dora

GALADITIS

Crocodilopolis

Strato's Tower

Scythopolis

Jordan River

PERAEA

Apollonia

Yarkon River

SAMARIA

AMMONITIS

Jaffa

Iamnia

Gezer

Jericho

JUDEA

Azotos

Jerusalem

Ascalon

Beth Zur

MOABITIS

Gaza

DEAD SEA

IDUMEA

Raphia

SINAI COAST (to Pelusium)

0   20 Miles

0   20 Kilometers

1.   Phoenicia, the coastal plain, and the regions of the interior in the Hellenistic period.

Before commenting on the statement itself, the meaning of "Phoenicia" in this context should be elucidated. There was no substantial Jewish settlement in Phoenicia proper—that is, in the area of Tyre and Sidon—nor even on the coast north of Mount Carmel, at any period in the days of the Second Temple.[152] At the same time we have ample evidence for a great concentration of Jews in the coastal plain south of the Carmel during certain periods.[153] Greeks indeed had applied the term "Phoenicia" as a geographical name to the coast of the Holy Land since the late Persian period,[154] a usage that was also preserved under Hasmonean[155] and Roman[156] rule. It was also the official administrative

152. This is evident from Josephus's accounts of the Great Revolt in the *Bellum* and *Vita* and from his geographical excursus in *Bell.* III.35–40. The later information in rabbinic sources about several Jewish sites on the west coast of Galilee is irrelevant to the period of the Second Temple. Syncellus I.559 mentions a siege of Tyre by Alexander Jannaeus, which is not recorded by any other source. Be the historicity of this information as it may, there is no reason to believe that Jannaeus made territorial gains in the neighborhood of the great Phoenician cities. Ptolemaïs (Acre) and its *chōra*, which were much closer to Judea proper, were not occupied by the Hasmoneans.

153. See pp. 124–28 below.

154. In the first half of the Persian period, the Greeks used the term "Phoenicia" for the northern coast of Syria and the Holy Land, while the southern coast was called "Palaestina" (Hdt. III.5.91, VII.89). As a result of the attachment of a number of southern cities to Sidon and Tyre in the late Persian period, the whole coastal plain seems to have been regarded as one unit named after its rulers, the Phoenicians. See Kahrstedt (1926) 5, 37, 39–40, based mainly on Pseudo-Scylax (*GGM* I.79). This is also accepted by M. Stern (1974–84) I.290. The counterarguments of Leuze (1935) 204–7 (supported by Galling [1964] 168) fail to convince. They also ignore the statement of Strabo XVI.2.21 (see nn. 156, 158 below), which, reflecting the Ptolemaic period, may also be indicative of the principal arrangements in the late Persian age.

155. See *Ant.* XIII.350, 395–96 (both references based on Strabo); Syncellus I.548. On the later source, p. 125 below.

156. Herennius Philo *ap.* Steph. Byz. s.v. Ἰόπη (cf. Pliny *NH* V.69 on *Iope*); Alexander Polyhistor *ap.* Stephanus s.v. Γάζα (*FGrH* IIIA 273 F 117). Although the administrative borders of Phoenicia specified in Strabo XVI.2.21 reflect those of the period of Ptolemaic rule in the region (see n. 158 below), one can assume that Strabo and Artemidorus, his source, would not have inserted this piece of information unless the geographic term "Phoenicia" was popularly applied to the whole Palestinian coast in their day. The same applies to the passages in *Ant.* XIII.350, 395–96, drawn from Strabo (Hölscher [1904] 15–16, 40), and the account of Phoenicia by Dionysius Periegetes (*GGM*

designation under the Successors,[157] Ptolemies,[158] and Seleucids,[159] and possibly also in the late Persian period,[160] but under the Hasmoneans and the Romans the political-administrative border was pushed northward to the Carmel coast.[161] Whether a geographical or an administrative term, the author refers to the coastal plain to the west and northwest of the Judean Hills.

Turning back to the sentence under consideration, the explanation provided for the Jewish emigration to Phoenicia seems rather odd. It

---

II.160), written in the first half of the second century A.D., which is likewise based on Strabo (see U. Bernays [1905] 6).

157. See Diod. I.78.5, drawing on Hecataeus.

158. On the borders of Phoenicia during the Ptolemaic period, see Strabo XVI.2.21. The specification "from Orthosia to Pelusium" was taken from Artemidorus (according to 2.33), who flourished ca. 100 B.C. It can only refer to the Ptolemaic period, when the coast up to Pelusium was under one rule. The northern border of Phoenicia as described also accords with the available information on the Ptolemaic border in the north (see, on the line Tripolis-Heliopolis or the river Eleutherus, Tcherikover [1937] 110; Bagnall [1976] 11–13). The inclusion of the Sinai coast in Phoenicia is somewhat surprising, but it may have its demographic and military reasons; and in any case, Ptolemaic Phoenicia certainly was subdivided into smaller units. It should be added that Strabo's account of Coile Syria and Phoenicia is, by and large, a contamination of data on the Hasmonean kingdom (e.g., 2.28) mixed with information from the Ptolemaic period (see, e.g., the names Bucolopolis and Crocodilopolis in 2.27; the mention of Strato's Tower and the absence of Dora in the same paragraph, which accords with the data from the Zeno papyri of 259 B.C.).

159. See II Macc. 4.21–22. The administrative district called Paralia founded by the Seleucids in the wake of the Maccabean Revolt, or perhaps even earlier, to the south of the old Phoenician cities (I Macc. 10.50, 15.38; II Macc. 13.24), was still part of "Phoenicia." The latter was after all one of the two components of "Coile Syria and Phoenicia," the official name of the Seleucid satrapy that included the Holy Land. On Paralia, see Bengtson (1964) II.176; Bar-Kochva (1989) 239.

160. So Kahrstedt (1926) 37 on the Phoenician *synedrion* according to Diod. XVI.41.1. It stands to reason that the council naturally held authority over the annexed cities on the Palestinian coast, although each of the major cities constituted a political unit in itself (on which see Avi-Yonah [1966] 23–31, [1971] 233–34).

161. On the Hasmonean period: *Ant.* XIII.324–25; *Bell.* I.66; Strabo XVI.2.28. For Roman rule: Jos. *Vit.* 31, *Ap.* II.116, *Bell.* III.35; Pliny, *NH* V.69; Ptol. *Geogr.* V.14.3. On the latter, see Z. Safrai (1981) 272.

must have been much safer for Jews to stay in the Judean Hills than to move nearer the sea.[162] The struggle between the Successors, like the later one between the Ptolemies and the Seleucids for control of Syria and the Land of Israel, was mainly concentrated on the coastal plain (including the area of Tyre and Sidon). That strip of land was most important for the Successors because of its position on the road leading to Egypt and because of the Phoenician naval tradition. Almost all the military confrontations took place along the coast. The Jewish population was clustered mainly in the Judean Hills, which were isolated and relatively remote from the main arena. The statement that the Jews left for Phoenicia to escape the "disturbance" just proves that the author was not properly cognizant of the circumstances in the area after Alexander's death. This certainly would not be expected of Hecataeus.

Even without this observation, the very statement about a massive migration of Jews to Phoenicia in the time of the Successors is unacceptable. The available information indicates that Jewish settlements on the coastal plain at the time preceding the Hasmonean state were few and rather small.[163] The statement is thus anachronistic, reflecting later developments in the region.

7. "MANY FORTRESSES OF THE JEWS"

After the passages on Jewish religious devotion and fanaticism and the Jews' great natural increase, Josephus quotes a number of passages dealing with the geography of the Jewish land (*Ap.* I.194–99). One of the passages refers to the defense of the country (*Ap.* I.197):

> There are many fortresses of the Jews [τῶν Ἰουδαίων ... πολλὰ ὀχυρώματα] throughout the country, as well as villages, but only one fortified city, ... called by them Jerusalem.

162. So Willrich (1900) 94: "Weiterhin hören wir, nach Alexanders Tode seien nicht wenige Myriaden Juden nach Ägypten und nach Phönizien geflohen wegen der Kämpfe in Syrien. Aber haben diese Kämpfe nicht Phönizien viel mehr betroffen als das abseits der grossen Heerstrasse gelegene Jerusalem? Nach Phönizien zu flüchten wäre ungefähr das verkehrteste gewesen, was die Juden damals hätten tun können, wenn sie Ruhe finden wollten." Cf. Hengel (1971) 303.

163. See p. 124 and n. 7 below.

Willrich argued that neither the Persians nor the Successors had any reason for building many fortresses in Judea, since it was situated off the main road to Egypt.[164] It has rightly been added that only with the foundation of the chain of fortresses by Bacchides, the Seleucid commander, after the death of Judas Maccabaeus in 160 B.C. (I Macc. 9.50–52), were there relatively "many fortresses" in the small territory of Judea.[165] The only fortresses in the country before that were the Jerusalem *Akra*, Beth Zur on the southern border, and Gezer in the west,[166] this last being then probably still outside the borders of Judea.

But there is much more in the sentence. The fortresses are said to have belonged to the Jews, which means that at that time the Jews had sovereignty over them. Yet a foreign ruler naturally would not have allowed the Jews to maintain "many fortresses" in their territory, a sure prescription for rebellion, and certainly not amid the delicate situation in the region during the struggle of the Successors.[167] The sentence could not have been written before the Jews gained their independence, and thus possessed fortresses of their own.[168] A similar anachronistic statement with regard to the Jerusalem citadel appears in Pseudo-Aristeas (102–4).[169]

This anachronistic information cannot be excused by saying that Hecataeus was not familiar with the country.[170] The existence of

---

164. Willrich (1900) 96–97. Cf. Reinach (1930) 37 n. 4; Stein (1934) 10.

165. So Walter (1976) 156 n. 197a. Gauger (1982) 42 argues that the word "many," referring to both fortresses and villages, does not mean that there were many fortresses. This is a mistaken reading of a simple, clear-cut sentence (πολλὰ ὀχυρώματα).

166. On Beth Zur, see Bar-Kochva (1989) 287; I Macc. 9.52. The last verse refers to the reinforcement of existing fortresses (see F. M. Abel [1949] 172–73). On the Jerusalem citadel, see Bar-Kochva (1989) 445–65 and bibliography, 445 n. 1. On Gezer (Gazara): I Macc. 4.15, 7.45, 9.52, 13.43–48.

167. Klein (1939) 38 tries to explain the sentence as meaning that the fortresses in Judea were manned only by Jews, as with the employment of Jews in Ptolemaic fortresses in Egypt. This is, however, not what is written, and Hecataeus would have been aware of the difference. And in general, garrisoning fortresses in an occupied country with natives is incomprehensible for the period of the Successors. In any case, there were not "many fortresses" in Judea in the time of Hecataeus.

168. This is also realized, though not explicitly said, by Stein (1934) 8.

169. See below p. 273ff.

170. So argued by Gauger (1982) 42.

many fortresses held by the local population is a politico-military fact of vital importance, and Hecataeus, who served in the court during the period of Ptolemaic rule in the region, could not have been misinformed on that basic subject. The sentence itself seems to have been taken as it stands from the treatise *On the Jews*, and not paraphrased by Josephus: it opens a long quotation cited in direct speech.

8. THE GEOGRAPHY OF JUDEA AND JERUSALEM

The account of the Jewish land includes many details about Judea (*Ap.* I.194–95), the city of Jerusalem (196–97), and especially the Temple (198–99). Most of the geographical information is either entirely inaccurate or does not reflect the early Hellenistic period. This is not exceptional: a number of Hellenistic and Roman authors, notably Strabo, the celebrated Hellenistic geographer, report inaccurate information on the Jewish land. Geographical accounts of the neighboring countries were not much better.

However, the author included in his account geographical assertions of the sort that obviously would have had important military implications for the planning and execution of the Ptolemaic reconquest of the country and its day-to-day administration. One of these assertions, referring to the fortresses in the country, was discussed in the previous section. The remaining assertions include the following topics: the size of the country, its fertility and water supply, the circumference of Jerusalem's walls, the population of the city, the location of its Temple, and the size of its wall. All these are instructive for the question of authenticity: the author claims to have written the book sometime after the battle of Gaza (I.187). At that time, after two intervals of Ptolemaic rule in Judea (320–315, 312–311), the Ptolemaic authorities were certainly well informed on these matters, and Hecataeus would not have had any difficulty in acquiring this information. Whatever the purpose of such a treatise, he must have been aware that as the only extant monograph on Judea by a prominent courtier and ethnographer, it would be accepted as authoritative and would mislead his Ptolemaic patrons in the future. For this reason, the explanation that in the absence of accurate information Hecataeus tried to idealize the country and its capital, or that he relied on idealized accounts of Egyptian Jews,[171] cannot be accepted.

According to the account, the Jews possessed "almost three hundred myriad [i.e., three million] *arourae*. . . . Such is the extent of Judea" (I.195). This means approximately 8,300 square kilometers. The borders of Yehud (Judea) at the end of the Persian and beginning of the Hellenistic period extended from Beth Zur in the south to Beth El in the north, and from Jericho in the east to the Ayalon Valley in the west,[172] all in all only about 1,600 square kilometers, which is just a fifth of the above estimate. Even if one accepts the assumption (which is unwarranted) that in the time of the Successors Judea also included the southern toparchies of Samaria (Aphairema, Lydda, and Ramathaim),[173] the territory of Judea would have amounted to no more than one-quarter of that figure. It is noteworthy that this estimate more or less recalls the extent of the Jewish territory at a certain point in the last years of John Hyrcanus (the years 107–104 B.C.), after the attachment to the Jewish state of Samaria, Idumea, and part of the coastal plain, and before the occupation of Galilee.[174] Nevertheless, this correspondence must not be utilized for a precise dating of the book. In view of the numerous mistakes in other statements referring to Judea and Jerusalem, it may well be coincidental.

The three million *arourae* are described as the "best and most fertile land for all products" (I.195). However, the soil of Judea proper in the early Hellenistic period was for the most part rocky, and of its 1,600 square kilometers, 600 were desert. Only the narrow strip of the Jericho Valley accords with this description. An enthusiastic report also appears in the detailed account of the country in Pseudo-Aristeas (107, 112), and is based on the idealization of the Holy Land in the Pentateuch and the ideal city-state in Greek utopias.[175]

---

171. In contrast to Gauger (1982) 42. Cf. Stein (1934) 9–10. Hans Lewy, who did not realize that the geographical account is mistaken, went so far as to suggest that Hezekiah the High Priest was Hecataeus's source for the geography of Jerusalem ([1932] 122–23, 132). Notably, Hecataeus's Jewish excursus does not contain a geographical section. (See below, pp. 208ff.)

172. See Alt (1953–59) II.94–95; Avi-Yonah (1966) 13ff.; E. Stern (1982) 245–48. See also Map 4, p. 124 below.

173. Kallai (1960) 88ff., (1983) 78–79; and see p. 117 below.

174. On these occupations, see pp. 124–28 below, and Map 5, p. 126 below.

175. See p. 272 and nn. 4–6 below.

The image of Judea proper in Hellenistic and Roman literature was not that of a fertile land. On the contrary, it was customary to stress the scarcity of water, and the rocky soil. Timochares, who describes Judea in the period preceding the great Hasmonean expansion,[176] even writes that the region of Jerusalem is completely dry and barren for a radius of 40 or 60 stadia (7.5 or 11.2 km) from the city (Eusebius, *PE* IX.35). This account is twice paraphrased by Strabo (XVI.2.36, 40),[177] who uses it on one occasion to illustrate his statement that Moses easily took possession of Jerusalem and its surrounding region, since "it was not a place that would be looked on with envy, nor yet one for which anyone would make a serious fight" (XVI.2.36).

Only the Jericho Valley, one of the districts of Judea proper, was singled out in the Hellenistic and Roman periods for its fertility. We have the account of Diodorus, drawing on Hieronymus of Cardia, the contemporary of the Successors (II.48.9, XIX.98); Strabo, who based his version on Posidonius of Apamea (XVI.2.41); Pompeius Trogus in the generation of Augustus (epitomized in Justin XXXVI.3.1), and historians of the Roman period—Josephus (*Bell.* IV.456–75), Pliny (*NH* V.70), and Tacitus (*Hist.* V.6). All mention only palm trees and balsam, but no other plants. It is interesting that Josephus's detailed geographic excursus on the enlarged Jewish territory on the eve of the Great Revolt (*Bell.* III.35–58) elaborates on the agricultural qualities of Galilee (41–43), Samaria (48–50), and even the *Peraea* (44–47). Though he grossly exaggerates the fertility and population density of these regions in order to demonstrate the importance of Vespasian's achievements, he avoids any reference to agriculture in his detailed account of Judea proper (51–58). By and large, Hellenistic and Roman accounts do not even speak favorably of the agricultural features of the enlarged Judea. Apart from the Jericho Valley, Pompeius Trogus praises only the area of Tarichea on the shores of the Sea of Galilee (Justin XVI.2.45). Tacitus, who mentions in a general statement the

---

176. On the connection of this information to the siege of Jerusalem by Antiochus VII Sidetes in the early years of John Hyrcanus, see M. Stern (1974–84) I.134–35, and in detail, Bar-Kochva, *Anti-Semitism and Idealization of Judaism*, chap. VIII.

177. The number in Timochares, as recorded by Eusebius (*PE* IX.35.1), is forty. The paraphrase of Strabo reads "sixty." As the first figure recurs three times in Timochares' small fragment, Strabo's version may better reflect the original.

fertility of the land, refers specifically only to the vegetation of the Jericho region (*Hist.* V.6.1). He may have used the book of Antonius Julius, the last governor of Judea before the Great Revolt,[178] or drawn (directly or indirectly) on Josephus.[179]

Having alluded to the extent and agriculture of Judea, the author turns to a description of Jerusalem. According to the passage (*Ap.* I.197), the circumference of the city was more than 50 stadia (9.3 km). However, in the days of Hecataeus, when the city was limited to the south-eastern hill (the "City of David"), the Ophel, and the Temple Mount, its circumference stood at no more than 12 stadia (2.2 km). At the peak of the Hasmonean state, when it included also the Upper City, the circumference stood at about 27 stadia (5 km), and even on the eve of the Great Revolt, when the city reached its greatest extent, being protected by the "Third Wall," its circumference did not exceed 33 stadia (about 6 km).[180] The statement attributed to Hecataeus is thus highly exaggerated and does not accord with any period in the history of the city. The figure is even higher than that quoted by Pseudo-Aristeas. The latter lauds the holy city, but apologizes for its small size—only 40 stadia (105)—and even tries to explain why it was not larger (107, 108-9). It stands to reason that what actually bothered Pseudo-Aristeas was the comparison of Jerusalem to Alexandria, his native city. The circumference of Alexandria was about 76 stadia.[181] He had to admit that Jerusalem was smaller, for which he offered his original explanation. But despite the apology, an accurate estimate would have considerably detracted from the importance of the city in the eyes of his readers: hence a figure that is more than half the circumference of Alexandria. Pseudo-Aristeas, who was well versed in Hellenistic literature, could also have been acquainted with the figure 40 quoted by Timochares (Eus. *PE* IX.35). Direct influence by Pseudo-Aristeas,

---

178. See J. Bernays (1861) 56 (= *Gesammelte Abhandlungen* II [1885] 256ff.); Norden (1913) 664ff.

179. On the question whether Tacitus used Josephus in one way or another, see M. Stern (1974–84) II.3–4, and bibliography in n. 3.

180. On the circumference of the Jerusalem wall at the time of Nehemiah and its extension under the Hasmonean rulers, see Tsafrir (1983) esp. 69. For the Hasmonean period, see Avigad (1984) 64ff.; and for the time of the Great Revolt against the Romans, see Avi-Yonah (1957) 319; Broshi (1982) 22.

181. Strabo XVII.1.8; Pliny, *NH* V.62–63. See the discussion of Fraser (1972) I.11ff.

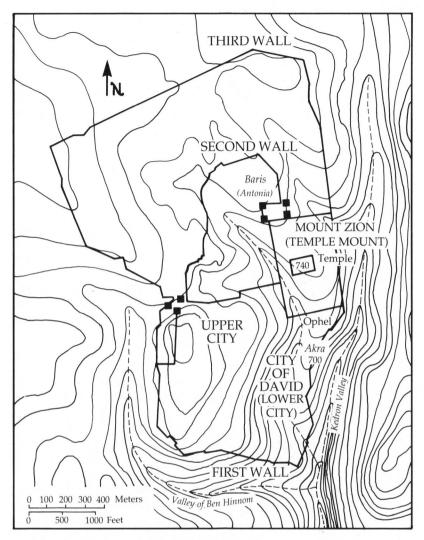

2. Jerusalem in the period of the Second Temple.

or similar considerations, may have inspired the figure in the treatise *On the Jews*.[182]

182. Additional estimates of the size of the Jerusalem wall are known from other sources. The *Schoinometrēsis Syriae*, written around the year 100 (see M. Stern [1974–84] I.137), mentions 27 stadia (Eus. *PE* IX.36.1), which

The number of the city's inhabitants—120,000 persons (*Ap.* I.197)—
is even more inflated. At the beginning of the Hellenistic period, the
inhabited area of the city extended over no more than 30 acres.[183]
The maximum estimate of population density for urban areas in the
ancient Near East and the Hellenistic Orient stands at 250 persons per
acre.[184] Jerusalem in Hecataeus's days could thus not have numbered
more than 7,500 inhabitants.[185] The figure of 120,000 does not accord
with that of Hasmonean Jerusalem (160 acres; about 40,000 persons
at the most), nor with that of the period of the Great Revolt against
the Romans (450 acres; about 100,000).[186] This great exaggeration is

---

correctly records the circumference of the city at the peak time of the Hasmonean state. Josephus is accurate in relating 33 stadia to the wall of Herod
Agrippa I (*Bell.* I.159). Timochares' 40 stadia (Eus. *PE* IX.35.1; see n. 177
above) is a quite exaggerated figure for his time, the early Hasmonean period,
his intention being to exalt the achievement of Antiochus VII Sidetes in sub-
duing the city. (Cf. his statements that the city was enclosed on all sides by
steep ravines, and that the city's source of water was inside its walls while the
region outside was extremely arid.)

183. According to Avi-Yonah (1954) 239–48; Broshi (1975) 9–10, (1977) 68;
Avigad (1984) 61–63.

184. See the summary of the various methods of calculating the size of
urban populations in antiquity by Broshi (1975) 5–9, (1977) 66–67; Broshi
and Gophna (1984) 184ff., (1984a) 4–5.

185. And see Broshi's estimate ([1975] 13, [1977] 71) for the late Persian
period: 4,800 inhabitants. Klein (1939) 13 draws attention to Nehemiah
chap. 12, from which it appears that after the reinforcement of the city
population by Nehemiah, the number of its adult male inhabitants stood at
3,044. Klein estimates the overall population at around 15,000, on the basis of
5 persons per family. However, it is still doubtful whether the list does indeed
belong to the time of the Second Temple; even if it does, it is not inevitable that
the priests, numbering 1,192 (verse 12), and the 284 Levites (v. 18) served in
Jerusalem in rotation (see v. 20) and therefore did not live in the city with their
families. It is also possible that at least part of the reinforcements from the
tribes of Judah and Benjamin did not stay permanently in the city, because
their fields were in the "cities of Judea" (so perhaps according to verse 3).

186. See the summary of the various data on the size of the city in Broshi
(1977) 68–69. His population estimates, based on 200 persons per acre (p. 71),
are somewhat low. The numbers offered by Josephus for the casualties
and captives in Jerusalem at the time of the Great Revolt (*Bell.* VI.420; cf.
V.567)—all in all 1.2 million—are grossly exaggerated and irrelevant for the
discussion. Josephus himself states that most of them were not permanent
residents of the city, but pilgrims who were trapped by the siege, and that

well in line with the tendency to magnify the importance of the city, reflected in the estimate of its circumference. It also accords with the author's earlier note on the overpopulation of the Jews in their land (I.194).

The account of the Temple, which has been preserved at relatively great length, includes information about its location, as well as on its cult and vessels. The topographical details have military significance. The Temple is said to have been located "nearly in the center of the city," being surrounded by "a stone wall" (I.198). The author goes on to give impressive measurements for the wall: "five plethra long, and a hundred cubits wide" (ca. 154 × 51 m). In the absence of any information on the very existence of a wall around the Temple before the days of Judas Maccabaeus (I Macc. 4.59–60), these figures cannot be verified.[187] One thing is sure: the Temple was not located "nearly in the center of the city," but to the north of the residential areas. It was built on a hill separate from the "City of David," where most of the population was concentrated. If the Temple was indeed protected at that period by such a wall, as claimed by the author, it was a fortress of formidable magnitude. Its location would not have been described so erroneously by Hecataeus.[188]

9. THE ANNEXATION OF SAMARIA TO JUDEA BY ALEXANDER

Separately from the passages discussed so far, which all appear in Book I of *Against Apion*, Josephus attributes to Hecataeus in Book II the following sentence (*Ap.* II.43):

---

the abnormal population density led to epidemics. See also Tac. *Hist.* V.13.3 (600,000). On the more reliable data in *Bell.* V.248, VI.420, see Broshi (1982) 23.

187. Ezra 6.3 obviously cannot be of much help (see also Zipser [1871] 79). Jeremias (1934) 110 argues that the figures are authentic, quoting as evidence Ezek. 40.47 and 41.13–14. However, the perimeter of the holy precinct according to the vision of Ezekiel stood at 500 × 500 cubits (about 250 × 250 m; see 45.2 and 40.5).

188. On the author's source of inspiration for locating the Temple, see p. 146 n. 23 below.

> Because of the fairness and loyalty shown to him [Alexander the Great] by the Jews, he annexed the land of Samaria [*Samareitis*][189] to them free of tribute [*aphorologētos*].

Before discussing the historical reliability of the statement, its context and source should be clarified. The sentence is quoted in the context of Josephus's campaign for the rights of the Jews in Alexandria. He states that Alexander settled the Jews in the city and granted them civil rights (II.12). The reference to the assignment of Samaria to the Jews appears as the only evidence to that effect, indicating Alexander's favorable treatment of the Jews.[190] It is thus evident that the quotation was taken from a work in which there was no intimation of Alexander's involvement in settling the Jews in Alexandria.

As for the source of the sentence, the suggestion has been made that it was taken from another lost work, which had been ascribed to Hecataeus.[191] However, no valid reason has been put forward to

189. The region is named by the sources *Samareia* and *Samareitis*. The first form appears in Polybius (V.71.11, XVI.39), the Septuagint references to Mt. Shomron throughout the entire biblical period, the narrative of Judith (4.4), and the first two books of the Maccabees (I.3.10, II.15.1), and *Samareitis* is known from the documents of I Maccabees (10.30; 11.28, 34) and Pseudo-Aristeas (para. 107). Josephus uses both forms (see the concordance, Schalit [1968] 105). *Samareitis* was the official name under the Ptolemies (see Avi-Yonah [1971] 239–40, 449–50), and therefore that form was sometimes preferred by authors and translators living in Egypt, especially with regard to documents. Josephus uses *Samareitis* even in his geographical excursus on the districts of Judea on the eve of the Great Revolt against the Romans (*Bell.* II.37, 48), which may indicate that both forms were current in the Roman period (cf. the preservation of the ending -*itis* for the districts of Trans-Jordan in the Roman period, Avi-Yonah [1971] 449–50).

190. Doran (1985) 913–14 is puzzled by the connection between Josephus's statement and the quotation, and suggests that the reference in the sentence is to a district named Samaria in Egypt. However, Samaria of Egypt was just a single settlement, not a district (*CPJ* I.22, 28, 128), and the word προσέθηκεν does not make sense in an Egyptian context. Josephus occasionally supports his statements by quotations that do not directly prove the point; cf., e.g., *Ant.* XII.131–34 as compared with the quotations in paras. 135–36; *Ant.* XVI.144 (see paras. 145–48).

191. Thus Jacoby (1943) 74; Wacholder (1974) 265–66; Goodman in Schürer et al. (1973–86) III.672 n. 268; Gauger (1982) 38–39. Cf. Holladay (1983) 284–87.

substantiate this suggestion,[192] and one would have expected that if such a work did indeed exist, Josephus would have indicated its name or contents, to distinguish it from the treatise of Hecataeus from which he quoted earlier in great detail. This was especially required as the title of the latter treatise is implied by Josephus, if not explicitly named (I.183).[193] The content of the sentence under discussion does not contain anything that could not have been included in *On the Jews*.[194] Quite clearly, the book did not include any information directly relevant to the relationship between Alexander and the Jews of Alexandria.[195]

192. Only Wacholder and Gauger (*locc. citt.*, n. 191) have tried to prove their claims. The first mistakenly assumes that the quotation from Hecataeus (para. 43) also included the subsequent passage (paras. 44–47), which reports, *inter alia*, the favorable attitude of Ptolemy II toward the Jews. The latter passage also refers to the freeing of Jewish slaves by Ptolemy II, which indicates that they were enslaved by his predecessor. This contradicts the enthusiastic report in the Hezekiah story of the relationship between Ptolemy I and the Jews. Wacholder therefore concludes that the sentence on the attachment of Samaria to Judea was not taken from the same work as the Hezekiah story. However, Josephus attributes to Hecataeus only the sentence about the attachment of Samaria. Paragraphs 44–47 are based on Pseudo-Aristeas (see esp. the mention of Demetrius of Phaleron, Andreas, and Aristeas in para. 46; and cf. *Ant.* XII.12–118). Cf. *Ant.* XII.9, where Josephus quotes information from the book attributed to Hecataeus, following a sentence based on Pseudo-Aristeas (paras. 7, 8; and see p. 226 below). The same mistake lies behind Wacholder's other arguments (nos. a and b, p. 265). Cf. Walter (1976) 148 n. 25, 157 n. 43a. See further below, and p. 220 n. 99.

193. See pp. 188–89 below.

194. Gauger ([1982] 38–39) argues that had the sentence been taken from the same work as the quotations in *Ap.* I.183–204, it would have been incorporated there, and not separately, as it could well have served his purposes in quoting those passages. However, Josephus had to choose where to put it. The sentence was the only evidence (as indirect and flimsy as it may be) to substantiate his statement that Alexander settled the Jews in Alexandria, a key point in his struggle for the rights of the Jews in Alexandria. On the other hand, the quotations in I.183–204 were quite sufficient to support his main claim in that context, that the Jews were already a mature nation by the time of Alexander and the Successors (I.22, 175, 185).

195. Such information would have been quoted in Book II of *Against Apion*, and could well have supported Josephus's argument in Book I, certainly more than the references to two waves of Jewish immigration to Egypt (I.188–89, 194).

Now to the question of authenticity. Some scholars have gone so far as to regard this quotation as clinching evidence for the inauthenticity of the book.[196] It has generally been argued that the information does not make sense historically and politically. At the same time various attempts have been made to explain the sentence in one way or another according to the circumstances of the period, although even the advocates of authenticity admit that it cannot be accepted as it stands.

The alleged annexation of Samaria to Judea is not confirmed by any of the relatively abundant sources on Alexander's period. Even the anti-Samaritan stories in Josephus, which elaborate on the triangular relations Alexander-Jews-Samaritans (*Ant.* XI.302–46), do not mention an annexation of Samaria to Judea. Nor does the sentence agree with available knowledge on the administrative divisions of the region in the Ptolemaic and Seleucid eras. Judea and Samaria/Samareitis were separate eparchies, each having its own governor. This is clearly indicated for the Ptolemaic period (Polyb. V.71.11, XVI.39; Jos. *Ant.* XII.133, 154) and is explicitly stated for the Seleucid reign (*Ant.* XIII.264, II Macc. 14.12).[197] The first change known in the territorial arrangements occurred at the time of Jonathan (152/1 B.C.): the Seleucid rulers approved the annexation to Judea of Aphairema, Lydda, and Ramathaim, three toparchies in southern Samaria, settled by many Jews (I Macc. 10.38; cf. 11.34). A more drastic political change took place late in the reign of John Hyrcanus, when all of Samaria was occupied by the Jews in two military campaigns and integrated in one way or another into the expanding Jewish state.[198] The first campaign (112/111 B.C.) was directed at the south of the region centering around Shechem and Mount Gerizim (*Ant.* XIII. 255–56).[199] The second (108/7 B.C.) was launched against the north and against the city of Samaria (*Ant.* XIII.275–83).[200]

---

196. See esp. Stein (1934) 3–8; Momigliano (1975) 94. Cf. Willrich (1900) 97; Jacoby (1943) 62; Hengel (1971) 302; Walter (1976) 147–48. Even Lewy (1932) 120 n. 4, 131 doubts whether the passage is Hecataean.

197. See further Bar-Kochva (1989) 202–3, 353.

198. For the status of *Samareitis* under the Hasmoneans, see Schalit (1969) 201–2. Cf. *Ant.* XIV.48 (if Josephus uses there Hasmonean terminology). For the Roman period, see *Bell.* III.48–51; Pliny, *NH* V.70.

199. For the dating of the destruction of the Samaritan temple on Mt. Gerizim, see p. 131 n. 29 below.

200. On the date see p. 132 n. 30 below.

A number of scholars have called attention to the reference in Curtius Rufus (IV.8.9–11) to the Samaritan revolt against Alexander and the severe punishment that ensued (corroborated by the findings from the Wadi Dâliyeh caves), and have argued that the Samaritans were also punished by having their territory given to the Jews.[201] However, this does not make much sense from the military and administrative point of view: an effective measure to counter further unrest would be to tighten direct control over the rebellious region, certainly not loosening it by appending the region to a neighboring semiautonomous nation or district. Such a step would have slowed down and complicated any direct intervention by the central authorities. One would envisage measures such as increasing the military forces stationed in the region, splitting it into small administrative units under military governors, appointing a high-ranking military officer as governor-in-chief, and the like. These principles and practices of imperial rule were demonstrated by Alexander himself, as well as by later Hellenistic kings and governors, and are well known in later times from the provincial policy of Roman emperors.

Other scholars, describing the sentence as "exaggerated," have claimed that the original information referred to an annexation of the three toparchies in southern Samaria. The phrasing of one paragraph in the royal document of Demetrius I, declaring their annexation in the days of Jonathan (I Macc. 10.38), may indicate that the Seleucid king simply restored former arrangements. It has therefore been suggested that these toparchies were annexed by Alexander to Judea mainly because they were populated by Jews, and were later severed from it either by the Seleucids as a punitive measure for the Maccabean Revolt, or perhaps even earlier, by the Ptolemies. Hence their subsequent annexation to Judea in the time of Jonathan.[202] However, the phrasing of another paragraph in the same document (I Macc. 10.30) suggests that the attachment of the three toparchies to Judea was an established fact already

---

201. Kahrstedt (1926) 9, 43; Lewy (1932) 120–21; Grintz (1969) 13; Gager (1969) 136; M. Stern (1974–84) I.44; Gauger (1982) 39.

202. Thackeray (1926) 309 n. d.; Beyer (1933) 233ff.; Zeitlin (1950) 172; Alt (1953–59) II.348, 352; Gager (1969) 136; M. Stern (1974–84) I.44; cf. Kahrstedt (1926) 64–66; Kallai (1960) 99–105; Holladay (1983) 334 n. 55. And see the variation in Schlatter (1925) 311; M. Stern (1965) 110; Sterling (1992) 86 n. 120.

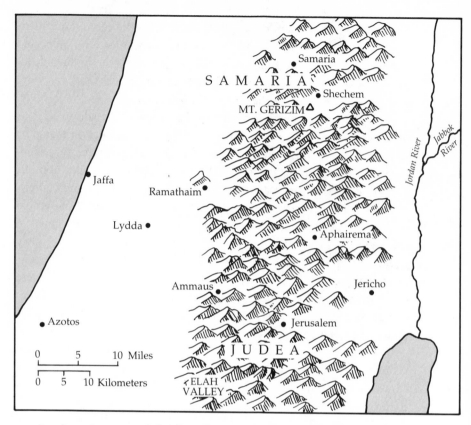

3.   Southern Samaria and the three districts in the time of Jonathan.

by the time of that document. Accordingly it has been assumed that the document recognizes a situation that was earlier created by actual Jewish domination of the three toparchies.[203] But it is even more likely that the document refers to privileges bestowed by Alexander Balas that preceded the proclamation of the concessions by Demetrius I, his rival for the throne.[204] In the absence of real evidence to the contrary, it seems

203. M. Stern (1965) 110; Avi-Yonah (1966) 56; Goldstein (1976) 410; Gauger (1982) 39 n. 79. As a parallel example of a retroactive confirmation Gauger quotes II Macc. 11.25 (which is not exactly the same).

204. The letter of Alexander Balas to Jonathan as quoted in I Maccabees (10.18–20) is extremely brief and only announces the appointment of Jonathan as High Priest. Since Jonathan was by then in control of the Temple in any case (10.7–14), this recognition alone could not have been tempting enough

rather that the three southern toparchies were annexed to Judea for the first time only in the days of Jonathan. The new territorial division came in the wake of demographic change: the constant infiltration of Jewish settlers into the border areas during the pre-Hasmonean period gradually created a Jewish majority in the three toparchies.[205]

Be that as it may, what matters is that an author like Hecataeus, who was well acquainted with court and state affairs, would not have confused the administrative-political status of a relatively large region like Samaria (which also included Galilee)[206] with that of three small toparchies on its southern fringe. He certainly would have been careful not to inflate the territory, thereby providing a precedent that might commit the Ptolemaic administration in the future, especially with the annexation attributed to Alexander.

What is even more instructive is the second part of the sentence under discussion, stating that Samaria was given to the Jews *aphorologētos*, which means "exempt from tribute [*phoros*]" and possibly other payments. In the Persian and Hellenistic periods, the annual collective *phoros* symbolized the submission of ethnic groups and nations to

---

to secure Jonathan's support for Alexander Balas in the face of Demetrius's previous generous concessions (10.3–6), not to mention the succeeding ones (10.25–45). It seems therefore quite clear that the document of Alexander Balas is sharply abbreviated, and it may well have originally included the attachment of the three toparchies. Significantly enough, the paragraph in I Macc. 10.30, which is one of the first paragraphs of Demetrius's letter, declares that the three toparchies, together with Judea as a whole, are to be exempt from taxes, but does not proclaim their attachment. This is referred to as an established fact. A confirmation of the new situation appears only at the end of the document (10.38). Cf. 11.34, where Demetrius II refers to the concession offered by his father.

205. See, e.g., Alt (1953–59) II.99ff., 420; Avi-Yonah (1966) 55–56; M. Stern (1965) 110; Schalit (1969) 197; Goldstein (1976) 410. In view of the use of formulas and the special historical circumstances, there is no justification for the argument that the documents in I Macc. 10.25–45 and 11.30–37 were falsified (so, e.g., Willrich [1924] 39; M. Smith [1971] 199). For arguments in favor of their authenticity, see M. Stern (1965) 85–86, 95–110, and further references on p. 86 n. 2; Goldstein (1976) 405ff. At the same time, some allowance must be made for minor mistakes in the translation of the document from the original Greek to the Hebrew of I Maccabees and back again.

206. See I Macc. 10.30; Hölscher (1903) 54, 82; F. M. Abel (1933–38) II.134; Avi-Yonah (1966) 25. Jos. *Ant.* XIII.50 is an inaccurate free paraphrase (see F. M. Abel [1949] 187; Goldstein [1976] 407).

the ruling state or empire. To free them from the *phoros* meant actually granting independence. Would Hecataeus have indicated that Alexander recognized the Jewish right to independent rule of Samaria, with all its implications for Ptolemy I? Even if Josephus was not accurate in transmitting the text, and the original in fact only referred to exemption from taxes and duties, such a total and permanent exemption of a nation or a province, or even of a polis, was quite rare and was granted only under very special circumstances or when imperial rule was only nominal.[207] In the case of the Jews it was granted only by Seleucid kings who already had lost control over the Jews and badly needed their help against internal rivals.[208] More common was a temporary exemption after a devastating war,[209] or to help a military settlement establish itself.[210] With regard to the days of Alexander, Josephus states in the story of the reception of Alexander by the High Priest that the Jews were freed from taxes in the sabbatical year (*Ant.* XI.338; cf. XIV.202, 206). The enthusiastic tone of this dubious legend merely indicates that an exemption in the fallow year was the most the Jews in Judea could expect from and ascribe to Alexander and other Hellenistic rulers who were in real control of the country. And if Judea proper was not totally exempted from these taxes, such exemption is even less likely for an annexed territory, much larger and more fruitful than Judea itself. Hecataeus would not have confused remission from taxes in the fallow year (which in itself is still doubtful) with an unprecedented permanent exemption, thus committing his notoriously greedy patrons to such a major economic concession. The sentence is thus a later Jewish fabrication.

The two components of the sentence have indeed seemed unacceptable even to some supporters of the authenticity of *On the Jews*. They have therefore suggested that Josephus or a Jewish adapter greatly

---

207. On the polis and royal taxes see Heuss (1937) 108–24, 186–87; Bickerman (1938) 118ff.; Rostovtzeff (1940) I.528; Jones (1940) 101–2. See, e.g., *OGIS* I.223, 228; Polyb. IV.84, XV.24.

208. See I Macc. 10.29–30, 11.34–35, 13.39, 15.8. On the question of the *phoros* in the time of Jonathan, see p. 134 n. 42 below.

209. Jos. *Ant.* XII.143. Cf., e.g., *P. Tebt.* I no. 5, line 93; *SIG*³ I no. 344, line 70; Holleaux (1938–57) II.109.

210. *Ant.* XII.151; cf. *OGIS* I 229, lines 100, 104. And see Schalit (1960) 308ff.; Bar-Kochva (1976) 57–58; G. Cohen (1978) 60–62; Ihnken (1978) 118–22; Bar-Kochva (1989) 85 n. 49.

distorted an original text by Hecataeus.[211] It is true that the structure of the passage may suggest that the sentence was shortened and rephrased by Josephus himself. However, imputing to Josephus such gross errors, both in the definition of the annexed territory and in the exemption, makes efforts to verify the general authenticity of the sentence extremely labored. And after all, it is just one of a fair number of anachronistic and unreliable statements, most of which could not have been invented by Josephus.[212] Similarly, the theory that the text underwent a slight adaptation by an unknown Jew cannot resolve all the difficulties.[213] To assume that it was a consistent adaptation is to deny the value of the passages as a reliable source for Jewish history in the early Hellenistic period.[214]

In conclusion, at the risk of repeating myself: there are too many statements and pieces of information which sound anachronistic, or contradict the information at our disposal, or cannot be attributed to Hecataeus; there is hardly one piece of real, positive evidence that the passages originated with Hecataeus or from his period, or were at least written by a gentile.

211. See p. 5 n. 11 above. Particularly referring to the sentence under discussion: M. Stern (1974–84) I.44; Goodman in Schürer et al. (1973–86) III.673 n. 272.

212. See esp. pp. 70–71 and 100–1 above. There is no reason to think that Josephus misunderstood or misinterpreted any of the other paragraphs.

213. Loc. cit.

214. P. 101 above.

IV   Date of Composition

The scholars who regard *On the Jews* as a forgery have put forward various dates for its composition, ranging from the end of the fourth century B.C. to the first century A.D.[1] The following discussion suggests dating the book between the years 107, or rather 103/2, and 93, that is, during the last years of John Hyrcanus and/or the first decade of Alexander Jannaeus's reign.

1.   THE ANACHRONISTIC REFERENCES

A *terminus post quem* for the dating of the book can be provided by five anachronistic references: the religious persecutions and Jewish martyrdom, the destruction of the pagan cult, the Jewish expansion to Phoenicia, the existence of many Jewish fortresses, and the annexation of Samaria to Judea (Chap. III.4–7, 9, above). The first reference proves that the book could not have been composed before the religious persecutions of Antiochus IV Epiphanes (168 B.C.). The other four point to the time of the Hasmonean state (142/1–63 B.C.). In order to be more precise in determining a *post quem*

---

1. End of the fourth century: Wacholder (1971) 236–37, (1974) 269–73. End of the third century: Schürer (1901–9) III.607. Ca. the year 160: Hengel (1971) 301ff., (1989) 50. "Before year 100 B.C.": Stein (1934) 8–9; Jacoby (1943) 67; Schaller (1963) 26–27; Walter (1976) 148, (1989) 402; Feldman (1993) 208–9. Close to the year 100: Willrich (1895) 25; W. Schmid and Stählin (1920) II.619. Beginning of the first century A.D.: Willrich (1900) 126–27. Cf. the survey by Holladay (1983) 287, 296 n. 59.

date, a short survey of these major developments in the Hasmonean state is necessary.

⁓

The statement that there are "many fortresses of the Jews" in the country (I.197) may reflect the situation found from the later days of Simeon, the last of the Hasmonean brothers.[2] In the time of Judas Maccabaeus, after the purification of the Temple (164–160), Beth Zur was the only fortress controlled by the rebels, and even this only intermittently.[3] His brother Jonathan (160–143) is said to have fortified Beth Basi, near Bethlehem, in 159 (I Macc. 9.62ff.). Seven of the fortresses established in the Judean Hills by Bacchides in 160/59 (I Macc. 9.50–52) were deserted by their garrisons in 152/1 (I Macc. 10.12, 11.41). They may well have been regarrisoned by Jonathan's standing army.[4]

A comprehensive fortification project was launched by Simeon (143–135). He is reported to have fortified the Temple Mount (I Macc. 13.53), Beth Zur (14.33), Adida on the fringe of the Shephela (11.38), Gezer (13.48, 14.34), Jaffa, on the sea (13.11, 14.34), and Dok, near Jericho (14.16). He also positioned Jewish soldiers in the former Seleucid *Akra* in Jerusalem (14.36–37) shortly before totally demolishing it.[5] The covenant between Simeon and the people (Sept. 140) praises him for fortifying the "cities of Judea" (14.33; cf. 13.33, 38; 15.7). Apparently this also refers to other fortresses, perhaps to those deserted by Bacchides' garrisons. The later territorial expansion in the time of Simeon's successors added to Jewish control more Hellenistic fortresses.[6] Their number considerably grew under his successors.

⁓

2. This is also implied by Willrich (1900) 96–97.

3. I Macc. 4.59–60; and see Bar-Kochva (1989) 287.

4. This is possible in view of Jonathan's standing army and the need to find new tasks for it. On these questions, see Bar-Kochva (1977) 169ff.

5. On the sequence of events in Simeon's handling of the *Akra*, see Bar-Kochva (1989) 453–54.

6. The most recent discussion of the Hasmonean fortress is Shatzman (1990) 36–97. With the exception of Galilee it contains a comprehensive survey of the available material, especially the archaeological, and modern views as well. I disagree, however, with many of Shatzman's statements and conclusions (e.g., pp. 37, 42, 45, 59, 63, 79, 84–86).

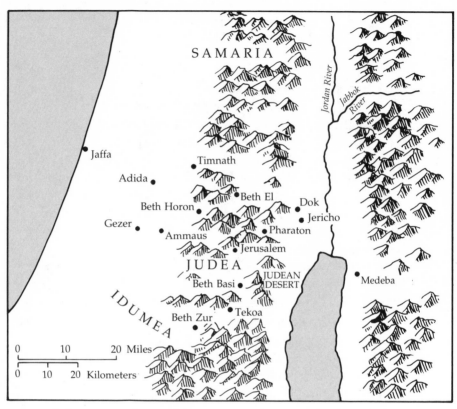

4.   Jewish fortresses in the time of Simeon.

The paragraph about the great settlement drive of the Jews in Phoenicia (I.194) brings us to the days of John Hyrcanus, Simeon's son (135–104).   In the period preceding the Hasmonean conquests there were just a few small Jewish enclaves on the coastal plain.[7]   Massive Jewish settlement of the region could have started only after its occupation by the Hasmonean rulers.   The conquest was carried out in several

---

7. See Ezra 2.32; Neh. 11.34–36; I Macc. 5.23 (Narbatta), 11.34 (the Lydda toparchy); II Macc. 12.3, 8. The sources clearly indicate that except for the Lydda district, which was situated on the eastern edge of the coastal plain and the low hills of the Shephela, the other settlements and enclaves were too small to defend themselves. The survey by Klein (1939) 68ff. is in places rather speculative.

stages. Simeon opened a narrow corridor to the sea via Gezer to Jaffa, and expelled the local population (143–142).[8] There is no direct reference to the precise date and extent of Hyrcanus's westward expansion. However, the information about the early conquests of Alexander Jannaeus, Hyrcanus's son, indicates that by the late days of John Hyrcanus, the coast between Strato's Tower in the north and Ascalon to the south was in Jewish hands.[9] This means that the Hellenistic cities of the region, Apollonia, Iamnia (Jabneh), and Azotos (Ashdod), mentioned in the general summary list of the Hasmonean occupations (*Ant.* XIII.395), were conquered by Hyrcanus.[10] Notably, in summing up Hyrcanus's achievements, Georgius Syncellus, the Byzantine chronographer, states (I.548, ed. Dindorf):

> He distinguished himself by many successes and victories against the neighboring Arabs, the Idumeans, the coastland of Phoenicia [παράλου Φοινίκης] and Samaria.

The sentence, like two others on the days of Alexander Jannaeus, may well have been drawn from a knowledgeable source.[11] The reference to the region as "Phoenicia" is also instructive for interpreting the sentence in Pseudo-Hecataeus.[12]

---

8. Gezer: I Macc. 13.43–48; 14.7, 34; 15.28. Jaffa: I Macc. 13.11; 14.5, 34; 15.28. The mention of Iamnia (Jabneh) among Simeon's conquests in *Ant.* XIII.215 and *Bell.* I.50 may be a mistaken interpretation of I Macc. 16.8–10 in relation to 15.40. The account by Nicolaus of the time of Simeon, the sole source of Josephus's version (see Hölscher [1904] 10–11; Bar-Kochva [1989] 452–53), was a hasty, inconsequential, and badly organized summary of I Macc. 13.31–16.22, supplemented from another source by the story about the destruction of the *Akra*.

9. *Ant.* XIII.324, 357; *Bell.* I.61, 87.

10. So also Avi-Yonah (1966) 64; Kasher (1990) 121 n. 18.

11. These data corroborate information on the days of Jannaeus that does not appear in Josephus, and at least once even contradicts his account. For the possible origin in Justus of Tiberias (via Julius Africanus), see Gelzer (1885) I.225–26, followed by many others. See, e.g., Schürer (1901–9) I.62–63; Schürer et al. (1973–86) I.37. But see the objections of Rajak (1973) 365–68, (1987). The latter underestimates the historical significance of the differences between Syncellus and Josephus. They cannot be mere paraphrases of the Josephan text. See also M. Stern (1981) 44 n. 100; and esp. S. Schwartz (1990).

12. On the usage of the term, see pp. 103–4 above.

Key:
- Judea at the time of Judas Maccabeus
- Annexations under Jonathan
- Annexations under Simeon
- Annexations under Hyrcanus I
- Possible annexations under Hyrcanus I
- Annexations under Aristobulus I
- Annexations under Alexander Jannaeus

5.   The Hasmonean expansion.

The chronology of Hyrcanus's conquests in the region can be established on the basis of two Roman documents and the general background. At the same time, without additional archaeological evidence
we may not yet determine which parts of the region were occupied in
the various phases. It seems that at least some parts had already fallen

into Jewish hands in the early days of Hyrcanus's reign, probably in the years 135–132. They were temporarily lost with the invasion of Antiochus VII Sidetes in 132. Hyrcanus regained his territorial conquests and seems to have expanded them between 127 and 125. In 113 the Jews again lost control of the area when Antiochus IX Cyzicenus made his brief drive to the south. It was soon restored, in 112, and Hyrcanus may have made some new encroachments in that year, as well as taken further steps to consolidate Jewish control of the region.[13]

Alexander Jannaeus (103–76) expanded Jewish dominance in the north during the first year of his reign,[14] occupying the cities of Strato's Tower and Dora on the Carmel coast (*Ant.* XIII.326, 335; *Bell.* I.61). In 102, Jannaeus turned to the area south of Ascalon.[15] He conquered Anthedon, Raphia, and Gaza, the later flourishing city being thoroughly destroyed (*Ant.* XIII.357–64, *Bell.* I.87). Ascalon was the only gentile city on the coast south of Mount Carmel to retain its independence.[16]

The pace of Jewish settlement in the region cannot be ascertained. It can only be said that in the time of the Hasmonean state the demography of the region changed decisively in favor of the Jews. This is well attested by Strabo (XVI.2.28), who drew on a Hellenistic source from the time of the Hasmoneans,[17] and is evident from Josephus's accounts of the occurrences in the region at the time of the Great Revolt against the Romans.[18] The Jewish community in the Judean Hills in the period of the Maccabean uprising suffered from overpopulation and

13. See the discussion in Extended Notes, n. 2 p. 291.

14. On the sequence of events in the year 103/2, see M. Stern (1981) 33ff., (1985) 98ff.; cf. van't Dack and Clarysse in van't Dack et al. (1989) 109–10. For the absolute chronology, see Schürer (1901–9) I.256 n. 1; Schürer et al. (1973–86) I.200 n. 1.

15. On the dating of the destruction of Gaza to around the year 100 B.C., see Extended Notes, n. 3 p. 292.

16. On the special status of Ascalon and its historical background, see Kanael (1955) 10ff.; Avi-Yonah (1966) 62–68; Rappaport (1970); M. Stern (1985) 22.

17. The reservation must be noted that Strabo's additional statement that the "village" Iamnia and its surroundings could supply 40,000 armed men is certainly grossly exaggerated. Assuming the 10%–15% standard recruiting rate in antiquity (see Bar-Kochva [1989] 56–57), this means a population of 275,000–400,000 inhabitants.

18. See, e.g., Jos. *Bell.* II.509, 513–16; III.9–28, 414, 428–31; IV.443–49; *Lament. Rabba* 2.2 (= *BT Gittin* 57a).

land scarcity.[19] The newly occupied fertile plains near the sea obviously offered new possibilities. Determining the chronology and development of the settlement drive would involve a number of unanswerable questions. Which areas and cities of the region were occupied in each of the above-mentioned phases? Were the Hellenistic cities destroyed? And if so, when?[20] And what happened to the local inhabitants? Were they deported as were the inhabitants of Jaffa in the time of Simeon, or the people dwelling in the Scythopolis Valley in the later days of Hyrcanus and elsewhere in the time of Alexander Jannaeus?[21] And if so, were they driven out immediately after the occupation? Or were all these drastic measures taken only after the year 112, when Hyrcanus became more confident of himself in view of growing crises in the Seleucid kingdom? Whatever the answers to such questions, the settlement of "many tens of thousands" as per Pseudo-Hecataeus (Jos. *Ap.* I.194) could not have taken place overnight. This reference could indeed reflect the demographical situation in the coastal plain as early as the middle of John Hyrcanus's reign (ca. 120 B.C.), but it may also indicate a later *post quem* date.

A later date does in fact appear from the statement about pagan cults. The Jews are said to have destroyed *all* (ἄπαντα) temples and altars constructed by "those coming to the land" (τῶν εἰς τὴν χώραν ... ἀφικνουμένων, *Ap.* I.193). The sentence indicates an organized, comprehensive campaign against pagan religious monuments and the destruction of a significant number of temples. The reference in the paragraph to "newcomers" and the "satraps," as well as the evident restriction of the scope of the treatise to the Persian and Hellenistic periods, excludes the possibility that the Israelite invaders of Canaan and Joshua son of Nun are actually meant (cf. Deut. 12.2–3). As there were no pagan temples in Judea proper, the sentence refers either to the

19. See Bar-Kochva (1977) 168ff. The population of Judea at the time of the Maccabean Revolt seems to have been even larger than assessed in that article; see Bar-Kochva (1989) 56–57; and cf. 50–56.

20. Cf. the case of Gadara, which was occupied early in Jannaeus's reign (*Ant.* XIII.356) but destroyed only toward the end of his reign (XIV.74).

21. Pp. 125 above and 132–33 below. See further Extended Notes, n. 4 p. 294.

enlarged borders of the Hasmonean state or to the Holy Land as a whole. Such a campaign is indeed known from the time of the Hasmonean state and has been referred to in one way or another by modern scholars. However, its chronology and development have yet to be clarified.

Acts of violence against the cults of the gentile population became increasingly common after the death of Antiochus IV (end of 164 B.C.). In his expedition to rescue Jews in the enclaves outside Judea (163 B.C.), Judas Maccabaeus punished the city of Azotos by destroying its altars and idols (I Macc. 5.68), and burned the temple of Karnayim, in Trans-Jordan, because the enemy found refuge there (5.43–44). For the same reason Jonathan, his brother (160–143), destroyed the temple of Dagon in Azotos in the year 148/7 (10.84, 11.4). All these acts, however, do not seem to have been motivated by a preconceived policy, but were a response to special, local circumstances. They were launched outside the Jewish-controlled area and certainly would not be described as the destruction of "all temples" in the Holy Land.[22]

A systematic destruction of foreign cults was first carried out by Simeon, who is explicitly said to have "cleared out" the idolatry, prob-ably statues and cult objects, of Gezer (Gazara) and the *Akra*, the Jerusalem citadel (I Macc. 13.47–48, 50). The same certainly happened in Jaffa, where the local population was expelled, and Jews settled in their place (I Macc. 13.11). However, since the "corridor" occupied by Simeon was rather small, the scale of these operations was still rather limited. And what is more important, there is no reference to the de-struction of temples in his time. As the achievements of Simeon were comprehensively recorded by his contemporary admirer the author of I Maccabees,[23] and his operations against pagan cult especially lauded (14.7), the absence of such a reference cannot be accidental. It seems, therefore, that there were no impressive temples in the rural areas of the "corridor." As for Jaffa, Simeon, who actually recognized Seleucid

22. Contrary to Willrich (1895) 21–22, (1900) 95. Cf. Schaller (1963) 27; Hengel (1971) 303; Holladay (1983) 329 n. 25. In their view the sentence under discussion reflects the aggressive opposition of Mattathias and Judas Maccabaeus to the pagan cult imposed on Judea by Antiochus IV and the destruction of two temples outside Judea by Judas Maccabaeus and Jonathan (see below).

23. The only significant undertaking of Simeon that was not recorded was the destruction of the *Akra* (see *Ant.* XIII.215–17, *Bell.* I.50). On the reason for this, see Bar-Kochva (1989) 454.

supremacy over the city (15.35), was perhaps careful enough not to provoke too much antagonism at that stage and therefore refrained from demolishing the temple or temples of that celebrated harbor city. This may have taken place sometime later, in the days of John Hyrcanus.

Much more extensive was the destruction of pagan cults by his successors John Hyrcanus (135–104), Aristobulus I (104/3), and Alexander Jannaeus (103–76), covering more regions of the Holy Land. In contrast to the abundant information on the days of the Hasmonean brothers, our knowledge of the days of these later rulers is mainly based on excerpts from secondhand sources, which were badly adapted and arranged by Josephus.[24] Consequently not all the conquests are reported, and the destruction of temples is only occasionally mentioned. However, as appears from a number of references, the general policy of the Hasmonean rulers toward pagan cults is quite clear, and we can accordingly assume that after becoming confident of their ability to face possible Seleucid retaliation, they did not spare pagan temples and cults in the occupied territories. This was certainly done in the Hellenized cities reported to have been partly or utterly demolished or whose populations were sent into exile. The same obviously applies to regions whose inhabitants were forced to convert to Judaism.

Hyrcanus's expansion took place in the early and later days of his reign. His campaigns on the coastal plain (in the years 135–132, 127–125, 112) have been referred to above.[25] The occupied stretch of land between Ascalon and Strato's Tower included three Hellenistic cities—Apollonia, Azotos, and Iamnia. At least in the first two there were respectable temples of considerable magnitude.[26] However, it could be that Hyrcanus was careful, like his father, Simeon, and refrained from destroying temples as long as there was an immediate danger of a Seleucid reaction. The opportunity may have come in the year 112/11, when the Seleucid kingdom sank ever deeper into its longest internal

---

24. On the sources used by Josephus, see Hölscher (1904) 11ff.; on their confused adaptation by Josephus, see nn. 29 and 49 below.

25. See pp. 126–27 and esp. Extended Notes, n. 2 p. 291.

26. On the temple of Azotos, I Macc. 10.84. Apollonia, as appears from its name, most likely dedicated a temple to Apollo, who replaced Rešef, the old Canaanite god of fire, after whom the site had first been named. The excavations of the site so far cover only a tiny part of the Roman city, and therefore are not of any help for the present discussion (see Roll and Ayalon [1989] esp. 34–38).

crisis, the struggle between Antiochus IX Cyzicenus and Antiochus VIII Gryphus.[27]

For this reason, the second stage of his campaigns, which covered a larger area, was launched at about the same time (112/11–107). At that stage Hyrcanus turned to the regions south and north of the Judean Hills. He first conquered Idumea, totally destroying Marisa and Adora, its main cities, and converting the Idumeans to Judaism (*Ant.* XIII.257–58, XIV.88).[28] This campaign was followed by an expedition against the Samaritans (in the year 112/111). Hyrcanus occupied southern Samaria, demolishing the Samaritan temple at Mount Gerizim (*Ant.* XIII.254–58).[29] In 108/7, Hyrcanus carried out the second phase

27. On the background and main developments, see the survey by Bellinger (1949) 66ff.; Will (1967) II.373–74; Cohen in van't Dack et al. (1989) 15–16, 121–22. The later devastation of Jewish territories by Antiochus Cyzicenus, in the year 107, which was an attempt to force Hyrcanus to raise the siege of Samaria (*Ant.* XIII.278), just shows the readiness of the Seleucid contenders for the throne to come to the aid of their Hellenistic allies even when they were themselves in dire straits. This further emphasizes the need for restraint on the part of the Jewish ruler before the year 112/11.

28. The date of the occupation of Idumea has recently been established by the excavations in Marisa. The lower city, occupying about 75 acres, was totally destroyed by Hyrcanus, and the latest coins, belonging to Antiochus IX Cyzicenus, are from the year 200 of the Seleucid calendar, i.e., 113/12 B.C. The same date appears on an inscription found in one of the nearby burial caves, and the Rhodian handles scattered in the lower city cannot be dated later. The many ostraca and inscriptions, and the recurrence of Kos, the Idumean deity, show that the population included a substantial Idumean element, in addition to the Phoenicians known from the celebrated cave inscription found at the beginning of the century by Peters and Thiersch. The unsystematic excavations carried out on the acropolis at the beginning of the century did not definitely identify the site of the temple, but this still may be located. See a preliminary report: Kloner (1991) esp. 33, (1991a) 82–83. On the numismatic evidence, see Barkay (1992/3). On the inscriptions: Oren and Rappaport (1984).

29. The destruction of the Samaritan temple and its city should be dated to 112/11 in view of the hoard found on the site. See Magen (1989) 31–37, 48–51; id. (1990) 87, 96. The same date appears from the coins found in nearby Shechem, which was also destroyed (Wright [1965] 172, 184). It appears from the excavations that the city on the top of Mt. Gerizim was totally destroyed by Hyrcanus. This dating, as well as that of the occupation of Idumea, definitely proves that the passage in *Ant.* XIII.254–58, drawing on Nicolaus (see *Bell.* I.62–63; cf. Hölscher [1904] 12), was not incorporated in the correct chronological sequence already by the time of Nicolaus.

of his northern campaign.[30] He first laid siege to the city of Samaria and at the same time occupied northern Samaria as well as Scythopolis. The inhabitants of Scythopolis and "its valley" are said to have gone into exile (Scroll of Fasting, 15–16 Sivan), and Jewish settlers were presumably introduced.[31] The temple of Zeus in the city (*SEG* VIII.33) and other cult monuments were certainly destroyed. After a year of siege, the Hellenistic city of Samaria was conquered, and Josephus reports in detail how the Jews obliterated all traces of this great city by flooding it (*Ant.* XIII.281). The nearby Esdralon (Jezreel) Valley and probably also Lower Galilee may well have been occupied shortly afterwards.[32]

Hyrcanus's son, Aristobulus I, expanded to the north in his single year as ruler (104/3). He launched a campaign in Galilee (*Bell.* I.76), probably Upper Galilee, and forcibly converted the Itureans (*Ant.* XIII.318–19), Arabs residing mainly in the Lebanon Valley.[33]

Alexander Jannaeus (103–76), the great Hasmonean conqueror, pursued the antipagan policy with much vigor. In the year 102 he occupied Strato's Tower and Dora (*Ant.* XIII.324, 335, 395), the Hellenized Phoenician cities on the Carmel coast, treating the inhabitants harshly (Syncellus I.558, Jos. *Ant.* XIV.76).[34] Shortly afterwards (in the year 102/1) came the turn of Anthedon, Gaza, and Raphia, the coastal cities south of Ascalon (*Ant.* XIII.357–64, *Bell.* I.87). The detailed account of the Gaza siege records the killing of the city councilors in the temple

---

30. For the date see Avi-Yonah (1966) 72–73; Schalit (1969) 201–2; Schürer et al. (1973–86) I.210 n. 22; van't Dack and Clarysse in van't Dack et al. (1989) 22.

31. On the fate of Scythopolis, see Fuks (1983) 64, referring to *Ant.* XIII.355. This also appears from Strabo XVI.2.40.

32. See Klausner (1950) III.89 and others. The reference to Jewish settlements in Lower Galilee at the beginning of Jannaeus's reign in *Ant.* XIII.337–38 (though the number of captives is grossly exaggerated; cf. XIII.344) indicates that Hyrcanus occupied the region at the time of his Samarian campaign, or even earlier (*Ant.* XIII.322–23). See also Bar-Kochva (1977) 191–94; Rappaport (1993) 28–29. On the evacuation of the region by the Assyrians, cf. recently Gal (1990) 142–43 and Na'aman (1989) 46ff., as opposed to former views.

33. For their location according to the unique ceramics attributed to them, see Dar (1991). However, Dr. R. Fränkel of Tel Aviv University has found similar ceramics in various places in the Israeli Upper Galilee. See M. Stern (1993) 8ff. on the occupation of Upper Galilee.

34. References for the date: see p. 127 n. 14 above. Syncellus explicitly names only Dora as one of the places where a total massacre had taken place.

of Apollo and the destruction of the temple itself (*Ant.* XIII.364). The Hellenistic temple at Beer Sheva may have been destroyed shortly afterwards.[35] In the next stage, which took place between the years 96–93 and 83–76,[36] Alexander Jannaeus occupied almost all the gentile territories in Trans-Jordan. A fair number of Hellenized cities, as well as Moabite sites, are listed as being destroyed or having their inhabitants deported (*Ant.* XIII.395–97, XIV.74–76, 87–88), and massacres of the entire population are recorded for most of them (Sync. I.558). In the case of Pella, it is explicitly asserted that the city was destroyed because its inhabitants refused to convert to Judaism (*Ant.* XIII.397). Excavations at Tel Anafa, an unidentified Hellenistic city on the slopes of the Golan Heights, show that the site was completely destroyed in the year 80.[37] This suggests that more Hellenistic cities than those listed in the sources suffered the same fate (perhaps also implied in *Ant.* XIV.76).[38] The campaign against pagan witchcraft conducted by Jews in Ascalon (which was never occupied by them), at the time of Alexander Jannaeus,[39] indicates that certain manifestations of idolatry in the Holy Land were persecuted on private or royal initiative even outside the borders of the Jewish state.

The above survey suggests that the statement of Pseudo-Hecataeus, reporting systematic and total destruction of temples, can record events already in the time of John Hyrcanus. A *terminus post quem* would seem to be provided by his later major campaigns in Idumea and Samaria (112/11–107), rather than by his early conquests on the coastal plain. We do not know whether all the Hellenistic cities between Ascalon and Strato's Tower were already occupied during the early expeditions, and one cannot be sure that their temples were demolished immediately after the conquest. In any case, just a few temples were involved, and such an operation affected only a small part of the Holy Land. However, the total number of temples destroyed by the Jews in 112/11–107 during the conquest of Marisa, Adora, Shechem and Mount Gerizim, Samaria,

35. See Shatzman (1990) 56.
36. See pp. 138–39 below.
37. See Weinberg (1971) 97; Herbert (1979); Fuks (1979/80). For possible identifications, see Fuks, ibid. (Arsinoë); and Bar-Kochva (1976) 70 n. 44 (Antioch in Ḥulata).
38. Cf. Schürer et al. (1973–86) I.240 n. 25.
39. See Hengel (1984); Efron in Kasher (1990) 318–41.

Scythopolis, and their *chōrai*, and the size of the newly occupied areas, which was twice as large as Judea proper, are more likely to have inspired the statement of Pseudo-Hecataeus.

The last and perhaps most instructive anachronistic reference is the statement that Samaria was annexed to Judea by Alexander "free of tribute" (*Ap.* II.43). For its historical background, some scholars have suggested that the sentence reflects, in exaggerated form, the territorial changes in the later years of Jonathan's leadership (from 152 B.C.), when the Seleucids certified the annexation of the three southern toparchies to Judea, free from many taxes.[40] However, the exaggeration is too great, the three toparchies occupying no more than a quarter of the Samaritan Hills and less than 15 percent of the district of Samaria as a whole.[41] Moreover, Pseudo-Hecataeus uses the term *aphorologētos*, which refers to exemption from the *phoros*, the symbol of foreign rule, while the Seleucids waived only duties and income taxes. Jonathan even offers to pay the *phoros* when asking for exemption from other taxes (I Macc. 11.28).[42]

40. See Willrich (1895) 21–22; Hengel (1971) 302; Walter (1976) 147–48; Holladay (1983) 334 n. 55.

41. The district included also Galilee; see p. 119 n. 206 above.

42. The only document that mentions exemption from the *phoros* is I Macc. 10.29, 33. This never came into effect. Though it is mentioned in a list of unprecedented concessions, it is quite doubtful whether the original Greek document had the Hellenistic *phoros* in mind. In I Macc. 11.28 Jonathan is said to have asked to "make Judea free of tribute [*aphorologētos*]" but according to the same verse he promised to pay 300 talents, which was the amount of the annual *phoros* (cf. I Macc. 13.15; II Macc. 4.8; *Ant.* XIII.247; prob. also Diod. XXXIV–XXXV.1.5). And indeed there is no reference to the *phoros* in the subsequent document (I Macc. 11.30–37). The word *aphorologētos* in I Macc. 11.28 is based on a mistranslation of the vague Hebrew word מס, which appeared in the Hebrew original of the book (cf. Bar-Kochva [1989] 228–29). The same may well be the case in I Macc. 10.29, 33. Notably, I Macc. 11.28 also contains another mistranslation, which has universally been acknowledged (the original text was "the three toparchies of Samaria"; see, e.g., F. M. Abel [1949] 208; Goldstein [1976] 431). However, Pseudo-Hecataeus, writing in Greek, would not have applied the term *aphorologētos* in a sense that excludes the *phoros*.

It remains therefore to accept the assumption of other scholars that the sentence was written under the influence of the occupation of the districts of Samaria by John Hyrcanus, that is, in 112/11–107 B.C.[43] An instructive typological parallel can be found in the famous Talmudic legend that attributes to Alexander the Great the destruction of the Samaritan temple, although it was actually carried out by John Hyrcanus concurrently with the annexation of Samaria.[44]

The purpose of *Against Apion* II.43 is obviously to legitimize the occupation of Samaria by implying that the Jews only restored rights granted to them by Alexander the Great. The principle of precedent played a major role in Hellenistic diplomacy and literary polemics, and had its effects also on Jewish literature. The tendency among Jews and Samaritans to relate some of their later achievements to Alexander can be observed in the series of stories in Josephus on Jewish and Samaritan relations with Alexander (*Ant.* XI.313–46) and the above-mentioned Talmudic parallel. At the same time one should not rule out the possibility that the author was also inspired by at least some general knowledge of the hostility between the great Macedonian conqueror and the Samaritans.[45]

The occupation of northern Samaria, or rather the end of the siege of the city of Samaria in the year 107, which completed the conquest of the region, should thus be taken as a *post quem* date. We could go one step further and ask where and when such a legitimation of the conquest was asked for. The author, an Egyptian Jew,[46] was certainly aware of the grievances harbored by the Samaritans against the Jews for destroying the Samaritan temple and annexing their land. The inhabitants of Coile Syria, including the Samaritans, were used to appealing to Hellenistic rulers to spare them from Hasmonean oppression,[47] and disputes between Jews and Samaritans in Egypt arising out of events that occurred in the Holy Land are recorded to have been brought before and decided

43. So Willrich (1895) 21–22, (1900) 97; Stein (1934) 7–8; Schaller (1963) 27; Walter (1976) 148.

44. *BT* Yoma 79a; and the parallel in the medieval scholion to the Scroll of Fasting, 21 Kislev.

45. On the persecution of the Samaritans by Alexander, see Cross (1963) 118–19; Coggins (1975) 106–8; Egger (1986) 74–75.

46. See pp. 145–47 below.

47. See, e.g., I Macc. 11.4–5; *Ant.* XIII.275–80, 328ff.

by the Ptolemaic king (*Ant.* XII.10, XIII.74).[48] In the year 107, at the time of the siege of Samaria, Antiochus IX Cyzicenus applied for help on behalf of the Samaritans to Ptolemy Lathyrus, who was still co-regent with his mother, Cleopatra III (*Ant.* XIII.278).[49] Though Cleopatra was against any intervention, Lathyrus dispatched six thousand troops to support the Syrian king. This was one of the reasons for the breach with his mother (ibid.). It stands to reason that Samaritans as well as Jews would have presented their arguments on that occasion.

Another opportunity for the Samaritans to appeal to the Ptolemaic queen came immediately before and during her expedition to Palestine in the year 103/2 (*Ant.* XIII.348ff.).[50] The expedition was indeed meant to counter the advancing troops of Lathyrus, who from his base in Cyprus invaded Judea, but she also considered deposing Alexander Jannaeus and renewing direct Ptolemaic rule in Judea. It is told that Cleopatra's counselors advised her not to allow the accumulation of too much power in the hands of Alexander Jannaeus and recommended that she occupy his kingdom, though the Jewish commanders of the Ptolemaic army warned that in doing so she might lose the support of her Jewish soldiers (*Ant.* XIII.353–54). Egyptian Jews thus played a major role in the discussions about the future of Judea (and Samaria). One would assume that deputations of the local populations, including the Samaritans, were also allowed to present their case. A legitimation of the conquest of Samaria was badly needed for Egyptian Jews in the year 103/2, even more than it was in 107. Year 103/2 as a *terminus post quem* will also appear from an analysis of the sources of inspiration for

---

48. On these traditions, see Fraser (1972) I.285–86; Rappaport (1990) 378–87.

49. The Josephus story about the intervention of Antiochus IX Cyzicenus (XIII.275–80) includes two versions. The first (paras. 275–77), which was taken from Nicolaus (see *Bell.* I.64–66; Hölscher [1904] 13), does not mention the participation of Ptolemy Lathyrus. The second (paras. 278–80), based on another source, probably Strabo, differs in several respects from the Nicolaus version. Josephus tried to harmonize the two versions in para. 277b.

50. The date has been established on the basis of a demotic inscription from Karnak dated to 27 Sept. 103. It clearly shows that by then Cleopatra was already in control of Ptolemaïs. See the reading of the text by Winnicki (1981) and in van't Dack et al. (1989) 53–61, and the comments of van't Dack (1981); M. Stern (1985) 100; Cohen in van't Dack et al. (1989) 122–24; van't Dack and Claryssc, ibid. 109.

the unique explanation provided by the author of Pseudo-Hecataeus as to the purpose of Jewish residence in the Egyptian Diaspora.[51]

2. *TERMINUS ANTE QUEM*

An approximate *ante quem* date can be determined in light of the absence of any echo of the conquests and annexation of districts in Trans-Jordan by Alexander Jannaeus. This cannot be accidental: the Trans-Jordanian campaigns added a new, imperial dimension to the Hasmonean expansion and required far more justification than did the former, much smaller territorial achievements, the annexation of Samaria and the expansion in the coastal plain (*Ap.* I.194, II.43). All the more so with regard to Moabitis, which had never previously been Jewish or Israelite (apart from a short period of occupation in the tenth century B.C.), and which the Bible itself does not consider part of the Promised Land. In the case of Ammonitis, likewise not included in the Promised Land, it was even easy to prove former rights by referring to the settlements of Tobias there, which had strong ties with Ptolemaic Egypt and its Jewry.[52] An author like Pseudo-Hecataeus would certainly have striven to legitimize these occupations by inventing a precedent or the like. Such a reference would not have escaped Josephus's notice in his persistent polemical effort in *Against Apion* to demonstrate the good will of Hellenistic rulers toward the Jews and the antiquity of the Jewish nation.

It is true that the occupation of Hebron Hills–Idumea was not recorded either, but that annexation did not require legitimization. It was known in the Hellenistic world that the Idumeans were newcomers to the Hebron Hills (e.g., Strabo XVI.2.34). There is no indication that they ever claimed to be autochthonous, and even Jews who were not well versed in the Bible hardly needed to be reminded of this.

Hasmonean penetration into Trans-Jordan commenced probably in the time of Jonathan, who may have gained official control over the *Peraea*, the Jewish-inhabited district in the central Jordan Valley and the western slopes of Ammonitis (perhaps according to I Macc. 11.57).

---

51. See pp. 242–43 below.

52. On the Tobias settlements near Philadelphia (Ammonitis) and their connection with Egypt, see the surveys by Tcherikover (1961) 64ff., (1961a) 59ff.; Hengel (1973) 486ff. On the origin of the story about Joseph son of Tobias among the Egyptian Jewry, see M. Stern (1962) 38ff.

Late in his reign, John Hyrcanus obtained a further foothold, occupying the north of Moabitis (Medeba and Samaga, *Ant.* XIII.255).[53] Alexander Jannaeus carried out his campaigns in the region in three stages. Shortly after year 102/1 or so, he occupied Gadara (*Ant.* XIII.356, *Bell.* I.86–87),[54] which provided him with a bridgehead for further operations in northern Trans-Jordan.[55] The second stage was the most significant: it consisted of the conquest of Ammonitis (Syncellus I.558–59), Moabitis, and Galaditis, as well as the uprooting of the gentile strongholds in the *Peraea*, the old Jewish enclave east of the Jordan (*Ant.* XIII.374, *Bell.* I.89). This stage took place sometime in the years 96–93.[56] Most of these territorial gains were given away by Jannaeus in about the year 87, toward the end of the long internal upheaval in Judea (*Ant.* XIII.382).[57]

53. On the identification of Samaga, see Foerster (1981) 353–55. Whatever its identification, the conquest did not allow Hyrcanus more than a foothold. The date of the event is unclear (see Bar-Kochva [1989] 560–62), and the subsequent reference in Josephus to the destruction of Mt. Gerizim and the occupation of Idumea, known from the recent excavations to have occurred in 112/11 (see p. 131 nn. 28, 29 above), may indicate that it took place in the later years of John Hyrcanus. On the purpose of this conquest, see Kasher (1986) 77.

54. For the sequence of events and absolute chronology, see above (p. 127 and nn. 14, 15). The occupation of Amathos in the *Peraea*, which is mentioned in the same paragraph, was only temporary. See the reference to Theodorus's subsequent military success (*Ant.* XIII.356) and to the destruction of the fortress only in the second stage of Jannaeus's campaigns (*Ant.* XIII.374 = *Bell.* I.89; cf. Schürer et al. [1973–86] I.223; M. Stern [1981] 40 n. 84).

55. For Amathos in the *Peraea*, see the previous note. The list of Jannaeus's occupations in Moabitis (*Ant.* XIII.395–97), which is included in the summary of his conquests toward the end of his reign, certainly goes back to the second stage of his conquests. On this list, see Schalit (1967/8) 3–50; Kasher (1986) 97–98.

56. The expedition is recorded by Josephus after a reference to the murder of Antiochus VIII Gryphus (*Ant.* XIII.365), dated to 96 B.C. (see Schürer [1901–9] I.176–77; Schürer et al. [1973–86] I.134). It is said to have preceded the battle against Obedas I in Gaulanitis, which was followed by six years of insurrection in Judea (para. 376). The rebellion actually came to an end with the intervention of Demetrius III Eucaerus (paras. 376–79). As Demetrius III lost his throne in Damascus in 87 (Schürer et al. I.134–35; cf. Bowersock [1983] 24 n. 47 on Antiochus XII), the conquest of Moabitis and Galaditis has to be dated no later than 93.

57. See the expression τὸ τελευταῖον. The rebellion took place from about 93 to 87 B.C. (See the previous note.)

Jannaeus succeeded in restoring his achievements in the third stage of his Trans-Jordanian campaigns, which seem to have started in the year 83, and even strengthened his hold by occupying Gaulanitis and the remaining independent cities in Galaditis (*Ant.* XIII.393–94, *Bell.* I.104–5; Syncellus I.558–59).[58] We can therefore say that the *terminus ante quem* for the composition of Pseudo-Hecataeus is to be found in the years 96–93.

This conclusion finds support in the Egyptian background: in the year 88 Ptolemy Lathyrus deposed his brother and gained control over Egypt. He seems to have taken revenge on the Jews, who consistently supported his mother, Cleopatra III, and his brother, Ptolemy X Alexander. There is indeed some evidence for persecutions in the same year.[59] The favorable account of the Ptolemaic regime and the general atmosphere of Jewish-Ptolemaic cooperation reflected in the passages could hardly be imagined under Ptolemy Lathyrus.

3. PSEUDO-ARISTEAS AND PSEUDO-HECATAEUS

Further evidence for the dating of Pseudo-Hecataeus can be provided by comparing his book with that of Pseudo-Aristeas and elucidating the sequence of each. In the discussion of the relations between Ptolemy I and the Jews (Chap. III.2) it was pointed out that the Hezekiah story was unknown to Pseudo-Aristeas.[60] The story opened the treatise *On the Jews* and played a major role in it.[61] This suggests that Pseudo-Aristeas was the earlier of the two. Pseudo-Aristeas, who was *au courant* with the daily problems and literature of Alexandria and Egyptian Jewry, would have been familiar with Pseudo-Hecataeus's treatise, one of the few literary works composed by an Egyptian Jew, if Pseudo-Hecataeus had preceded the composition of his book. At the very least, he would have become aware indirectly of the Hezekiah story, which would have served his account very well.

---

58. See M. Stern (1981) 45ff.; Schürer et al. (1973–86) I.226 and n. 25; Kasher (1986) 95–97. The dating is to be established on the basis of the reference to the death of Antiochus XII Dionysius (*Ant.* XIII.391), which according to his coins occurred around the year 84 (see Bellinger [1949] 77 n. 84).

59. See Tcherikover (1957) I.25 and n. 63; followed by Kasher (1985) 12.

60. Pp. 78–79 above.

61. See below, pp. 226–30.

This conclusion seems at first sight to be contradicted by a quotation said by Pseudo-Aristeas to have been taken from Hecataeus (para. 31). It has been assumed by many scholars that the citation originated in the treatise *On the Jews*,[62] and its contents were adduced to deny the authenticity of the book. In order to examine its implications for the dating of Pseudo-Hecataeus, a close look at this text is required. The passage in Pseudo-Aristeas raises and answers the question why Greek authors did not mention the Jewish holy books:

> It is for this reason that authors and poets and the mass of historians have abstained from mentioning these aforesaid books and the men who have lived and are living in accordance with them, because the conception presented in them is somewhat pure and exalted [διὰ τὸ ἁγνήν τινα καὶ σεμνὴν εἶναι τὴν ἐν αὐτοῖς θεωρίαν], as Hecataeus of Abdera said.

Had the passage as a whole been ascribed by Pseudo-Aristeas to Hecataeus, one could indeed relate it only to a forged book. But even so, that could hardly be the treatise *On the Jews*: Josephus would not have missed the opportunity to include such an enthusiastic comment in his citations, especially as the passages he does quote do not contain any reference to the Jewish holy books.[63] Moreover, in the preface to *Against Apion* Josephus says that the absence of any reference to biblical history in Greek literature was the main argument raised by anti-Jewish authors against the antiquity of the Jewish people (I.2). As it is, Hans Lewy has decisively proved on comparative and philological grounds that the implicit question in the passage was asked by Pseudo-Aristeas himself, and the quotation comprises only the last sentence.[64] The quotation from Hecataeus thus reads: "The conception presented in

---

62. Eichorn (1793) 438–39; Dähne (1834) 216–19; Willrich (1900) 98–99; Schürer (1901–9) III.604ff.; Lewy (1932) 119–20 (though not explicitly); Jacoby (1943) 62, 65–66, 79; Murray (1967) 343, (1973) 165; Fraser (1972) II.968–69; Walter (1976) 194; Goodman in Schürer et al. (1973–86) III.674–75. And see Holladay (1983) 293 n. 13; and the variations of Wacholder (1974) 266; Doran (1985) 911–12.

63. Cf. the paraphrase of Pseudo-Aristeas 31 in Josephus's abridged adaptation of the "letter" (*Ant.* XII.37–38).

64. Lewy (1932) 119–20; cf. Geffcken (1907) p. xii n. 6; Gager (1969) 133 n. 15; Meisner (1973) 39, 50; Walter (1976) 146; Gauger (1982) 37–38; Doran (1985) 911–12. Other interpretations: Schaller (1963) 30; Wacholder (1974) 264.

them is somewhat pure and exalted." It should be added to Lewy's arguments that the cautious language of the sentence ("somewhat") at the outset discounts the possibility that it was originally an answer to the preceding questions. Pseudo-Aristeas obviously utilized a statement that appeared in his source in a different context.

A quotation of this nature is even less likely to have been taken from the treatise *On the Jews*. An enthusiastic Jewish forger would not have used this cautious language in appreciating the Jewish Holy Scriptures. Besides, Josephus would not have missed the sentence, even in this form, in his quotations,[65] as nothing he does quote or paraphrase contains any reference to the Jewish holy books. The first argument also applies to the possibility that the sentence was taken from the book *On Abraham* (if it were composed so early) or from another forged book that may have been attributed to Hecataeus, or that it is a free invention of Pseudo-Aristeas.[66] On the other hand, the sentence accords with the general tone of the genuine excursus on the Jews in Hecataeus's Egyptian ethnography,[67] which adheres to an unbiased and detached presentation.[68] Moreover, its phrasing recalls the style of Hecataeus in his moderate criticism of Jewish customs, which used the same diminutive adjective: "He [Moses] introduced a [way of] life that is somewhat unsocial and hostile to strangers" (ἀπάνθρωπόν τινα καὶ μισόξενον βίον, Diod. XL.3.4).[69] The sentence could well have been added to Hecataeus's reference to the Jewish laws: "There is even appended to the laws, at the end, the statement 'These are the words that Moses heard from God and declares unto the Jews' " (XL.3.6),[70] or elsewhere. The sentence is indeed not included in the Jewish ethnography as recorded by Diodorus, but Diodorus evidently abbreviated the original Hecataean excursus.[71] Nor is there anything in the contents of the excursus as it stands now that requires us to reject the attribution

---

65. So Gauger (1982) 37.

66. Suggested by Hengel (1971) 303 n. 1; Walter (1976) 146; Gauger (1982) 38; Goodman in Schürer et al. (1973–86) III.674–75.

67. So also Walter (1976) 146; Gauger (1982) 37.

68. Cf. above pp. 39–40.

69. Gager (1969) 134 points out in another context the use of τις in both cases, but his basic interpretation and conclusions are different because he believes in the authenticity of the passages ascribed to Hecataeus in *Against Apion*. Similarly Doran (1985) 912. See also p. 39 and n. 98 above.

70. Cf. Walter (1976) 145–46.

71. See above p. 23 and esp. n. 45.

of the quotation to Hecataeus. The statement by itself does not necessarily express Hecataeus's own attitude but may reflect in his own
words Jewish explanations either for their reverent handling of their
Scriptures (cf. *Ap.* I.42),[72] or for the restrictions imposed on gentiles
wishing to gain access to them, or the like.[73] There is thus no reason
to date Pseudo-Hecataeus before Pseudo-Aristeas.[74]

Returning to the question of the date of Pseudo-Hecataeus: in
Appendix B at the end of this monograph it is suggested that Pseudo-
Aristeas's book was written between the years 116 (or 118) and 113.
This sets another *post quem* date for Pseudo-Hecataeus, and shows
that the author of the *Letter of Aristeas* was his elder contemporary.
Accordingly, one to two decades separated the composition of the two
books. Writing in the same generation and in the same community,[75] it
stands to reason that Pseudo-Hecataeus was acquainted with Pseudo-
Aristeas. After all, only few literary works were by then written by
Egyptian Jews, and as Pseudo-Aristeas was occupied with the legitimacy
of the Septuagint, one of the most controversial issues in the life of
Egyptian Jewry, one would suppose that the book gained fame among
his contemporaries. There are indeed some striking similarities between
Pseudo-Hecataeus and Pseudo-Aristeas.[76]

72. Cf. Gauger (1982) 37. However, his emendation of the text must be
rejected. Pseudo-Aristeas certainly did not insert the qualifer τις.

73. See other possibilities in Gauger, ibid.

74. In contrast to Willrich (1900) 99; Wendland (1900a) 2–3; Jacoby (1943)
61, 66, 69; Wacholder (1974) 267. Their other arguments are invalid; see
Meisner (1973) 39; Walter (1976) 48, 145–46; and n. 76 below.

75. See pp. 143–47 on the descent and provenance of Pseudo-Hecataeus.

76. The resemblance between the dominant role of the Ptolemaic king and
the Jerusalem High Priest in the Hezekiah story and in Pseudo-Aristeas can
hardly be accidental. The possible influence of Pseudo-Aristeas can be discerned with regard to the circumference of Jerusalem (*Ap.* I.197; Pseudo-
Aristeas 105; see pp. 110–11), the fertility of the land (*Ap.* I.195; Pseudo-
Aristeas 107, 112), the statement that there was just one city in Judea (*Ap.* I.197;
Pseudo-Aristeas 113), and the location of the Temple (*Ap.* I.198; Pseudo-
Aristeas 83). However, these similarities do not necessarily prove direct
dependence, and they may be based on a common literary tradition. The
differences are not decisive: Pseudo-Hecataeus deliberately avoided any reference to the golden table and to the Septuagint (pp. 166–67 below), and there
is no contradiction with regard to the Temple walls: Pseudo-Aristeas 84 refers
to the partitions separating the three courts; Pseudo-Hecataeus (*Ap.* I.198),
to the exterior wall only (thus Hadas [1951] 132).

V   The Author: Origin, Education, and Religious Group

1.   DESCENT AND PROVENANCE

The scholars who regard *On the Jews* as spurious naturally assume that the author was Jewish. This is indeed unquestionable: a gentile would not have attributed his treatise on the Jews to Hecataeus of Abdera and disguised the anachronistic statements as he did. Nor would he have attempted to justify the Hasmoneans' antipagan policy (the destruction of temples and altars) and to legitimize their territorial expansion (the settlement in the coastal plain; the annexation of Samaria). The analysis of the Mosollamus story also showed that it could hardly have been written by an educated Greek, and the same holds for the author's praise for Jewish violence against pagan cults.

Nonetheless, attention should be given to the arguments of the proponents of authenticity, who have pointed out what they consider to be basic errors in Jewish history and religious practice. These may at first sight suggest that the book was not written by a Jew. Above all, it has been noted that the book speaks about a deportation of Jews to Babylonia by the Persians (Jos. *Ap.* I.194). If the Judean exile after the destruction of the First Temple in the year 586 is meant, this would seem to be too elementary a mistake to have been made by a Jew.[1] However, a similar mistake appears in the Second Book of the Maccabees

---

1. See J. G. Müller (1877) 175; Lewy (1932) 126; Guttman (1958–63) I.69. Cf. Wendland (1900) 1200.

(1.19–20).[2] Referring undoubtedly to the exile of 586, II Maccabees states that the Jews were deported to Persia. It has been suggested that the mistake in II Maccabees originates in a statement by Eupolemus, the Jewish Hellenistic author of the generation of Judas Maccabaeus, that Jerusalem was destroyed by a Babylonian-Median alliance.[3] As a matter of fact, the context of the sentence in Pseudo-Hecataeus indicates that it does not refer to the great Babylonian exile. The subsequent sentence states: "After Alexander's death, no less immigrated to Egypt and Phoenicia" (*Ap.* I.194). The author, then, could not have had in mind the almost total banishment of Judea to Babylonia after the destruction of the First Temple. It therefore seems correct to accept the view that he is referring to a deportation of Jews from Judea to Babylonia and Hyrcania by Artaxerxes III Ochus (359–338), which was recorded in a number of later sources.[4] The deportation has been related to the aftermath of the rebellion led by Tennes, the Sidonian king in the year 348,[5] or an earlier event.[6] Worthy of note is a tradition about a forced deportation of Jews to Egypt by the Persians, which has been preserved in Pseudo-Aristeas (para. 35).

Hans Lewy draws attention to two references about Jewish practice that in his view are mistaken and reflect Egyptian rituals.[7] First, the Jewish priests are said to abstain from drinking wine while in the Temple (*Ap.* I.199).[8] This is, however, explicitly demanded by the Torah, and the penalty for failing to comply is death (Lev. 10.8–11).[9] Lewy further argues that the same paragraph speaks of the mortification of the flesh by Jewish priests in the Temple, a practice alien to Judaism. But this is a misrepresentation of the phrase ἁγνείας τινὰς ἁγνεύοντες, which simply means "purifying themselves by certain

---

2. This has already been noted by Willrich (1900) 94; Reinach (1930) 37; Wacholder (1971) 236–37, (1974) 235–36, 270; Holladay (1983) 329 n. 27.

3. See Wacholder (1974) 236.

4. See Reinach (1895) 231, (1930) 37; Lewy (1932) 126 and n. 2; Klausner (1950) II.13; M. Stern (1974–84) I.43; Gauger (1982) 44; Doran (1985) 918 n. k; see the sources in Schürer (1901–9) III.7 n. 11.

5. See p. 87 n. 104 above.

6. See E. Stern (1982) 280 n. 77.

7. Lewy (1932) 127–28; followed by Doran (1985) 915–16.

8. On the Egyptian practice, see Plut. *De Is. et Os.* 353A–B; cf. Hecataeus *ap.* Diod. I.70.11. Cf. Iambl. *Pyth.* 97–98.

9. Cf. Ezek. 44.21; Jos. *Bell.* V.229, *Ant.* III.279; Philo, *Spec. Leg.* I.98.

[rituals] of purification."[10] Purity is indeed repeatedly demanded of the priests by the Pentateuch,[11] and there is no reason to reject the statement by Pseudo-Hecataeus, as Lewy does, that the priests were engaged in these rituals "night and day":[12] priests also performed guard duties at night (Middot 1.2, Tamid 1.1), which required constant purity. Purification rituals were carried out even at night (Middot 1.9).[13] There is thus no reason to doubt that the author was Jewish.

The Greek language and the use of the name of a Hellenistic author as a pseudonym, as well as the relative familiarity with Hellenistic polis life and customs by a Jewish author at the turn of the first century, suggest that the book was written in the Diaspora. That it was the Egyptian Diaspora is evident from the author's apparent admiration for the Ptolemaic king,[14] the stress laid on Hezekiah's emigration and Jewish settlement in Egypt,[15] and the use of the Ptolemaic measure *aroura* in describing the size of the Jewish land (*Ap.* I.195).

Though it is universally agreed that the book was written in Ptolemaic Egypt, a few scholars argue that it was composed by a Palestinian Jew who had emigrated to Egypt. They further claim that he was a Jerusalem priest.[16] The suggestion is based on the accurate description of the altar stones in the Temple (I.198). We shall later see that the author is indeed well acquainted with a number of other cult objects, but all these could easily have been known, in one way or another, to practicing Jews in the Diaspora. On the other hand, the elementary mistakes of Pseudo-Hecataeus with regard to the geography of the Holy Land and the city of Jerusalem[17] do not permit us to accept that he was a Palestinian priest. Unlike the geographical account of Pseudo-Aristeas,

10. Besides, Plutarch's account of the Egyptian priests (*De Is. et Os.* 6) does not necessarily refer to mortification of the flesh, as thought by Lewy (1932) 127 and n. 6, but merely to purification.

11. See Lewy (1932) 128 n. 2.

12. Esp. Lev. 21–22.16; cf. Exod. 29–30.21; Lev. 6–10, 13–16.

13. Cf. Zipser (1871) 87–88; Schlatter (1893) 94; Klein (1939) 121.

14. See, e.g., Jacoby (1943) 65; Hengel (1971) 303; Walter (1976) 148; Holladay (1983) 289.

15. See Holladay, ibid.

16. See Jacoby (1943) 61–63; Denis (1970) 266; Wacholder (1974) 267, 273.

17. See in detail pp. 107–13 above.

the mistaken description of Jerusalem cannot be excused as an idealization inspired by Hellenistic utopias or biblical associations.[18] This applies to the circumference of the city (about 50 stadia, I.197), the number of its inhabitants (120,000, I.197), and the location of the Temple "*nearly* in the center of the city" (I.198).[19] The first two mistakes indicate too large a city, which does not accord with the ideal Greek city-state[20] and does not recall any biblical verse. The third differs from Greek utopias, which place the main temple (or the most important one) *exactly* in the center of the city.[21] The latter difference, however slight, spoils the religious-moral principle underlying the location of temples in utopian fictions. For the same reason it also cannot be based, as suggested by one scholar, on a possible but unknown early Jewish midrash.[22] The three mistakes seem to be influenced, in one way or another, by personal acquaintance with the demography and geography of Alexandria.[23] A respectable Jewish priest from Jerusalem would hardly have so misinformed the reader about his native city, the holy city of the Jewish people, no matter how impressed he was by the great city of Egypt.

It is doubtful whether the author had ever even visited Jerusalem. It is reported in the Mishna that pilgrims usually circled the Temple wall, bowed toward each gate in turn, and then, after the Temple service, made

---

18. On the tendency toward idealization in Pseudo-Aristeas, see pp. 272–73 and nn. 4–7 below.

19. For this meaning of κατὰ μέσον μάλιστα τῆς πόλεως (and not "especially" or "certainly"), see H. G. Liddell, R. Scott, and H. S. Jones, eds., *A Greek-English Lexicon*, 9th ed. (Oxford, 1968), s.v. μάλα III.5. This meaning of μάλιστα is evident in the previous paragraph (197).

20. Arist. *Pol.* 1326[a-b]. Cf. Plato, *Leges* 737d–e, 740d–e, 745a.

21. See the sources in Lewy (1932) 128 n. 4; Guttman (1958–63) I.69. They, however, do not notice the difference. The main sources: Plato, *Leges* 778c–d, 848c–d, *Crit.* 116c; Diod. II.9.3. Cf. Arist. *Pol.* 1331[a].

22. In contrast to Wacholder (1974) 270 and n. 47.

23. The temples of Alexandria were concentrated in the *basileia*, the royal city, situated in the north-central area of Alexandria. This accords with the description "nearly in the middle of the city." On the sanctuaries of Alexandria and the location of the *basileia*, see Fraser (1972) I.14–15; Hoepfner (1990) 277–78. (See esp. p. 278 on the location of the *Paneion*.) On the influence of the size and demography of Alexandria on the account of Pseudo-Hecataeus, see pp. 110–11 above.

a tour of the city.[24] This would surely have provided a basic knowledge of the city's topography as well as of the location of the Temple. Thus Philo, who visited Jerusalem as a pilgrim,[25] quite accurately describes the relative height of the Temple Mount and the Temple,[26] despite the rather complicated topography. There is, however, no equivalent piece of information in Pseudo-Hecataeus. Even so, Pseudo-Hecataeus may well be, like Philo,[27] of priestly descent, which would help to explain his relative accuracy with regard to the cult objects of the Temple.

The question whether the author belonged to the Alexandrian community or resided in the country (the Egyptian *chōra*) seems to remain open. His apparent acquaintance with Alexandria cannot be used as conclusive evidence. At the same time, the absence of any explicit reference to the settlement of Jews in Alexandria in the original treatise,[28] which elaborated on the beginnings of Jewish settlement in Egypt,[29] still does not prove the opposite. This lacuna may be explained in a variety of ways.[30] Even so, Willrich's hypothesis that the author belonged to the settlers or to the "supporters" of the Oniad priestly family at Leontopolis[31] must be rejected. The account of the Jerusalem Temple contains veiled criticism of certain practices in the Leontopolis temple.[32]

24. See S. Safrai (1981) 180–85. The main references: Middot 2.2, 3, 6; Sekalim 6.1.

25. *Spec. Leg.* I.69, *De Providentia* II.22, 24.

26. See *Spec. Leg.* I.73; and cf. Middot 4.6; *Bell.* V.207.

27. See Hieronymus, *De Viris Illustribus* 11. On the question whether Philo was indeed a priest, see the discussion (and positive answer) of D. R. Schwartz (1984). At the same time it must be said that Philo himself, who does have some autobiographical remarks, does not say that, and neither does anyone else before Hieronymus.

28. See p. 227 below.

29. Pp. 226–28 below.

30. Thus one may perhaps argue that the tradition about the participation of Jews in the foundation of Alexandria at the time of Alexander (*Ap.* II.35, 42; *Bell.* II.487) could not properly be integrated into a story of settlement that used for its background the events of the year 312 and claimed to be based on the personal experiences of Hecataeus.

31. See pp. 90–91 and n. 114 above.

32. See pp. 166, 247 below.

2. GREEK EDUCATION

The author was accordingly a native of the Jewish Egyptian Diaspora. In view of his origin, his knowledge of Greek, the use of the name of a celebrated Hellenistic ethnographer as his pseudonym, and what appear to be Hellenistic features in the fragments, it has been assumed that he was a "Hellenistic Jew,"[33] and the book has been classified in the category of Jewish Hellenistic literature. Our examination of this assumption will at first avoid the question what Hellenistic Judaism actually was. It should be noted only that the Jewish community in Hellenistic Egypt was not homogeneous, and its major streams advocated diverse and often conflicting approaches to the relationship between Judaism and Hellenism. The traditional image of a Hellenistic Jew has, however, been shaped according to the surviving literary contributions of Alexandrian Jewry, especially the works of Philo. Therefore, the question that will occupy us at this juncture is whether Pseudo-Hecataeus was a Hellenistic Jew similar to the enlightened Hellenistic Jews Aristobulus, Pseudo-Aristeas, and Philo, who utilized their profound mastery of the Greek heritage, each in his own way, to reconcile the two cultures and explain the Jewish Holy Scriptures according to the methods, ideas, and achievements of "Greek wisdom." To answer this, it must be established whether the author's Greek education and knowledge of the Greek literary corpus (especially the philosophical one) was profound and on a level with that of the above-mentioned Jewish authors, and whether Pseudo-Hecataeus indeed tried to apply Greek thinking and traditions to an understanding of Judaism.

The evidence available for answering these two questions is closely related. From the contents of the fragments and testimonia it appears that the author did not have any philosophical education and that his acquaintance with the Greek heritage and Hellenistic life was limited to popular ideas and practices, and that even this knowledge was rather superficial. In addition, there are no associations, parallels, or references to the great corpus of Greek literature, which were so common in contemporary prose writing. What the author knew of Hellenistic culture and civilization was, by and large, no more than could be expected of

33. This is implied or stated explicitly by Freudenthal (1875) 165–66; Graetz (1888) III.2.608–9; Willrich (1895) 32, (1900) 105, 115–16, 127; Hengel (1971) 303; Walter (1976) 148; and others.

an intelligent oriental, living in Hellenistic Egypt or residing in the greatest and most civilized city of the Hellenistic world, who had not completed a comprehensive program of Greek education.[34] A grammatical and stylistic analysis of the text corroborates this impression. The author's acquaintance with Greek literature thus fell considerably short of the standard set by the Hellenistic Jewish authors mentioned above. In addition he made no attempt to apply "Greek wisdom" to the interpretation of Jewish beliefs and religious practices.

One is especially struck by the total absence of any philosophical terminology or argument and the ignorance of the Greek philosophical heritage. It would suffice, for instance, to select at random a few passages from Jason of Cyrene, the Wisdom of Solomon, or Pseudo-Aristeas (not to mention Philo and IV Maccabees) to see the difference. Given the wide range of topics mentioned in the surviving material, the fact that only a small part of the original work has come down to us is no excuse. The passages about the Jews' strong adherence to their religion, martyrdom, the destruction of pagan altars and temples, and even the allusions to Jewish overpopulation invite some philosophical interpretation, justification, or parallels. They are lacking here, although their inclusion was a common practice for most Jewish Hellenistic authors. The author, who paraded himself as Hecataeus and must have known that Hecataeus was a philosopher, does not even try to imitate Hecataeus's Jewish excursus, which is full of philosophical and social reasonings. It is true that these passages may be abbreviated, but Josephus had no reason to be so consistent in omitting "philosophical" explanations. On the contrary, he was keen on offering reasons for Torah precepts. In the preface to the laws of Deuteronomy he states that he plans to write a book on Jewish practices and their reasons (*Ant.* IV.198), and his version in the *Jewish Antiquities* provides explanations for many laws.

No less instructive is the absence of any philosophical-moral explanation in the references to the construction of the Jewish altar solely of unhewn stones (*Ap.* I.188). The Torah itself indicates the existence of such a reason: "If you make an altar of stones for me, you must not build it of hewn stones, for if you lift up your sword on

---

34. On the question whether there was a Hellenistic *enkyklios paideia* and on its regular disciplines, see Marrou (1937) 211–35, (1956) 223ff.; Koller (1955); de Rijk (1965); Mendelson (1982) 1–47.

it, you will profane it" (Exod. 20.25, Deut. 27.5–6). Philo provided two symbolic explanations (*Spec. Leg.* I.275, 287), and later Judaism interpreted it in various moralistic ways (e.g., Middot 3.4, Mechilta *ad loc.*). Pseudo-Hecataeus's description of the Temple is detailed and given in direct speech, and Josephus, who was evidently puzzled about this instruction of the Torah,[35] would not have missed the opportunity to give an explanation had he found one in the original text. Josephus himself gives allegorical explanations in Book III of the *Antiquities* for various aspects of the Temple and of the priestly service.

The absence of Greek philosophical terms in the characterization of Jewish personalities is also noteworthy. Hezekiah the High Priest is described as "not unintelligent" (τὴν ψυχὴν οὐκ ἀνόητος), "an able speaker," and "experienced ... in the affairs" (*Ap.* I.187), and Mosollamus, the Jewish archer, as "a man with a robust mind and ... the best archer among Greeks and barbarians" (I.201).[36] Hans Lewy claimed that these qualities characterize "a perfect Greek" and a man "Hellenic in spirit," respectively.[37] But they represent not even one of the four Platonic cardinal virtues, which were universally accepted in the Greek world, nor do they echo the twelve (or thirteen) Aristotelian good qualities (*Eth. Eud.* 1220[b]38ff., *Eth. Nic.* 1114[b]10ff.). Their first quality would not have impressed a Greek reader, for it is far from excellence. Neither of them is defined as *sophos*, *phronimos*, or *epistēmōn* ("wise," "prudent"), and even *eusebeia* ("piety"), a subclass (or "part") of "justice" (Plato, *Euthyphro* 11e; cf. *SVF* III.64.40), which is naturally to be expected of a High Priest, is not mentioned. The cardinal virtues and the Aristotelian "middle-way" qualities had deeply influenced the characterization of ideal leaders in Greek and Jewish

35. See *Ant.* IV.200. Josephus does not allude to the explanations of the Torah, but adds in an apologetic manner (see the preceding ἀλλά, "but") that the stones were carefully selected, neatly arranged, and coated with white plaster "to make them look comely and nice." He obviously felt that an altar of simple unhewn stones would seem to the reader too humble. To include a philosophico-moral justification for the appearance of the altar would have lent it greater dignity. Josephus was uneasy, for one reason or another, about the explanation of the Torah.

36. For the correct reading and translation, see p. 51 n. g above.

37. Lewy (1932) 122, 129, 131, twice employing the Greek expression Ἑλληνικὸς τῇ ψυχῇ.

Hellenistic literature, including that of biblical heroes.[38] This applies also to Moses and the High Priest in Hecataeus's Jewish excursus (Diod. XL.3.3, 5). Eulogies (*enkōmia*), which were among the first school exercises of the rhetorical curriculum and played an essential role in public competitions and funerals, included the virtues as a regular component.[39] The personality of Hezekiah seems to reflect the obvious qualities of a good politician or leader in a Hellenistic city and oriental community alike, or of a secular leader in the Jewish Diaspora, rather than to have been inspired by a Greek literary model or reference.[40]

A direct proof of the author's incomplete and superficial acquaintance with Greek conceptions and practices is provided by the Mosollamus story. The analysis of the episode in Chapter III.1 showed that Pseudo-Hecataeus misrepresented the belief in bird omens, as well as the rules of interpretation, and that he failed to mention either the common term for a bird of omen or the particular species. One may of course argue that he disregarded the Greek features in order to simplify the story for his less knowledgeable Jewish readers and thus make the joke more effective. This explanation may be valid as far as the theological conception is concerned, but not with regard to the practical details. The arguments already raised above in the discussion of the authenticity of the book[41]

---

38. See, e.g., Plato, *Leges* 965; *Politeia* 427e ff., 439d ff., 480ff.; *Plt.* 311; Xen. *Ages.* III.5, IV.1, V.5, VI.1, 4, VIII.1, 4, and esp. XI; *Anab.* I.9; *Cyr.* I.3.10–11, 16–18, 4.18–24, 5.6–7, 6.1–6, and many parallels in the other books of that work; Pseudo-Aristeas 122, 212–27; Jos. *Ant.* I.256, IV.327–31, VII.390–91. Many parallels can be found in references by Philo to biblical figures. Cf. also the *rector* in Cic. *Rep.* V and VI.

39. See Marrou (1956) 272–73.

40. Literary influence of *Il.* IX.443 (cf. Cic. *De Or.* III.15.57) on the characterization of Hezekiah is rather a remote possibility, especially in view of the absence of further associations with the epic tradition and the many other references to the ideal leader. Moreover, the terminology is quite different, and the distinction between doers and talkers is a common *topos* in Greek literature. Josephus's description of Joshua's personality may suggest the existence of a *topos* that also included the three qualities of Hezekiah. He attributes to Joshua wisdom, eloquence, piety, courage, endurance, dexterity in directing affairs, and adaptability to every situation (*Ant.* III.49, V.118; cf. Feldman [1989]). However, the other qualities are still missing in the characterization of Hezekiah, and the absence of piety shows even more forcibly that the author had in mind a practical, not a literary, model.

41. See pp. 68–69, 70 above.

are also applicable here: referring to one or two of the real rules for interpreting omens would have contributed greatly to ridiculing gentile divination. And why would a knowledgeable Hellenistic Jew refrain from specifying the bird in question, or from using the word *oiōnos*, the technical term for a bird of omen, and instead repeat four times the general term *ornis* ("bird")? The Homeric epics stood at the forefront of Hellenistic education in Egypt in all its stages, including the first writing exercises.[42] An author who received a systematic Greek education would easily have been inspired by certain Homeric verses to fill these gaps in his story, even if he was not personally acquainted with the practical side of Greek mantics. Whatever the reason for the absence of a real challenge to the theology underlying Greek omens,[43] the author certainly differed from Pseudo-Aristeas, his older contemporary, who took great pains to undermine the theological foundations of gentile practices mentioned in his book.

Hans Lewy, in his endeavors to prove the authenticity of the treatise, pointed to a number of references that in his view proved that the author was well acquainted with Greek classical and contemporary literature and trends.[44] This has generally been accepted, even by scholars who deny authenticity, and has led them to describe the author as a Hellenistic Jew. It has been shown above that Lewy was mistaken in describing the characterization of the Jewish individuals in the book as typically Greek. Of the other features that have been taken to indicate a broad knowledge of Greek culture, some are known from Jewish literary tradition, while others were commonplace and conspicuous in a Hellenistic city and the Ptolemaic kingdom. Two references were also influenced by Hecataeus's Jewish excursus, a knowledge of which by a Diaspora Jew is only natural and does not indicate that he had an extensive Greek education.

The *philanthrōpia* attributed to Ptolemy I (*Ap.* I.186) indeed appears in Hellenistic literature as one of the basic notions of ideal kingship,[45]

42. See Marrou (1956) 226–28.

43. Philo in *Spec. Leg.* I.60–63 refers only to the belief of the ignorant mob (para. 60), because in that context he was eager to illustrate the moral and religious dangers facing Jews who turn to pagan mantics. This would have been less convincing had Philo seriously discussed the theological background of Greek mantics.

44. Lewy (1932) 122ff.; cf. Guttman (1958–63) I.69.

45. See p. 74 n. 65 above.

but this does not prove direct acquaintance with Greek political writing. The term was common in the *koinē* and recurs in Hellenistic documents,[46] as well as in Jewish Hellenistic literature,[47] including Pseudo-Aristeas (paras. 208, 265, 271), which may well have been known to the author,[48] and even in III Maccabees (3.18), which was extremely hostile to the pagan world and its culture.[49]

According to the Hezekiah story, the High Priest "possessed in writing their settling [*katoikēsis*] and *politeia*" (*Ap.* I.189). Chapter VI.4 will discuss what is actually meant in this context by *katoikēsis* and *politeia*.[50] But whatever the author had in mind, he was influenced by similar terms used by Hecataeus himself in his Jewish excursus (Diod. XL.3.3),[51] and by their current and even daily use in Ptolemaic Egypt. The influence of the Hecataeus excursus also appears in the passage on the large Jewish population (*Ap.* I.197; cf. Diod. XL.3.8).[52] In addition, it simply records the demographic pressures in the Judean Hills at the time of the first Hasmoneans,[53] as well as the first precept of the Pentateuch. It is not necessarily meant, as might be argued, to be an antithesis to the old Greek practice of infanticide (*ekthesis*).[54]

The account of Jerusalem contains two details that were thought to have been influenced by Greek literary models:[55] the city is described as "most beautiful" (*Ap.* I.196), and the Temple is said to be located

46. See Schubert (1937); Zuntz (1959) 25. Cf. Welles (1934) 373 on φιλαν-θρωπέω and φιλάνθρωπον.

47. See esp. Meisner (1970) 162–78. See also Feldman (1989) 152–53.

48. See p. 142 and n. 76 above.

49. On the author of III Maccabees and his circle, see pp. 176ff.

50. See below pp. 221ff.

51. Regarding Hecataeus's influence on the Hezekiah story, see pp. 227–28 below.

52. See Lewy (1932) 127; M. Stern (1974–84) I.43.

53. On the overpopulation of Judea, see Bar-Kochva (1977) 170, 174–75, 191–94; *id.* (1989) 56–57.

54. On references to high Jewish birth rates in Hellenistic and Roman literature and their purpose, see M. Stern (1974–84) I.33. To the sources quoted add Diod. I.77.7, 80.3 (Hecataeus on the Egyptians); Strabo XV.1.59 (Megasthenes on the Indians). On the new trend with regard to child rearing in Hellenistic literature and practice, see Rostovtzeff (1940) II.623–24; Deissmann-Merten (1984) 276–78; Golden (1990) 173.

55. See Lewy (1932) 128ff.; Guttman (1958–63) I.69; M. Stern (1974–84) I.43; Doran (1985) 918, n. k.

"nearly in the center of the city" (I.198), while in fact it was built on the northeastern hill. However, the beauty of the city and its surroundings are lauded in the celebrated verses of Psalm 48, and could well have been reported by pilgrims from the Egyptian Diaspora. Coming from a flat land, they would certainly have been impressed by the hilly surroundings of the city. As for the location of the Temple, I have already mentioned that the Temple is not said to have been "in the center" as in a number of Greek utopian and philosophical works, but—significantly—"nearly in the center," and that this description accords with the topography of Alexandria.[56]

With regard to the report on the Temple, it has been argued that it is based on stereotypical temple accounts found in Hellenistic literature. Lewy tried to prove this by a comparison with Euhemerus's imaginary description of the Panchaean temple (preserved in Diod. V.42.6–44.5, VI.1.6).[57] However, there is no similarity whatsoever between the two accounts, neither in structure nor in detail.[58] A note that closes the report of the Jerusalem Temple has also been quoted as reflecting acquaintance with the "characteristics of a Greek temple":[59] Pseudo-Hecataeus states that in the Jewish Temple there are "no statue, nor any votive offerings, and absolutely no plants, resembling neither a grove nor anything similar" (*Ap.* I.199). However, the predominance of all these in Greek (and Egyptian) temples could not have escaped the notice of Jewish inhabitants in Egypt and in a mixed Greek polis.[60]

56. See p. 146 and n. 23 above.

57. Lewy (1932) 127.

58. Lewy (ibid.) quotes the references in Euhemerus to the antiquity, splendor, and "favorable location" of the Panchaean temple of Zeus Triphylias as well as those to its size (Diod. V.42.6–44, VI.1.6–10). However, Pseudo-Hecataeus mentions antiquity, beauty, and size only with regard to the city of Jerusalem (para. 196), not the Temple. These details are missing in Euhemerus's account of the Panchaean city. As far as the Jerusalem Temple is concerned, the size of its wall is given, but not of the building itself, and the rest of the description bears no resemblance to Euhemerus's detailed account of the location, splendor, decoration, architecture, and surroundings of the Panchaean temple. Thus, for instance, the latter is located on the top of a lofty hill, 60 stades from the city (Diod. V.42.6, VI.1.6).

59. See Lewy (1932) 129–30.

60. To offer just one parallel: Jewish inhabitants of Haifa in Israel know quite well that the temple of the Persian Baha'i sect on Mt. Carmel is surrounded by

Hans Lewy tried to trace typically Greek features even in the Mosollamus story (I.201–4). That Mosollamus's characterization is not typically Greek, and that the author was ignorant of the theological background, terminology, and practices of Greek divination has been shown above. Lewy's additional argument, that the literary features of the story disclose the direct influence of Greek tragedy,[61] is also unwarranted.

Lewy seems to have indicated as an influence the anecdote about Diogenes the Cynic ridiculing a seer,[62] but this must be rejected: it is narrated in a fictitious epistle written in the first century B.C.[63] At the same time, although it may have been quite a popular motif, I would not rule out the possibility that the author drew some inspiration from one of Aesop's fables containing a similar moral.[64] Fables were, in any case, elementary reading and composition material in Greek education.[65]

Finally, the linguistic and stylistic quality of the fragments should be examined. The very use of the Greek language is in itself no evidence: Demetrius the chronographer (second half of the third century B.C.), who wrote a stylistically dull and poor account of Jewish history, certainly does not belong in the same category as Pseudo-Aristeas, Jason of Cyrene, or Aristobulus. The same applies to Eupolemus, whose Greek is rightly characterized as "pompous, crude, and poor," and tending to Hebraic structure.[66] The Greek of Pseudo-Hecataeus can be evaluated only on the basis of the passages quoted in direct speech, mainly the two longest and most complete fragments, the account of Jerusalem and the Temple (I.197–99) and the Mosollamus story (I.201–4). This does not provide much material, but the general features are quite clear.

---

beautiful gardens, and its shrine is decorated with marvelous carpets, while only a few of them know anything about the Baha'i religion and its literature.

61. Lewy (1932) 129–30. See also Holladay (1983) 334 n. 52.

62. See Lewy (1932) 129 and n. 4. The letter: *EG*, Diog. no. 38 (p. 253). The contents are summarized on p. 64 above.

63. See the summary of research on the origin and dating of the "epistle" by Malherbe (1977) 14–22, esp. 14 n. 1.

64. See fable no. 170, ed. Hausrath (Leipzig, 1970). While the fable may have influenced the story, I do not, of course, suggest that they have the same point; see pp. 64–65 above.

65. See, e.g., Marrou (1956) 215, 239.

66. See, Jacoby, *RE* s.v. "Eupolemos," 1229; Goodman in Schürer et al. (1973–86) III.519.

The vocabulary by and large lives up to the norms of the contemporary literary *koinē*. The grammar is, however, less satisfactory; there are a number of instances of grammatical awkwardness. To be on the safe side, here are a few examples just from the Mosollamus episode:

1. *Ap.* I.201, ἐμοῦ ... βαδίζοντος συνηκολούθει τις ... : (συν)α-κολούθει requires dative, not genitive. If ἐμοῦ ... βαδίζοντος is a genitive absolute, συνηκολούθει remains without an indirect object. Such a loose construction would not have been used by anyone who had mastered his Greek.[67]

2. I.201, ἱκανῶς κατὰ ψυχὴν εὔρωστος: whether one reads the adverbial ἱκανῶς of codex I of Eusebius or the adjectival ἱκανός of manuscript L and the transmission, the Greek would be rather strange. The author—here—might be saved from blame if we assume a serious corruption of the archetype.[68]

3. I.201, ὁμολογουμένως ... ἄριστος: an adverb can be used as an attributive adjective even in Attic (οἱ ἐνθάδε στρατιῶται and the like), but not in a context where one would expect a verb to follow (for example, with this adverb, ἐνομίζετο). Even if the reading ὁμολογούμενος of L and Eusebius is correct (which is rather doubtful),[69] the combination of two adjectives like ὁμολογούμενος ἄριστος is not Greek. One would have expected at least ἄριστος εἶναι.

4. I.204, πῶς γὰρ ... ἀπήγγελεν: the whole sentence is ungrammatical. Assuming that τὴν αὐτοῦ σωτηρίαν οὐ προϊδών is in a sense causal ("since it did not foresee ..., then how could it," etc.), one would have expected an apodosis such as πῶς ἄν ... ἡμῖν τι ὑγιὲς ἀπαγγείλειεν, with the verb in the aorist optative, to express future potentiality. As the text stands, we find ἀπήγγελλεν, which is in the imperfect indicative, expressing a plain "rejected condition" in the present. This is inappropriate in the context. A confusion in dictation between ἀπήγγελλεν and ἀπαγγείλειεν is unlikely, if only for reasons of pronunciation. The next sentence, which is a proper "rejected condition" in the past, makes this clear, together with the fact that our author was not sure of his conditional sentences.

---

67. On loose genitive absolute in the *koinē*, see Blass and Debrunner (1967) §423, but none of their examples is quite like this sentence.
68. Cf. p. 51 n. *g* above.
69. See the apparatus, p. 50 n. 18 above.

The style of the fragments is an odd mixture: the geographic fragment is written in a fluent paratactic style, using simple sentences without subordinate clauses. It resembles the traditional style of itinerary literature. The style of the Mosollamus story is different and syntactically rather diverse: the introduction (I.201) comprises a long, complicated period, employing extended clauses, a common rhetorical device. The episode itself (202–4), which should have been recounted in an entertaining and exciting manner, is told in a monotonous and boring style, two paragraphs (202–4a) sounding especially cumbersome. They contain a cluster of ten participial constructions (including seven genitive absolutes). The use of many participles can be expected in an *epitomē,* and may occur in a historical narrative that tries to compress years and events, but the text is not an abbreviation, since it records in great detail occurrences that took place within a very short time, and even includes an imaginary dialogue. The unusual frequency of the participial forms, the change of the cases, and particularly the recurring changes of subject, make the sentences extremely strained. The style of these paragraphs recalls that of a *grammatikos* trying to summarize the plot of a tragedy or the like. Only the dialogue between Mosollamus and the seer (203–4) is of a much higher literary quality, using a fluent and simple "periodic" style. Josephus clearly did not rephrase the narrative part of the episode. This is not his style, even when abbreviating accounts of other authors. Moreover, it was pointed out above that Josephus himself stresses that the text of the episode is a quotation (200, 201); that subsequently referring the reader to the treatise itself (205), he must have striven to be accurate; and that the contents of the paragraphs show that they are not an abbreviation.[70]

This mixing of styles and standards is occasionally also discernible in the employment of expressions and phrases: thus, on the one hand, the author three times uses, in a complimentary context, the word ἄνθρωπος (186, 187, 201), which in literature (as well as in Hellenistic papyri)[71] can have a somewhat pejorative sense, instead of the common ἀνήρ. On the other hand, the author also uses a slightly more literary expression such as εἴπερ τις ἄλλος (187, "if indeed anyone was"), and understatements such as τὴν ψυχὴν οὐκ ἀνόητος (187, "not unintelligent in his mind").

70. See pp. 70–71 above.
71. See Preisigke (1924) I.122–23, 126.

One must conclude that the author imitated various (even extremely different) styles. These were known to him from historical, geographical, rhetorical, and "grammatical" literature. While having attained some proficiency in these styles, he was obviously no very gifted writer, employing them inconsistently, and at least once not in the right context. The impression is of an author who had received tutoring in the primary subjects of Greek education, but by no means comprehensively. His education did not include, for example, basic poetical texts, and it certainly did not extend to philosophical literature. Consequently the overall effect is only partly satisfactory.

The standard of vocabulary and the very ability to employ a variety of styles should not mislead us in evaluating the author's degree of Hellenization. Even without attending the educational system of the gymnasium, linguistically talented orientals who were brought up using their mother tongue would have been capable of attaining a sufficient degree of proficiency to express themselves in a reasonable Greek style after taking private tuition or the like. The Greek of Pseudo-Hecataeus is far superior to that of Berossus the Babylonian,[72] but not to that of Manetho.[73] These two, who served in oriental temples at the beginning of the Hellenistic period, had fewer opportunities to communicate with Greeks and practice their language than would a Jew from Alexandria (or even from the rest of Egypt) of the late second or early first century B.C. For determining the position of the author in relation to the cultural and religious divisions within the Jewish community, it is important to stress that his Greek is less impressive, certainly less sophisticated (not necessarily always

72. On the poor language and style of Berossus, see von Gutschmid (1893) IV.449ff.; Schnabel (1923) 29–32. On his life: Burstein (1978) 5–6; Kuhrt (1987) 48ff. Burstein's conjecture that at one time or another Berossus had served in the Seleucid court is doubtful and does not accord with some of his own assumptions. For an evaluation of Manetho's Greek, see von Gutschmid (1893) IV.419.

73. On Manetho's life, see Waddel (1940) ix–xiv; Helck (1956) 15ff.; Fraser (1972) I.504–5; Mendels (1990). Josephus's great appreciation of Manetho's Greek culture (*Ap.* I.73) cannot be substantiated by the surviving fragments. From the following sentence it appears that Manetho's frequent criticism of Herodotus (cf. Waddel fr. 88) is what mainly impressed Josephus. No wonder Manetho was eager to become acquainted with the celebrated Greek account of ancient Egypt.

less accurate), than that of a number of Jewish Hellenistic authors: Aristobulus and Artaphanus in earlier generations, Pseudo-Aristeas in his time,[74] and Jason of Cyrene, who may have written his great work in those years; not to mention later Jewish authors such as Philo, or the authors of the Wisdom of Solomon,[75] IV Maccabees, and Joseph and Asenath. A similar level of familiarity with Greek language and culture (though dissimilar in style) is evinced in III Maccabees.[76]

3. JEWISH EDUCATION

Just as the author's Hellenistic education has been overestimated, the breadth of his Jewish education has not yet been properly appreciated.[77] This appears from the references to Jewish ritual practices. Some of them allude to the priests; others to the Temple. With regard to the priests we have established above the accuracy of the statements about their abstention from wine in the Temple and their indulgence in rituals of purification "night and day" (*Ap.* I.199).[78] To these must be added the reference to the tithes. The author states that the priests receive "the tithe of the produce" (I.188), while according to the Pentateuch tithes were to be given to the Levites (Num. 18.21, 24). The sentence has been much discussed, and scholars have tried to apply it to the controversy over the authenticity of the book.[79] Taken by itself, it can support neither of the two opposing views.[80] The conclusion that the book was written in the time of the Hasmonean kingdom puts the sentence in the right perspective: it records the practice of the Hasmoneans, which

74. On the Greek of Pseudo-Aristeas, see the comprehensive study of Meecham (1935) 46ff., 154ff., 311ff.; cf. Tcherikover (1961a) 320.

75. See the analysis of its style by Gärtner (1912); Reese (1970) 1–30; Winston (1979) 14–18.

76. On the author's Greek education and knowledge of the Greek language, see Tcherikover (1961a) 350–51, 356–58.

77. The scholars who hold the author to be a priest (see pp. 145–46 and n. 16 above) mention only the reference to the stones of the altar (para. 188; see esp. Wacholder [1974] 270). The only detailed discussion of the account of the Temple is by Zipser (1871) 79–88, who accepts the book as authentically Hecataean. His analysis is, however, sometimes inaccurate, and he often draws the wrong conclusions.

78. See pp. 144–45 above.

79. See esp. Schaller (1963) 22–26; and the response of Gager (1969) 137–38.

80. So, rightly, M. Stern (1974–84) I.41; Holladay (1983) 326 n. 13.

was contrary to the rules of the Pentateuch. The new practice may already have been introduced before the Hasmonean period, but this cannot be proved. It can only be said with certainty that the Hasmonean rulers insisted on compliance with the new practice and employed tough administrative measures to enforce it.[81] We thus see that in this case Pseudo-Hecataeus follows the current practice of his age, and not the old written law.

The number attributed to the Jewish priests (*Ap.* I.188) also deserves attention in this context, although it is irrelevant to the question of the author's education. Pseudo-Hecataeus states: "All the Jewish priests who receive the tithe of the produce and administer public matters number at most about one thousand five hundred." This estimate considerably falls short of the number of priests at the time of the Restoration (Ezra 2.36–38). It has therefore been assumed that the figure approximately reflects the number of the Jerusalem priests alone (cf. Neh. 11.10–14; I Chron. 9.13).[82] The statement, however, refers to "all the priests." As the sentence qualifies the priests as those who are engaged in public matters, it behooves us to accept the alternative that Pseudo-Hecataeus gives only the number of the priests who were occupied in public administration.[83] This interpretation gains support from the context: the sentence does not appear in the framework of the account of ritual duties of the priests and the Temple, but follows the passage that elaborates on the leadership and administrative skills of Hezekiah the High Priest (*Ap.* I.187). The number quoted cannot be verified, but integration of such a number of priests in the royal administration of the Hasmoneans in the generation of Pseudo-Hecataeus does make sense, especially in view of the pro-Sadducean policy of Alexander Jannaeus and his father, John Hyrcanus, in his last years.

The author's knowledge is rather impressive when referring to cult objects of the Temple. Two points deserve attention. First, his version does not contain any allegorical interpretation or any Hellenistic feature. This stands in sharp contrast to Philo, Pseudo-Aristeas, and Eupolemus, the Jewish Hellenistic authors who elaborate on the Temple's

---

81. See, e.g., Alon (1957) 83–92; Oppenheimer (1977) 38–42; Bar-Kochva (1977) 185ff. Cf. M. Stern and Holladay, *locc. citt.* (n. 80).

82. So Büchler (1895) 49; M. Stern (1974–84) I.42; Doran (1985) 917 n. d.

83. Similarly Schlatter (1893) 94; Klein (1939) 37–38.

cult objects.[84] Second, the fragment basically accords with the available information about cult objects of the Second Temple. They partially differed from those known from the time of the First Temple. This shows that the author drew his information not from the Pentateuch or the Books of Kings, but from contemporary reports.

His account opens with the stone altar. According to Pseudo-Hecataeus it was made of unhewn stones, placed outside the main building, and measured "twenty cubits long and ten cubits high" (I.198). At the time of the First Temple there were stone altars only in the provinces. The offering altar in the Tabernacle and the First Temple was made of bronze. It was replaced in the visionary temple of Ezekiel and at the time of the Second Temple by a stone altar.[85] The altar was placed near the entrance to the shrine (Jos. *Bell.* V.225; Philo, *Spec. Leg.* I.274). The construction of this altar of unhewn stones, based on the Torah instructions for provincial stone altars (Exod. 20.25; cf. Deut. 27.5–6),[86] is known from the period before and after the defilement of the Temple by Antiochus IV (I Macc. 4.47; Josephus, *loc. cit.*; Philo, *loc. cit.*; Middot 3.4).

No less instructive are the measurements quoted by Pseudo-Hecataeus. They equal those of the bronze altar, its predecessor, built by Solomon, as listed by II Chronicles (4.1), and differ from both the much smaller bronze altar of the Tabernacle (Exod. 27.1) and the visionary altar of Ezekiel (43.13–17). According to Josephus, the stone altar of the Herodian Temple measured $50 \times 50 \times 15$ cubits (*Bell.* V.225), but the Mishna gives other measurements: for the lower base, 32×32; and for the upper surface, 24×24 (Middot 3.1). The latter information, which originated from a knowledgeable eyewitness,[87] is much more detailed and elaborate, and may therefore be more accurate. As far as the pre-Herodian stone altar is concerned, the only direct piece of

84. See Philo's allegorical interpretations of the cult objects in *Spec. Leg.* I.74ff., and esp. *Quaest. Exod.* II.52ff. For the Hellenistic features in Pseudo-Aristeas, see paras. 50ff.; and in Eupolemus: Lieberman (1962) 173.

85. See the survey of M. Haran in *Encyclopaedia Biblica* (Jerusalem, 1962) IV.772–73; Yadin (1977) I.186. Cf. esp. Exod. 38.1–7, I Kings 8.64, Ezek. 9.2; and the references below.

86. Cf. pp. 149–50 above.

87. On Rabbi Eliezer ben Ya'acov as the source of the anonymous statements (סתם משנה) in tractate Middot, see Epstein (1957) 31–36; Albeck (1959) 85–86, 220. Cf. esp. *PT* Yoma 2.2. (39d), *BT* Yoma 16a.

information that may be relevant[88] is the number, 20, that survived in a fragmentary account of the stone altar in one of the Qumran Aramaic scrolls.[89] In addition to that, the author of the Books of Chronicles may well have based the measurements of Solomon's bronze altar on the size of the stone offering altar of his time, in the late fifth century, as he frequently does when his source, the Books of Kings, does not contain the necessary information.[90] It seems probable, therefore, that Pseudo-Hecataeus indeed properly recorded the measurements of the stone altar of his time. That he relied on the information given in Chronicles is a less acceptable possibility: readership of this book was always rather limited. Philo, for instance, hardly ever refers to any biblical book outside the Pentateuch.[91]

The next item is a golden altar, located in "a great edifice" (*Ap.* I.198). The reference is to the golden incense altar (Exod. 30.1–10) that was placed inside the Temple.[92] The existence of this altar, known from Philo and Palestinian Second Temple sources,[93] is not recorded by Pseudo-Aristeas, who was familiar with Jewish religious practices and elaborates on the Temple and its objects. It is noteworthy that even the Mishnaic

---

88. The minority opinion of Rabbi Yosi in Middot 3.1 about the upper surface of the altar in the time of the Restoration (24 × 24 cubits) is an attempt to harmonize conflicting biblical references (including Ezekiel) and give the impression of a continuity between the periods. This appears from his terminology and argumentation. Rabbi Yosi ("the Galilean") belongs to the generation of the Bar-Kokhva Revolt, and his original comment underwent a later adaptation (see Epstein [1957] 36).

89. See Yadin (1977) I.186, referring to Baillet et al. (1962) 88–89.

90. The description of the Book of Chronicles as a midrash of the Book of Kings has been commonly accepted. The question is only whether and to what extent the author supplemented it by reliable sources for the period of the First Temple. See the survey of research in Japhet (1977) 334–36. For a new wave of contributions reviving the old extreme negative view, see Welten (1973); Mosis (1973); North (1974); Mackenzie (1984). Cf. Na'aman (1989).

91. On Philo's use of biblical books, see Knox (1940); Borgen (1981) 55, (1984) 258.

92. I Kings 6.22, II Chr. 4.19, I Macc. 4.49; Jos. *Bell.* V.215.

93. In addition to the sources mentioned above, see I Macc. 1.21; Jos. *Bell.* V.225; Philo, *Spec. Leg.* I.274; Temple Scroll, col. VIII (see Yadin [1977] II.23–26; the column describes the incense altar, though the word "gold" has not survived in the few barely legible lines that have come down to us).

tractate Middot, devoted to the Temple, fails to mention the golden altar. Only Mishna Hagiga (3.8) alludes to it.

Together with the golden altar, the author lists the celebrated golden lamp, which is mentioned by many Jewish and gentile sources. This is followed by the statement that the gold of these two objects weighed two talents (*Ap.* I.198). The lamp of the Tabernacle is said to have weighed one talent (Exod. 25.38–39), but there is no indication as to the weight of the gold of the incense altar. Pseudo-Hecataeus may have conjectured or known that the weight of the gold cover of the altar was equal to that of the lamp. At the same time I would not rule out the possibility that the original text referred only to the weight of the lamp. The Temple Scroll indeed states that the lamp, together with its various utensils, weighed two talents (col. IX, line 11). This may be an interpretation of the biblical verse,[94] but it can also accord with the real weight of the lamp and its utensils at the time of the Second Temple.

The allusion to the incense altar and the lamp ends with the sentence "Upon these [ἐπὶ τούτων; i.e., both the golden altar and the lamp] there is a light that is never extinguished night and day" (*Ap.* I.199). This is reported, at least for the time of the Second Temple, with regard to the lamp,[95] as well as the offering altar.[96] The information in Pseudo-Hecataeus may suggest that the same practice was also observed for the golden altar. However, it is also possible that the author confused the two altars, or that there is a slight copying error in the text (ἐπὶ τούτων instead of ἐπὶ τούτου), the original referring to the golden lamp alone.

Following the account of the main objects of the sanctuary, the author stresses that there were no statues, votive offerings, plants, or grove in the Temple (*Ap.* I.199). That statues were forbidden everywhere in the Temple does not require references, and an explicit prohibition on planting trees within the Temple precincts is known from the Pentateuch (Deut. 16.21) and seems to have been strictly

94. See Yadin (1977) II.28–29 on the dispute over the interpretation of Exod. 25.38–39.

95. See, e.g., Jos. *Ant.* III.199; Tamid 3.9, 6.1; *BT* Yoma 39b; Sabbat 39a–b. The practice in the Tabernacle was probably different; see Exod. 30.7–8, Lev. 24.2–3, I Sam. 3.3. But see Exod. 27.20.

96. See Philo, *Spec. Leg.* I.285; and see Lev. 6.9, 12, 13. Cf. II Macc. 1.19–22; Maimonides, *Temidim* II.1.

observed.[97] The reference to votive offerings requires more elaboration. Oriental and Greek temples abounded with these objects. They were carefully registered in official lists, some of which have come down to us.[98] For a monotheistic religion, which also rejected material representation of the divine, votive offerings must have presented an obvious threat. Though the Pentateuch regulates only dedications to the Temple treasury (Lev. 27.1–8, 16–24, 28), there is no explicit prohibition on the public display of votive offerings. On the contrary, Moses is said to have constructed a bronze serpent (Num. 21.8–9), which indeed was soon sanctified and acquired a cult of its own. There is sufficient evidence that votive offerings were not entirely absent from the two Temples, but the impression is that there were not many of them, nothing similar to the numbers found in pagan temples.

At the time of the First Temple we read only of the bronze serpent, which was finally destroyed by King Hezekiah (II Kings 18.4). The weapons of King David were also placed in the Temple (II Kings 11.10; cf. I Sam. 21.9). One may assume that at least during the time of the kings who introduced pagan cults into Jerusalem and the Temple, greater numbers of votive offerings were to be seen.

The only extant piece of information about votive offerings in the pre-Herodian Second Temple refers to "crowns" (I Macc. 1.21–22, 4.57).[99] They were placed there already at the time of the Jewish Restoration (Zech. 6.9–15, Middot 3.8). As they are the only items mentioned besides the ordinary Temple cult vessels later plundered by Antiochus IV, it may be that there were no other costly votive offerings in the Temple. If this is correct, it indicates that in the wake of the increasing monotheistic strictness at the time of the Restoration there was opposition to the display of votive offerings in the Temple. The crowns may have been regarded as a special case since they symbolized

---

97. The references quoted to support a contrary view by Zipser (1871) 86–87 are irrelevant for the Temple itself. The prohibition is also mentioned by Philo, *Spec. Leg.* I.74; *Leg. Alleg.* I.48–52.

98. On votive offerings in the Greek world, see Rouse (1902), which still remains the standard work on the subject.

99. The ἀσπιδίσκαι mentioned in the same verses are not small shields but משבצות זהב (gold rosettes? gold settings?) listed in the description of the original decoration of the Tabernacle (Exod. 28.13, 36.23). For the translation of משבצת as ἀσπιδίσκη, see the Septuagint, Exod. 28.13, 14, 25; 36.23, 26 (36.16, 18).

the authority of the High Priest as well as hopes for the return of the Davidic dynasty.[100] At the same time, allowance must be made for the possibility that the paucity of references to votive offerings in the pre-Herodian Temple is only accidental.[101]

Much more information about votive offerings is available for the Herodian Temple. A huge golden vine was located at the entrance (Jos. *Ant.* XV.394–95, *Bell.* V.210–12; Tac. *Hist.* V.5), and small private donations were placed on it (Middot 3.8). The vine seems to have symbolized first and foremost the Jewish nation.[102] A golden chain donated by Agrippa I was hung in the forecourt of the Temple (Jos. *Ant.* XIX.294), and the above-mentioned crowns were displayed inside the shrine. The presence of votive offerings in the Temple is also explicitly mentioned in the New Testament (Luke 21.5).[103] Philo, who mentions the prohibition on trees within the precincts of the Temple, does not refer to the question of votive offerings, although he endeavors to offer an allegorical explanation for the bronze serpent.[104]

100. On the textual question involved in the interpretation of Zech. 6.11, 14, and the meaning of the two crowns, see, e.g., Kaufman (1937–56) VIII.262–66; Uffenheimer (1961) 117–18; Meyers and Meyers (1987) 349–50, 362–64.

101. Jos. *Ap.* II.48, if it is to be trusted, does not say that the votive offerings were exhibited in the Temple. They could have been kept in the treasury, as was done with private donations (see n. 103 below). Goodenough's conjecture ([1953–68] V.99–103; already anticipated by Zipser [1871] 86) that the huge vine of the Herodian Temple actually replaced the vine donated by Aristobulus II to the Romans (Jos. *Ant.* XIV.34–36) is unwarranted. Moreover, if the reading of the MSS "from Alexander the Jew" is correct, that vine could not have been taken by Aristobulus from the Temple. On the textual question and the historical interpretation, see M. Stern (1974–84) I.275.

102. First suggested by Holtzmann (1913) 87ff. Cf. Isa. 5.1–5, Jer. 2.21, Ezek. 17.5–8, Ps. 80.9–12. However, the vines on Jewish coins and ossuaries need not be understood in the same sense. On the symbolism of the vine, see also Goodenough (1953–68) XIII *passim.* The golden chains mentioned in Middot 3.8 may have their origin in the description of the Tabernacle (Exod. 28.14).

103. The dedication of a "leg," "hand," scepter, etc., made of precious metals (Mishna, ʿArachin 5.1; Tosefta, ʿArachin 3.1) obviously refers to the Temple treasury (הקדש), as do all other dedications listed in that Mishna and Tosefta. Decorated doors (like the Nicanor Gates) donated to the temple, and possibly also such other immovable structures, are not votive offerings in the strict sense and therefore do not concern us here.

104. On trees, see n. 97 above. On the bronze serpent, see Philo, *De Agricultura* 97. Cf. Sap. Sal. 16.5–6.

The statement in Pseudo-Hecataeus, which refers to the pre-Herodian Temple, may then be basically correct, or it may reflect a strict sectarian approach that opposed votive offerings. The danger of votive offerings' tending to acquire a cult of their own was certainly well known to Diaspora Jews. The wish to avoid any resemblance between Jewish and gentile cults is evident in the statement under discussion. Moreover, it may well be that the author wished to express a negative opinion about the practice of the Oniad temple in Leontopolis. Josephus stresses that Onias IV decorated his temple with votive offerings (*Bell.* VII.428). In a letter said to have been sent by Onias IV to Ptolemy VI, asking for permission to build a temple in Leontopolis, the site chosen for the temple is praised for being "most suitable, ... full of [a variety of] colorful trees" (Jos. *Ant.* XIII.66). Whether the letter is authentic or not, it may indicate that the trees were later left in the precinct of the temple. If this is true, the reference to the absence of trees in the Jerusalem Temple is also meant to deplore the practice in Leontopolis.

In view of the author's relatively abundant knowledge about the Temple, the absence from the list of the golden table ("show-bread table"), one of its three most celebrated cult objects (Jos. *Bell.* V.216, Menahot 11.5),[105] is rather surprising.[106] I would venture to guess that he was reluctant to refer to the golden table because of the detailed (and imaginary) account by Pseudo-Aristeas, his older contemporary, about its design, construction, and decoration by the artisans of Ptolemy II (paras. 51–72). Pseudo-Hecataeus, who was strongly against gentile influence in religious matters, must have been uneasy both about the role of a Ptolemaic king and workmen in constructing one of the holiest objects of the Jewish Temple and about its sources of inspiration in pagan art, no matter which table was in fact used in his time.[107] He may have felt that listing the table

105. The golden table was also commemorated on Jewish coins from the short reign of Mattathias Antigonus (see Meshorer [1982] I pl. 55 nos. Z.1–3).

106. It is less likely that Josephus omitted a reference to the table (cf. Schlatter [1893] 94). After describing the vessels, the quotation goes on to note the absence of statues, plants, and votive offerings.

107. On the possible influence of the Dionysian cult, see Büchler (1899) 198–99 n. 28; and on the similarity of certain features with those of utensils described by Callixenus (Athen. V.196ff., esp. 199b–c), see Hadas (1951) 47–48. But see Fraser (1972) I.697, II.975 n. 133. Cf. Rice (1983) 72. There is no

would also require some reference to the story circulated among Egyptian Jews concerning its origin, and therefore preferred to omit it altogether.

Another omission can enhance our appreciation of the author's knowledge of the Temple in his day. He does not mention the Ark of the Covenant. The ark played a central role in the Tabernacle and the First Temple, but disappeared at the time of the Babylonian exile and was not replaced in the Second Temple (Sekalim 6.1; cf. Jos. *Bell.* V.215–21). We see again that Pseudo-Hecataeus did not rely uncritically on the Bible, but based his information on up-to-date knowledge.

The author's acquaintance with Jewish traditions and cult, on the one hand, and his mediocre Greek style and ignorance of "Greek wisdom" and mantic practices, on the other, naturally raise the question of his mother tongue. Analysis of two "sensitive" cult terms suggests that Pseudo-Hecataeus used the Hebrew original of the Holy Scriptures and not the Greek translation. Thus he calls the temple altar *bōmos* (*Ap.* I.198) after applying the same term to pagan altars (I.193). In the Septuagint the word designates only gentile altars. Wishing to distinguish the latter from the legitimate altars of the Jewish God, the translators invented the term *thysiastērion* for the Temple altars. They were even careful to differentiate between pagan altars and the "illegal" Israelite altars (*bamōt* in Hebrew) located in the provinces, which were so deplored by the Books of Kings, and consistently refrained from employing the Greek *bōmoi* (despite the obvious similarity with the Hebrew), always using the literal translation *hypsēla*.[108] The other case is the word *neōs*, which is used by Pseudo-Hecataeus to designate gentile temples (I.193),[109] while the

---

resemblance between the table of Pseudo-Aristeas and that of the Pentateuch, the Hasmonean coins, and the Mishna (contrary to Meshorer [1982] I.95–96: the legs are different; there is no figure for the width in Pseudo-Aristeas, and his table is not necessarily rectangular [see paras. 58–60]). Be the historicity of the report of Pseudo-Aristeas as it may, the show-bread table was stolen by Antiochus Epiphanes in his outburst to the Jerusalem Temple in the year 168 (I Macc. 1.22), and a new one was brought to the Temple shortly after its purification by Judas Maccabaeus in 164 B.C. (ibid. 4.49).

108. See the discussion in Daniel (1966) 27–53.

109. The word *neōs* in para. 196, which refers to the Jewish Temple, appears in an introductory sentence phrased by Josephus, but it could be influenced by a similar usage in Pseudo-Hecataeus.

Septuagint reserves it for the Jewish Temple alone (also in the forms *naos* and *naios*).[110]

The terminology of the Septuagint influenced early Jewish Hellenistic authors like Pseudo-Aristeas and Jason of Cyrene, who applied only *naos*, and even the Jewish neologism *thysiastērion*, to the Jerusalem Temple and altar, respectively, though they wrote an idiomatic and sophisticated Greek and the former even pretended to be a gentile author.[111] As Pseudo-Hecataeus demonstrates extreme zealousness against pagan altars and temples and devotion toward the Jewish faith and cult, one cannot believe that he had been brought up on the Septuagint or that he used it regularly. The concurrent use of identical Greek terms for the Jewish and pagan cults would have imposed difficulties mainly in respect to religious services in synagogues. The conclusion is therefore that Pseudo-Hecataeus was brought up on the Hebrew Bible, and used it in religious ceremonies and for study and reference. He would not have felt the need to differentiate in Greek between Jewish and pagan altars and temples, and would have had no theological inhibitions on this point. It is, however, difficult to affirm that Hebrew was his mother tongue or the language he used daily at home.

4. THE RELIGIOUS DIVISION OF EGYPTIAN JEWRY AND THE AUTHOR'S AFFILIATION

The conclusions about the author's Greek and Jewish education, together with a number of explicit statements in the fragments, make

---

110. *Hieron*, the other Greek word for "temple," appears in the Septuagint for both gentile and Jewish temples. The same applies to Pseudo-Hecataeus (paras. 192, 199).

111. Cf. also, e.g., Sap. Sal. 9.8. Philo, however, uses *naos* and *hieron* interchangeably, and his common word for "altar" is *bōmos*. He even indicates that the word *thysiastērion* was a Jewish invention (*Leges* I.290) and offers an etymological explanation (*Vit. Mos.* II.106). This should not come as a surprise: Philo did not hesitate to employ pagan divine terms and titles in his account of the Jewish faith and its institutions (see Wolfson [1948] I.27ff., esp. 38ff.). In this respect, as in many others, Philo differs from other Jewish Hellenistic authors. Notably, *bōmos* appears once in II Maccabees (2.19) to designate the altar in Jerusalem, in the introduction to the book written by the epitomator, although elsewhere he uses *thysiastērion*.

possible a reconstruction of the religious-cultural position of this Egyptian Jew. The following points are essential:

1. Pseudo-Hecataeus did not have any knowledge of Greek philosophy.

2. He does not apply the Greek cultural and literary heritage when interpreting Jewish traditions.

3. The author's acquaintance with Greek culture and customs is rather superficial.

4. There is no trace of allegorical or symbolical interpretation of the Pentateuch.

5. The Hebrew Bible is his book of study and reference, not the Greek Septuagint.

6. He demonstrates a relatively good knowledge of the cult of the Jerusalem Temple.

7. His book expresses absolute loyalty to the Jewish faith and its religious practices, even to the extent of expressing a readiness to undergo persecution and martyrdom.

8. He advocates extreme intolerance toward pagan cults and even physical violence against their cult objects and places of worship.

In order to realize the significance of these points, it is worth comparing him briefly with Philo Judaeus, the most eloquent and prominent spokesman of Hellenistic Judaism. With regard to points 1–5, Philo differs entirely from Pseudo-Hecataeus. Points 6 and 7 are well in line with Philo's writings. Point 8 stands in sharp contrast to recurring statements by Philo.[112] Points 1, 2, and 4 are known to have been matters of contention within the Jewish community of Alexandria. These contrasts and parallels can guide us in locating Pseudo-Hecataeus among the various religious streams and groups of Egyptian Jewry.

The internal religious division of Egyptian Jewry appears from indications and a number of explicit references that have come down to us, mainly in Philo's works, Pseudo-Aristeas, III Maccabees, and the Wisdom of Solomon. They can be supplemented by statements and views expressed in other books and literary fragments of the Egyptian Jewish community, as well as by archaeological findings. It should,

---

112. See the sources, p. 100 n. 146 above. The erection of the altar in Iamnia at the time of Caligula is described by Philo as a deliberate provocation (*Leg. ad Gaium* 200–202); hence the implied justification of its destruction.

however, be stressed that the precise dating of these sources and the question of the integrity of certain literary works impose considerable difficulties. Most of these are to be dated to the first century A.D., a number of generations after the composition of Pseudo-Hecataeus.

There is still no comprehensive study of the subject. Some important papers have been devoted to certain aspects,[113] and others are referred to in the numerous studies on Jewish Hellenistic literature (mainly on Philo),[114] or on the history of the community and its external struggles.[115] This is not enough: essential questions have not been discussed, or the evidence offered has been unsatisfactory.[116] However, despite the difficulties connected with the sources and the lacunae in research, a general picture can be sketched of the main streams and the characteristics of certain religious groups belonging to Egyptian Jewry. As the subject deserves a comprehensive study, which cannot be made within the framework of this book, I shall try to avoid making references to information and conclusions that are well known, and shall refrain from technical discussions that cannot significantly change the general picture. At the same time, it must be admitted that not all the statements made in this survey are supported by firm textual evidence. Some are based rather on general impressions and historical deductions.

Scholars usually refer to three main streams among the Jews of Hellenistic Egypt: conservatives, allegorists, and nonpracticing Jews. They are also named "orthodox" (or "traditionalists," "literalists"), "Hellenistic Jews" (or "liberals"), and "atheists" (or "assimilators"), respectively. To these should be added another stream (or rather trend): the "syncretists."[117] Each of these streams was divided into groups and

---

113. See esp. Friedländer (1903) 56–74; Shroyer (1936); Goodenough (1953–68) II.153ff.; Feldman (1960). Of a more general character are the discussions by Tcherikover (1957a), (1958) 59–85, (1961a) 294–315, 366–92; Schürer et al. (1973–86) III.126–37.

114. See, e.g., Goodenough (1935) 7ff.; Stein (1937) 290–92; Tcherikover (1961a) 339–65; Wolfson (1948) I.55–86 *et passim*; Bickerman (1976–80) I.246–81; Collins (1983) 2–24 *et passim*; Mendelson (1982) 2–28.

115. Tcherikover (1963) 116–59; Smallwood (1970) 3–14; Alberro (1976) 100–212; Kasher (1985) 208ff.

116. On some of the lacunae, see Tcherikover (1961a) 291–315, esp. 309ff.

117. For somewhat different classifications see Friedländer (1903) 56–57; Stein (1937) 290–92; Wolfson (1948) I.55ff.; Feldman (1960). Cf. Jacobson (1983) 19–20; Feldman (1993) 65–83. The existence of syncretistic groups was

subgroups. The "syncretists" and the different nonpracticing groups ("Yom Kippur Jews," apostates, hedonists, assimilators, atheists, etc.) do not concern us in this context. I shall also skip over the extreme conservative (or "orthodox") group and the extreme groups of allegorists such as the antinomians, on the one hand, and the *therapeutai*, who sought solitude and kept strictly to the religious precepts, on the other. In order to locate the author of Pseudo-Hecataeus among the religious divisions of Egyptian Jewry, we must concentrate our attention on the moderate allegorists and on two conservative groups, the "moderates" and the "progressives."[118]

It should be stressed that we are still puzzled about certain essential questions, and there is some uncertainty in the definitions suggested for the various groups. The boundaries between them were not always clear-cut, and they were not homogeneous. People who belonged to one group could also show features characteristic of the other groups. There were also splinter groups. This was reflected in the communal organization. It is recorded that there were many synagogues in Alexandria (Philo, *Leg. ad Gaium* 132; cf. *Spec. Leg.* II.62), each serving as a community center.[119] As was customary in later generations, membership in a synagogue was determined first and foremost by a person's affiliation to a religious subgroup, and only secondarily by socioeconomic class and place of residence.[120]

---

stressed by Feldman, and it seems that there is enough material to believe that they had their own synagogues and organization. Grouping them with the conservatives or the allegorists cannot be justified. Artapanus may perhaps have been their representative in literature, and there is ample evidence for their existence in epigraphical findings and art objects. The dominance of syncretistic elements in the archaeological material may indicate the numerical strength of this stream. Some of them who were even initiated into the Greek and Egyptian mysteries are mentioned in Philo's writings.

118. It stands to reason that there was also a group of extreme conservatives, along lines somewhat similar to the extreme orthodox Jewry of the modern Diaspora. However, we have no explicit references to this effect.

119. On the various activities in the synagogue, see the summaries of Friedländer (1903) 26–32; Alberro (1976) 157–66; Kasher (1987).

120. On the arrangement of the seats in the celebrated, magnificent synagogue of Alexandria according to trades, see *PT Succa* 5.1 (55a), *BT Succa* 51b. We do not know which stream this synagogue belonged to, and it is difficult to assess the reliability of the Talmudic tradition according to which the court of the Alexandrian community was located in this synagogue (which means

The many synagogues in Alexandria represented the streams, groups, and subgroups.

The moderate allegorists are considered to have been the most important and distinguished group among the Jews in Egypt. Their great contribution to literature, especially the copious works by Philo that have been preserved, is mainly responsible for this evaluation. In contrast, only a few writings of their opponents have reached us, and they are of lesser merit. For this reason many scholars tend to identify the moderate allegorists with Alexandrian Jewry by and large, and unjustifiably regard them as the numerically dominant group among the Jews of the community.

The most characteristic feature of the moderate allegorists was their language of religious study and cult: the Pentateuch was read in synagogues in the Greek versions of the Septuagint. Greek was also the liturgical language of the synagogue, used in prayer, biblical exegesis, and sermons. The allegorists even argued for a divine inspiration and special sanctity of the Septuagint and its advantages over Hebrew copies of the Pentateuch that were available in Alexandria (Pseudo-Aristeas 30;[121] Philo, *Vit. Mos.* II.37–40). Their mother tongue and literary language was Greek. For most of them this was their only language, and even the few who had knowledge of Hebrew did not all use it correctly.

The allegorists acquired a comprehensive knowledge of Greek culture. This included the basic disciplines of the Hellenistic curriculum (grammar, dialectics, geometry, arithmetic, astronomy, and music),[122] and beyond these, first and foremost, philosophy. Such a Jew had broad acquaintance with Greek literature from Homer onwards. Consequently he was at home with both Greek mythology and Greek philosophical writings. His practical training and reading provided him with an adequate style and vocabulary.

The allegorists employed their acquaintance with Greek tradition (particularly with Greek philosophy) in the interpretation of the Holy

---

that it was the central synagogue). Philo, *Leg. ad Gaium* 134, mentions a synagogue that was larger and more splendid than the others, but does not designate it as the central synagogue. On the role of this synagogue and its arrangements, see the hypothesis of Krauss (1922) 261–63.

121. The meaning of the words relevant to our case are disputed. See the interpretation of Bickerman (1976–80) I.228; and also Howard (1971) 399ff. Cf. *BT* Megilla 9a.

122. See the detailed discussion of Mendelson (1982) 4–24.

Scriptures. Their explanations filled the Pentateuch with new meanings and created a fusion between the two cultures. The purpose of this was to make the old tradition more acceptable to contemporary Jews so as to prevent assimilation, while at the same time helping Jews to integrate themselves into the life of Hellenistic society. Certain Jewish Hellenistic authors, like Philo, seem to have believed sincerely that this was theologically the right method and that they thus correctly served the divine. In order to reach their goal, the allegorists applied the interpretive methods customary in the Greek world that were so favored by the interpreters of Homer. Philo was not the first Jewish allegorist, and he mentions interpreters who preceded him.[123] The allegorical interpretation supplemented the literal meanings of Pentateuch verses with new and entirely different meanings. Among the allegorists there were authors who applied more moderate methods of interpretation, such as Aristobulus the philosopher (second century B.C.), who preferred the "metaphorical explanation," the interpretation mainly of biblical anthropomorphisms as metaphors, and the author of Pseudo-Aristeas who offers symbolistic explanations for certain precepts without neglecting their literal meanings.[124] The name "allegorists," which employed to designate this stream, is thus somewhat misleading. At the same time it may well be that in the first century A.D., in the wake of Philo's monumental contribution, the allegorical interpretation became the dominant method among Jews who were trying to build a bridge between Judaism and Hellenism.

Alongside their "flexible" method of interpretation, the moderate allegorists adhered to the main theological principles of Second-Temple Judaism. They invested much effort in refuting pagan beliefs, including the more enlightened versions like the Euhemeristic interpretation and the Stoic religious conception.[125] Nevertheless they refrained from advocating violence, both physical and verbal (apart from references to the Egyptian animal cult and the mysteries), and explicitly warn against publicly insulting and ridiculing pagan beliefs and cults.[126] Ph

123. See Stein (1937) 175–76 and the references there.
124. See Stein (1929) 6–12, (1937) 23–30. Another conception and definition Heinemann (1948/9).
125. See, e.g., Pseudo-Aristeas 135–37; Philo, *Deca.* 52ff.; *Spec. Leg.* I.13 *De Contempl.* 3–9; *De Congressu* 133.
126. See p. 100 n. 146 above, and n. 112 on p. 169.

was even uneasy about the violent conquest of Canaan by the Israelites and its "purification," and therefore explained that the "Syrian and Phoenician" natives had left their lands to the Israelites of their own free will, out of respect and reverence for the Israelites' spiritual superiority (*Hyp. ap.* Eus. *PE* VIII.6.6–7).

As for the practical precepts, we are less certain. At least Philo strictly adhered to the precepts and treated the trivial commandments with as much care as the cardinal ones.[127] There is no doubt that the moderate allegorists observed the basic religious practices such as Sabbath, holidays, circumcision, and dietary laws. However, it may be that others (like mezuzah, fringes, and tefillin)[128] were neglected by some of them. Certain scholars think that the allegorists had a good knowledge of their Jewish past and that they were acquainted with Palestinian halachic and midrashic traditions.[129] The nature of their halachic system is a matter of controversy: though there is no doubt that they were influenced by Palestinian Pharisees as well as Sadducees, it seems that they developed certain local practices of their own.

The moderate allegorists were well integrated into the economic systems and administration of Hellenistic Egypt, and some of them held senior positions in the government. A man such as Philo attended the theater, chariot races, and boxing and wrestling competitions.[130] If one can judge from Pseudo-Aristeas, the "allegorists" did not refrain from dining in the company of gentiles and participated in symposia after taking the necessary precautions with regard to kosher food.[131] The range of their occupations is not known, but there are reasons to

127. See, e.g., the explanations of Philo, *De Migr. Abrahami* 92–93. This is also well reflected in the treatises *Deca.* and *Spec. Leg.* Cf. Pseudo-Aristeas 127. See also the survey of Alberro (1976) 172–81.

128. Some scholars tend to deduce this from Pseudo-Aristeas 158–60. But these paragraphs can also be taken to indicate the contrary.

129. Philo's acquaintance with Pharisaic and Sadducean traditions has been much discussed in modern research. His deviations can be considered as reflecting local practices and interpretations. For grave historical mistakes, see, e.g., *Vit. Mos.* II.31, where he states that the High Priest who was involved in the translation of the Pentateuch into Greek was also king of Judea. However, this refers to a period that was not covered by the Bible.

130. See, e.g., Philo, *De Ebrietate* 177; *Quod Omnis Probus Sit* 26, 141; *De Provid.* II.58 (*ap.* Eus. *PE* VIII.14.58); Pseudo-Aristeas 284. See further Harris (1976).

131. See, e.g., Pseudo-Aristeas 121–22, 182–84.

believe that they belonged to the upper class.[132] The heavy expenses involved in acquiring a comprehensive Greek education support this assumption. It is hard, therefore, to think that the allegorists comprised a majority in the Jewish community of Alexandria, and they certainly did not in the country as a whole. At the same time, it seems that the socioeconomic status of the allegorists, as well as their relations with the governments, made them the most influential group in the community, to an extent greatly disproportionate with their numbers. Good examples of this are Philo himself and his brother Alexander, the rich customs agent, who both served as leaders of the Alexandrian community.

Despite the relatively abundant information scattered throughout Philo's writings on pedagogical matters, we are in the dark with regard to the institutional framework in which his group (and Egyptian Jews by and large) received their Greek and Jewish educations.[133] The regular educational institution in Hellenistic cities was the gymnasium, or rather the *ephēbeion*, the gymnasium for adolescents. As pagan cult occupied an important role in the life of the gymnasium, a number of scholars find it difficult to believe that Jews who strictly adhered to Jewish beliefs and precepts sent their children to the gymnasium. They think, therefore, that the Jewish community had its own institutions for Greek education, or that this education was acquired through private tutoring. As for Jewish education, it is thought that it was mainly based on attendance in the synagogue for many hours on the Sabbath, where the Torah was publicly read and interpreted and sermons were delivered (Philo, *Hyp. ap.* Eus. *PE* VIII.7.12–13; *Spec. Leg.* II.62). One scholar has suggested that a day school was operated in the synagogue. Private tutors and the transmission of traditions from fathers to sons certainly also played an important role in providing Jewish education. It seems that among the private tutors and preachers there were also Palestinian Jews.[134]

---

132. See esp. Tcherikover (1961a) 314–15.

133. See Colson (1916–17); Stein (1937) 49ff., (1938) 192–99; Marcus (1938); Wolfson (1948) I.78ff.; Alexandre (1967); 'Amir (1973) 240ff.; Alberro (1976) 166–72; Sandmel (1979) 12ff.; Borgen (1981) 108ff.; Mendelson (1982); Feldman (1993) 57–59, 63–64.

134. See Stein (1937) 61–62.

The characteristics of the moderate allegorists help us to understand the positions of the "moderate" and "progressive" conservatives.[135] The information available on the conservative stream is quite scant in comparison with the material on the allegorists. The sources are mainly casual references by opponents like Philo and Pseudo-Aristeas. These references find proper illustration in III Maccabees, which was probably written by a moderate conservative,[136] and the Wisdom of Solomon, which could be attributed to the "progressive" conservatives.

The moderate conservatives rejected the use of the Septuagint in the synagogue. They read and studied the Pentateuch in its original Hebrew, as they did prayers that consisted of selected passages from the Holy Scriptures. We do not know whether interpretation and preaching in their synagogues was also done in Hebrew. It may well be that there was no uniformity of practice. In the synagogues of recent immigrants from Palestine, however, Hebrew was surely the dominant language.

Just as they opposed the use of the Septuagint, the moderate conservatives also rejected the allegoristic method. According to Philo, they adhered strictly to literal exegesis and even paid particular attention to every word and letter.[137] This approach, differing as it did from that of the allegorists, accorded with the methods of the Sadducees and Pharisees alike. Groups and individuals who belonged to these two trends immigrated to Egypt from Palestine during the Hellenistic and Roman periods. The constant flow of traffic between the Holy Land and the Diaspora also helped to spread the influence of these major trends in Egypt. The moderate conservatives in Egypt may also have been divided between Sadducees and Pharisees, although there is no evidence to that effect. It is only natural that both subgroups held strictly to the practical precepts, presumably more than the moderate allegorists did.

The moderate conservatives not only rejected the allegorical method of interpretation; they also refrained from any attempt to explain Jewish faith and practices according to conceptions and ideas taken from the

---

135. On the orthodox Jews of Egypt, see Friedländer (1903) 56ff.; Shroyer (1936) 262–64, 283–84; Stein (1937) 292; Wolfson (1948) I.38–43; Feldman (1960) 227–30.

136. See Tracy (1928); Hadas (1951) 32–38; Tcherikover (1961a) 362–64.

137. See the sources and discussion of Shroyer (1936). Cf. Wolfson (1948) I.55–56.

Greek heritage. Moreover, they avoided the study of philosophy, which occupied a major role in the thinking of the allegorists. Philosophy was not included, as a matter of principle, among the disciplines studied by the moderate conservatives. It has to be borne in mind that philosophy was not one of the basic disciplines of the Hellenistic curriculum, being left to the discretion of the more talented students who had the proper intellectual abilities and the interest to pursue it after graduation.[138]

However, even the study of the basic Greek disciplines posed great difficulties for the moderate conservatives. The Homeric poems, which were the cornerstone of Greek education even in the first stages of learning to read and write, contained too much mythology and paganism to be suitable for their children in their formative years. It seems possible that the Greek curriculum was modified for the use of these conservatives. They may have preferred as reading material historical narratives, geographical and ethnographical works, and rhetoric as opposed to poetry. This was also more practical for everyday needs in Hellenistic Egypt. An examination of III Maccabees reveals that the author had a reasonable knowledge of Greek prose, but there is no sign that his education had included philosophy, poetry, or mythology.[139]

There is no possibility of knowing how these Jews acquired their Greek education—certainly not in the Hellenistic gymnasium. The various possibilities mentioned above for the Jewish education of the allegorists apply also to the conservatives. The need to study Hebrew probably required an additional framework for Jewish studies.

An important element of the conservatives were people who arrived as refugees and immigrants from the Holy Land in the Seleucid and Hasmonean periods, when there was already a flourishing Jewish community in Egypt. Just to mention a few: Onias IV and his family escaped to Egypt in the time of the religious persecutions and founded the temple in Leontopolis;[140] Pharisee sages who fled from Alexander Jannaeus found refuge in Alexandria;[141] the grandson of Ben Sira emigrated to

---

138. See Marrou (1956) 282ff.

139. On his language and general knowledge, see Hadas (1951) 22–23; Tcherikover (1961a) 356–57.

140. The syncretistic features found in the Jewish cemetery at Leontopolis do not necessarily reflect the practices of the Oniads, and they may be dated to the first century A.D. See on them Feldman (1960) 217–18. For further bibliography on that necropolis, see Schürer et al. (1973–86) III.146 n. 33.

141. On them, see Stein (1937) 60–62; Tcherikover (1957) 2–3.

Egypt. This last then translated the book of his grandfather into Greek, but found it necessary to express in the prologue his reservations about the Greek translations of the Bible; a priest named Dositheus, together with two others, arrived from Palestine in 77 B.C. and brought with him a Greek translation of the Esther Scroll. The translation itself had been made by a Jerusalem Jew.[142]

As appears from III Maccabees and the Wisdom of Solomon, the socioeconomic status of the conservatives, or at least of a substantial proportion of them, was lower than that of the allegorists.[143] This also makes sense in view of the expenses involved in acquiring a comprehensive Greek education and the number of recent immigrants among the conservatives. Nevertheless, among these immigrants were also to be found people like the Oniads, who soon found ways of integrating themselves into the Ptolemaic system, mainly as senior and influential army commanders; and it may well be that they brought their fortunes with them from Palestine. We do not know to what extent the conservatives adopted Greek manners, clothing, and the like in everyday life and in their contacts with gentiles.

As was said above, the convictions of the "progressive" conservatives can be inferred from the pseudepigraphic Wisdom of Solomon. They differed from the moderate conservatives mainly in their favorable attitude toward Greek philosophy and its application to the understanding of Jewish theological principles. Similar contrasts in the attitudes of orthodox groups toward philosophy are well known from later periods in Jewish history, *inter alia* from Egypt itself in the Middle Ages. It also seems that the Greek education of the progressive conservatives was more comprehensive and included poetic-mythological literature. In addition, they were well acquainted with the Septuagint and used it in their writings, if not for services in the synagogue.[144] On the other hand, they shared the opposition of the moderate conservatives to allegorical interpretation, their strict fulfillment of everyday precepts, and their aggressive attitude toward paganism.

142. See the analysis of the colophon by Bickerman (1976–80) I.225–46.

143. See Tcherikover (1957) 47, 50–52, 67–68, 74–75; *id.* (1961a) 314 n. 53, 362–64; Mendelson (1982) 27.

144. On the favorable attitude toward the Septuagint of certain conservative circles in the Talmudic period in contrast to the hostility of others, see Gooding (1963); Gruenwald (1986) 71–78. For another approach, see Veltri (1992).

The author of the Wisdom of Solomon explicitly lists philosophy among the disciplines he studied (7.17), and his book abounds in philosophical terminology, as well as in philosophical arguments and ways of thinking.[145] Philosophy is applied by him mainly to the explanation of the Creation and the meaning and role of Wisdom as described in Proverbs and Job. In his list of the Greek disciplines, in addition to philosophy he mentions astronomy, dialectic, psychology, zoology, and botany (7.17–20). He demonstrates a good knowledge of Homer and Greek tragedy, and integrates mythological terms into his verses.[146] The Holy Scriptures are known to him from the Septuagint, which he uses even in cases where it differs considerably from the Hebrew original.[147]

As opposed to all these, there are features shared by the author and the moderate conservatives that distinguish him from the allegorists. He usually refrains from applying philosophy to the interpretation of the Pentateuch, and reserves it for the interpretation of Wisdom. Moreover, he avoids allegorical interpretations, despite the many quotations and references to historical events in his book and his detailed midrashic version of the Ten Plagues of Egypt. The few symbolic interpretations he makes[148] do not exclude him from the camp of the literalists. He uses strong expressions, recording in detail the harsh treatment of the poor by the rich of the community, the contempt of the latter for the Jewish faith and its practices, and their hedonistic and immoral way of life (chaps. 1–3). He insists on one's absolute duty to fulfill strictly the precepts of the Torah (e.g., 2.12, 6.10), and does not think it necessary to explain and justify them.

The attitude of the author toward Greek and Egyptian religions is very aggressive. He advocates all-out war against paganism (chaps. 2, 14). Like Pseudo-Aristeas and Philo, he criticizes the rationalization of the Greek gods. However, unlike them, he does this in an extremely intolerant way. Against the Stoics he employs insulting language, and against the Euhemerists he argues that the cult of the heroes and kings involved the practice of a number of moral crimes, including ritual murder and sexual perversion (13.1–9, 14.15). Moreover, in contrast

145. Stein (1937) 33–45; Winston (1979) 18–20, 25ff.
146. Winston (1979) 15 and n. 20, p. 20.
147. Winston (1979) 17–18.
148. For instance 15.6; 16.5–7, 28; 17.21; 18.24. See Stein (1929) 12–15; Winston (1979) 61–62; Goodman in Schürer et al. (1973–86) III.573.

to Philo he praises the annihilation of paganism and of the peoples of Canaan by the Israelites and justifies these in much detail (12.3ff.). His aggressive campaign against paganism and his loyalty to the precepts of the Torah, on one hand, and the frequent use of mythological terms, on the other, find parallels in the Third Sibylline Book. Other noteworthy features of the latter book are the absence of allegorical interpretations and the stress on the need to help the poor. At least part of that book originated in the same circle that produced the Wisdom of Solomon (though in another generation).[149]

On the basis of the features of the three groups surveyed above, we can say that Pseudo-Hecataeus belonged to the moderate conservatives. He read and wrote Greek, and was acquainted with certain genres of the Greek literary corpus (historiography, ethnography, geography, rhetoric, and the grammarians), but the stylistic quality of his work does not rise to that of the allegorists'. He deliberately refrains from using Greek wisdom and culture to explain Jewish tradition, does not suggest any synthesis of Greek and Jewish culture, and adheres to the literal interpretation of the Scriptures. Furthermore, it seems that he did not have any philosophical education, and there are signs that he was not acquainted with Homer or later poets, at least not where the content was primarily religious or mythological. He studied the Torah only in its Hebrew original, and not in the versions of the Septuagint. It may well be that he belonged to a synagogue in which Hebrew was also the liturgical language.

Living in Hellenistic Egypt, Pseudo-Hecataeus was acquainted with basic Hellenistic practices. However, it seems that his direct contacts with Greek society did not include cultural relations. From the fragments it appears that contacts had to be limited to economic and state affairs alone. These contacts were necessary for everyday existence, and, moreover, they served the national goal that in his view justified the very residence of Jews in Egypt.[150] The Greek language was a necessary instrument for maintaining contacts with the regime and the local population. At least part of the Greek literary corpus was an aid to acquiring the proper means of expression and gaining knowledge about the practical world of the ruling nation.

149. On his circle, see, e.g., Friedländer (1903) 59ff.; Collins (1974) 44ff., (1983) 148–52; Goodman, *op. cit.* (n. 148) 632–39.
150. See pp. 238ff. below.

Pseudo-Hecataeus opposes any philosophico-theological dialogue with the Greek world and any possibility of profiting from its achievements. Pagan religions, their cult, practices, and beliefs, are portrayed by him as harmful superstitions. Nothing can be learned from them; there is no point in trying to understand them, and they deserve only mockery and disdain. The Jews must avoid them and, if possible (as in the Holy Land), annihilate them from the face of the earth. This justification of contemporary physical violence stands in sharp contrast to the view of the allegorists, who prohibit even verbal violence and insults. Pseudo-Hecataeus displays no semblance of elementary political sensitivity in his references to the customs and institutions of the state religion.

The celebrated statement by Pseudo-Aristeas according to which God "fenced us about with impregnable palisades and walls of iron, to the end that we should mingle in no way with any of the other nations" (para. 139) properly expresses the point of view of Pseudo-Hecataeus. In the case (and context) of Pseudo-Aristeas this sounds rather exaggerated and does not accord with the positions presented in his book.[151] We can thus conclude that the author of Pseudo-Hecataeus was not a "Hellenistic Jew" in the strict sense. The term has been specifically reserved (and so it should remain) for the circles that created a synthesis between Hellenism and Judaism. Pseudo-Hecataeus can be listed in the category of Jewish Hellenistic literature only if the term designates merely language and place of composition.

151. It may well be that Pseudo-Aristeas felt the necessity of such a radical definition in view of the dangers involved in the adaptation of Greek manners and culture he recommended. He may be referring mainly to the less gifted, who were not able to absorb the foreign culture properly, rather than to the elite of the allegorists. Even Philo was cautious and restricted the study of allegorical interpretation to qualified and talented individuals.

VI The Framework,
Literary Genre, Structure, and Contents

The dating of Pseudo-Hecataeus's treatise and the clarification of its provenance and cultural-religious background have brought us closer to an understanding of the purpose of the work, which can be further advanced by reconstructing the structure and basic contents of the treatise.

An examination of the passages in *Against Apion* does not by itself provide a clear picture. They are fragmentary and appear garbled and unrelated to each other, lacking historical or thematic sequence. In order to arrive at the structure and contents of the treatise, we have to determine the framework from which the passages were taken, its literary genre, and the conventional scheme of works belonging to that genre.

1. MONOGRAPH OR EXCURSUS?

Josephus emphatically states that Hecataeus wrote a book that was devoted entirely to the subject of the Jews. He does this in three places. (a) In the preface to the quotations, Josephus contrasts Hecataeus with Clearchus, who had been quoted by him before. (He also implicitly contrasts him with other Greek authors quoted from *Ap.* I.161 onwards.) He states that while Clearchus mentioned the Jews only "in a digression" (ἐν παρεκβάσει), Hecataeus did not refer to the Jews "incidentally" (παρέργως), but "wrote a book about the Jews themselves" (I.183).[1] (b) At the end of the passages quoted (I.205), Josephus adds an

---

1. The similar assertion of Eusebius (*PE* IX.9, p. 408a) is only a paraphrase of Josephus, like the quotations that follow it (pp. 408b–409b).

instructive note: "To those who want to learn more the book is readily available." (c) Farther on, Josephus notes that Hieronymus of Cardia, though he was the governor of Syria, did not mention the Jews at all, while Hecataeus "wrote a book about us" (I.214).[2]

A number of considerations rule out the possibility that Josephus exaggerated in describing an excursus as a monograph. The statement that Hecataeus wrote a book on the Jews would have aroused particular curiosity among his potential readers and a desire to check it. *Against Apion* was written for Greco-Roman intellectuals who had an interest (positive or negative) in the Jews, and for emperors, governors, and political personalities who had to decide on the status and rights of Jewish communities (mainly in Alexandria). Even casual readers who were not involved with the Jewish question would have been interested in information about the existence of an independent monograph by an author of Hecataeus's reputation. These readers could easily have ascertained whether or not such a book existed: they could have used bibliographical handbooks like those based on the *Pinakes* of Callimachus and later works. These handbooks provided data about all Greek books collected in the Library of Alexandria, such as the title, the author, a short biography, the opening words, the number of lines, and so forth.[3] Guides of this sort were available in Roman public libraries, as well as in the two large libraries of Alexandria.[4]

Josephus would therefore have been careful in stating that Hecataeus wrote a book on the Jews, and that it was "readily available." Certainly he would have been even more cautious in advising his readers to consult it further. Reference to a nonexistent book would have undermined his credibility. The note that the book was "readily available" also discounts the possibility that Josephus did not use the treatise directly but found the passages in a secondary source.[5]

---

2. On the latter reference, cf. Reinach (1895) 227.

3. On the *Pinakes* of Callimachus, see Susemihl (1891) I.337ff.; Schmidt (1924); Turner (1968) 100–106; Fraser (1972) I.333–35; Reynolds and Wilson (1974) 7, 16; and esp. Blum (1991) 124–81, 226–46.

4. On these handbooks, see Blum (1991) 182–225, 244–46. On the continued activity of the Museum library despite the fire in 48 B.C., see Fraser (1972) I.452–54.

5. In contrast to Mendels (1983) 97 n. 7, and others, Josephus's widely recognized shortcomings in citing or paraphrasing other sources are irrelevant at this point. The factors that caused Josephus's negligence (and likewise

In addition to Josephus, Origen refers in his *Against Celsus* to a book on the Jews attributed to Hecataeus. The passage, which has a number of implications occupying us more than once, reads (*C. Cels.* I.15):

> And it is also said that there is a book on the Jews [περὶ Ἰουδαίων βιβλίον] by Hecataeus the historian in which still more is attributed to the wisdom of the nation, so much so that Herennius Philo in his treatise *On the Jews* [ἐν τῷ περὶ Ἰουδαίων συγγράμματι] first doubts whether the treatise [σύγγραμμα] belongs to the historian, and then states that if it is his, it seems likely that he had been carried away by the persuasiveness of the Jews and conformed to their principles.

Herennius Philo, accordingly, called the work "a book," or at least a "treatise." The question is whether this was based on direct acquaintance with Pseudo-Hecataeus or only through the Josephan testimonia and quotations. The balance tends in favor of the first possibility: the passages in *Against Apion* alone would hardly have created the impression that the author exaggerated in referring to Jewish "wisdom," of all things, and this also applies to the Mosollamus episode. The exaggerated admiration of Jewish hostility toward pagan cult is much more striking, and, after all, the "wisdom" of ancient nations was a rather common motif in ancient ethnographic literature.[6] One should note that at the beginning of the same paragraph Origen elaborates on the "wisdom" attributed to the Jews by a number of Greek writers, especially Hermippus and Numenius, who posited a decisive Jewish influence on Greek philosophers such as Plato and Pythagoras and stressed the uniqueness of Jewish lawgivers and prophets.[7] Origen further states that the Jewish "wisdom" was emphasized by Hecataeus even more than by those authors. This evaluation may be based on some further comments by Herennius Philo. Origen himself certainly

---

that of other ancient authors) made it even more difficult for the reader to compare his version to the original. Frequently the original was not available in the vicinity of the potential reader, and checking a quotation was always inconvenient because of the scroll form of books. The reader would have had to be especially motivated to try to check the original version. All this is irrelevant to the statement about the very existence of a book on the Jews by an author of Hecataeus's stature.

6. See Trüdinger (1918) 27–28.

7. See their fragments in M. Stern (1974–84) I nos. 23–26, II nos. 363a ff. Cf. Strabo XVI.2.35–36.

was not directly acquainted with Pseudo-Hecataeus.[8] Some clear and far-reaching expressions about "Jewish wisdom" must have been found in the original treatise of Pseudo-Hecataeus.

In this context it should be made clear that Herennius Philo referred only to the same treatise quoted by Josephus in *Against Apion*: the spuriousness of the book *On Abraham*, which was also attributed to Hecataeus, is evident even from the single preserved extract, since it contains forged verses of Sophocles promulgating the unity of the divine and abolition of idolatry.[9] Herennius Philo would have disqualified this book with more decisive arguments, and would not have raised the possibility that Hecataeus "had been carried away by the persuasiveness of the Jews." There is no justification for positing another forged book attributed to Hecataeus.[10]

The trustworthy testimonia of Josephus and Herennius Philo (besides a number of other reasons) thus finally discount the view (obviously of scholars who support authenticity) that Josephus took the material from an excursus included in a comprehensive historiographical work,[11] from Hecateus's Egyptian ethnography,[12] or from a travelogue.[13]

8. Origen was eager to quote such references; see Feldman (1990) 115–20. However, he alludes only to the Mosollamus story (IV.90).

9. See the bibliography, p. 3 n. 3 above.

10. For a rejection of the last possibility, suggested by some scholars, see M. Stern (1974–84) II.142.

11. So Gauger (1982) 26–27, who tries to prove this from the references to the battle of Gaza and its date (*Ap.* I.184–85). His arguments do not hold water, and the questions raised by him on the sequence and logic of the passage can be resolved by a more careful reading of the text. On the other hand, Josephus explicitly says that Hecataeus "mentions" (μνημονεύει) the battle of Gaza (para. 189), which indicates that it was referred to only in passing as background for the special connection between Hezekiah and his followers and Ptolemy I. The need to rely on Castor, who was less known than Hecataeus and lacked his authority, for the dating of the latter (para. 184) further shows that the passage was not drawn from a comprehensive historiographical book.

12. Guttman (1958–63) I.69–71. This suggestion has to be rejected at the outset, in view of the evident differences in the general attitude toward the Jews, as well as in various details, between Hecataeus's Jewish excursus and the passages quoted by Josephus.

13. Lewy (1932) 122–23, 131–32, followed by others. Lewy points to the pronouns "I" and "we," which are repeated twice in the passages (paras. 189, 201), and suggests that the book described Hecataeus's travels in Ptolemy's service. However, the claim of being an eyewitness (whether authentic or

The conclusion that the treatise was not written by Hecataeus, but by an Egyptian Jew at the time of the Hasmonean state, is in itself sufficient to show that Josephus's source for these quotations was primarily concerned with Jews and Judaism.

At the same time, the argument raised by those scholars who claim that the material contained in the Josephus passages is too brief to have comprised an independent work deserves examination. Josephus does not claim to have quoted the whole book, but explicitly states that he intends to quote only "the highlights of some of the things said" (*Ap.* I.183; cf. 205). The phrasing of a number of passages, some of which appear in indirect speech, clearly indicates abbreviation and condensation of the original text.[14] Furthermore, the passages do not embrace all the subjects covered by Pseudo-Hecataeus. In the second book of *Against Apion* Josephus quotes a sentence from the treatise that recounted the granting of Samaria by Alexander to the Jews (II.43),[15] and we have already inferred that some references of Pseudo-Hecataeus to Jewish "wisdom" were not quoted. Josephus, in accordance with the purpose of his book (I.57–59), chose to cite only passages that demonstrated the maturity of the Jewish people at the beginning of the Hellenistic period (I.186): their good relations with Ptolemy I, their numerical strength, their well-established settlements, the role and importance of the Temple, and their profound faith. As can be seen from the absence of the reference to Samaria in Book I of *Against Apion*, even the coverage of these subjects was not comprehensive.

As a matter of fact, the extant passages alone may indicate a quantity of material equal to that of a typical book of the Hellenistic-Roman period. The length of books was variable and may have been no more than that of a modern pamphlet. A papyrus scroll could have contained even more than two such books, and even works of different authors (*symmigēs*). After the standardization of the scrolls by the scholars

---

fabricated) is still not evidence for a travel book. These expressions, typical of the ethnographic literature as a whole (cf. Jacoby [1943] 66), are lacking in the account of Jerusalem and Judea, although they would be expected in a travel book covering Hecataeus's experiences in the area in the years 312–311. The personal tone in paras. 189 and 200 was merely intended to create an impression of authenticity.

14. Cf. p. 221 below.

15. On the attribution of that sentence to the same treatise, see pp. 114–15 above.

of the Alexandria Museum, an average scroll measured thirty feet in length and contained about fifty thousand letters.[16] There were scrolls that were far shorter, and Pliny states that a scroll was no more than fifteen feet long (*NH* XIII.72). The number of letters in the Josephus material, a quarter of which is occupied by the Mosollamus story (I.201–4), is 10 percent of a standard Alexandrian scroll, or 20 percent of a standard book. In contrast to other passages, the Mosollamus story is quoted at relative length, but it illustrates just one feature (and not a central one) of the Jewish people—their disdain for pagan techniques of divination. The Hezekiah story and the description of Jerusalem, Judea, and the land of Israel, for instance, were certainly much longer than Mosollamus's episodic anecdote. We can thus be quite sure that the original treatise was of a length acceptable for a Hellenistic book, if not for an "unmixed" scroll.

2. THE TITLE OF THE TREATISE AND THE LITERARY GENRE

The passages in Josephus, which deal with Jewish customs and traditions, suggest that the book had an ethnographic character. This, however, is not enough to establish its genre. Besides ethnographic material, the book contains a report of a fictitious historical event—the Hezekiah story. This combination may at first sight recall Pseudo-Aristeas, a story (which could even be disguised as a letter) centered around an event in Jewish life in the Hellenistic period, and supplemented, in one way or another, by plentiful ethnographic material, as well as symposia, travelogues, and the like. We must therefore clarify whether the book belongs to the ethnographic genre *par excellence*, or to a related genre that also included ethnographic features.

The title of a book in Hellenistic and Jewish Hellenistic literature, if not just fanciful in an attempt to catch the eye (Plin. *NH* pref. 24–25), indicates its literary genre.[17] To mention just a few titles: *Philippica, Hellenica, Anabasis, Chronicon, Periplous,* "For ...," "Against ...," "Letter to [or "of"] ...," "Memories of ...," "History of ...," "Art

16. This calculation is based on the data in Kenyon and Roberts (1970) 173–74. See also Schubart (1921) 50–59; Reynolds and Wilson (1974) 2; Turner (1971) 8; Kenney (1982) 16–18; Blum (1991) 107–8.

17. See, e.g., Kenney (1982) 16, 30–31; Geiger (1984) 3ff., (1985/8) 125ff.

of...." It is clear from some of the titles that they were modeled after the scheme of a celebrated book, while others simply specify the genre or the contents.

Scholars who have accepted that the passages were taken from a monograph devoted to the Jews alone assume that the book was named *Peri Ioudaiōn* ("On the Jews").[18] However, as it is not clearly stated in the sources, the question of the title requires some elaboration.

Josephus's statement that Hecataeus of Abdera "wrote a book about the Jews themselves" (περὶ αὐτῶν Ἰουδαίων συγγέγραφε βιβλίον, *Ap.* I.183) is again relevant. The sentence, as it stands, may appear to refer to the subject of the book and not to its title. But it has already been mentioned that Josephus recommended consulting the book for further information (I.205). Hecataeus wrote books on various subjects,[19] and Josephus even believed that the forged book *On Abraham* was written by him (*Ant.* I.158–59). Could he have encouraged his reader to consult the complete book without giving any indication of its title? We can thus assume that the name "Jews" or some variant appeared in the title. To judge by parallel titles, it could be either *On the Jews* or *Ioudaika*.

No less instructive is the passage in Origen (*C. Cels.* I.15), quoted in the previous section, where Hecataeus's book is referred to without the article ("there is a book on the Jews by Hecataeus"). The words περὶ Ἰουδαίων βιβλίον, which were certainly taken from Herennius Philo, must indicate the book's contents, title, or both. An allusion to the contents is understandable in view of the context (and see I.14), while the use of an identical reference in Josephus lends support to understanding it rather as a title. The latter alternative is suggested by the title of Herennius Philo's own treatise referred to in the same passage: the preceding article (τῷ, I.15) indicates that it was *On the Jews*. The same formula for Philo's work is also mentioned by Eusebius (*PE* I.10, p. 42).[20] One may suppose that Herennius Philo would not

18. See Jacoby (1943) 61; Schürer et al. (1973–86) I.41; Goodman, ibid. III.671–72; Holladay (1983) 279.

19. See pp. 10–11 above.

20. On the doubts about the present readings of Eusebius's text and their rejection, see M. Stern (1974–84) II.140, 143. Schürer et al. (1973–86) I.41–43 plausibly argue that Eusebius mistakenly attributed a quotation from Philo's Phoenician history to his treatise *On the Jews*. This does not affect our conclusion.

have used the same phrase in referring to a book by someone else unless it was indeed its title. Finally, Hecataeus's known ethnographical books were named *On the Hyperboreans* and *On the Egyptians*, or *Aegyptiaca*.[21] The wish to create an impression of authenticity would have led the forger to imitate external features of Hecataeus's books such as their titles. We can thus conclude that though there is no unequivocal statement to this effect, the name of the book was *On the Jews*, or less probably *Ioudaika*.

These names indicate that the book was an ethnographic work. Hellenistic ethnographies were usually entitled with the name of the nation or the land in one of two basic forms: "[Affairs of] ..." (*Aithiopikē, Indikē, Persikē, Skythikē,* and the like) or "On the ..." (*Peri tōn Indikōn, Peri Kyprou, Peri Sikelias, Peri tōn Aithiopeōn, Peri Aiolikōn*).[22] Significantly enough, almost all the ethnographic books devoted to the Jews known to us were called *Peri Ioudaiōn*. They were written in the Hellenistic period by both Jews and gentiles. The best-known among them is the book by Alexander Polyhistor (Eus. *PE* IX.17), a gentile contemporary of Pompey and Sulla, who compiled material from monographs on the Jews by Jewish as well as gentile authors.[23] This was probably also the name of Apollonius Molon's anti-Jewish book.[24] The treatise *On the Jews* by Herennius Philo, written in the first half of the second century A.D., belongs to the same category. From the brief fragments of two books called *On the Jews* by two otherwise unknown authors, Damocritus the Tactician and Nicarchus son of Ammonius, it also appears that they belonged to the ethnographic genre, and were perhaps written in the first century A.D.[25] Of the Jewish authors who

---

21. See p. 9 n. 9 above.

22. Cf. Fornara (1983) 12. See also the *Peri Ethnōn* of Hellanicus (*FHG* I.57, 92, 93) and Damastes (*FHG* II.64.1). But see Pearson's reservations ([1939] 194) about the name and contents of Hellanicus's work.

23. On Alexander Polyhistor see the monograph by Freudenthal (1875). Cf. also M. Stern (1974–84) I.157ff.

24. Alexander Polyhistor introduces him as "Molon who composed the invective against the Jews" (ὁ δὲ τὴν συσκευὴν τὴν κατὰ Ἰουδαίων γράψας Μόλων, Eus. *PE* IX.19.1). A title Κατὰ Ἰουδαίων is less likely for a book written in the first century B.C.

25. On the last two, see M. Stern (1974–84) I.530–33.

wrote books entitled *On the Jews*,[26] we know about Artapanus, Aristeas the Exegete, Theodotus the Poet,[27] and Pseudo-Eupolemus, who was probably a Samaritan.[28] These books were written between the middle of the second and the middle of the first century B.C.[29]

The fragments of the works named *On the Jews* confirm that they were indeed ethnographic works containing the common components of the genre.[30] Those written by Jewish authors report on the patriarchs, leaders, and kings: Abraham, Job,[31] Joseph, Moses and the Exodus, Solomon and the building of the Temple, the last kings of Judea, and the destruction of the First Temple. Stress is laid on the theoretical and practical wisdom of Moses and the patriarchs. Thus the invention of astrology is attributed to Abraham, and that of philosophy, together with a number of useful technical inventions, to Moses. In addition to stories about the leaders, we hear about Jerusalem, the Jewish holy books, the origin of the name "Judea," and the like.

The books named *On the Jews* written by gentiles contain similar topics, although the contents and attitudes frequently differ. Alexander Polyhistor probably did not contribute much of his own and was content with quotations from earlier ethnographies. The fragments and

26. See Eus. *PE* IX.17, 18, 22, 23, 25; Clem. *Strom.* I.23, 154.2–3.

27. On the question of whether Theodotus's epic was indeed originally titled *On the Jews* as stated by Alexander Polyhistor, see the summary of the pros and cons in Holladay (1989) 53–58, 81–82, and the references included there to earlier bibliography. The negative arguments are by no means decisive. That Alexander Polyhistor named the work by Philo the epic poet *On Jerusalem* is still the most relevant fact for the discussion. It indicates that Alexander Polyhistor would not have applied the general title *On the Jews* to Theodotus's epic, from which he quotes only verses on a non-Jewish city (Shechem), unless this was indeed its real name.

28. On the origin of Pseudo-Eupolemus, see Freudenthal (1875) 82ff.; Guttman (1958–63) II.96; Wacholder (1963) 112; Hengel (1973) 162 n. 233; Walter (1965) 282ff., (1976) 137–43; Holladay (1983) 157–59; Doran in Charlesworth (1985) II.873ff.

29. See the summaries in Holladay (1983) 159, 190, 262; *id.* (1989) 68–76, 208–10; Goodman in Schürer et al. (1973–86) III.521–24, 526, 529–30, 561–62.

30. Of these works, the epic of Theodotus does not concern us here. Because of its poetic form, it would certainly have differed in its structure and content from prose monographs.

31. Job appears in Aristeas's book (Eus. *PE* IX.25.1–4). Since Job is presented as the son of Esau, there is no doubt that he was mentioned in the context of the patriarchal traditions.

testimonia of Herennius Philo contain mainly folkloristic-etymological notes: the origin of the words "Judea" and "Jews," the name of the Jewish God, a derogatory nickname ascribed to Moses,[32] and reservations about Jewish "wisdom" and the authenticity of the treatise attributed to Hecataeus. From the works of Damocritus and Nicarchus we have references to the "blood" libel against contemporary Jewish cult and the leper libel against Moses and the Israelites in Egypt. The remaining fragments of the works entitled *On the Jews* thus reassure us that they were indeed ethnographical books commenting on the beginnings of the nation and the achievements of its leaders, as well as on the customs (including faith and religious practices) and the land of the Jews. The last two components are also to be found in Pseudo-Hecataeus.

3. THE STRUCTURE OF AN ETHNOGRAPHICAL WORK

We have seen in this chapter that the passages quoted by Josephus were taken from an independent monograph called *On the Jews*. The title and the contents of the material indicate that it was an ethnographical treatise. Pseudo-Hecataeus was acquainted with ethnographical literature, certainly with the writings of Hecataeus. Even Berossus, the Babylonian historian-ethnographer, and Demetrius, the Jewish chronographer, whose knowledge of Greek language and culture was far worse, were influenced by Greek literary models.[33] Like other genres of ancient literature, the ethnographical work had a conventional scheme and structure, so much so, that their elucidation can contribute to an understanding of the structure of Pseudo-Hecataeus's treatise and the nature of its contents. The few extant discussions of Greek ethnography do not provide a satisfactory and comprehensive analysis of the structure.[34] We must therefore digress from the discussion of the treatise itself and examine the structure of works belonging to this genre. Other features of the genre were surveyed above, at the beginning of this book.[35]

---

32. See the fragments in M. Stern (1974–84) II.138–45.

33. On Demetrius, see Sterling (1992) 157–62.

34. See Jacoby (1909) 88–96; Trüdinger (1918); K. E. Müller (1972–80); Sterling (1992) 20–102.

35. See pp. 10–13 above.

The following discussion will attempt to establish the conventional scheme of the genre by analyzing the structure of several independent monographs, as well as that of a few ethnographical excursuses that properly represent the genre. The difference between the two is by and large only one of length, although occasionally the structure of an excursus is dictated by the context in which it is inserted and may therefore differ somewhat from the conventional scheme. The discussion does not deal with works of a semiethnographical character. These actually belong to other genres: for example, Ctesias's *Persica*, classified as a historical novel; the book of Manetho on Egypt, apparently an expanded chronicle;[36] or Berossus's monograph, which is largely a historical account of Babylon and its people.[37] In order to follow the development of the genre, the survey is arranged in chronological order, and includes examples of various types of nations described in this literature: nations residing in the centers of civilization as against peoples (including legendary ones) on the periphery of the known inhabited world, and autochthonous nations as against nations of immigrants. To keep the discussion within reasonable bounds, it is limited to the four outstanding ethnographical authors preceding Pseudo-Hecataeus: Herodotus, Hecataeus of Abdera, Megasthenes, and Agatharcides. In addition, the structure of half a dozen ethnographical accounts of the Jews will be analyzed.

The genre seems to have originated in Ionia during the late sixth and the early fifth century. Hecataeus of Miletus is universally acknowledged as its originator. However, only relatively short fragments of his writings have survived.[38] The first real evidence for the rules and structure of ethnographical works is to be found in the excursuses on various nations included in the *Histories* of Herodotus. The most detailed of these excursuses, and the ones most similar to Hellenistic ethnographies, are the *logoi* on the Egyptians (II.2–182) and the Scythians (IV.5–82).

36. Cf. Jacoby (1909) 91.
37. See Burstein (1978) 6–8; Kuhrt (1987) 44ff.; in contrast to Murray (1970) 208–9; K. E. Müller (1972–80) I.94–105.
38. On Hecataeus of Miletus, see Trüdinger (1918) 8–14; Pearson (1939) 25ff., and bibliography on pp. 106–8; Sterling (1992) 22–33.

Many conjectures have been proffered as to the sources and original forms of the two excursuses, which by themselves contribute to our understanding of the development of the ethnographic genre. It has been suggested that the contents of the Egyptian excursus were basically influenced by the Egyptian ethnography of Hecataeus of Miletus included in his *Periēgēsis*. If this is correct, the structure of the Herodotean excursus may resemble that of its predecessor. However, the extent to which the "father of ethnography" influenced the "father of history" is disputed.[39] Similarly, there is no unanimity as to the stages of composition of Herodotus's ethnographies. In the past many scholars were of the opinion that the two excursuses were originally written as independent *logoi* and only later incorporated by Herodotus into his great work. Others think that the excursuses were never meant to be independent, but were first written as "rough drafts" planned for inclusion in existing sections of the *Histories*.[40] Be that as it may, the composition of the excursuses, as they now stand, was dictated by a clear conception as to the structure and contents of the ethnographical work.[41]

The Egyptian excursus, which is the longer of the two, contains the following sections:[42] (a) the *origo* of the Egyptian people, or rather their *archaeologia*, describing the antiquity of the Egyptians and their contribution to the beginnings of civilization (II.2–4);[43] (b) the geography of Egypt (5–34); (c) customs (35–98), with Egyptian cult and beliefs described in the middle of the section (37–76); (d) history, recounting stories about famous Egyptian rulers and their major achievements (99–182). The first three sections appear in the same order in the Scythian excursus: (a) the *origo*, offering various speculations on the descent of the Scythians, who are introduced, unlike the Egyptians, as

39. On this, see, e.g., Heidel (1935); Pearson (1939) 81ff.; and the detailed survey by Lloyd (1975–78) I.127–39. Recently: Sterling (1992) 36–39.

40. See the summary in Lloyd (1975–78) I.66–68; Sterling (1992) 40–44.

41. Cf. Trüdinger (1918) 14–34, esp. 21; Sterling (1992) 36ff.

42. The divisions and titles suggested by Trüdinger (1918) 18–19, K. E. Müller (1972–80) 107–15, Lloyd (1990) 219–20, Sterling (1992) 46, based on the general conception of Jacoby (1909) 89, are inaccurate.

43. Sterling (1992) 46 *et passim* does not mention the *origo* section. Although he rightly states that the Egyptian *logos* opens at II.2, his division of the sections starts only from II.4.3, leaving chaps. 2–4.3 without any title.

the youngest of all nations (IV.5–15);[44] (b) the geography of the various Scythian regions and tribes (16–58: this section is interrupted by two accounts that do not directly relate to the Scythian territories [32–36; 36–45]; a description of the Scythian coast and borders appears separately in the course of the historical narrative that follows [99–101]); (c) customs (59–82), including at the beginning an account of cults and beliefs (59–63). In contrast to the Egyptian ethnography, there is no survey of Scythian rulers and their achievements, presumably because of a lack of sufficient material.[45]

Close acquaintance with the oriental world in the wake of Alexander's expedition naturally stimulated much ethnographical writing and set new standards for the genre.[46] The pioneer of the new ethnography was Hecataeus of Abdera, who provided a model for ethnographical writing and was for many years widely imitated by Hellenistic ethnographers.[47] Nevertheless, Hellenistic ethnography did not entirely depart from the Ionian tradition. The basic schematic structure of the Herodotean ethnographical excursus (especially that of the Egyptian *logos*) still guided Hellenistic ethnographers.[48] This applies not only to authors like Agatharcides of Cnidus, who expressed admiration for Herodotus's achievements, but also to Hecataeus, who did not greatly appreciate him. The latter even occasionally drew on Herodotus, although he had opportunities to consult much better sources.

Of Hecataeus's two ethnographical books known to us, *On the Egyptians* was the longer and more important. It was preserved, in an abbreviated form, in Book I of Diodorus's *Historical Library*, which contains the ethnography of Egypt.[49] Diodorus's lack of originality

---

44. Sterling, ibid., again disregards the *origo*. He entitles the contents of chaps. 5–15 "History." However, this section appears in Herodotus at the head of the *logos*, while "history" is usually located in the third or fourth place (see the puzzlement of Sterling about this). Furthermore, the content is that of an *origo*, and there are no dynastic lists or accounts, which characterize historical sections in ethnographies. On this, see, e.g., Sterling 14.

45. On the absence of certain sections in the shorter excursuses, see Jacoby (1909) 89 n. 1; and the table in Sterling (1992) 48.

46. See pp. 11–13 above.

47. See above pp. 13–18.

48. See Murray (1972) 204ff., esp. 207–8. Cf. Fraser (1972) I.504; J. Hornblower (1981) 152; Sterling (1992) 65–69.

49. See pp. 14ff. above, and Extended Notes, n. 1 p. 289.

in transmitting the narrative material of his sources must also be characteristic of the structure of his books. We can therefore assume that the scheme of the ethnographical account in Diodorus's Book I reflects that of Hecataeus's original work.

The structure of Hecataeus's book has already been surveyed and analyzed by quite a number of scholars.[50] The general division is supported by the captions (*epikephalaia*) that precede Diodorus's Book I, the internal division of that book into two parts, and the prefaces and endnotes to the sections (I.29.6, 41.10, 42.1–2, 69.1–2; II.1–2). Consequently, there are no significant differences between the various reconstructions. All of them assume that Hecataeus's book was divided into four sections: (a) *theologoumena*, that is, theology (Diod. I.10–29);[51] (b) geography (30–31; on 32–41 see below); (c) history (42.2–68); (d) *nomima*, or customs and manners (69–98). In the following pages the titles of the sections will be examined, as well as the arrangement of material and emphasis in each of them.

The title *theologoumena* for the first section is derived from an expression used by Diodorus in its closing sentence: "This is what can be said about the theological matters [περὶ μὲν τῶν θεολογουμένων] of the Egyptians" (I.29.6). At first sight, it may appear that the section differs from the *origo-archaeologia*, the first section of Herodotus's Egyptian ethnography. However, a close look at the contents shows that its primary purpose was much the same. The section opens with the genesis of life in general, and goes on to the creation of the human species and subsequent development of society. According to Hecataeus all these occurred in Egypt as a result of its special climate and soil (I.10). The Egyptian people are thus autochthonous, as indicated by Herodotus. The section ends with an appendix on the beginnings of other nations through dispersal from Egypt (28–29), which further proves that it was an *origo-archaeologia*. In the middle of the section there is indeed an account of the creation and origin of the Egyptian religion. This is why Diodorus named the whole section *theologoumena*. It includes an explanation of how belief in the celestial bodies arose in Egypt (11), an identification of certain Egyptian gods with the five basic

50. Susemihl (1891) I.312 n. 17; Jacoby (1943) 34–36; Murray (1970) 150ff., (1972) 207ff.; Fraser (1972) I.497ff.; Burton (1972) 33; J. Hornblower (1981) 138; Sterling (1992) 61–64.

51. See Extended Notes, n. 5 p. 295.

elements (12), the deification of past Egyptian heroes and kings and their achievements (13), the introduction of civilization to Egypt and the inhabited world by Osiris (14–20), and a series of mythological tales about Osiris and Isis (21–27). However, all these components are clearly meant to show the development of early Egyptian civilization in the mythological age, before the historical period of the kings, and particularly its great contribution to the beginnings of humanity. The contribution is demonstrated by the very creation of belief in gods, and by a number of useful inventions attributed to Egyptian personalities, said to have been consequently deified. Similarly, the Egyptian contribution to early civilization (including the invention of religion) occupies a substantial part of the first section of Herodotus's Egyptian ethnography (II.4), which is only natural for an *origo-archaeologia* section on an autochthonic nation. Significantly Hecataeus does not describe the role of the animal gods according to Egyptian beliefs in this section, which would have been expected of a proper theological account, nor does he elaborate on Egyptian cult (apart from occasional references and etiological hints).[52] He does these, and with much detail, only in the fourth section, the *nomima*.

In contrast to the first section, the Diodorean titles of the other sections properly reflect their purpose and contents. Nevertheless, some clarification is still necessary. The second section of Diodorus's version, the geography (30–41), opens with an account of the boundaries of Egypt and refers to its great population (30–31.8). This was taken from Hecataeus. Then comes a sentence by Diodorus (31.9) in which he indicates that although his source (i.e., Hecataeus) passed on to the history section, he will insert a detailed report on the Nile. It is assumed that the long digression on the Nile, which follows (32–41), was drawn from Agatharcides of Cnidus.[53] Hecataeus did not devote much attention to the subject, presumably because it could not contribute much to the social and political purposes that guided him in writing his book.[54] If so, we see that an ethnographical work does not necessarily include a comprehensive account of all geographical features, even if they are in themselves of special interest. Their inclusion

52. See 12.9, 15.3–5, 18.1, 21.9–10.
53. See Jacoby (1943) 75; Murray (1970) 147; Fraser (1972) I.499; Burton (1972) 20–21.
54. See other explanations in Murray (1970) 147–48; Sterling (1992) 70.

depends on their relevance to the purposes of the ethnographical work as a whole.

The third section comprises the major achievements of outstanding kings (I.42.2–68). Diodorus himself so defines the contents of the section (I.44.4–5), which is actually neither a history nor a chronicle. Like Herodotus, the author mentions only those kings whose achievements included impressive, monumental, building projects (temples, palaces, pyramids, dams, canals, etc.) as well as leading military expeditions beyond the borders of Egypt (cf. 71.5). In addition, he refers here and there to kings known for such curious and exceptional actions as the accumulation of numerous treasures, excessive cruelty, hospitality to foreigners, metamorphosis into animals or trees, and the like.

The fourth and last section (I.69–98) is defined by Diodorus as *nomima* ("customs," 69.2), "habits and laws" (69.6), and even "everyday life" (*bios*, 41.10). According to the contents it should rather be called "customs, laws, and institutions." The location of the *nomima* in the fourth place is exceptional. In other ethnographies it precedes the history, and sometimes even the geography. The reason for this may be that part of the customs are explained by the section about the rulers (especially the account of the practices of the Egyptian royalty, which opens the *nomima*). Naturally that section also includes many typical Egyptian customs (e.g., the building of pyramids).

The material included by Hecataeus was rather selective, and consisted only of curiosities or information that might be "most useful" (69.2). Diodorus made a further selection from this material (72.6, 84.4, 89.4). The section contains the following subjects: everyday life of the kings, describing regular daily sacrifices and the role of the priests, subordination to laws, the loyalty of the people, funerary and mourning ceremonies (70–72); agrarian arrangements and social classes (73–74); jurisprudence, including judges, procedure, offenses, and penalties (75–80.2); marriage and child rearing (80.3–81); health and medicine (82); animal worship (83–90); mourning and funeral customs of ordinary people (91–93); a list of Egyptian lawgivers (94–95); and finally, famous Greek poets, lawgivers, and philosophers who visited Egypt and were inspired by its customs and culture (96–98). As was mentioned above, Egyptian cult was not included by Hecataeus in the first section, but among the *nomima*. The survey indeed refers only to animal worship, but one can assume that it also included other cult forms. Diodorus hints that he abbreviated the account of Egyptian cult (84.4, 89.4), presumably deleting practices that were not "curious" enough.

Far less has been preserved of Hecataeus's second ethnographical work, *On the Hyperboreans*. It was not just a short treatise, but, as appears from a reference in a scholion to Apollonius Rhodius (*FGrH* IIIA, 264 F 10), it comprised at least two books. However, all we have is a brief summary by Diodorus (II.47) and a few short fragments and testimonia in Hellenistic and Roman authors, as well as ones found in Byzantine lexicons and scholia.[55] Diodorus's summary suggests the following sections: geography (II.47.1–2); *nomima* (2–6)—beliefs and cult (2–3); customs and other characteristics (4–6).[56] The inclusion of the *origo* section can be deduced from a scholion to Pindar (*FGrH* IIIA, 264 F 9). It quotes different views of the origin of the Hyperboreans, and says that Hecataeus had another version of their descent. Hecataeus's version itself is not recorded. The scholion to Apollonius Rhodius states that according to Hecataeus there were three Hyperborean tribes (*ethnē*). One can consequently assume that Hecataeus discussed the origin of the three Hyperborean tribes and the foundation of Hyperborean society.[57] The Hyperboreans being an imaginary, utopian nation, their *origo* may well have been described as autochthonous, considered the ideal descent, as was that of the Panchaeans in Euhemerus's celebrated ethnography-utopia (Diod. V.42.5). The other fragments provide additional material on the geography of the Hyperborean country (e.g., Strabo VII.3.6; Pliny, *NH* IV.94), on their religion (mainly Ael. *NA* XI.1), and on other customs (Plut. *QC* IV.3.1).

In view of the structure of other ethnographies, it is very likely that Hecataeus's Hyperborean ethnography also opened with an *origo* section. Its absence in Diodorus's summary does not impose a particular difficulty: Jacoby has already shown that Diodorus was not directly acquainted with Hecataeus's treatise, but rather knew of it through

---

55. *FGrH* IIIA 264 F 8–14. On the various motifs and the cultural and literary background for the composition of the book, see esp. Rohde (1876) 209–14; Susemihl (1891) I.314; Jacoby (1943) 57ff.; Guttman (1958–63) I.42–45.

56. For a different division, see Sterling (1992) 60 and n. 26. *Pace* Sterling, I doubt whether Diod. II.47.6 is a remnant of a historical section. Fragments 10 and 12 (*FGrH* 264), in any case, are no evidence: they refer to tribes and priests, not to kings.

57. See Jacoby (1943) 57. On the three "nations": *FGrH* IIIA 264 F 10 line 4.

a secondary source that preceded the abstracts with the question of whether the Hyperboreans lived in Asia or in Europe.[58] It is therefore only natural that the intermediate source omitted the *origo*, and opened with the geographical section. From geography it continued on to customs (including religion). That author did not return to the *origo*, either through negligence or because it was not important for his case.[59] It should be noted that the *origo* section heads Euhemerus's Panchaean ethnography, and is followed by geography and customs (Diod. V.42.4–46.7).

Hecataeus's counterpart at the Seleucid court in the first generation of the Hellenistic kings was Megasthenes.[60] Like Hecataeus, he also went on diplomatic missions, first and foremost to the Indian king Sandracottus (Candragupta). His *Indica* served as the main source of information for the accounts of India written by Diodorus, Strabo, and Arrian, and its influence can also be traced in fragments from other authors.[61] The work was not exactly an eyewitness account, as might be expected, but was based on hearsay, folklore, and local legends, as well as on information drawn from Megasthenes' predecessors—Herodotus, Ctesias, Nearchus, and others. All these were occasionally supplemented by the author's own experiences. Hecataeus's influence

---

58. See Jacoby (1943) 54.

59. Jacoby (1943) 52ff. suggests that *On the Hyperboreans* was written as a travel book. The fragments and summary do not, however, support this conjecture. It should also be remembered that according to the accepted tradition it was impossible to reach the Hyperborean country. Only exceptional personalities like Aristeas of Proconnesus, who possessed divine traits (Hdt. IV.13.1), managed to get there. According to Diodorus's summary of Hecataeus, some Greeks did indeed visit the Hyperboreans, but these cases occurred in "most ancient times," and the information on them originates in the "authors of mythology" (II.47.4).

60. On Megasthenes, see Müller, *FHG* I.397–401; Susemihl (1891) I.547–52; Trüdinger (1918) 75–80; Bevan (1927) 358; Timmer (1930); Stein, *RE* s.v. "Megasthenes (2)," 230–326; Breloer (1933); Brown (1955) 18–33; Dahlquist (1962); Altheim and Stiehl (1970) 284ff., 318ff.; K. E. Müller (1972–80) I.245–52; Derrett (1975) cols. 1150–54; Kalota (1978); Karttunen (1986) 84ff.; Zambrini (1982, 1985); Sterling (1992) 92–103.

61. The first attempt to form a corpus of Megasthenes' fragments was made by Schwanbeck ([1846], inaccurately translated by McCrindle [1877]). See also Müller, *FHG* II.397–439. Much more precise is the collection by Jacoby in *FGrH* IIIC no. 715. See also Karttunen (1986).

can be recognized in the structure, the author's approach and etiological techniques, and above all in his tendency to idealize the political and social structure and practices of the subjects of his ethnography.[62]

Of all the accounts that drew on Megasthenes, the most important for our discussion is Diodorus's Indian excursus, included in Book II of his *Library* (II.35–42). It was taken solely from Megasthenes,[63] and so it stands to reason that Diodorus, more than others, preserved the original structure of Megasthenes' ethnography. The various attempts at reconstructing Megasthenes' *Indica* are consequently based chiefly on Diodorus.[64] This is, however, not particularly easy, since Diodorus drastically abbreviated the original work. Furthermore, the complementary extracts preserved by Strabo and Arrian are themselves part of concise versions (see, e.g., Arrian, *Indica* XVII.6), and what is worse, they evidently did not adhere to Megasthenes' sequence.

Diodorus's excursus opens with the geography of India (II.35–37). He surveys the borders, terrain, flora and fauna, minerals, precipitation, and rivers. To these has to be added the description of Palimbothra (Pāṭaliputra), the capital of Sandracottus (Arr. *Ind.* X, Strabo XV.1.36, Ael. *NA* XIII.18). The influence of physical geography on the development of a country's civilization and history and on the characteristics and customs of its people was stressed by Megasthenes more than by other ethnographers. Such references already recur in the geographical section itself (e.g., Diod. II.35.4; 36.1, 4, 6–7; 37.3). The geographical section thus also serves as a preface to the following sections; hence its location at the head of the work.

Diodorus's second section deals with the *origo-archaeologia* (II.38–39; cf. Arr. *Ind.* VII.1–3)—the inhabitants' being autochthonous and the

---

62. See esp. Murray (1972) 207–8, (1973) 166. There is some exaggeration in his statement that Megasthenes' work was conceived as a Seleucid response to Hecataeus's Egyptian ethnography. Seleucus I did not, after all, rule India, and the center of his kingdom was geographically distant from India.

63. This view, which is accepted by the majority of scholars, has been challenged by Majumdar (1958, 1960, 1960a). But see Sethna's reply (1960). However, the exchanges between the two, both Indologists, ignore the contribution of classical scholarship to the understanding of Diodorus's literary methods.

64. See Susemihl (1891) I.548 n. 131; Trüdinger (1918) 75–80; Derrett (1975) col. 1151; Sterling (1992) 95–101 (despite his statement on p. 94); in contrast to Stein, *RE* s.v. "Megasthenes (2)," 271–72.

life of the first human beings—and, as in Hecataeus, it elaborates on the development of civilization. In this framework the role of Dionysus and Heracles in introducing civilization to India is described in detail. There is also a reference to religious matters: Dionysus is said to have taught the Indians to respect the gods (Diod. II.39). It may well be that in this context, Megasthenes, like Hecataeus, expanded on Indian beliefs, although he later returned to the subject in the account of Indian castes, included in the section on customs. Further supplements, especially with regard to the contributions of Dionysus and Heracles, are mainly provided by Arrian (*Ind.* V.9–13, VII–IX.8).[65]

The determination of the *origo* as the second component in Megasthenes' work faces an obstacle: Josephus writes in the *Jewish Antiquities* (X.227) and *Against Apion* (I.144) that in Book IV of his *Indica* Megasthenes tried to prove that Nabuchodonosor (Nebuchadnezzar) "exceeded Heracles in his heroism and the greatness of his deeds." This statement has been brought forward as (sole) evidence for the accepted view that Megasthenes' work consisted of four books. As it mentions Heracles, it was naturally assumed that the reference is to the account of his Indian expedition, recorded by Diodorus in the *origo* section. Hence the conclusion of some scholars that the *origo* was included in the fourth book of the *Indica*.[66] As we shall see later, the *nomima* were undoubtedly included in Books II and III. It therefore may appear that the *origo* was placed at the end of the ethnography. This by itself would be rather strange,[67] and would not correspond with the location of the *origo* in Diodorus.

65. Sterling (1992) 95, 100 ignores the existence of an *origo-archaeologia* component in his survey of the contents, describing Diod. II.38–39 as "an historical summary" (p. 98); but elsewhere he defines these paragraphs as *archaeologiae*, making them the second section, while "History" appears in his list as the fourth and final section (pp. 99–100).

66. See esp. Stein, *RE* s.v. "Megasthenes (2)," 235, 272, followed by many others.

67. This may be why Jacoby (without explanation) suggested emending Josephus's text to read "in the first book" (*FGrH* IIIC p. 665 and n. 1). Some legitimization for emending the text can be found in the fact that Josephus was probably not directly acquainted with Megasthenes' work: Josephus does not quote his complimentary comment on the Jews, which introduces them as "philosophers" (Clem. *Strom.* I.15), though it could have contributed greatly to his purposes in writing *Against Apion*. However, as we shall see, the emendation is unnecessary. Jacoby may also have thought that the original

An examination of the reference to Nebuchadnezzar indeed suggests that it was not included in the *origo*: a similar allusion to Nebuchadnezzar, which is attributed to Megasthenes, appears in Strabo (XV.1.6–7), in an extract much longer than the Josephus reference. Megasthenes states that the Indians never undertook military expeditions and had never been occupied by foreigners, apart from the occupations by Dionysus, Heracles, and Alexander the Great. He then continues by listing a number of celebrated oriental emperors, including Nebuchadnezzar, saying that despite their great achievements elsewhere, none of them had invaded India.[68] In this context he notes that the Babylonian emperor had a greater reputation among the Chaldaeans than even Heracles and that he led an expedition to the Pillars. The context indicates that the passage was taken not necessarily from the account of Heracles' contribution to the development of Indian civilization (i.e., from the *origo*), but from a section on the kings and their achievements.[69] A passage quite similar to that quoted by Strabo (though making no mention of Nebuchadnezzar) indeed appears in Arrian at the end of a short survey of the Indian kings (*Ind.* IX.10–12; cf. V.4–8), based on Megasthenes (VIII.6, IX.8).

The contents of this survey (*Ind.* VIII–IX) in themselves prove that Megasthenes' work did include a section on the kings and their achievements, though it is missing from Diodorus's Indian excursus. The extract records the names of several kings who reigned after Dionysus, their years of rule, the number of generations from Dionysus to Heracles, the rise of the dynasty related to Heracles' daughter, the number of kings and years from Dionysus to Sandracottus, Megasthenes' contemporary, and some notes on attempted invasions and foreign occupations. The references to Dionysus and Heracles in this survey, and especially to the role of the former in introducing civilization to India, which

---

location of the sentence was in the geographical section (according to Diod. II.36.3). Müller (*FHG* II.399, 417) suggests for another reason the emendation "in the second book." But see the counterarguments of Susemihl (1891) I.548 n. 131. Cf. Sterling (1992) 59 n. 168.

68. On the development of the story about the attempt by Semiramis to conquer India, see Brown (1955) 24–29.

69. This conclusion may be supported by the reference to Heracles in the *origo* as a native Indian (Diod. II.39.1), while in the passage under discussion he comes from outside to conquer the country. However, two versions of Heracles' descent could still be included in the same section.

were described in detail in the *origo* section (Diod. II.38–39), do not prove that it was taken from the *origo*. Similarly Hecataeus opens his section on Egyptian kings with a short recapitulation of the main stages in the development of Egyptian civilization and the roles (and reigns) of mythological god-kings like Isis and Horus (I.43–44) before elaborating on the historical kings, although the former were already described in detail in the *origo* section. Like Megasthenes, he appends on this occasion summary numbers of kings and years, and even briefly mentions the foreign occupations.

Arrian refrains from quoting the subsequent detailed account of the Indian kings. As he himself testifies, the ethnography in his *Indica* is only a preface to the main purpose of the book—recounting the story of the naval expedition initiated by Alexander from Persia to India. Therefore he recorded only the "most notable" of the *nomima* he had found in Nearchus and Megasthenes (XVII.6–7). The emphasis was accordingly laid at the outset on customs, and even these were carefully selected and considerably abbreviated. He was not interested in the detailed history of the nonmythological kings. Diodorus, on his part, did not incorporate the section on the kings in his version, probably assuming that the names of Indian kings would not mean anything to the Greek reader, in contrast to those of the Egyptian and Mesopotamian kings. The detailed report by Herodotus (and possibly also by his predecessors) about the achievements of the latter introduced them into the corpus of Greek historical knowledge.

Diodorus's ethnographical excursus closes with a section on customs (II.39.5–42.2). It briefly comments on the absence of slavery in India (39.5), surveys the seven castes (40.1–41.5), and gives a long description of Indian elephants and their habits (42.1–2). Apart from the description of Indian elephants, Diodorus greatly abbreviated the *nomima*, omitting most of them. A number of subjects that Strabo explicitly attributed to Megasthenes can help in reconstructing this section: the simple life of the Indians, their self-restraint, oral laws and their characteristics, abstinence from alcoholic drinks, eating in solitude, physical activity, burial customs, body ornaments, clothing, attitude toward elderly people, marriage customs, and court practices (XV.1.53–55). Some of these subjects have parallels in Arrian, who supplements them with descriptions of urban construction, transportation, courting customs, and dining practices (*Indica* VIII.17). All these are likewise said to have been taken from Megasthenes.

The tenets and practices of Indian religion, which were already briefly referred to in the *origo*, are scattered among the *nomima* (e.g., sacrifices), mainly in the framework of the account of classes. Especially detailed is Strabo's version of the first caste, that of the philosophers (XV.1.58–60), drawn from Megasthenes (58.1, 59.1). It proves their connection with the Dionysian religion (58), distinguishes between the Brachmanes and the Garmanes, and elaborates on their unique ethics, way of life, and beliefs, especially on death and the creation and governance of the universe.

The account of elephants, their characteristics and habits, and elephant hunts appears in Diodorus after the survey of classes (cf. Arr. *Ind*. XIII–XV). In contrast to the views of some scholars, I do not think it was taken from an independent section dealing with *thaumasia* ("wonders," "curiosities"). In Strabo's version it is included in the account of the third class—that of farmers and hunters (XV.1.42–45)—and this may well have been its place in Megasthenes' ethnography. It could also be that the account of hunting and taming methods, which were described in particular detail, was attached as an appendix to the survey of the classes, as in Diodorus and also in Arrian (*Ind*. XIII).[70] An appendix to a section is also known from Hecataeus's Egyptian ethnography. It is almost certain that Megasthenes' work included accounts of hunting methods and the behavior of various wild animals: Strabo, attributing his information to Megasthenes, describes wild animals that had been domesticated in other countries, as well as unusual horses, monkeys, tigers, snakes, and scorpions (Strabo XV.1.37, 44–45, 56; cf. Ael. *NA* XVI.41; Pliny, *NH* VIII.14.1). Parallels for these descriptions can be found in references to wild animals, birds, and reptiles by Strabo and Arrian, which are attributed by them to Nearchus (Strabo XV.1.15; Arr. *Ind*. VIII.15.1–2, 8–12).[71]

---

70. In contrast to Stein, *RE* s.v. "Megasthenes (2)," 271, who thinks that the account of the elephants followed that of the customs of the kings. In his view, the latter account was included in the *nomima*, preceding the description of castes. The reference to elephant hunting in Strabo XV.1.55 is, however, rather flimsy evidence, and it seems that the kings' customs themselves appeared together with the classification of the officials (ibid. 50–52) at the end of the report on the seventh class (ibid. 49), or in the section on the history of the rulers.

71. At the same time, it seems that the Herodotean tale about the ants (Hdt. III.102–5, Arr. *Ind*. XV.5–7, Strabo XV.1.44) was incorporated by Megas-

Which of Megasthenes' books included the *nomima* section? Athenaeus (IV.153d) quotes a piece of information from Megasthenes' Book II about table setting as practiced by Indians. Clement of Alexandria (*Strom.* I.15) takes from Book III of the *Indica* a comparison between the views of Greek philosophers on nature and those of the Indian Brahmans. It can hence be accepted that Book II included the customs that were common to Indian society as a whole, and that Book III was devoted to those of individual castes.

To conclude: Megasthenes' work on India included the following sections: geography, *origo*, customs, and history of kings. The geography appeared in Book I; the *origo*, in the second part of that book or at the beginning of Book II. The *nomima* section was located in Books II and III, and the history of kings in Book IV. Wild animals were surveyed at the end of the *nomima*, as an appendix to the description of the castes, and the Indian religion in the *origo*, as well as in the *nomima* (in the latter section in relation to the class of philosophers). Geography was located at the head of the work, because Megasthenes believed it to exert a decisive influence on the other components.

Having dealt with Hecataeus and Megasthenes, the two great ethnographers of the beginning of the Hellenistic era, let us turn to Agatharcides of Cnidus, the most important figure in Alexandrian historiography, geography, and ethnography of the second century B.C.[72] Most of the fragments and extracts from his works are preserved in Diodorus's Book III, in Photius's *Bibliotheca* (213, 250), and in various books of Athenaeus's *Deipnosophistae*. The ethnographical passages deal with regions to the south of Egypt. The longest and most complete of them is the ethnographical account of the Ethiopians residing on the Upper Nile (Diod. III.2–10).

Diodorus himself states at the end of his excursus on the Ethiopian state that he drew his material from Agatharcides (III.11–12), adding that it was included in Book II of the work *On Asian Matters*. In the same sentence he also mentions Artemidorus of Ephesus as his source. It has already been accepted that Diodorus used Agatharcides indirectly

---

thenes within the account on mines, included in the geographical section (Diod. II.36.2). *Contra*, Stein, *RE* s.v. "Megasthenes (2)," 271.

72. For an evaluation of Agatharcides' achievements and his standing in the literature of the period, see Dihle (1961) 213ff.; Fraser (1972) I.539–53; K. E. Müller (1972–80) I.281–90. See also Murray (1970) 153–55.

through the work of Artemidorus, who himself held closely to the original account by Agatharcides.[73] There is no reason not to assume that Diodorus's version properly reflects the structure of Agatharcides' ethnographical account, despite the obvious abbreviation.[74]

The excursus by Diodorus-Agatharcides opens with the *origo-archaeologia* of the Ethiopians (III.2–7). They are described as an autochthonous nation, and as the first human beings (2.1). The author stresses that they were the originators of religious beliefs and cults (2.2–3) and emphasizes their piety, and the resultant difficulty of conquering and controlling them (2.4–3.1). The section closes with an appendix similar to that attached to the *origo* of Hecataeus's Egyptian ethnography, on the origin of mankind from Ethiopia. However, only the colonization of Egypt by Ethiopians is described, with Agatharcides clearly accepting Hecataeus's version on the dispersion of other nations from Egypt. As evidence for the Ethiopian origin of the Egyptians, the author points out similarities in customs, physical features, and the development of script (3.1–5.4). Religious beliefs and cult are referred to in both this section and that on customs. There is a great resemblance between this *origo* section and the first section of Hecataeus's Egyptian ethnography, which indicates the influence of the latter,[75] and supports the conclusion above that Hecataeus's first section is not a *theologoumena* but is an *origo-archaeologia*: both sections open with the autochthonous origin of the nation described and the creation of mankind there. Next they discuss the development of civilization, laying stress on the rise of religious beliefs and the family of gods. The accounts close with migration from the country and the creation of new nations. Evidence is provided mainly by comparisons of customs.

The second section describes the Ethiopian *nomima* (Diod. III.5.1–9.4). The first part deals with the civilized Ethiopians (5–7), the second with the wild tribes (8), and the third with practices common to all the Ethiopians (9). The section concentrates on unique, curious customs

73. On the origin of Diod. III.2–10 in Agatharcides, see Schwartz, *RE* s.v. "Diodoros (12)," 673; Jacoby (1943) 152. On Agatharcides as the source for chaps. 5–10, see Schwartz, *loc. cit.*; Leopoldi (1892) 32–34. On Artemidorus as an intermediate source and his adherence to the original text, see Jacoby, *loc. cit.*; Fraser (1972) II.773 n. 160, and also I.549–50; Dihle (1961) 222–23.

74. See, e.g., Peremans (1967).

75. On the influence of Hecataeus's Egyptian ethnography on the Ethiopian ethnography of Agatharcides, see also Murray (1970) 152–57.

attributed to the Ethiopians. It also includes the Ethiopian belief in various gods interpreted according to the Euhemerist conception (9.1–2), though the religious originality of the Ethiopians was already surveyed in the *origo*. The last section deals with geography (10). It appears in Diodorus in an extremely abbreviated version, which certainly does not properly reflect Agatharcides' original account.[76] The excursus does not include a section on Ethiopian rulers, perhaps because Agatharcides was acquainted only with the names and deeds of the kings of the Hellenistic period (see on Ergamenes, Diod. III.6.3–4). As he could have sought support in royal Egyptian records (see III.38.1), it is possible that he did not bother to incorporate them into his account because the ancient Ethiopian kings had not had contacts with the Greek world in the past,[77] and were not mentioned by Herodotus. It may also be that it was Diodorus who omitted the section on the kings, for similar reasons, as he had done with regard to the survey by Megasthenes on the Indian kings.

Other fragments of Agatharcides, which also refer to Ethiopia (Photius, *Bibl.* cod. 250; *GGM* I.111–95), were taken from his book *On the Red Sea*. They do not deal with political entities, but with primitive tribes in the region. The account includes only geography and customs, and lays stress on *thaumasia*, namely miracles, curiosities, and exceptional phenomena. This focus indicates a shortage of authoritative information. The narrative inclines to the paradoxographical, rather than to ethnographical writing,[78] and therefore does not concern us here.

Having so far discussed some of the most important ethnographical monographs and excursuses of the classical and Hellenistic periods, we turn now to excursuses on Jews and Judaism in Hellenistic and Roman literature. The first comprehensive account on Jews and Judaism was the Jewish excursus by Hecataeus of Abdera, preserved by

76. See also the indication in Diod. III.10.6.

77. See Diod. III.37.5, taken as well from Agatharcides.

78. Cf. the evaluation of Susemihl (1891) I.691, which is certainly based on the fragments from the book *On the Red Sea*, and not on the Ethiopian ethnography (though he exaggerates in underrating the former work). A more detailed discussion: Burstein (1989) 23–29. On the ethnographical-paradoxographical literature, see Trüdinger (1918) 34ff.

Diodorus (XL.3.1–8) as an ethnographic introduction to the first Jewish confrontations with the Romans (63 B.C.). The variety of subjects connected with this version concerning ancient Judaism was discussed above in Chapter I.2. With regard to the genre it was argued that the excursus is basically an ethnography and not a "foundation story" (*ktisis*), despite the evident influence of Greek colonization traditions.[79] In the framework of the present chapter, I shall refer only to the general scheme of the excursus and related questions.

The excursus, as explicitly stated by Diodorus (XL.3.1), comprised a *ktisis* ("foundation") section (1–3) and a *nomima* section (3–8). The titles may well have recorded Hecataeus's original nomenclature. The excursus does not include sections on geography and history. Despite the abbreviation of Jewish daily practices by Diodorus,[80] it is quite certain that the two sections were missing in the original version. Diodorus would not have omitted historical and geographical accounts, had there been any, when he incorporated the excursus into Book XL. They would have served to introduce the reader to the geographical background of the Roman occupation. The absence of a historical section is not exceptional. A geographical section, however, is included in the conventional scheme of an ethnographical work, and in all later Jewish ethnographical excursuses. To understand this lacuna, the original location of the Jewish account in Hecataeus's work must be established. The discussion may reveal a subtype of the ethnographical excursus.

As has been universally accepted, the excursus could be taken only from Hecataeus's great Egyptian ethnography. It has been suggested by Jacoby that its exact location was in the framework of the appendix to the *origo* section, which described the migration of various nations from Egypt (Diod. I.28–29).[81] To examine this suggestion and its implications for the structure of the original Jewish excursus, let us take a closer look at the appendix.

The appendix opens with the statement "Now the Egyptians say that also after these events a great number of *apoikiai* were spread

---

79. See p. 32 above.

80. P. 24 above.

81. See Jacoby (1943) 49–52; cf. Murray (1970) 146–47, 158; Gager (1972) 28–29; Sterling (1992) 76–77. The counterarguments of Guttman (1958–63) I.49 are mistaken, esp. his references to the passage on the Babylonians (Diod. I.28.1).

from Egypt over all the inhabited world" (28.1; cf. 29.5). Then comes a short account of an emigration from Egypt to Babylon, led by the eponymous Belus, his appointment of priests, and the establishment of their rights and practices (28.1). It is followed by a short sentence about the emigration to Argos led by Danaus (28.2) and a statement that the Colchi in Pontus, as well as the Jews, were also emigrants from Egypt (28.2). To justify this statement, the author mentions the practice of circumcision as common among the Egyptians, the Colchi, and the Jews (28.3; cf. Hdt. II.104). The discussion then turns to the Athenians (Diod. I.28.4–29.5). Diodorus provides evidence as to their origin in Egypt: linguistic parallels, the similarity of political institutions and religious rituals, the Egyptian descent of some Athenian rulers, and some evidence for an Egyptian origin of two Athenian families. The appendix closes with the observation that the Egyptians attributed Egyptian origin to many other nations, but since they did not provide real evidence, he chose to ignore their claims (29.5).

It seems rather clear that the appendix was drastically abbreviated by Diodorus. Writing a universal history, he did not find it appropriate to include in the framework of the Egyptian ethnography detailed accounts about nations or cities that were to figure later in the course of his historical narrative. The passage on the Babylonians is evidently a shortened version of an ethnographical account that included their *origo* and *nomima*. Diodorus, for his own reasons, preferred to preserve only the information concerning the priests originally included in the *nomima* section. There is no reason not to think that the references to the Jews and the Colchi are likewise remnants of more detailed accounts. The case of the Athenians was different: Hecataeus was content with quoting evidence for their Egyptian descent, because there was no point in introducing an Athenian ethnography (or a comprehensive *nomima* section) to his prospective Greek readers. The same may apply to the Argives. It is difficult to know whether the original appendix included accounts of other nations. On the one hand, the note at the end of the appendix (29.5), casting doubt on Egyptian stories about the descent of other nations and cities from Egypt, does not seem to be Diodorean. On the other hand, the Jewish excursus mentions Cadmus as one of the leaders of Greek emigrants from Egypt, which indicates some account concerning Thebes. Be that as it may, the references to nations in the appendix reflect two types of account in the original text: (a) ethnographical accounts containing only the *origo* and *nomima*; (b) statements concerning migration and evidence pointing to it, especially common customs and institutions, and linguistic similarities. The absence of a geographical section and an account of rulers in both types is not accidental: after all, the author was primarily concerned in this context to stress the origin of certain nations in Egypt, with the evidence of Egyptian influences on their customs to prove it. Moreover, historical and especially geographical sections on foreign lands would have been quite out of place in a work on Egypt and the Egyptians.

The suggestion made by Jacoby, that the Jewish excursus had been taken by Diodorus from Hecataeus's appendix to the Egyptian *origo*, was based on the conclusion that the appendix included a series of ethnographical accounts of nations said to have migrated from Egypt; on the reference to the Jews in the appendix; on the reference in the excursus to the expulsion of foreigners to "Greece and other regions" and the explicit mention of Danaus (3.2), which recalls the information about the emigration to Greece and Asia Minor headed by Danaus found in the appendix (28.2); and finally, on the appearance of the phrase τὸ παλαιόν ("in ancient times") both at the beginning of the excursus (3.1) and in the appendix with regard to the Jews (28.3). These points can be supplemented by further observations. First, there are striking parallels between the passage about the Babylonians in the appendix and the Jewish excursus (migration; leader-lawgiver; appointment of priests; privileges conferred upon the priests; duties and qualifications of the priests). Second, the excursus contains only the *origo* and *nomima*, like the Babylonian passage.[82]

It should be added that the absence of any reference to circumcision in the Jewish excursus as preserved by Diodorus, though it is mentioned in the appendix (I.28.3; cf. 55.5), does not detract from the validity of the above conclusion. The passage in the appendix about circumcision among the Egyptians, the Jews, and the Colchi may have been a general preface by Hecataeus to his more detailed account of the latter two nations, which made the listing of circumcision among their *nomima* rather redundant. It could also be that it was Diodorus who omitted circumcision from the excursus, as he had done with all Jewish practices re-

---

82. The reference to the location of the Jewish land in the appendix is not a remnant of a geographical section but a necessary orientation note (cf. n. 98 below).

lating to private life (XL.3.8). Citing these practices could not contribute to the main purpose for which the excursus was quoted by Diodorus.

Another difficulty with Jacoby's suggestion is the apparent discrepancy between the excursus and the appendix with regard to the cause of the emigration: the excursus speaks about the expulsion of Jews and Greeks from Egypt (Diod. XL.3.1–2), while the appendix does not mention an expulsion, but describes the settlements founded by the Jews and other nations as *apoikiai* ("colonies") "spread from Egypt" (I.28.1) and "founded by emigrants from Egypt" (28.2). However, the absence of a reference to the expulsion can be attributed to the drastic abbreviation of the appendix by Diodorus, which is especially evident in its first paragraphs.[83] As for the terminology, the fact is that even a settlement of exiles was called an *apoikia*.[84] Moreover, such inconsistency exists in the excursus itself, which shortly afterwards uses the same term for the settlement of Jews by Moses in Judea (XL.3.3). We have already seen that the terminology, like other features in the excursus, was deeply influenced by foundation traditions.[85] The same naturally applies to the appendix, which deals with emigrations.

To sum up: Diodorus took the excursus from Hecataeus's appendix, and like other ethnographical accounts in that appendix, the original text contained only two sections: the *origo* and the *nomima*. With regard to the general question of the structure of ethnographical works, it appears that there was a subtype of ethnographical excursus, which, because of the special context, consisted of only two of the major components: the *origo* and the *nomima*.

Hecataeus's Jewish excursus deeply influenced, directly and indirectly, the contents of almost all ethnographical accounts of and references to the Jews and Judaism written by Hellenistic and Roman authors. Although they had the possibility of acquiring better and more accurate knowledge, they preferred to adhere to the earliest account. A similar tendency can also be observed in ethnographies of other nations, which are merely expanded adaptations of earlier ethnographies.[86] However, the structure of later Jewish ethnographies

---

83. Another explanation for the discrepancy is suggested by Jacoby (1943) 49–50. Cf. Gager (1972) 28–29; Conzelmann (1981) 57; Sterling (1992) 76–77.

84. See Graham (1982) 143.

85. See pp. 30–34 above.

86. See Jacoby (1909) 92.

follows the conventional scheme of an ethnographical treatise, as reflected in Hecataeus's account of the Egyptians, and not the shortened, exceptional one of his Jewish excursus and his other "miniatures." As the Jewish ethnographies were written in the time of the Hasmonean state and afterwards, a section on Jewish rulers was also included.

Strabo's ethnographical excursus on the Jews, incorporated in his *Geography* (XVI.2.34–39), is the best example of Hecataeus's influence. The excursus, which was taken from Posidonius of Apamea, is a consistent adaptation (frequently also a deliberate reversal), following Hecataeus step by step. Hecataeus's information is reshaped in the spirit of the Middle Stoa. Mosaic Judaism, which Posidonius contrasts with later Judaism, is clearly a utopian society intended to serve as a model. Its way of life is actually a reflection of the social, religious, and political ideals of Posidonius himself. Posidonius's purpose from the outset was not to provide information on the Jews, but to show that his own theoretical ideals were not impractically utopian but could be (and were) realized in practice.[87]

Strabo's excursus opens with the statement that Moses was an Egyptian priest. Then follows a description of the Jewish faith and the story of the migration from Egypt (XVI.2.35–36). The integration of theology into the *origo* is necessary for his original explanation of the Exodus: Moses and his followers, who are introduced as what might be called "intellectual Egyptians," left Egypt because they were dissatisfied with the local cult and aspired to establish a new religion, free of any material representation of the divine. In order to explain why the Jews chose to settle in Jerusalem, the author includes a few sentences on the water supply and soil of the city and its surroundings (2.36).

A comprehensive geographical account of the Jewish land appears in the sequence of Strabo's general geographic narrative, preceding and following the Jewish excursus (2.34, 41–45), but not in the excursus itself. This geographical account combines two sources, Posidonius and Artemidorus,[88] and is artificially separated into two parts by the ethnographical excursus. It includes, among other things, a repetition

---

87. The question of the source of Strabo's ethnographical excursus has been touched on by a number of scholars. For a detailed discussion with new evidence, see Bar-Kochva, *Anti-Semitism and Idealization of Judaism*, chap. VI.

88. On Artemidorus, cf. p. 104 n. 158 above. Posidonius as a source is mentioned in Strabo XVI.2.43.

(with one addition) of the references to Jerusalem and its surroundings that have already appeared in the ethnographical excursus (2.40). Thus it is possible that in Posidonius's original Jewish excursus there was a detailed section on the geography of Judea that followed the *origo*, and not just a few sentences on Jerusalem.

The next section, the *nomima*, lists a number of Stoic-influenced practices and ideals, which the author attributes to Moses: refraining from military exercises and armament, from excessive expenditures on the religious cult, and from establishing governmental institutions (2.36). The section is rather short in comparison with its equivalents in other Jewish ethnographies. This is not surprising in view of Posidonius's purpose: he took from Hecataeus only those customs that he could bring into conformity (or reverse to fit) with his Stoic conceptions and ideals. The excursus closes with a section on Jewish rulers after Moses, the founder. The author refers mainly to the Hasmonean leaders and kings, described as tyrants who departed from the Mosaic heritage (2.37, 39). An appendix to the section on the Jewish rulers elaborates on famous ancient prophets and lawgivers. The appendix was taken by Strabo not from Posidonius but from an unknown source.[89]

A Jewish excursus that ignored the Hecataean tradition altogether was written by Pompeius Trogus, the Augustan historian. The excursus, originally included in Trogus's *Historiae Philippicae*, has come down to us in an abbreviated version in the *epitomē* of Justin, from the third century A.D. (XXXVI.2.1–3.8), and it appears to be a rather confused mixture of information from various sources.[90] The structure is, however, identical to the conventional scheme of Hellenistic ethnographical works.

The excursus opens with a complicated, long version of the Jewish *origo*, which combines several traditions (2.1–14): the Jews are said to have arisen from a royal dynasty ruling in Damascus. The author refers specifically to Abraham, Israel and his twelve children, and the creation of the twelve tribes (in Damascus?). After this he goes on to describe the sale of Joseph to the Egyptians and Joseph's success in Egypt. Moses, according to Trogus's story, was Joseph's son, and is said to have left

---

89. See Bar-Kochva, *Anti-Semitism and Idealization of Judaism*, chap. VI.

90. On the basic sources of Pompeius Trogus, see M. Stern (1974–84) I.332ff., 339; *id.* (1991) 470ff., (1993) 12–13; Gager (1983) 70ff. On his ethnographical writing, see K. E. Müller (1972–80) II.60–67.

Egypt at the head of all the Egyptians who suffered from pestilence and leprosy. The account of the Jews wandering in the desert and the relation of the Jews to Mount Sinai is no less distorted.

The second section is devoted to Jewish customs (2.14–15). It is directly connected with the *origo*: Jewish practices are explained by the circumstances of the residence in and expulsion from Egypt. Thus, for instance, the Sabbath is said to have been established as a fast day to commemorate a seven days' fast at the time of the wanderings in the desert. Moreover, Jewish religious practices are characterized as typically Egyptian. Consequently the excursus devotes just one short sentence to the Jewish faith and cult. Egyptian beliefs themselves were probably described, in a manner similar to that of Hecataeus, in the framework of the Egyptian *origines* known to have been included in Book I of Pompeius Trogus's historical work (according to his *Prol.* I). The Jews are said to be ruled by kings who also served as priests. Pompeius Trogus was informed on this point by sources referring to the Hasmonean period. Contrary to the accounts of other gentile authors, however, this system of government is presented by him as traditionally Jewish, originating with Arruas (Aaron, Moses' son in his version).

After the customs comes the geography (3.1–7). Justin's version is not comprehensive. It relates only to what he calls the sources of Jewish wealth—the balsam of the Jericho Valley and the natural resources of the Dead Sea. It is possible that the original account included a comprehensive geographical section and that Justin omitted most of it, as he had done with other geographical excursuses.[91] Justin preserved only the passages that described the districts and features unique to Judea. The references to Jewish wealth may indicate that Pompeius Trogus also used the geographical excursus to illustrate and explain other features of Jewish life.

Justin closes the excursus with a short passage on the period of Jewish subjection, from Xerxes (instead of Cyrus) up to the gaining of independence, dated to the time of Demetrius (I or II; unspecified). The section does not record the deeds of Jewish rulers, because in this case an account of the Hasmonaeans would have been redundant: the excursus was preceded in the same book by a description of the campaign of

91. See Klotz, *RE* s.v. "Pompeius Trogus," 2304; M. Stern (1991) 473.

Antiochus VII against John Hyrcanus (*Prol.* XXXVI), and the same book later recorded events in the days of his successors (*Prol.* XXXIX, Justin XL.2.4). Those chapters in Pompeius Trogus's original book must certainly have expanded on the characteristics of the Hasmonean dynasty from the viewpoint of the Hellenistic world.

The best-known and most detailed Jewish ethnography at our disposal is Tacitus's notorious excursus in Book V of his *Histories* (V.2–10). It served as a preface to his account of Titus's siege and conquest of Jerusalem and the destruction of the Temple.[92] The contents of the excursus were influenced by Hecataeus, as well as by later hostile references and rumors about Jews and Judaism, all carrying Tacitus's strong imprint. The structure follows the conventional scheme of four sections. However, their sequence and contents, and the internal order of each section, differ from those of other Jewish ethnographies. They are dictated by the context of the excursus, Tacitus's tendency to arrange topics associatively in his ethnographical works,[93] and his extremely negative opinion of Jews and Judaism.

The excursus opens with the *origo*. Tacitus raises a number of conjectures as to the origin of the Jews. All are connected with stories of migration, expulsion, or flight from Crete, Ethiopia, Assyria, and Asia Minor (*Hist.* V.2). Tacitus himself accepts the anti-Semitic Egyptian-Greek versions of the Jewish Exodus from Egypt (3). The *origo* is followed by customs (4–5), and not by the geography as is usual in Tacitus. The reason is first and foremost the thematic association: Tacitus opens the customs section with those Jewish cult practices that could be explained by events from the time of the expulsion. Furthermore, contrary to his practice in other ethnographies (e.g., *Germania* 5.1ff., *Agricola* 11), Tacitus does not apply geographical explanations to Jewish customs. He therefore did not have any reason to place the geography before the customs.

The customs section breaks down into two parts: the first (*Hist.* V.4) deals with Jewish cult and religious customs (some alleged), which are explained by the Jewish *origo*. The second (5) contains customs that are not connected with early Jewish history, but arise from what

92. On the excursus as a whole, see M. Stern (1974–84) II.1–6, 17, and detailed bibliography there.

93. On this tendency as a decisive factor in the structure of Tacitus's ethnographical accounts, see Trüdinger (1918) 163, 168; Norden (1922) 457, 461.

Tacitus calls the Jewish *pravitas* ("corrupted character").[94] It ends with a reference to Jewish monotheism, which is followed by the statement that the Jews refrained from making graven representations of the divine and from deifying kings. These features of the Jewish cult and creed were discussed at the end of the section because of association with the preceding material on Jewish customs.[95] Since Tacitus mentioned there the similarity between the burial customs and the belief in immortality of Egyptians and Jews, he also found it appropriate to stress the fundamental differences in the cults of the two nations. It stands to reason that Tacitus deferred the account of Jewish beliefs to the end of the customs section because of his lack of appreciation for Jewish religion: in his view Jewish religious conceptions did not originate in authentic, positive religious and moral thinking, but from hatred for mankind and anything sanctified by the civilized world. In his view this negative motivation also characterized most Jewish religious practices (mainly 3.1; 5.1, 5).

The geography occupies the third part of the work (*Hist.* V.6–8). The survey covers the borders of Judea, climate, flora, and terrain—soil, mountains, rivers, and lakes. Special attention is given to the balsam of Jericho and the unique phenomena of the Dead Sea. The description of Jerusalem (8) is rather short, relative to the rest of the section, because the report on the beginning of Titus's siege, which follows the excursus, is accompanied by a detailed description of the city: its hills and walls, and the Temple fortifications (11–12). As was said above, in contrast to other ethnographies, Tacitus in the *Histories* does not use the geography in any way to explain Jewish character and customs. He was obviously unable to connect the pleasant features of the land and its climate with his hostile characterization of its inhabitants. The account, therefore, remains cool and "neutral," unlike the other sections of the excursus.

The historical discussion makes up the fourth section, the very last in the excursus (*Hist.* V.8–10). Contrary to the usual practice in non-Jewish ethnographies, it is not an account of rulers alone, but a summary of later Jewish history. In this respect Tacitus's version is similar to other Jewish ethnographies, but it differs from them in the emphasis laid on periods of foreign rule. The report opens with

94. On this division and its literary and ideological background, see Lewy (1960) 123 n. 37.

95. On the associative process in para. 5, see Lewy (1960) 175 n. 254.

the subjection of the Jews to the oriental empires and the Macedonian kingdoms (8.2–3), continues with a brief, condensed reference to the Hasmonean rulers (8.3), and closes with the development of Jewish-Roman relations from the occupation by Pompey up to the Great Revolt (9–10). Tacitus deviates from the accepted scheme in this section because of his overall purpose and because of the context. The first period of Jewish subjugation serves as evidence for the inferior, "servile" position of the Jews in history (8.2), and the period under Roman occupation is a preface to the story of the Roman-Jewish war. It ends in the Year of the Four Emperors and is thus naturally integrated into the account of the siege of Jerusalem. For reasons related to the context (although in an entirely different manner), Tacitus's excursus on the British in *Agricola* (13ff.) also expands on the history of Roman rule in Britain and mentions only in passing that in the past the British had had kings of their own.

To sum up the discussion: the above survey of ethnographical monographs and excursuses shows that the conventional ethnography was composed of three or four sections, in the following order: *origo-archaeologia*, geography, customs, and history of rulers. The *origo* almost always opened the ethnographical work, and only in one case was it replaced by the geography. The geographical account usually preceded that of customs, while in the Jewish excursuses the customs section comes before the geographical account. The fourth component, the history of rulers, was sometimes absent, and in a number of Jewish excursuses it takes the form of a concise history of the nation in the time of the Second Temple. A cursory glance at some Roman ethnographies suffices to show that they followed the same basic scheme (e.g., Tacitus's *Germania* and *Agricola*; Amm. Marc. XV.9–12).

The origin of the nation heads the ethnographical work because according to the conception of ethnographical literature the *origo* was the main clue to understanding the character, customs, and history of a nation. All these were thought to have been deeply influenced by the special circumstances of the nation's birth.[96] The origin may be autochthonous or connected with a migration. In the case of

---

96. See also Trüdinger (1918) 75, 147–48, 150; Norden (1922) 46ff.; Lewy (1960) 95–96, 131–39; Lloyd (1990) 225–26.

autochthonous peoples (Egyptians, Ethiopians, or Indians), the *origo-archaeologia* section includes the claim for the genesis of the human race (or life in general) in their countries and the early stages of civilization. These accounts include the beginnings of the belief in gods and the role of certain gods and mythological figures in the introduction of civilization. With regard to migrating nations, the basic beliefs are recorded in the customs section. Only Strabo's Jewish excursus records the Jewish faith and some basic religious practices in the framework of the *origo*, for, according to the author's view, the very migration was motivated by philosophical-religious aspirations.

The *origo-archaeologia* of an autochthonous nation is sometimes supplemented by appendixes on nations created by migration from its land. Such an appendix consists of a series of independent ethnographical accounts. Unlike the ordinary ethnographical monograph or excursus, they contain only the two sections required by the context: the story of the migration (i.e., the *origo*) and the *nomima*. Hecataeus's account of Jews and Judaism belongs to this exceptional category. In the case of famous Greek cities like Athens, the ethnographical account is replaced by a statement about the migration and indirect evidence that it did in fact occur, based mainly on language, customs, and institutions.

The geography usually appears as the second section. Ethnographers attributed to geography great influence (though usually less than to the *origo*) on the shaping and development of a nation. Climate, soil, topography, and water are described as decisive factors.[97] Hence the prominent position of the geographical section in second place, before customs. Geography was considered to have a greater impact on autochthonous than on migrating nations. In the case of Megasthenes this even caused him to place the Indian geography before the *origo*.[98]

---

97. See further Trüdinger (1918) 51ff.; Dihle (1961) 208.

98. Tacitus's ethnographies may seem to open with geography (*Agr.* 10, *Ger.* 1). However, he only records the borders of the country and then goes on to the *origo*. A comprehensive geographical account follows the *origo* section and includes all the other components of geography that were considered to have influenced the character of a nation (climate, soil, flora, fauna, etc.: *Ger.* 5, *Agr.* 11b–12). The placing of the borders at the head of the ethnography was thus intended only to give the reader the necessary basic orientation.

The section on customs, the *nomima*, is as a rule located third, after the *origo* and geography. In some cases, customs precede the geography, despite the influence of the latter component on the life of a nation. This happens, for instance, in the Jewish excursuses, where the connection between the customs and the *origo* is too evident to be deferred to a later stage in the account. The *nomima* are actually the "heart" of an ethnography. Ethnographical works were written first and foremost either to teach the reader about the characteristics and everyday life of a nation or to achieve some political, social, or religious goal. The customs section also includes religious creeds and practices, if these are not recorded in the *origo*.

An ethnographical work usually closes with a historical section. For reasons connected with the specific contents, Hecataeus's Egyptian ethnography places history before the *nomima*. The ordinary historical section covers only the most famous rulers, laying stress on their major achievements, especially great military expeditions and building projects. In the case of the Jews this is replaced by a general historical outline, mainly of the changes in the political status of the nation from subjection to independence and back to subjection, without naming individual rulers. Later ethnographers comment on the policies of the Hasmoneans.

The historical section is missing in the ethnographies of some nations. The authors either did not know much about their rulers, or assumed that the reader would not be interested in the names of rulers who were not mentioned by Herodotus or other classical authors.

For the sake of the following discussion on the structure of Pseudo-Hecataeus's treatise, it should be repeated that apart from one case, the surveyed ethnographical works all open with the *origo*. Only in Megasthenes' Indian ethnography does the *origo-archaeologia* appear in second place, after geography. It should also be stressed that the *origo* opens Hecataeus's two ethnographies, his excursus on the Jews, and all the surviving excursuses on Jews and Judaism.

4. THE STRUCTURE OF *ON THE JEWS:* THE PLACE AND ROLE OF THE HEZEKIAH STORY

Hecataeus's passages in *Against Apion* contain at least two sections of the four common in ethnographic literature: (a) customs (including religion: *Ap.* I.188, 190–94, 201–2; II.43;[99] Orig. *C. Cels.* I.15);[100] (b) geography (including descriptions of the Temple and demography, *Ap.* I.195–200).

The passages do not make any reference to the traditional Jewish *origo*—the patriarchs, the former Jewish residence in Egypt, Moses' personality and accomplishments, the Exodus, and the settlement in Canaan. Nor is there any mention of Jewish rulers, the kings or later secular and religious leaders (except for Hezekiah). There is no doubt that all these were absent from the treatise: the very quotation of the passages by Josephus is meant to prove that Greek and Hellenistic authors were acquainted with and acknowledged the antiquity of the Jewish people (*Ap.* I.22, 175). Had there been any account of these events and personalities, Josephus would certainly have quoted it at length. His emphatic statement that Hecataeus's report about Hezekiah proves that the Jewish people were already flourishing by the time of Ptolemy I (*Ap.* I.185) further strengthens this conclusion.

The Hezekiah story cannot belong to the two components inherent in the other passages. Hezekiah being the only Jewish leader mentioned, the story could not be part of a section on rulers' histories either.[101] What then is the role and place of the story in the schematic structure of the book? In order to answer this question we have to understand the contents of the story precisely, especially the passage about Hezekiah's activity in Egypt.

---

99. The granting of Samaria to the Jews was presented by Hecataeus as a compensation for Jewish loyalty. It therefore appears that the event was briefly referred to in the context of illustrations for the loyalty of Jews (esp. that of Jewish soldiers) under oath. This characteristic is also emphasized by Josephus (*Ant.* XI.318; XII.8, 147) and is mentioned in a document of Antiochus III (*Ant.* XII.150; and cf. 147; see also Schalit [1960] 298ff.).

100. Herennius Philo's note about the excessive elaboration of Pseudo-Hecataeus on "Jewish wisdom" obviously refers to the Mosollamus anecdote, and also summarizes the essence of other passages (see p. 184 above). Other views on the location of the Mosollamus story: Jacoby (1943) 66; Sterling (1992) 87, who considers it to belong to a historical section. See also the following footnotes.

101. *Contra* Sterling, ibid. Jacoby (*loc. cit.*, n. 100), who suggests that the story belongs (together with the Mosollamus episode) to a quasi-autobiographical framework of (what he considers to be) an ethnographic treatise, fails to take into account the absence of the *origo* component.

This, however, is not easy. The original text was only partly cited by Josephus. The quotations contain four separate excerpts (I.186–89), each paragraph constituting another excerpt. Certain conjunctions used by Josephus indicate considerable omissions between the excerpts.[102] As appears from the contents, significant omissions have been made at the end of the first excerpt, as well as at the beginning and the end of the fourth. In addition, the phrasing of the fourth excerpt is quite condensed, containing twice as many participles as finite verbs, which may indicate abbreviation by Josephus. The last two sentences are especially concise, and there is an evident lacuna in one of them. These shortcomings of the present text have to be taken into account in trying to understand it.

The general contents of the first and second excerpts (I.186–87) are quite clear: after the battle of Gaza, many Jews, among them Hezekiah the High Priest, decided to follow the king to Egypt and participate in the building of the kingdom. The third excerpt (I.188) refers to the number of priests engaged in public duties and does not concern us here. Hezekiah's activity in Egypt is described in the fourth excerpt, the text of which is rather problematic:

[189] οὗτος . . . ὁ ἄνθρωπος τετευχὼς τῆς τιμῆς ταύτης καὶ συνήθης ἡμῖν γενόμενος, παραλαβών τινας τῶν μεθ' ἑαυτοῦ τήν τε διαφορὰν ἀνέγνω πᾶσαν αὐτοῖς· εἶχεν γὰρ τὴν κατοίκησιν αὐτῶν καὶ τὴν πολιτείαν γεγραμμένην.

[189] This man . . . had obtained this *timē* ["honor"? "appointment"? "authority"? "reward"?], and being well acquainted with us, he assembled some of his men and read to them the whole *diaphora* ["difference"? "advantage"? "profit"?]. For [he? it?] held [εἶχεν] in writing their settling [*katoikēsis*] and *politeia*.

The great stumbling block is the word *diaphora*. Whatever its meaning, it can hardly stand alone as the object of "he read." Hans Lewy emends διαφοράν to διφθέραν (i.e., *diaphora*, "difference," to *diphthera*, "scroll").[103] He suggests that Hezekiah was reading the Torah, and that the following sentence refers to its contents: the story of the settlement of the Israelites in Canaan (*katoikēsis*) and the law of

102. πάλιν (186, 189), καίτοι (188), and also φασίν (187). Cf. Jacoby (1943) 66.
103. Lewy (1932) 132; and independently Cataudella (1933) 75. Cf. Février (1924) 70.

the Torah (*politeia*). Lewy's emendation and interpretation have been accepted by the majority of scholars.[104]

The emendation itself is not free from difficulties of grammar and substance. First, the particle τε indicates a lacuna in the text.[105] Second, according to the emendation, the subject of the verb εἶχεν, which opens the subsequent sentence, must be the "scroll," meaning "it contained" or the like. However, εἶχεν is not the right expression. The closest possible verb would be περίειχεν. Finally, the word γάρ ("for"), which connects the two sentences, would certainly not fit: the Pentateuch, especially the book of Deuteronomy, is anything but supportive of the idea of settling in Egypt.

To interpret the author as referring to the reading of the Pentateuch, and consequently the *katoikēsis* as the story about the settlement in Canaan, poses a number of other questions: Why did Hezekiah assemble only "some of his men" for the reading of the Pentateuch, which was usually performed before large crowds? How could Hezekiah have read "the whole scroll"—that is, the Torah—in one session? Moreover, the Pentateuch does not record the story of the settlement in Canaan, but closes at the eve of the occupation. The Jewish author, who demonstrates good knowledge of the Scriptures, must have known this basic fact, if only from the ordinary communal religious service.[106] And above all, would a leader who initiated Jewish emigration to Egypt have assembled his followers on that occasion just to read them the story of the Exodus and the settlement in the Holy Land, a story whose very

104. E.g., Jacoby (1943) 71–72; Guttman (1958–63) I.69–70; Zuntz (1958) 311; M. Stern (1974–84) I.42; Troiani (1977) 119; Millar (1979) 7–8; Gauger (1982) 30; Holladay (1983) 327 n. 17; Doran (1985) 917; cf. Conzelmann (1981) 169–70; Will and Orrieux (1986) 91.

105. For the benefit of readers who may not be at home with Greek syntax, some words of explanation may be of assistance. The particle τε has two usages (see Denniston [1954] 495ff.). The first usage, as simple connective, must be excluded for the sentence under discussion: τε can connect clauses only when they are of equal syntactical standing. A participial subordinate clause can in no way be connected to the main clause by τε or καί. The τε in the sentence must therefore have the second usage, which is far commoner in prose anyway: a preparatory particle in correspondsion. Its corressponsive particle is thus missing. Being a *lectio difficilior*, τε is not likely to have been a copyist's addition.

106. On his Jewish education and affiliation to the moderate conservatives, see above, pp. 159ff., 180–81.

essence is the negation of Jewish residence in Egypt? The author must have been aware of this, and would not have attributed to Hezekiah the performance of such a ceremony in the midst of the emigration and settlement in Egypt. Surely he would not have described it as the climax of Hezekiah's activity upon arriving in Egypt.

Consequently, the emended reading διφθέραν, "scroll," cannot mean the Pentateuch unless the lacuna is filled with the name of another written text, and this text is assumed to have contained the *katoikēsis* and *politeia*. It can therefore be concluded that whatever the correct reading of the word in question might be, the main essence of the last two sentences in the fourth excerpt could only be that Hezekiah introduced to his audience the "foundation decree," that is, an official document (or more than one) dealing with the Jewish settlement in Egypt. It contained the charter of the settlement, that is, permission to settle (*katoikēsis*) and a constitution (*politeia*).[107]

In view of all these considerations the existing reading, διαφοράν, deserves reexamination. On the assumption that the word *diaphora* in this context means "advantage," "profit,"[108] I would suggest *exempli gratia* the following to supplement the lacuna:

τήν τε διαφοράν ⟨ἀπέδειξε, καὶ τὴν συγγραφὴν⟩ ἀνέγνω πᾶσαν αὐτοῖς· εἶχεν γὰρ τὴν κατοίκησιν αὐτῶν καὶ τὴν πολιτείαν γεγραμμένην.
(He ⟨pointed out⟩ to them the advantage and read to them the whole ⟨*syngraphē*: "decree"? "charter"?⟩. For he possessed in writing their settling and *politeia*.)

Instead of καί, δέ and τε are also possible.[109] *Syngraphē* appears for decrees as well as for a charter of a settlement, which contains

---

107. On Greek "foundation decrees," see Graham (1964) 40–68, (1982) 144. For the Hellenistic period, see, e.g., Jos. *Ant.* XII.148–53; Welles (1934) no. 51.

108. Cf. Reinach (1895) 230; Willrich (1900) 91; Wendland (1900) 1200 n. 2; Conzelmann (1981) 169–70; Doran (1985) 917. Their interpretations of the sentence, however, fail to convince. They do not solve the difficulty in language and contents, and do not notice the existence of the lacuna. Thus Wendland suggests that *diaphora* refers to the advantage of the Jewish laws over those of other nations, which presumes that Hezekiah read the Torah.

109. On the usage of these particles as corresponsive to τε, see Denniston (1954) 497–505, 513–15. Note the appearance (*bis*) of the corresponsion τε ... τε in Antiphon II.3.3, where *diaphora* is used in the sense "advantage," "profit." Direct influence must not be ruled out: being almost free of religion and mythology, the fourth-century orators could well have served as reading

the permission to settle and the rights of the settlers,[110] but other terms and variations are also possible. The general meaning of the sentence remains the same. The lacuna may have been caused by a *homoiographon* (διαφορὰν ⟨...⟩ ἀνέγνω), or by jumping from a point in the first leg of a *parisōsis* to the equivalent point in the second leg (-ν [verb τὴν -ν] verb). The sentences thus mean that Hezekiah consulted his close friends, reading to them the decree or charter given by the court, pointing out to them the advantages of accepting the offer.[111]

The interpretation of the second part of the fourth excerpt illuminates its first part. They seem to be closely connected, the second resulting from the first. Hezekiah is said to have been "well acquainted with us" (καὶ συνήθης ἡμῖν γενόμενος).[112] This means that he carried out negotiations with the authorities over the settlement and its conditions. Consequently, he received a *timē*. In view of the general context, this does not seem to be merely an honorary title or gesture,[113] but the authority given to Hezekiah to settle the Jews. It can also be interpreted as "reward," namely the right to settle and the related benefits granted to the Jews in return for their loyalty mentioned in the previous excerpts

---

material in the educational framework in which Pseudo-Hecataeus was brought up (see p. 177 above; cf. p. 158).

110. On *syngraphē* in this sense, see, e.g., Minns (1915) 52; Mitteis (1915) 428; Griffith (1935) 160; Bar-Kochva (1979) 32–33.

111. It is tempting to suggest that the author is describing a public ceremony, possibly performed on the occasion of the foundation of an *apoikia*: Hezekiah, the leader of the community and its founder, would be reading before the assembly the text of a scroll that perpetuated the story of the foundation and laid down its constitution. However, such a ceremony would naturally have been performed in the presence of all the settlers, and not only a few followers of the leader. As we shall also see below, the story cannot refer to the establishment of just one settlement.

112. The translation according to the common usage of the phrase. Possible also: "being closely connected with us." For the various translations, see Doran (1985) 917 n. e. Doran suggests "who now was part of our society," i.e., that Hezekiah had the same *ēthos* as Greeks. This sense of *synēthēs*, if it exists at all, must be very rare.

113. J. G. Müller (1877) 172, Thackeray (1926) 239 n. b, Reinach (1930) 36, Millar (1979) 7, and Holladay (1983) 237 n. 15 suggest (some of them hesitantly) that the *timē* granted was the appointment of Hezekiah to the High Priesthood. However, the conclusion that the author describes a permanent emigration and not just a temporary mission discredits this suggestion. See further pp. 225–26.

(*Ap.* I.183, 186). Thus probably after negotiating with the Ptolemaic authorities, Hezekiah obtained the *timē*, authority or reward, and was able to present his achievements to his close friends. The contents and phrasing of the excerpt show that details about Hezekiah's negotiations and an account of the realization of the right to settle were included in the original version of the story preceding and following the excerpt, respectively.

⌐⌐⌐

We should at this point digress to examine a different interpretation of the whole story recently made by a distinguished scholar. Fergus Millar has argued that the phrasing of the text does not necessarily imply a permanent migration.[114] In his view, Hezekiah traveled to Egypt after the Ptolemaic occupation of Judea in the year 312 to negotiate with Ptolemy about his appointment as High Priest and about future arrangements in Judea. Accordingly he was accompanied on this mission by just a few friends and advisers.

This interpretation depends upon emending διαφοράν to διφθέραν, the assumption that Hezekiah was reading the Torah, and mainly that the *katoikēsis* and *politeia* referred to are the story of the Exodus and the settlement in Canaan. Most of the arguments raised above do not leave much room for Millar's hypothesis. There is also further evidence that the story indeed described an emigration, not just a trip.

First of all, the opening excerpt states that "many people" followed the king to Egypt (*Ap.* I.187). Given the context, the author could hardly have meant anyone other than Jews. Second, the sequence of events must be considered. After his victory at Gaza, Ptolemy stayed in Coile Syria for a few months to conduct various operations. He returned with his troops to Egypt only seven or eight months later, upon hearing the news of the arrival of Antigonus in Upper Syria (Diod. XIX.93.4–6).[115] According to the Hezekiah story, the Jewish High Priest and his men "followed" (I.186) Ptolemy to Egypt. What sense was there after the Ptolemaic withdrawal in carrying on negotiations in Egypt about the High Priesthood or other subjects relating to the Jews in Judea? And if the word "followed" is not to be accepted literally, and Hezekiah had

114. Millar (1979) 7.
115. See the detailed analysis of Winnicki (1989) 83–89, and on p. 56 n. 3 and pp. 65–76. For the absolute chronology, cf. *id.* (1991) 147.

come to Egypt before Judea was abandoned, would he have negotiated there on the affairs of Judea while Ptolemy himself and his staff stayed in Coile Syria?

Furthermore, Josephus, who could read the full text of the Hezekiah story, surely knew its correct meaning. His version of the story elsewhere in his writings may be instructive. In the consecutive account of the beginning of the Ptolemaic period in Judea in *Jewish Antiquities* (XII.3–9), Josephus deplores the attitude of Ptolemy toward the inhabitants of Syria, including the Jews, calling him *despotēs*, and elaborates on the occupation of Jerusalem by Ptolemy, his harsh rule in the city, and the banishment of many captives to Egypt and their settlement there. Immediately after this account, Josephus adds (*Ant.* XII.9):

> But not a few [οὐκ ὀλίγοι δ' οὐδέ] of the other Jews came voluntarily [ἐκουσίως] to Egypt, because the quality of the places and Ptolemy's prodigality [*philotimia*] "invited" them.

The sentence contradicts the preceding account: the immigration is a voluntary one and not a deportation, and the evaluation of Ptolemy's character is the opposite of the despotism stressed in the earlier paragraphs. It recalls the Hezekiah story:[116] a great number of people were involved, they went to Egypt voluntarily, and they were attracted by Ptolemy's generous character. It seems clear, therefore, that the sentence was written under the influence of the Hezekiah story, and we can thus conclude that Josephus understood the story as recording a permanent migration of a great number of Jews to Egypt. The fact that Josephus introduced this sentence, despite its blatantly contradicting his own preceding account, indicates that he was confident of the meaning of the story and that it was based on unambiguous statements. These must have been found mainly in the missing passages of the original story.

The next step required for understanding the role of the Hezekiah story would be to clarify the dimensions of the settlement and its status according to the author. It has been suggested that the Jewish

---

116. Marcus (1943) 6 n. 6 connects the sentence with the Hezekiah story, but ignores the obvious contradiction with the immediate context.

community in Alexandria or a certain military settlement is meant.[117] However, as was said above, Hezekiah's activity in Egypt—that is, the emigration and negotiations, and the very settlement—was certainly recorded in the missing sentences (or passages) preceding and following the fourth excerpt. Had it been the founding of the Jewish community in Alexandria, Josephus would not have missed such a reference. In Book II of *Against Apion*, where he strives to prove the antiquity of Jewish settlement in Alexandria and the rights granted to it, Josephus cannot adduce any direct evidence from Pseudo-Hecataeus, but only the scarcely relevant passage about the granting of Samaria to the Jews by Alexander (*Ap.* II.43). It also appears from Josephus that the Jews of Alexandria claimed to have been settled there earlier, since the founding of the city (*Bell.* II.487, *Ap.* II.35; cf. Philo, *Flacc.* 46).

As for the other suggestion: the High Priest and his followers are said to have emigrated to Egypt in order to "take part in the affairs [of the kingdom]" (*Ap.* I.186), and Hezekiah is introduced as a man especially competent in these matters (187). The placement of the immigrants in a single military settlement, which was normally relatively far from the center of the Ptolemaic regime, does not accord with the purpose of the emigration and the personality and status of Hezekiah. Moreover, the author mentions an emigration of "many people" (186), while the Ptolemaic military settlements were, naturally, rather small.[118]

In considering the two suggestions, it should be noticed that the story is a clear antithesis to the version of the Exodus in the Jewish excursus of Hecataeus of Abdera (Diod. XL.3.1–3), and the meaning of *katoikēsis* can therefore be deduced from its parallel in Hecataeus: Moses takes the people out of Egypt, and Hezekiah leads them back to Egypt; the Jews were expelled from Egypt by the Egyptians, while the Ptolemaic regime accepted them in Egypt most favorably; Moses is said to have established the Jewish *apoikia* in Judea and given it a *politeia*, while Hezekiah received both the right to establish Jewish settlements in Egypt and

---

117. Alexandria: J. G. Müller (1877) 172–73; Engers (1923) 237; Jacoby (1943) 66; Tcherikover (1961) 300. A military settlement: Kasher (1985) 40–41. The latter is mistaken in thinking that *katoikēsis* necessarily means the founding of a *katoikia*, a military settlement. It designates the process of establishing a settlement without specifying its status.

118. See, e.g., Crawford (1971) 122–23 on Kerkeosiris.

their *politeia*. Now, the term *apoikia* in Hecataeus means, as the author himself elaborates, not a single city or locality, but the whole settlement of the Jews in Judea, Jerusalem, and other cities (Diod. XL.3.3).[119] This parallel indicates that the author attributed to Hezekiah and his men a settlement undertaking of remarkable dimensions, certainly not a single rural settlement. The very modeling of the Hezekiah story after the Moses tradition and its place at the head of the original treatise also show how important it was to the author. Limiting Hezekiah's practical achievements to the foundation of just one military settlement or the like considerably reduces the story's importance.

Despite what might be thought, I do not believe the author presented the Hezekiah migration as the historical beginning of the Jewish Egyptian Diaspora. Jewish readers would not have accepted such an inaccuracy. The existence of a Jewish community in Egypt already in the time of the great oriental empires, recorded in the Bible and the Elephantine papyri, was well known to Egyptian Jews and was recorded in their literature (e.g., Pseudo-Aristeas 13, 36). In another passage, Pseudo-Hecataeus himself recounts Jewish emigration to Egypt "after Alexander's death," caused by the *stasis* in Coile Syria (*Ap.* I.194), which could not have meant the emigration attributed to Hezekiah, nor a later emigration. Thus according to Pseudo-Hecataeus, the settlement of Hezekiah and his followers was not the first emigration of Jews to Egypt, but a wave of emigration and settlement of special importance and considerable extent, which made the Jewish community there an important factor, well integrated in state affairs.

From the historical point of view, this seems to be a proper assessment. I have already noted in Chapter III.2 that the story about the voluntary emigration is a reversal of the deportation of many Jews from Judea by Ptolemy I and their forced settlement in Egypt.[120] As usual in deportations of this kind, which were intended to insure the future stability of the provincial regime, those exiled naturally comprised the elite of the Jewish community in Judea. Their arrival in Egypt not only made a major numerical contribution to the building of Egyptian Jewry, but, given their quality, must also have decisively influenced its future cultural, religious, and social development.

---

119. Notably Philo uses the term *apoikiai* (in the plural) for the whole Jewish Diaspora (*Leg. ad Gaium* 281; cf. *Flacc.* 45–46).

120. See pp. 79, 89–90 above.

With its contents clarified, the location of the Hezekiah story in the book requires attention. Josephus quotes it at the head of the passages cited. Along with the fact that the story is an antithesis to the Exodus story that opens Hecataeus's authentic Jewish excursus, this suggests that the Hezekiah story was the first subject dealt with by Pseudo-Hecataeus. Furthermore, the Hezekiah story is quoted by Josephus at the outset as evidence that the Jewish people were already "mature" at the time of the battle of Gaza. However, this could be proved by references to other events, which preceded the battle of Gaza and were adduced by Josephus in the context of Jewish customs, such as Jewish martyrology in the Persian period (*Ap.* I.191), the participation in Alexander's army of Jews firmly committed to their beliefs (I.192), the granting of Samaria to the Jews by Alexander (II.43), and the massive emigration to Phoenicia and Egypt after his death (I.194). The placing of the Hezekiah story at the head of the passages can thus be explained only by its original place in the treatise. Josephus just followed the original sequence of his source.[121]

The dimension and importance of the settlement attributed to Hezekiah and the place of the story in the book, and, even more, its formulation as an antithesis to the Exodus story in Hecataeus's excursus, lead to the inevitable conclusion that the Hezekiah story served as a substitute for the *origo* component, which heads most ethnographic surveys and usually centers around an emigration and foundation. The Hezekiah story does this in a unique way: it does not report the *origo* of the Jewish people as such, but only that of the hard core (both numerical and qualitative) of the Jewish Egyptian Diaspora. The odd mixture of an "*origo*" that deals only with Egyptian Jewry together with the geography of the Holy Land and a general Jewish *nomima* section will be understandable once we clarify the purposes of the book. And after all, one would not expect the author of a Jewish ethnography to replace in his treatise a Palestinian geography with an Egyptian one. Pseudo-Aristeas, admittedly not an ethnographical author in the strict sense, similarly opens the *Letter* with an account of an event in the life of the Egyptian Jewry and inserts a detailed geographic excursus on the Holy Land (83–120). For an ethnographic book proper this is certainly

---

121. It is worth making clear that the adverb πάλιν in para. 186, which serves as a conjunction, refers to the statement in para. 185 that Hecataeus mentions the battle of Gaza.

an extraordinary mixture, but the omission of the Exodus and the personality of Moses from a Jewish ethnography is also unparalleled.

The omissions of Moses and the Exodus could not have occurred accidentally. The author, apart from being well acquainted with Hecataeus's excursus, knew perfectly well that the beginning of a nation as a whole is always the first (and frequently the most significant) component of an ethnographical work, and this also applies to the story of the Exodus in Jewish ethnographies. The omission can be understood in light of the contents of the Hezekiah story. The laudatory story of emigration to Egypt initiated by the High Priest could not coexist with the tradition about the sufferings in Egypt, the Exodus, and the settlement in the Jewish land. This is also why the component of the rulers' achievements was omitted: a description of the glorious days of past Jewish independence in the Holy Land could not be harmonized with an idealization of the emigration and settlement in the Egyptian Diaspora—certainly not in the period of the Hasmonean state, when the treatise was composed. The omission of these fundamental traditions, together with the use of the Hezekiah story as the *origo* component, once more underlines the major importance of the story in the framework of the book, and indicates that it contains the main message.

It should be added that even if we are wrong, and the treatise was not an ethnographical work *par excellence*, the absence of any reference to Moses could not but be deliberate. Moses stands at the center of almost every paragraph in Hecataeus's Jewish excursus, and was described as the initiator and lawgiver responsible for all Jewish practices. How was it that the Jewish forger, who tried to convince his readers of the authenticity of his work, and was evidently acquainted with Hecataeus's original excursus, did not mention Moses in his detailed account of Jewish practices, not even in the report about the Jewish priests and their regulations (*Ap.* I.188), attributed by Hecataeus explicitly to Moses (Diod. XL.3.4)?[122]

A final note about the genre: despite the major role of the Hezekiah story, the treatise cannot be classified as a "foundation story" (*ktisis*). This genre, which saw its beginning in ancient Greece and acquired

---

122. Moses is, however, referred to more than once in Pseudo-Aristeas. In para. 144 he is mentioned explicitly by name; in 131, 139, 170, as the lawgiver. Moses is again indicated in 155, 158, 159, 162, and his contribution is emphasized in 131–44, 154–62.

considerable popularity in the Hellenistic period, was composed in metrical poetry, and only a few works were written in prose, using similar stylistic-artistic features. The books are named after a country, a region, or, most often, a city. Stress is laid on etiological explanations for the foundation of the settlement and its names, cult, and customs.[123] The account centers around the personality of the "founder," to whom the establishment of all institutions and customs is attributed.[124] None of these features can be found in Josephus's passages. Besides, inclusion of detailed accounts on the *nomima* and geography of a mother city is less understandable in a "foundation story" than in an ethnography. In preferring to use the ethnographic genre, for which Hecataeus was celebrated, the author was motivated, among other things, by the wish to create an impression of authenticity.

123. On the *ktisis* literature, see in detail P. B. Schmid (1947), and pp. 90–94 on the prose *ktiseis*.
124. See also pp. 30–32 above.

VII The Purpose of the Book

The book *On the Jews* evidently contained a number of messages. They are scattered in the surviving passages. However, as in other ethnographical books written in the Hellenistic period, there was certainly a major purpose that motivated the author to compose the treatise.

In the previous chapter (VI.4) we observed that the author placed the Hezekiah story at the head of his book, using it as a substitute for the *origo*, which in ethnographical literature served as a clue for understanding the customs and historical development of the nation concerned. To clear the way for the Hezekiah story, he even went so far as to avoid altogether any reference to Moses and the Exodus tradition, the *origo* component in all Jewish ethnographies, as well as any section on Jewish rulers. The evident shaping of the Hezekiah story as an antithesis to the Moses story as it appears in Hecataeus's Jewish excursus reiterates the importance of the former in the framework of the treatise.[1] All these indicate that the Hezekiah story contains the main message of the treatise.

The author devoted much thought to shaping the details of the story, and to changing the basic historical facts: he turned Hezekiah from a civil governor into a High Priest, the forced deportation of Jews to Egypt into a voluntary migration, and the maltreatment of Ptolemy I into *philanthrōpia*, and dated the events to the time of the battle of Gaza instead of that of Ipsus.[2] In view of the very contents of the story, especially the absurd attribution of an initiative

1. See above pp. 229–30.
2. See pp. 79, 89–90.

to emigrate to Egypt to the religious leader of the nation, as well as the strange explanation of his motive ("to take part in the affairs [of the kingdom]"), there seems little doubt that the story was designed to answer a major question or dilemma with regard to Jewish residence in Egypt.[3]

In order to expose the purpose of the story, it would be of advantage to take a look into the *Letter of Aristeas*. This work, which like Pseudo-Hecataeus's is pseudonymic and is ascribed to a gentile Ptolemaic courtier, was written by an Alexandrian Jew a decade or two before Pseudo-Hecataeus's *On the Jews*.[4] Although this cannot be decisively proven, the author of Pseudo-Hecataeus may well have been acquainted with the *Letter*.[5] Pseudo-Aristeas opens his book with a story that reveals typological features shared with the Hezekiah story: the Ptolemaic king is benevolent, and the Jerusalem High Priest cooperates with him. This cooperation is said to have produced the Septuagint, a major religious and cultural contribution to the life of Egyptian Jewry. The translation is ascribed to seventy-two representatives of the Israelite tribes ordained by the Jewish High Priest. As has been almost universally recognized, the story was invented first and foremost in order to legitimize the Septuagint and thus solve the quandary and internal controversy over the very translation of the Pentateuch into Greek, and especially over its use in religious services. We see that the alleged participation of the Jerusalem High Priest was used to lend legitimacy and respectability to a controversial project or issue in the life of Egyptian Jewry.

3. It is worth noting in this context that the conservative author should not have been too worried that a story about a High Priest who abandoned his position in the Temple would be disbelieved because of its practical implications. Pseudo-Hecataeus knew that a High Priest could be succeeded or replaced by his brother (see p. 34 n. 80 above), and he does not indicate that the whole clan of the High Priest emigrated to Egypt. Moreover, two generations before the composition of the treatise, the whole family of the High Priests, the Oniads, found refuge in Egypt and remained there, the worship being carried on under the guidance of other families. There was not even a question of interim arrangements before settling the matter of succession: a substitue High Priest had always been prepared seven days before Yom Kippur and was waiting in the wings (Mishna, Yoma 1.1).

4. See below, pp. 271ff., and pp. 139–42.

5. See p. 142 n. 76 above.

The Hezekiah story, then, in attributing to the High Priest the initiative and leadership in a substantial migration from Judea and settlement in Egypt, is clearly aiming at legitimizing Jewish residence in Egypt. This further explains why Moses and the Exodus story were not mentioned in the treatise. It is notable that religious legitimacy for an emigration was also required in Greek tradition: the founder of an *apoikia* was designated, authorized, and even sanctified by the Delphic Apollo.[6]

The legitimacy of residence in Egypt is expressed not only by the dominant role of the Jerusalem High Priest in the emigration, but also by his activity in shaping the document containing the *katoikēsis* and *politeia* of the Jewish settlers, namely, the charter that authorized their settlement and the set of rules that regulated it.[7] As in the legend about the Septuagint, legitimacy is strengthened by the Ptolemaic authorities' recognition of or involvement in the project. The very inspiration for legitimizing a controversial issue in the life of Diaspora Jews by a fictitious story centered around the Jewish High Priest and the Ptolemaic king could well have been taken from Pseudo-Aristeas. But it could also have been a typological motif current in other works of Egyptian Jews.

The composition of Pseudo-Hecataeus's treatise in the prime period of the Hasmonean state and his affiliation to the conservative groups in the community[8] explain why such a legitimization was needed. Emigration to Egypt was deplored in the Bible because of the memories of the Captivity and the Exodus. In the instructions to the future king, the Torah warns: "Nor, to add to his horses, shall he cause the people to go back to Egypt, for this is what the Lord said to you, 'You shall never go back that way' " (Deut. 17.16).[9] The list of punishments for

---

6. See Parke and Wormell (1956) 49ff.; Graham (1964) 25ff.; Parke (1967) 44–55; Fontenrose (1978) 137ff.; Leschhorn (1984) 86; Malkin (1987) 17ff. Cf. Hdt. V.42.2

7. See pp. 221–25 above.

8. See above, pp. 122ff., 180–81.

9. The precise original intention of this verse as a whole, which has been much discussed, does not concern us here. The second part of the verse was certainly understood as a prohibition to migrate to Egypt under ordinary circumstances. This appears in later sources. See *PT* Succa 55.5b, *BT* Succa 51b, and a number of parallels in the midrashic literature (see esp. Mechilta, Beshallah, Exod. 14.13). Cf. Maimonides, *Mishne Tora*, Judges, Kings, chap. V,

the nation that sins culminates in the threat "The Lord will bring you sorrowing back to Egypt by that very road of which I said to you, 'You shall not see that road again' " (28.68).[10] The prophet Jeremiah tried to prevent the remaining Jews in Judea from finding refuge in Egypt, and even threatened emigrants with severe punishment (Jer. 42.15–22). The same prophet, however, did encourage the deported Jews to settle in Babylon and to lead ordinary lives there until salvation came (29.4–7). This negative approach did not fade into obscurity. Far from it: the annual celebration of the Passover kept reminding the people of the meaning of residence in Egypt.

By and large, migration from the land of Israel to Egypt was usually brought about by some strong compulsion such as severe drought, forced exile, danger from the north, or panic flight from an enemy. Practicing Jews like Pseudo-Hecataeus, who strictly adhered to the precepts of the Torah, must have been puzzled about the legitimacy of their residence in Egypt. One may assume that so long as the community in the Holy Land was under foreign rule or in dire straits, the question was not pressing, and there was not much difficulty in excusing residence in Egypt. Principally, such Jews could have regarded Egypt as a temporary residence resulting from forced exile and insecure existence, and less out of economic hardship in the Holy Land, the Diaspora still being seen as a divine punishment. A good example is to be found in the Greek translation of Isaiah, dated to around the year 140, that is, a generation before Pseudo-Hecataeus.[11] The Hebrew Isaiah 10.24 says: "Be not afraid, my people who dwell in Zion, of Asshur, that will smite you with the rod, and lift his staff against you on the road to Egypt [בדרך מצרים]." The Septuagint renders the second clause completely differently: "For I [God] deliver a blow upon you, so that you may see the road of Egypt [τοῦ ἰδεῖν ὁδὸν Αἰγύπτου]." The translator clearly paraphrases the verse in Deuteronomy 28.68, which describes the Diaspora as a punishment and refers to the prohibition against returning to

---

7–8. Consequently Jos. *Ant.* IV.224 ignores the words "nor ... shall he cause the people to go back to Egypt," and Philo (*Spec. Leg.* IV.158) omits the word "Egypt." Cf. Philo's allegorical interpretation in *Agr.* 84ff.

10. Cf. Exod. 14.13. The Talmudic references mentioned in the previous note and Maimonides quote this verse as a warning not to return to Egypt.

11. See Seeligman (1948) 76–94, esp. 87.

Egypt ("Egypt ... road ... you shall not see"). Residence in Egypt is thus explained as a result of foreign pressure in Judea and the wrath of God.[12]

This situation changed considerably with the rise and successes of the Hasmonean state. Practicing Jews must, then, obviously have been uncomfortable about their continued residence in Egypt when the new Jewish state in the Promised Land established itself politically, considerably expanded its borders, and flourished economically (e.g., Jos. *Ant.* XIII.273–74). The traditional hope for the ingathering of the Diaspora was cherished among Diaspora Jews in the Hasmonean period, as can be detected in the Greek translation of Isaiah[13] and II Maccabees (2.18).[14] A recently discovered prayer from the time of Alexander Jannaeus reveals a sense of close identification between the Jews in the Holy Land and the Diaspora, and may even indicate that at least some circles in Judea regarded the Hasmonean king as the leader of the Jews in all four corners of the world.[15] Under these circumstances, the old

12. Seeligman (1948) 84–85 argues that the Asshur in the Greek translation of Isaiah symbolizes Antiochus Epiphanes and that the clause under discussion refers to the Jews who found refuge in Egypt in the time of the religious persecutions, esp. the Oniads.

13. See Seeligman (1948) 14–17. A good example is Isa. 11.16: "And there shall be a causeway for the remnant of His people that shall remain from Assyria as there was for Israel in the day he came up out of the land of Egypt." LXX translates: ἔσται διόδος τῷ καταλειφθέντι μου λαῷ ἐν Αἰγύπτῳ ("There shall be a causeway for my people left in Egypt").

14. It is agreed that the second epistle at the beginning of II Maccabees (1.10–2.18) is a fabrication. It seems to have been fabricated by the epitomator or someone of his circle. The epitomator was a Hellenistic Jew living in the early Roman period at the latest. The phrasing of verse 17 itself, as well as other verses, betrays its origin in the Diaspora. For a sober summary of the results of the copious research on this epistle, see M. Stern (1991) 353–54.

15. On this prayer and its reading, see Eshel et al. (1990/1); Flusser (1991/2); Qimron (1991/2); Eisenman and Wise (1992) no. 50. The relevant lines: "Watch, O Lord, over King Jonathan and all the congregation, your people of Israel in the four winds of Heaven." The reading עוּר and its interpretation as "watch" was suggested by Qimron. Harrington and Strugnell (1993) 498–99 suggest the possibility that the prayer was directed against Jannaeus. Their interpretation of the imperative עוּר as "rise up (against)" may sound better than "watch" (עִיר and שִׁיר read by others can be discounted). However, in this case, the following reference to the congregation "in all four corners of the

problem about residence in Egypt thus gained special relevance in the generation of Pseudo-Hecataeus.

This feeling was certainly aggravated even more by constant tension in the multinational cities and settlements of Egypt, under the psychological pressure of local anti-Jewish literature and rumors, and recurring mob outbursts. Moreover, Pseudo-Hecataeus wrote just two decades after the reign of Ptolemy VIII Physcon (145–116), with the exception of his two last years the worst period of Ptolemaic Egypt, and one of the darkest in the history of Egyptian Jewry in the Persian and Hellenistic-Roman periods.[16] Pseudo-Aristeas, his elder contemporary, explicitly complains about the misery of living in exile (para. 249). The same applies to the Greek translator of Isaiah and to the translators of other prophetic books.[17]

The establishment of Jewish settlement in Egypt by Hezekiah was, according to Pseudo-Hecataeus, a result not of deportation, but of voluntary migration. Nor was it caused by dire economic straits. The prosperity of the land of Israel should not therefore operate to eliminate the Diaspora. The attribution of the initiative to the High Priest legitimizes the existing situation, and the granting of the *politeia* by him sanctifies Jewish life and institutions in Egypt.

Jewish settlement in Egypt was thus sanctioned by the highest religious authority of the nation. This, however, was still not enough, and a justification of the move was required. The author must also have offered in the same context a convincing purpose for Hezekiah's migration, and thus for Jewish residence in Egypt in his time. The reason that Hezekiah and his men migrated to Egypt is recorded in just a few words: κοινωνεῖν τῶν πραγμάτων (*Ap.* I.186). In the given context and construction, the phrase can only mean "to take part in the affairs [of the kingdom]" or "in the [royal] administration."[18]

---

world" remains without a verb. See also Eshel et al. 310–11 on the favorable attitude reflected in the presentation of Jannaeus as "Jonathan, the king."

16. See p. 285 and Extended Notes, n. 9 p. 300 below.

17. See Seeligman (1948) 112ff.

18. τὰ πράγματα is common for state affairs; in Hellenistic Greek, esp. for royal administration (e.g., the position of ὁ ἐπὶ τῶν πραγμάτων). It also appears twice in *Against Apion*, specifically for (royal) administration (I.138, II.177). The Ptolemaic regime being an autocratic one, the verb should be translated as "to take part in" rather than "to have a share in" (although the biased Jewish author could also have used the latter expression to describe the

What is the practical meaning of this statement, and how could it help in justifying residence in the Egyptian Diaspora during the time of the Hasmonean kingdom? To be involved in the affairs of the Ptolemaic kingdom or its administration alone could not justify such a radical step as an emigration of the High Priest from the Holy Land to Egypt, the prohibited country. Nor could it be compared with the obviously more noble and demanding requirement in the time of the author to lend a hand in the building of the newly established state in the Holy Land and to take part in its affairs. It is quite clear that the quoted sentence was just the beginning of a statement about the purpose of the emigration. Its second part is missing. The quotation ends abruptly with the words "to take part in the affairs," and is evidently cut. The excerpts of the Hezekiah story suffer from other omissions and abbreviations as well.[19]

Jewish leaders in the literature and real life of antiquity and the Middle Ages volunteered for royal service (despite their religious, especially dietary, limitations), almost always in order to exert their influence on behalf of their compatriots. Mordecai and Esther are the classic examples. The Esther Scroll demonstrates how Jewish involvement in state affairs and royal service was seen as the only way to secure Jewish survival. Nehemiah, the literary figure of Tobias, and even Ezra—despite the differences between them—basically belong to the same category of Jewish leaders.[20] The lesson was well learned by a number of celebrated Jewish personalities in the Middle Ages from North Africa and Egypt to Iraq and Yemen, and in Europe from Spain to Germany and even in Poland.[21] Though some of them may

---

position of the Jewish generals at the time of the composition of the book). There is no room for interpreting the phrase in the sense "coming over to" the side of Ptolemy, or "sharing his fortune," as the phrase occasionally means, esp. in Polybius (e.g., II.61; III.60.11, 95.7; IV.22.5). This sense would require the addition of a personal pronoun (τινί, πρὸς ὄν, or the like), and it is hardly likely in the context: Ptolemy is said, in this sentence, to have become "master" (*enkratēs*) of Syria; would a native governor (or High Priest) wishing to side with the new regime have expressed it by emigrating to Egypt? This, in any case, does not appear from the construction and order of the clauses.

19. See above, pp. 221ff.

20. On Jews in royal service in the Persian period, see Weinfeld (1964) 231–32.

21. Just to mention a few outstanding figures: Maimonides and his son and the Tustari brothers in Egypt; Hisdai ibn Shaprut, Don Izhak Abarbanel, Samuel ha-Levi Abulafia, and Samuel ibn Nagrila (Samuel ha-Nagid) in Spain;

have striven mainly for private goals, they almost always explained their occupation as designed for the benefit of their brethren, and this was their image in the community. We thus have *a model of behavior* of Jewish leadership that can be utilized for the understanding of Hezekiah's purpose in wishing to be involved in "the affairs [of the kingdom]."

Since Hezekiah is described as the Jerusalem High Priest, the author would certainly not have gone so far as to argue that he had left the Holy Land and migrated to Egypt with many people in order to help the Jews in Egypt. Moreover, as the move headed by Hezekiah actually constituted (qualitatively and quantitatively) the most significant migration (in fact, deportation) of Jews to Egypt,[22] it would not have been described by the author simply in terms of its benefit to the Egyptian Diaspora. The conclusion must be that in the author's view Hezekiah and his people committed themselves to the royal service with a view to safeguarding the interests of Jews in the Holy Land itself. Given the date of composition, this means that Jews in Egypt were acting in the Ptolemaic court on behalf of the Jewish state. Such an explanation could be accepted as a proper justification for continuing residence in the Diaspora at the time of the Hasmonean state.

One can only speculate why Josephus chose to end the quotation before this point. After all, it was irrelevant for his purpose of proving the antiquity and uniqueness of the Jewish people, and may have confirmed traditional accusations about disloyalty and double loyalty of the Jewish community, especially of Jewish courtiers and other public figures. In Book II of *Against Apion* Josephus strives to refute similar accusations by Apion (e.g., II.43, 44, 52, 56, 64, 68). Pseudo-Hecataeus, for his part, would not have hesitated to clarify the meaning of his statement: the same author even went so far as to praise Jewish violence against pagan cult. The book of this conservative Jew was obviously written for a Jewish, not a gentile, audience.[23]

Abraham ibn 'Ata in North Africa; Shalom Iraqi in Yemen; Netira in Iraq; Esther, the mistress of Kazimierz III, in Poland; and the "court Jews" in Germany. On the latter, see S. Stern (1950); Schnee (1952–55).

22. See p. 228 above.

23. On his affiliation with the conservative stream, see pp. 180–81 above. On the book as directed to an internal and not an external audience, see pp. 246–47 below.

Be that as it may, what else could have been the purpose of becoming involved "in the affairs [of the kingdom]," a purpose that could justify for a conservative Jew deviation from an explicit warning of the Pentateuch? And it has to be remembered that the prohibition of Deuteronomy is explicitly directed at the leadership ("nor ... shall he cause the people to go back to Egypt," Deut. 17.16). Hezekiah is described as a religious as well as a secular leader. For conservative Jews, only a noble national or religious purpose could have justified the move and set aside the biblical prohibition. This rules out other, alternative explanations of the main purpose of the Hezekiah story, such as counteracting the impression created by Pseudo-Aristeas about the harsh treatment of the Jews by the founder of the dynasty (paras. 12–14), proving to Greeks in Egypt that Jews contributed to the building of the Ptolemaic empire, demonstrating their loyalty to the regime, or urging contemporary Jews to become more involved in state affairs. In addition, the first three of these explanations would not justify distorting the basic historical facts to such an extent, especially the turning of Hezekiah from a governor into a High Priest. As for the fourth possibility, Jews in the generation of Pseudo-Hecataeus were deeply involved in state affairs and did not need further exhortation.

The purpose of the story—to justify residence in the Diaspora during the time of Jewish independence by pointing to the political support provided by Diaspora Jews to the Jewish state—sounds rather familiar from contemporary history. The successful "Jewish (or "Israeli") lobby" in the United States is often used by American Zionist activists in their dialogue with Israelis to justify continued Jewish residence in America. This "lobbying argument" was raised there under circumstances similar to those of its appearance in Pseudo-Hecataeus: it became quite current in certain circles after the June 1967 ("Six-Day") war, when Israel considerably expanded its borders and entered an era of economic prosperity while it was, at the same time, in acute need of qualified manpower and put great pressure on Zionist organizations to commit themselves to a massive *aliyah*. The use of this explanation became even more popular after the October 1973 ("Yom Kippur") war, when Israel became more than ever dependent on American diplomatic and military support. However, the interpretation suggested is not a wild projection made from modern developments onto the remote past: in addition to the above analysis of the key sentence, the Hezekiah story, the treatise as a whole, and the historical model, it is substantiated by hard facts.

Egyptian Jews occupied key positions in the Ptolemaic administration and army. More than once Jewish officials exerted their influence in favor of Jews in the Holy Land, and involvement became especially effective in the prime period of the Hasmonean state. There is ample evidence for Jews' performing various duties in royal service. The material has been collected and discussed by a number of scholars, and there is no point in repeating it.[24] For the present context it deserves noting that the highest and most influential position held by Egyptian Jews was that of chief of staff. Significantly, employment of Jews as supreme commanders of the army is recorded during the sixty years preceding the days of Pseudo-Hecataeus and is unknown afterwards. The first pair of supreme commanders were Onias and Dositheus, in the time of Ptolemy VI Philometor (Jos. *Ap.* II.49).[25] Another Jew called Onias was the most loyal officer of Cleopatra II and led her army against Ptolemy VIII Physcon (*Ap.* II.51–52). In the early years of Alexander Jannaeus, two Jews named Ananias and Helkias stood at the head of the Ptolemaic army of Cleopatra III (*Ant.* XIII.284–87).[26] All these belonged to the family of Onias III, the Jerusalem High Priest who was executed at Daphne of Antioch on the eve of the religious persecutions by Antiochus IV Epiphanes. His son, Onias IV, found refuge in Egypt and established the military settlement at Leontopolis. He may be identified with one of the Jewish supreme commanders under Ptolemy VI.[27]

The great hour of the Jewish lobby came in the years 107–103/2, in the late days of Cleopatra III's reign. For reasons mainly connected with the aspirations and achievements of her rebel son, Ptolemy Lathyrus, the queen became absolutely dependent upon the support and good will of her Jewish supreme commanders and the Jewish troops (Jos. *Ant.* XIII.285–87), and at the same time had to be closely involved

24. See, e.g., Tcherikover (1957) 20ff., (1963) 30ff.; Alberro (1976) 142–51; Kasher (1985) 29ff.

25. On the papyrological material relating to Onias and the question of his identification, see Tcherikover (1957) 19–21, 244–45; *id.* (1961) 275ff.; Alberro (1976) 145ff.; van't Dack in van't Dack et al. (1989) 130.

26. For further details and sources, see van't Dack in van't Dack et al. (1989) 130–31.

27. The extraordinary situation of Jews' heading the Ptolemaic army may also perhaps have inspired Artapanus to describe Moses as commander-in-chief of the Egyptian army (*ap.* Eus. *PE* IX.27.7–8).

in the events in Coile Syria and Phoenicia. Josephus, drawing on Strabo, states that "Cleopatra did nothing without [asking for] their opinion" (XIII.286). The advice, pressure, and even threats of the Jewish commanders dictated the queen's policy toward the Jewish state.

The advice of the Jewish commander and its effects can first be traced in the events of the year 107. At the time of the siege of Samaria by John Hyrcanus, the Seleucid king, Antiochus IX Cyzicenus, came to the help of the Samaritans. He asked Ptolemy Lathyrus, who was still in Egypt, to send him a reinforcement of six thousand troops. Together with them, the Syrian king devastated Judea, trying in this way to force Hyrcanus to raise the siege (*Ant.* XIII.277–79). Cleopatra was so irritated by her son's intervention that, in Josephus's words, "she was on the verge of driving him from the kingdom" (XIII.278).[28] As in the same year Ptolemy Lathyrus was expelled from Egypt by his mother,[29] the author obviously indicates that his unauthorized involvement in the war against the Jews in Judea played a major role in his mother's later decision. The Jewish supreme commanders certainly expressed their view on that occasion as they had done, according to Strabo, all along, which could have influenced the queen's resolute reaction.

The most impressive case of Diaspora Jews' intervening in favor of the Jewish state is known from year 103/2: in the early days of Alexander Jannaeus, Ptolemy Lathyrus, sailing from his base in Cyprus, landed south of Ptolemaïs and decisively defeated Alexander's army in a great pitched battle in the Jordan Valley. He then carried on, ravaging the country and committing horrible atrocities against the Jewish population (*Ant.* XIII.331–47). Cleopatra III came from Egypt to confront her son, the army being headed by the Jews Ananias and Helkias (XIII.348–49). One can assume that the queen decided to intervene not only because of Lathyrus's intention to invade Egypt but presumably also because her commanders, whom she always consulted, were then eager to save the Jewish state. After all, judging from Egyptian and Hellenistic history, the safest thing for Cleopatra to do would have been to stop Lathyrus at the gates of Egypt. The position

28. The combination ὅσον οὔπω can also be translated as "almost," "all but," or the like. The word *archē* refers either to the co-regency or the Ptolemaic realm.

29. For the date of the expulsion, see Skeat (1954) 15–16; Mitford (1959) 104; Koenen (1970) 75–76.

of the Jewish commanders is explicitly recorded later on (351–55): after various developments, Ptolemy Lathyrus withdrew to Cyprus. Cleopatra then consulted her advisers about the future of the country. Alexander Jannaeus was virtually on his knees and could not offer real resistance. Certain Ptolemaic royal "friends" recommended occupying the country and thus bringing to an end the independent existence of the Jewish state. Ananias, the sole chief of staff now that Helkias had lost his life in pursuit of Lathyrus (351), warned the queen that such steps would turn the Egyptian Jews against her. Josephus, basing his version on Strabo, ends the report saying: "After Ananias exhorted her in these [words], Cleopatra was persuaded not to do Alexander any wrong, but [instead] she made an alliance with him at Scythopolis of Coile Syria" (355).

In the discussion about the dating of Pseudo-Hecataeus we have seen that the anachronistic statements and the absence of certain references indicate composition sometime between the years 107 or 103 and 93 B.C.[30] Is it too bold to suggest that the unique justification of Jewish residence in Egypt provided in the treatise was invented under the strong influence of the background to Cleopatra's treaty with Alexander Jannaeus and her withdrawal from the Holy Land? If such an influence is accepted, the year 103/2 rather than 107 can be considered the *terminus post quem* for the composition of *On the Jews*.

The influence of the Jewish lobby under somewhat similar circumstances may be traced even before the years 107–103/2. A presumably forged letter attributed to Onias IV, the founder of the settlement at Leontopolis, mentions his service to Ptolemy VI in his campaigns in Coile Syria and Phoenicia (*Ant.* XIII.65).[31] Ptolemy came twice with his troops to the region: in the year 151/0 he made an alliance with Alexander Balas in Acre. On that occasion Jonathan, by then the leader of Judea, approached the two kings. We learn from I Maccabees (10.51–65) that despite the grievances of his Jewish adversaries, Jonathan was accepted with great honor and recognized as military commander and governor of Judea (*stratēgos* and *meridarchēs*). Five years later, in 146/5 or so, Ptolemy came again to Coile Syria, this time in order to depose his protégé, Alexander Balas. The Hellenistic city of Azotos

---

30. See pp. 122ff. above.

31. On the identification of the events referred to, see Tcherikover (1961) 499 n. 30; Kasher (1985) 133–34.

complained about the brutal treatment of its population and sanctuary by Jonathan, but the king again ignored their complaints and came to terms with Jonathan (I Macc. 11.1–6). One would assume that Onias and other influential Jewish military commanders intervened on these two occasions in favor of the Jewish nationalists in Judea.[32]

It is worthwhile recalling that Ananias and Helkias belonged to the Oniad family, and probably were descendants of Onias IV. As we have seen, Onias IV himself probably advised the Ptolemaic king to side with Jonathan and ignore the complaints against him. The almost inevitable conclusion that the lobbying of the Oniads inspired the author in inventing the purpose of Hezekiah's migration lends some support to a suggestion made by a number of scholars that there is a close connection between the Hezekiah story and the migration of Onias.[33] However, contrary to their opinion, I believe Onias's migration was not the main source of inspiration for the Hezekiah story. The basic framework was the deportation of Hezekiah the Governor by Ptolemy I.[34] This event was reshaped according to the purposes of the author, being influenced by the later migration of Onias IV. This does not mean that the author belonged to the Oniad clan or to the settlement at Leontopolis, and there is some indication that he did not.[35]

As a matter of fact, the Hezekiah story is not the only explanation offered by the treatise for Jewish residence in Egypt. In a later section of his work, referring to overpopulation in Judea, the author notes: "After Alexander's death many Jews migrated to Egypt because of the turbulence [*stasis*] in Syria" (*Ap.* I.194). Be the historicity of this statement as it may, it implies another line of justification: the situation in the Holy Land was far from being stable, and Jews there were still in danger. The invasion of the country by Ptolemy Lathyrus, and the atrocities committed by his troops in the year 103, underlined this feeling. The hint at the current insecurity provided some temporary justification; the Hezekiah story, the legitimation and long-term justification in times of prosperity and peace.

---

32. Cf. Bar-Kochva (1989) 86–87, and there on the question why the author of I Maccabees passed in silence over the role of Egyptian Jews in the events.

33. See pp. 90–91 and nn. 112, 114 above.

34. See pp. 90–91 above.

35. See p. 166 above, and p. 247 below.

The phenomenon of Jews' residing outside their homeland occupied Egyptian Jews also in later periods, when on the one hand their brethren in the Holy Land were suffering under Roman occupation, and on the other hand Egyptian Jews were being persecuted by their neighbors. The conservative author of III Maccabees describes the Jewish people in Egypt as "a foreign nation in a foreign country, being unjustly oppressed," and indicates that Jewish residence abroad is only temporary (6.3).[36] The feeling is that the author returns to the old, traditional explanations of the Diaspora, namely that the situation in the Holy Land does not allow a return to it, and the Diaspora is a place where the nation is punished for its former sins.[37]

There is nothing of these explanations in Philo's writings, although he found it necessary to justify Jewish residence abroad to Jews as well as to gentiles. His explanation of the Second Passover clearly betrays the fact that the legitimacy of Jewish residence in Egypt remained disputable among Jews (*Mos.* I.232):

> The same [opportunities to celebrate the Second Passover] must be granted to those who are prevented from worshipping together with the whole nation, not [only] because of mourning, but [also] because of [their] living in distant countries. For people who live abroad or reside elsewhere are not wrongdoers, to be denied an equal honor, as the one country does not contain the nation because of overpopulation, but sends colonies [*apoikiai*] in every direction.

Philo repeats the same explanation, elaborating the Greek features, in his response to the hostile Greco-Egyptians of Alexandria (*Flacc.* 45–46; cf. *Leg. ad Gaium* 281):

> For one country does not contain all the Jews because of [their] great number. For this reason they inhabit most [of the lands] and [the] most prosperous in Europe and Asia, on the islands as well as the mainland, and while on one hand they consider as their mother city [*mētropolis*] the holy city, where the holy temple of the highest God is situated, on the other hand they regard the lands in which they have been fated by [their] fathers, grandfathers, forefathers, or even [their] earlier ancestors to dwell as [their] fatherlands [*patriai*], in which they were born and brought up. They came immediately to some [of the

---

36. See Heinemann (1948/9) 6–7.

37. On the various explanations, see Yankelevitch (1980); Gafni (1984); Rofé (1986); Seeligman (1948) 110–13.

places] while they were being founded, having sent a colony [*apoikia*], and pleased the founders.

Philo's comparison of the relationship between Jerusalem and the Diaspora to that between a *mētropolis* and its *apoikiai*, inspired by Greek colonizing traditions, has been much discussed and need not be reviewed here.[38] I would only add that the naming of Jerusalem as a *mētropolis* appears already in the Greek translation of Isaiah (1.26), which may perhaps indicate that the same reasoning was current, in one version or another, long before the generation of Philo. As for the prohibition of the Pentateuch, one can assume that Philo and his circle found some allegoristic explanations for the verses in Deuteronomy so as not to be too embarrassed by them.

The conclusion that the main purpose of the book is to legitimize and justify Jewish residence in Egypt shows that the book was not written for external, apologetic purposes. Scholars since Willrich who regarded the book as a forgery argued that the book was written for Greeks in order to present the Jewish people in a favorable way.[39] This also falls on a number of other counts: the author refrains from recording the glorious periods in Jewish history, and does not even mention the name of Moses; he does not apologize for or try to explain the main peculiarities of the Jews ridiculed and criticized by gentiles (Sabbath, circumcision, kosher food), nor does he deny accusations like the leper, ass, and blood libels.[40] He praises, on the contrary, the destruction of pagan temples and altars by Jews (*Ap.* I.193), whereas Jewish authors struggled to refute similar allegations and even ascribed to Moses an explicit prohibition against such acts.[41] The mockery of gentile divination (*Ap.* I.201–4) could hardly find place in an apologetic book, or in a book aimed at fostering the good will of Greeks toward Judaism. And finally: in his eagerness to present the Hezekiah migration as the formative and decisive stage in the establishment of Egyptian Jewry, the

38. See, e.g., Wolfson (1948) II.396ff.; Heinemann (1948/9) 3ff.; Kasher (1979); ʿAmir (1981).

39. See. Willrich (1900) 104; cf. Geffcken (1907) xi; Jacoby (1943) 62.

40. Cf. pp. 287–88 below on the absence of any reference to the libels in Pseudo-Aristeas.

41. See p. 100 and n. 146 above.

author refrains from recording the traditions about the role of Jews in the foundation of Alexandria and the rights given to them by Alexander (see, e.g., *Ap.* II.35, 42). A book written for gentile readers would not have missed these stories.

The only reference that may be seen as directed to an external audience is the statement about the annexation of Samaria to Judea by Alexander (*Ap.* II.43). This, however, is outweighed by the evidence quoted above to the effect that the book was not written for an external audience. It seems, therefore, that the statement was meant to provide Jews with additional historical arguments in their recurring controversy with the Samaritans in Egypt. Moreover, the question of the legitimacy of Hyrcanus's occupations in Samaria was raised by Samaritan envoys as well as by local Samaritans in the Ptolemaic court.[42] A historical precedent attributing to Alexander himself the annexation or the granting of privileges was taken in the Hellenistic world as a weighty argument.

The book obviously contains a number of secondary religious and national messages directed to a Jewish audience. The stress laid on the readiness of Jews to sacrifice themselves for their religious beliefs and practices (*Ap.* I.191) is intended to encourage Diaspora Jews in cases of persecutions in the future, as probably happened in the time of Ptolemy IV and Ptolemy VIII. This emphasis, as well as the sneering at pagan omens and beliefs, was also intended to combat trends of extreme Hellenization and even conversion among Egyptian Jews. The praise for the destruction of pagan cults in the Holy Land may be taken as a polemic against the warnings of the "allegorists" and other Hellenistic Jews against such actions. The description of the Jerusalem Temple as being clear of votive offerings and plants (*Ap.* I.199) may be directed against practices in the Oniad temple at Leontopolis.[43] The detailed account of the Jerusalem Temple and its cult objects and practices (I.198–99) reiterates the absolute commitment of Egyptian Jewry to the Temple in the Holy Land as against local temples in the Diaspora.

The secondary national messages of the author are also clear: the Holy Land is the heart of the Jewish people, and all the Jews in the Diaspora should contribute in their special way to the existence and security of their brethren in the motherland. The Jews received the

42. See pp. 135–36 above.
43. See p. 166 above.

authority to govern the Samaritan land from Alexander, and were entitled to conquer and settle in regions outside Judea proper, especially the coastal plain. The Holy Land had to remain clear of foreign cult, and the Jews had the right to uproot pagan temples and altars from the country.

The attribution to a gentile of a book designed for internal purposes has an appropriate parallel in Pseudo-Aristeas as well as in a number of pseudonymic Jewish works and poems.[44] This also applies even to a conservative (though more progressive) Jew like the author of the Third Sibylline Book,[45] which even went so far as to pretend to be the work of pagan prophetesses. The choice of Hecataeus as pseudonym was not accidental. He was known as an author who took an interest in Jewish affairs and described them in his Egyptian ethnography. Because he was a celebrated public and literary figure at the beginning of Ptolemy I's reign, his statements about that period would have been respected by readers and trusted as being objective and accurate. Moreover, Hecataeus could be described as an eyewitness of Hezekiah's migration and the Mosollamus episode. Jews would naturally be inclined to believe in the authenticity of a book that attributed to Hecataeus enthusiastic comments on their religion and nation. Ascribing the book to a Jew would have raised suspicion with regard to the Hezekiah story, the focal point of the book, as being contrary to many reports about the harsh treatment of the Jews by Ptolemy son of Lagus. Other statements might have been taken as anachronistic and tendentious.

44. See on them Schürer (1901–9) III.595ff., 619ff.; Denis (1970) 215–19, 223–38; Goodman in Schürer et al. (1973–86) III.617–704.

45. See p. 180 above and n. 149.

Conclusion

The passages attributed to Hecataeus of Abdera in *Against Apion* cannot be accepted as authentic. The discussion raises a number of major arguments against authenticity, based on the following points: the details of the Mosollamus episode as well as of the Hezekiah story; the mention of, and praise for, the destruction by the Jews of pagan cult centers; the description of religious persecutions and martyrdom; certain data of military significance in the geographical account of Judea; the reference to immigration to Phoenicia and the statement about the annexation of Samaria. The suggestion that Josephus used a Jewish adaptation that slightly altered the original text fails to save the authenticity of the treatise; the alternative that Josephus had done this himself does not stand up to criticism.

The anachronistic references, the striking absence of certain allusions, and considerations related to the purpose of *On the Jews*, all taken together, indicate dating the passages between 107 and 93 B.C., or rather taking 103/2 as a *post quem* date. This means that composition took place sometime between the late years of John Hyrcanus, or the first years of Alexander Jannaeus, and the great Jewish conquests in Trans-Jordan. For the Jews in Judea this was a period of territorial expansion and prosperity, with a setback in the year 103/2, when Judea was invaded by Ptolemy Lathyrus. An analysis of certain passages of Pseudo-Aristeas shows that it was written in the same generation as Pseudo-Hecataeus, preceding it by a decade or two.

The author of the passages was a Diaspora Jew living in Egypt. He seems to have belonged to the moderate conservative stream, which significantly differed from the "allegorists," the typical representatives of

Hellenistic Jewry. Pseudo-Hecataeus demonstrates a profound knowledge of Jewish tradition, particularly of the cult in the Jerusalem Temple, but his Hellenistic education is incomplete and suffers from significant lacunae. His Greek is a mixture of different styles, and in at least two paragraphs is rather poor. He evidently did not have any philosophical education, and probably avoided reading poetical-mythological literature. There are no traces of allegorical, moral, or philosophical interpretations of Jewish traditions, even when such are badly needed. The author was probably brought up with the Hebrew Bible and went on to use it in religious services, to the exclusion of Septuagint versions. The treatise strictly adheres to Jewish practices and Torah precepts, and advocates intolerance toward pagan cult and beliefs, even violence when possible. The author resides in Egypt, but his heart is given to the Holy Land, demonstrating constant interest in current events there as well as loyalty and reverence for the Jerusalem Temple.

The passages were quoted by Josephus from a book named *On the Jews*. It was an ethnographical treatise of a modest size, composed according to the basic scheme of the ethnographical genre developed in the classical and Hellenistic periods. Such a work is almost always headed by an *origo* section, which describes the descent and beginning of the nation concerned. This is usually followed by a geographical account of the land, and a section on *nomima* ("customs"). The closing section is often a historical sketch that concentrates on the achievements of outstanding rulers. The order of the four sections sometimes differs, and the historical section is occasionally absent. Pseudo-Hecataeus opened his treatise with something like an *origo*, went on to the *nomima*, and closed the treatise with the geography. The placement of the geography at the end is known also from other Jewish ethnographies.

The Hezekiah story serves as a substitute for a true *origo* section. It does not describe the descent of the Jewish people as a whole, but claims to record the origins of the Jewish Diaspora in Hellenistic Egypt, or rather the most significant migration (quantitatively and qualitatively) from Judea to Egypt at the beginning of the Hellenistic period. This "*origo*" is influenced by, and is actually a reversal of, the *origo* section in the genuine Hecatean excursus on Jews and Judaism in the Egyptian ethnography, which recounts the Exodus from Egypt and the settlement in Canaan, both said to have been headed by Moses. The very kernel of the Hezekiah story is the great deportation of Jews from Judea to Egypt by Ptolemy I in the year 302/1. The real historical facts were reversed by the author: Hezekiah, actually the civil governor of Judea, is described as High Priest, and the forced exile of many Jews to Egypt as a voluntary migration; Ptolemy I's harsh and cruel treatment of the Jews is turned into *philanthrōpia*, and the background—the time of Ipsus (302/1 B.C.)—into the time of Gaza (312). According to the story, Hezekiah the High Priest, who was touched by the benevolence of Ptolemy, initiated a great migration to Egypt in order to involve the Jews in "the affairs [of the kingdom]." He is said to have headed the move personally, and to have established Jewish settlements in Egypt after receiving from the authorities their charter and constitution.

The Hezekiah story is the focal point of the book and contains the main message. The book was written in order to legitimize and justify Jewish residence in Egypt. This was essential for conservative Jews in view of the implicit prohibition of the Torah against returning to Egypt. The quandary became acute in the generation of Pseudo-Hecataeus: the Diaspora could no longer be described as compulsion when the Jewish state had consolidated its independence, become economically prosperous, and considerably expanded its borders. Moreover, the Hasmoneans badly needed additional qualified manpower, especially Jewish military men, who were so successful in Ptolemaic Egypt. The role of Hezekiah, the so-called High Priest, in the migration and settlement of Jews in Egypt provided the religious legitimization, just as the involvement of the High Priest, according to Pseudo-Aristeas, in the preparations for the translation of the Pentateuch legitimized the Septuagint.

But legitimation of the existing situation was not enough. Contemporary Jews needed a justification for remaining in Egypt. The justification was also provided by the Hezekiah story. Hezekiah's purpose in emigrating to Egypt was to create there a great concentration of Jews occupying key positions in the army, court, and economic life. In this way, local Jews would be able to exert their influence on the Ptolemaic authorities on behalf of the Jews in the Holy Land. The justification for the continued residence of Jews in Egypt is thus their contribution to the existence and security of their brethren in Judea. This certainly was not why Jews migrated to and remained in Egypt. But the fact is that they were deeply involved in state affairs at certain periods, and in the two generations preceding the composition of Pseudo-Hecataeus they even held the highest positions in the royal army. These Jews, indeed, used their "lobbying power" on various occasions to help the Jewish state. At least in one case—in the year 103/2—their influence upon a Ptolemaic sovereign saved the Jewish state from Ptolemaic occupation, when Alexander Jannaeus was virtually on his knees. The events of the year 103/2 may have inspired the author to provide this justification for the existence of the Diaspora. Pseudo-Hecataeus thus contains the oldest extant evaluation of the secular, national role of the Jewish Diaspora.

The treatise also carries a number of other religious and national messages. Most of them concern Diaspora Jews. Thus, for instance, it preaches adherence to Jewish traditions in the way of the contemporary conservatives and commitment to the Jerusalem Temple by the Diaspora, and justifies the territorial expansion of the Hasmonean rulers, even their brutality toward religious centers of the occupied population. The treatise attended to the basic facts and concerns of Egyptian Jewry and the Hasmonean state from the viewpoint of a conservative Diaspora Jew. Pseudo-Hecataeus's *On the Jews* can thus be regarded as a manifesto of conservative Judaism in Hellenistic Egypt.

APPENDIXES

Appendix A
The Hezekiah Coins

B. BAR-KOCHVA AND A. KINDLER

The Hezekiah coins form a special category among the Yehud-Judea coins dated to the second half of the Persian and early Hellenistic periods. They are divided into two groups of various types and denominations, which clearly differ from each other.[1] In the first group the legend is יחזקיה הפחה ("Hezekiah the *pehah*" ["governor"]); the obverse shows a frontal portrait of an unidentified male, and the reverse an owl (Pl. I.1–6). The second group (Pl. II) has a different type (or different types) of male portrait on the obverse, and a winged animal, probably a lynx, on the reverse. The legend reads יחזקיה ("Hezekiah"), without any title (Pl. II.8–11). The two groups have a number of variations. Like the majority of the Yehud coins, the two Hezekiah groups are tiny silver coins, weighing on the average around 0.2 g, and having a diameter of 6 mm.

The first group is unanimously dated to the end of the Persian period.[2] This means that on the eve of the Macedonian conquest, a Jew named Hezekiah served as *pehah*, that is, as the Persian governor

1. For comprehensive discussions on this series, and on the Yehud coins as a whole, see Mildenberg (1979) 183–96, (1988) 727–28; Rappaport (1981) 1–17; Meshorer (1982) 13–34, 184–85; Barag (1986/7) 1–21. For reference to discussions of the historical implications of the Hezekiah coins, see also p. 85 n. 97 above. The contributions of Kochman (1982) 3ff. and Betlyon (1986) 633–42 are highly speculative and ignore basic numismatic data. Good reproductions of the Yehud coins can be found in Mildenberg (1979) pls. 21, 22; *id.* (1988) pl. 23; Meshorer (1982) pls. 1–3.

2. See Mildenberg (1979) 187–88, (1988) 727; Rappaport (1981) 226; E. Stern (1982) 226; Meshorer (1982) 17–18, 20, 33–34; Barag (1986/7) 8–9. The

of Judea. However, there is no agreement with regard to the second group. Some date it as contemporaneous with the first group, or at least before Alexander's conquest,[3] while others place it after the first group, relating it to the period of the Successors.[4]

1. THE DISPUTE OVER THE DATING OF THE SECOND GROUP

Those numismatists who prefer the earlier dating have raised two arguments. Meshorer pointed out that of five coins that were found connected by their patinas in a hoard south of Gaza, three belonged to the first group of the Hezekiah coins, and one to the second.[5] As these tiny coins tended to wear out quickly, Meshorer thinks that they were struck at the same time. However, one need only accept that they were struck within a period of some years, but not necessarily at the same time. Moreover, variations and other types of these coins could be separated from each other by quite a number of years. The second group could thus have been struck after the Macedonian conquest.

Rappaport has put forward another argument:[6] it appears from the first group that Hezekiah served as governor and not as High Priest; but during the period of the Successors even secular authority was held by the High Priest. Indeed Hezekiah was not High Priest,[7] but the second statement is unwarranted: the literary sources do not offer any information on the identity and descent of the person at the head of the administration in Judea under the Successors up to 302.[8] The question may be decided on numismatic grounds.

---

recent reading of the coin of Johanan the High Priest (see pp. 263–64 below) actually provides the clinching evidence.

3. Rappaport (1981) 6, 16; Meshorer (1982) 17, 34. However, in his classification of the Yehud coins (p. 13) Meshorer lists the second group of Hezekiah's coins as issued "during the Macedonian occupation."

4. Elaborated by Mildenberg (1979) 188–89. This is assumed by all the scholars who identify the Hezekiah of the coins with Hezekiah the High Priest.

5. Meshorer (1982) 17.

6. Rappaport (1981) 16.

7. See pp. 82ff. above.

8. See Extended Notes, n. 6, pp. 297–98.

The main evidence proffered by the scholars who have dated the second group after Alexander's conquest is the absence of the title *pehah* on the types of that group bearing the name Hezekiah. They assume that this Persian-Aramean title was replaced by a Greek one under the Macedonians.[9] At least under Antigonus Monophthalmus the Greek title could well have been *hyparchos* (Diod. XIX.58.1, 95.2). To support this assumption, it may be suggested that the new Greek title was not inscribed either because it was too long to be struck onto the limited space on the coin, or, what is more likely, because the Jewish population, for whose daily use the coins were issued, still referred to the governor by the old, oriental, title, as it had done for two centuries.

This argument has been challenged by the suggestion that the title *pehah* was omitted because of apparent lack of space.[10] In view of the high technical skill of the engraver and the small size of the letters of the name Hezekiah in the second group (in comparison with the first), we are not convinced that he could not manage to insert such a short word, or adjust the position of the animal on the reverse to make room for the letters. The engravers of the first group, whose work was of considerably poorer quality, did this even though the space at their disposal was just as limited.[11]

Nevertheless, it should be noted that occasionally the title *pehah* is not attached to individuals, known to have served as governors, who appear on jar-handle stamps and bullae of Yehud and Samaria of the Persian period; nor is the title "Priest" always applied to persons who occupied the position of High Priest.[12] Similarly, most of the larger Persian silver coins of Mazdi, the famous satrap of Eber Nahara and Cilicia in the Persian period (and of Babylonia under Alexander), display only the legend "Mazdi" (or "MZ"). His title appears only on

9. See Mildenberg (1979) 188; followed by other scholars.

10. Rappaport (1981) 6.

11. See, e.g., יחזקיה in Pl. I.2, 4 and הפחה in Pl. I.3, 5.

12. The title "High Priest" is lacking on a recently discovered coin of Yaddua (Spaer [1986/7] 1–3). The same applies to a coin of Jeroboam, perhaps a Samaritan High Priest (Spaer [1979] 218; Meshorer [1982] 31–33; Meshorer and Qedar [1991] nos. 23–27). The title "Priest" appears, on the other hand, on a coin of Johanan the High Priest (Barag [1986/7] 10–12). On the nonoccurrence of the title *ha-pehah* on stamps and bullae of persons who served as governors of Yehud, see Avigad (1976) 6–7, 32–35.

one type ("the [one] who is [in charge] of *'Ever Naharā* and *Ḥalak̲*"),
while the tiny coins do not even bear his name.[13] The omission of
Mazdi's long title from most of the coins is indeed more understandable
than the absence of the short title *peḥah*, but the stamp material
from Judea and Samaria certainly casts some doubt on the validity
of this argument.

Besides the absence of the title *ha-peḥah*, Mildenberg has pointed
to direct numismatic evidence: the winged lynx on the reverse of
the second group also appears on a coin without a legend that in
Mildenberg's view bears a portrait of Ptolemy I on the obverse (Pl.
II.11a). This link may prove that Hezekiah's coins were struck at
some date very close to the Ptolemaic period.[14] It must, however,
be said that there is not a real similarity between this portrait and
the common representation of Ptolemy I struck in Egypt.[15] At the
same time, the Judea mint also produced different local versions of
Ptolemy's portrait with which the aforesaid portrait does fit in quite
well.[16] Although our strong feeling is that it was indeed meant to
represent Ptolemy I, this evidence does not by itself appear sufficient

13. See Babelon (1893) 28–44; and also Bellinger (1963) 60ff.; *BMC Lycaonia, Isauria, Cilicia* p. 170 no. 48. On Mazdi, see Berve (1926) I.245. The title
of Mazdi appears only on one group of his staters.

14. See Mildenberg (1979) 188, referring to pl. 22 no. 23 in his article
(see p. 195 n. 23). His second argument (p. 188 n. 30), based on a coin
published by Kindler ([1974] 75 and pl. II, no. a), is irrelevant: the coin was
discovered in Acre, and seems to have been minted in Tyre, not in Judea.
Furthermore, it bears Alexander's effigy, is not similar to any of the portraits
on the Judean coins, and shows not a lynx (as suggested by Mildenberg) but a
hippocamp.

15. The common representations show a large, protuberant chin and fleshy
lips and nose, as well as a protruding eye orbit and a deep-set eye. All these are
entirely different from the portrait under discussion. See the many examples
in Svoronos (1904) III pl. IX, and Kindler (1978) pls. 41–43. For a medical
explanation of these features as symptoms of acromegaly, see Hart (1973) 127.
Cf. Jeselsohn (1974) 78.

16. The regular representation of Ptolemy I can be found with some variations on three of the Yehud coins (Pl. III.14, 15, 17). However, on others
Ptolemy's portrait is quite different and is of "barbaric" style. See Pl. III.16,
18, 18a; Mildenberg (1979) pl. 22 no. 24; and a specimen known from the
Kadman Museum (cat. no. K-26989).

to decide the issue, and further evidence for the dating of the second group is required.

2. ARTISTIC STANDARD, STYLE, TYPES, MOTIFS, AND SEQUENCE

The dating of the second group to a time after that of the first group, and in the Hellenistic period, can be proved, in our view, by an examination of the artistry of the two groups, the style of the portraits in the second, the appearance of the various motifs in the coinage of the region, and considerations relating to the sequence of the late Yehud coins.

First, the examination of the artistry. There is a great difference in the artistic standards of the two groups. The portrait and figure as well as the general design of the first group are poor imitations, and the technique is rather primitive. The group has one issue that seems to belong to a prototype (Pl. I.1). The quality of its lettering and the shape of the owl are clearly superior to those of the others. However, even the prototype is considerably inferior to all the types of the second group, even to the early Yehud coins. The portrait on the obverse is quite "amorphic."[17] The owl on the reverse is a primitive local imitation of the standard Athenian owl, and the lettering is, in certain cases, of "barbaric" style.

In order to appreciate the artistic qualities of the second group, one has to examine the coins that present the best style and seem to be the prototypes of that group (Pl. II.8, 8a). The lettering is fine and styled,

17. Mildenberg (1979) 187, (1988) 723, suggests that the portrait is influenced by the Arethusa modeled by Cimon, the celebrated Syracusan engraver. However, the only similarity to Cimon's engravings is the appearance of a head *en face*, but this also appears on other Greek coins such as the various gorgoneia and the coins of Larissa, which are chronologically closer to the Hezekiah coins than the Cimonean types. For Cimon's Arethusa, see, e.g., *BMC Sicily* p. 177. Barag (1986/7) 9 suggests that the obverse in the coin of Johanan the High Priest (Pl. II.3; and see p. 263 below) represents his portrait. This would mean that Johanan also appears on the first group of the Hezekiah coins, carrying the latter's name as well as his title, which is out of the question. Besides, similar *en face* portraits are known from the Samaria hoard of the late Persian period (see Meshorer and Qedar [1991] pls. 23–31 nos. 71–153; most of the variations are rather distorted). See also the attempts at identification by Meshorer and Qedar, p. 22. The portrait, being so "amorphic," cannot be identified with any historical personality or a known type of the classical coinage. By and large it seems to be a stereotypical mask-shaped male head.

and the obverse shows a well-shaped Greco-Macedonian male profile. The excellent technique and the creative imagination of the artist stand out even more in the winged lynx, which is a combination of various elements: the body and wing remind one of a hippocamp known from Cilician and Phoenician coinage of the fourth century.[18] The head, probably of a lynx, or griffin, is somewhat similar to lion heads on the coinage of Asia Minor.[19] A combination of such a head with a hippocamp is otherwise unknown, but the body of a hippocamp (unwinged) with the face of wolf or a dog appears on a tiny coin from Tarsus of the time of Mazdi's governorship.[20] The wing differs from those of known hippocamps: the feathers are hatched throughout, and they recall the wing of a man-headed lion of Assyrian or even Persian type, current on the Greco-Persian coins found in Israel.[21] (Some scholars call these coins Philisto-Arabian.) The combination of all these elements in one imaginary creature may well be the artist's original contribution. The execution is amazingly accurate, especially as the diameter of these coins is only 6.5 to 8 mm and their weight 0.23 to 0.25 g.

A comparison of the two groups thus shows that the prototype of the second group is the creation of an artist of a caliber entirely different from that of the designer responsible for the first group. To the gap in artistic quality must be added the facts that the portraits and animals in the two groups are completely different, and that in the first the portrait is a frontal view and in the second a profile.[22] Two "schools" differing so greatly could not have developed together for the coinage of the same governor in the mint of Yehud, small as it was. One must

18. See Plant (1979) nos. 1299–1308; *BMC Cilicia* pl. XXXII nos. 8, 9; *BMC Phoenicia* pl. VII no. 305; Lambert (1933) pl. I nos. 39, 40; Kindler (1974) p. 75 and pl. II no. a; Cross (1974) pl. 80 no. 2 (from Wadi Dâliyeh in Samaria). The wing of these hippocamps is not hatched with alternating dots and dashes.

19. See, e.g., Kraay (1970) pl. 186 nos. 629–34 and esp. pl. 190 no. 55.

20. *BMC Cilicia* pl. XXXII nos. 8, 9; *SNG Lycaonia, Cilicia* pl. XII nos. 317, 318. The legs resemble those of a hippocamp; it is not winged, and its rear part is cut off.

21. *BMC Palestine* pl. XIX nos. 25, 26.

22. Contrary to the accepted method in regard to Athenian coins, the last difference cannot by itself be a chronological criterion. The profile already appears on the first Yehud coins. For the Athenian coins, see Robinson's well-known dictum, (1948) 43–59. Buttrey's counterevidence, (1982) 137ff., is based on Egyptian imitations, and therefore cannot apply to the original Athenian material.

have postdated the other. It stands to reason that had the "perfected" group antedated the primitive one, it would have influenced it in one way or another. No such influence is visible.

The great difference in the same small mint may also indicate a politico-cultural shift that brought about a creative momentum and provided new sources of inspiration. This suggestion may be confirmed by an analysis of the portraits of the second group (Pl. II.8, 8a, 11). That they are Greek is obvious from the hairstyle, but what decides the dating is their artistic realism. They stress the personal features (e.g., the neck) and the boniness of the face (cheekbones, nose, chin) in a way that is typical of the early Hellenistic period, as against the idealization of classical Greek art of the fifth and fourth centuries B.C. The same artistic features can be observed in another portrait (Pl. II.11a), which, if not to be identified with Ptolemy I, belongs to the second group of the Hezekiah series.[23]

The motifs, in addition, should be compared with those current on the coinage of Yehud and the surrounding region. All these coins show a portrait on the obverse and a bird on the reverse, the overwhelming majority carrying variations of Pallas Athene and the owl, known from traditional Athenian coinage. The Athenian types are sometimes replaced by the portrait of the Persian king and a falcon, and a single type replaces Pallas Athene with the (presumably) Jewish lily.[24] The coinage of the Levant in the Persian period was thus basically an imitation of the celebrated Athenian coinage, depicting a head on the obverse and a bird on the reverse. However, after the Macedonian conquest the Pallas Athene–owl type was only rarely minted in the East, and even in Athens it ceased to be struck after 322.[25] The Alexander coins, dominant between 332 and 302, do not have any bird on the reverse.[26] Hezekiah

23. See p. 258 above.

24. See Meshorer (1982) pls. I–III.

25. See *BMC Attica* pp. 13–23 nos. 129–247, pp. 25–27 nos. 263–80. The Athene-owl type, revived in Athens around 220 B.C., is of a new style, which differs from the classical type (see *BMC Attica* pl. VIII).

26. The appearance of the eagle standing on a thunderbolt on the Ptolemaic coins after 305 was exceptional and was motivated by propaganda purposes. It actually represents Zeus, following the Alexander coins that show an eagle on the hand of Zeus, thus indicating that Ptolemy was the only legitimate successor of Alexander, as was also demonstrated by the early coinage of Ptolemy I and other Ptolemaic initiatives and projects. It may also have served

coins of the first group do indeed always have an owl on the reverse; but those of the second have neither the owl (or any other type of bird), nor Pallas Athene, nor the head of a Persian king.

No less decisive are considerations relating to the sequence of the Yehud mintings. Most of these (and all the Hezekiah coins) are silver *minimae*, of the lowest denomination. Tiny silver coins are not known from Egypt of the Persian period,[27] but they were then regularly struck in Cilicia, Phoenicia (Byblos, Arados, and especially Tyre and Sidon), Acre, Samaria, Azotos, Ascalon, and Gaza.[28] Their production was stopped in most of these places under Alexander's rule, and in the remaining centers (Acre, Sidon, and Babylon) ceased no later than 307 B.C.[29] The Judea mint, however, continued to strike such denominations in the early Ptolemaic period, bearing the legend "Yehud" (or "Yehudah").[30]

A dating of all the Hezekiah coins to the Persian period thus creates a large gap of at least thirty-one years in the coinage of Yehud. It makes little sense to posit renewed production in Judea, after such a long interruption in the work of the local mint, of tiny silver coins whose production had started to decline in the Levant some decades earlier, and completely ceased shortly before. This point is strengthened by a further consideration: tiny coins can remain in circulation only for a limited time, because of their rapid abrasion through frequent use. The gap mentioned above must have led to the virtual disappearance of these coins, and within a few years of their issue being terminated. This rules out the possibility that the Judea mint, after resuming production, simply returned to its former practice. Continued use of the Persian-Aramean term "Yehud," in palaeo-Hebrew letters, in the early Ptolemaic period, when there seems to have been no Jewish governor, further strengthens the conclusion that there was

---

the purpose of presenting Ptolemy as the successor of the pharaohs, for the eagle was a royal bird in Egyptian Thebes (Diod. I.87.9).

27. Noted by Mildenberg (1988) 727.

28. See many examples in *BMC Phoenicia*. For Gaza, *BMC Palestine* pp. 176–83 nos. 1–31; Azotos and Ascalon, Meshorer (1989); Samaria, Meshorer and Qedar (1991).

29. For Sidon, see Newell (1916) 15 n. 37 and pl. II no. 26; Bellinger (1963) 26–27. Acre: Newell (1916) pl. VI no. 14. Babylonia: *BMC Arabia, Mesopotamia, Persia* 182–83, nos. 9–16 and pl. XXI nos. 8, 9.

30. See further pp. 266–70 below.

no gap in the production of the Judean mint. The second group of Hezekiah coins must therefore be dated to the period of Alexander and the Successors.

3. THE DURATION OF THE HEZEKIAH COINS

We have seen that the first group is unanimously dated to the late Persian period, while the second must be dated to the early Hellenistic period. The above-mentioned considerations with regard to sequence also seem to indicate that the Hezekiah coins were still being issued close to the time of the Ptolemaic occupation of Judea in 302/1 B.C., when they were replaced by the Ptolemaic Yehud series. This conclusion is supported by the appearance of the winged lynx that recurs on the reverse of the second group of Hezekiah, and also on a coin that seems to carry the portrait of Ptolemy I (Pl. II.11a).[31] What then is the *terminus post quem* for the Hezekiah coins?

The quantitative data do not offer much help. The first group includes about eight variations, and the second group four or five. In both of them the imprint of quite a number of dies can be discerned. However, the number of types or variations does not provide decisive evidence for the duration of coinage: a small number may have resulted from the wish to standardize the coins in order to lend them more credibility (as well as from the random nature of the findings), while a great number can be explained by special economic circumstances, changes in imperial rule, or the ambition of a particular personality to establish his image or eliminate those of his predecessors.[32] For similar reasons, neither can the number of dies serve as a guide.

Hard evidence for dating is provided by a coin of Johanan the High Priest (Pl. I.7). It was first attributed to Hezekiah the Governor, but Dan Barag has recently proved conclusively that the legend reads

---

31. See p. 258 above.

32. To offer just one illustration of these well-established rules from Jewish numismatics: so far at least twenty-five variants of the lamp-table type from just the first year of Mattathias Antigonus are known, all in all four types. And there are some dozen variants from the three years of this last Hasmonean king (40–37 B.C.), who tried to reestablish the Hasmonean state after a generation of Roman conquest.

יוֹחנן [[]] הכהן ("Johanan the Priest").[33] The portrait and owl on that coin are slight variations of those seen in the first Hezekiah group. Barag rightly concluded that the coin was struck simultaneously with Hezekiah's first group, and that Johanan was High Priest.[34] This means that he served when Hezekiah was governor.[35]

A close examination of the types of the first group supports Barag's chronological conclusion. We have already shown that one of them was the prototype, while all the others are just variations. This applies also to the coin of Johanan. The beginning of Hezekiah's governorship cannot, therefore, be dated after the High Priesthood of Johanan.

When did this High Priest serve? Josephus records events in the time of a High Priest named Johanan who served in the last generation of Persian rule (*Ant.* XI.297–302). From the context it appears that he died shortly before Alexander's accession in Macedonia in 336 B.C. (*Ant.* XI.302–4).[36] Some scholars have denied the reliability of Josephus's list and chronology of High Priests at the end of the Persian period, but as the first group of Hezekiah's coins is inevitably from that period, the Johanan coin provides direct confirmation for Josephus's list.[37]

33. Barag (1985) 166–68, (1986/7) 4–21; cf. Mildenberg (1988) 726; see also Cross (1983) 274 n. 50, quoting Meshorer.

34. See Barag's arguments, (1986/7) 10–12 and n. 41, on the recurrence of the title "the Priest" for the High Priests in the sources of the period. (See also the reference to Simeon the Righteous in Sirach 50.1.) Johanan's position as High Priest is apparent from the very right to mint coins and to do so concurrently with the governor, as well as from the recurrence of this name among the High Priests of the late Persian period. The dating of this coin, compared with Josephus's list of High Priests, further suggests that Johanan was indeed the acting High Priest. (See further below.)

35. See Barag (1986/7) 7–8, 10.

36. On the phrase "about this time" (*Ant.* XI.304), which recurs in Josephus's works, and its importance for source analysis, see D. R. Schwartz (1982) 246ff., and 248 on *Ant.* XI.304–5 (cf. S. J. D. Cohen [1982/3] 43), and there also on the ending of the passage ("as was narrated elsewhere"). The passage was indeed quoted from a subsidiary Hellenistic source, and not from the main source on the Yaddua-Menasseh affair. However, it stands to reason that the synchronization was based on some chronological indication in the main source.

37. See also p. 87 above.

The concurrent period of service of Hezekiah and Johanan must therefore have taken place before 336 B.C. The termination of the Hezekiah coinage close to the year 302/1 obliges us to date the start of minting as late as possible. It would be reasonable to assume that the coins were first struck around 340. Hezekiah entered office about 340 and continued to serve as governor until 302/1 (with some possible breaks due to changes in foreign rule). This is a long period of office for one man, but not exceptional or unparalleled in that period. Thus, for instance, of the four Persian kings who died in their beds, three reigned for periods of thirty-six to forty years (Darius I, Artaxerxes I, Artaxerxes II), one of them being a usurper. If Hezekiah the High Priest of Pseudo-Hecataeus is indeed a reflection of Hezekiah the Governor,[38] the statement that he was sixty-six years old at the time of his arrival in Egypt (*Ap.* I.187) may mean that he entered office at the age of twenty-eight. However, reliance on the data and figures offered by Pseudo-Hecataeus is rather questionable.

It should be noted here that concurrent coinages of a governor and a High Priest are not exceptional, and indeed, a coin of an earlier High Priest, named Yaddua, has recently been found.[39] The coins of the High Priests were intended to serve the current economic activities of the Temple and its treasury, and may have been issued only occasionally. Parallel temple coinage is known from the Orient in that period,[40] and one would assume that it required the approval of the governor,[41] especially because of the use of the same types and mint.

This observation naturally raises the wider question of the practical use and purchasing power of the Hezekiah coins.[42] Three considerations have to be taken into account. First, the governor and (sometimes) the High Priest were the minting authorities. Second, economic activity in Judea seems still to have been based mainly on barter: according to

38. See pp. 89–90 above.

39. See the coin in Spaer (1986/7) 1–5. He convincingly argues for the identification of Yaddua with the High Priest Yaddua II, born ca. 420.

40. On temple mints in Babylonia and Persia, see Newell (1938) 106, 117, 122, 171; Rostovtzeff (1940) I.435, III.1427 n. 234. In Syrian Hieropolis: Babelon (1893) 45, 51–54; Seyrig (1971) 11–21.

41. Thus Mildenberg (1988) 726.

42. See, e.g., Rappaport (1981) 13–14, who describes these coins as "small money."

the Book of Nehemiah, provincial and Temple taxes were paid partly in kind, partly in money (5.15). Third, there is no trace of bronze coins in circulation concurrently with the tiny silver coins. These considerations, taken together, may suggest that the Hezekiah coins were originally issued to serve as change money in return for provincial and Temple taxes, but had a relatively high purchasing value when reused in current commerce.[43]

4. THE DATING OF THE PTOLEMAIC YEHUD COINS

In the above discussion we have briefly referred to the dating of the Yehud coins from the Ptolemaic period. While scholars naturally attribute them to the days of Ptolemy I,[44] Meshorer argues for a later dating, to the time of Ptolemy II.[45] The connection between the dating of the Hezekiah coins and the Ptolemaic Yehud coins justifies a closer examination of the exact dating of the latter series.

Meshorer raises two arguments. First, a king who cruelly suppressed the Jews, as did Ptolemy I, would not have allowed Judea to strike coins of its own. He further mentions two silver hemidrachms (triobols) that were discovered recently and assumes that the striking of such a denomination indicates that the Jews were granted autonomy, which was unlikely under Ptolemy I. As for the historical argument, at the beginning of the Hellenistic period (contrary to the practice during the period when the empires were well established), the act of minting did not necessarily reflect the ruler's attitude toward the local population. Minting could be carried out by the local administration under any form of imperial government, whether this took the form of autonomy, semiautonomy, a Ptolemaic governor, or direct rule from Alexandria. Thus traditional local-style coinage of the time of Ptolemy I (and only in

---

43. Their high purchasing value can be deduced from comparison with the rates of the annual provincial and Temple taxes in Neh. 6.15, 10.33. Thus if the shekel followed the Persian standard (5.6 g), the annual "third shekel" donated to the Temple contained on the average nine tiny silver coins, and if Judea followed the old biblical shekel (11.3 g), which is less likely, it would have contained nineteen.

44. Kindler (1974) 73–77; Jeselsohn (1974) 77–78; Mildenberg (1979) 189–90; Rappaport (1981) 11–12, 14–15; Barag (1986/7) 6–7, esp. n. 20; Mildenberg (1988) 727; Mørkholm et al. (1991) 70.

45. Meshorer (1982) 18–20, 184–85.

large denominations) is known from the mints of the Ptolemaic realm in Asia Minor, Cyprus, Cyrenaica, and Phoenicia. The coins carry monograms that indicate the location of the mint, and almost all these places were treated harshly by Ptolemy I, as was Judea.[46] The use of the name Yehud, and in Hebrew letters, originated from the continuing practice of the Judean mint, which developed over a period of about eighty years. It continued because the Jewish population, for whose use these coins were produced, was still unaccustomed to the Greek language.[47] The striking of tiny silver coins by the High Priest in the Persian period shows that part of this coinage was struck for religious-administrative purposes, which further explains the continuing use of the Hebrew script.

By and large, the continued striking of the Yehud coins after 302/1, despite the change in foreign rule and governing system, is not unparalleled. Numismatic traditions tend sometimes to continue in periods of transition and not to disappear overnight, as has been seen above with regard to the second group of Hezekiah coins. To cite just a few instructive illustrations: golden double darics were still struck in Babylonia under the Successors, with the traditional depiction of the Persian king in a running pose.[48] Late Byzantine coinage had an even longer duration: the Arab occupation of Palestine in 636 A.D. did not change the monetary system, and for seventy years thereafter cities like Aelia Capitolina and Tiberias continued striking the typical Byzantine *follis*, divided into forty *nummi*. The Greek letter M (= 40) is topped by a cross, and the effigy resembles those of earlier Byzantine emperors, even bearing a cross on his headdress and on the end of his scepter.[49] In Persia the Arab governors continued striking the typical Sassanid types with Zoroastrian symbols.[50] These practices ceased only in 705 A.D. with the numismatic reforms of 'Abd al-Mālik ibn Marwān. And a modern example: after the deposition of Kaiser Wilhelm II in 1918, the Weimar Republic continued until 1922 to strike the traditional coins

46. See pp. 72ff. above.

47. See also Rappaport (1981) 12, who thinks that the mint in Judea acted as a "contractor" for the Ptolemaic regime, and pp. 12–13 on the absence of any political significance in the minting of *minimae* in the Persian period.

48. See *BMC Arabia, Mesopotamia, Persia* pl. XXII nos. 1–13.

49. See Walker (1956) pls. 1–4.

50. See the plates in Walker (1941).

of the Second Reich, with the German eagle and the crown of the German empire.

It should be noted that the use of silver hemidrachms (triobols) only weakens Meshorer's case: hemidrachms were struck in the region, although not frequently, under Alexander and the Successors,[51] and disappeared in the Ptolemaic period. Only a single specimen is known from Egypt at the time of Ptolemy II.[52]

Meshorer's second argument draws attention to the portrait of Berenice I, the wife of Ptolemy I, on the reverse of one of the types of the Ptolemaic Yehud coins (Pl. IV.19–21). It is generally accepted that the very first appearance of Berenice I on coins of the Ptolemaic dynasty was in Cyrenaica in 277 B.C. during the revolt of Magas.[53] Meshorer argues that her portrait could not have been struck in the local Judean mint before being circulated on royal coins. This assumption by itself is not compelling: on the Yehud coins of the second group of Hezekiah, as well as of the Ptolemaic period, one observes Hellenistic portraits unknown from the coinage of the Successors (and, so far, unknown even from local coinage or the art of the period: Pl. II.8, 8a, 11; III.12, 13). A portrait of Berenice could likewise have been introduced, in one way or another, to the Judean coinage. Moreover, her portrait seems to have appeared on coins of at least one place long before Ptolemy II's reign, even before the Ptolemaic occupation of Judea in 302/1: some types of coins bearing a female portrait identified as Berenice I are known from

51. Some examples: one specimen from Acre of the type of Alexander the Great (in the Kadman Museum, Tel Aviv, cat. no. K-30791); two types from Sidon of 325/4 B.C. (Newell [1916] 13 no. 28) and from Acre (ibid. 41 no. 8); other types from the time of Seleucus's governorship in the Babylonian satrapy (*BMC Arabia, Mesopotamia, Persia* 189 no. 49, 190 no. 54); a hemidrachm of Ptolemy I from 311–305 of the Alexander type (Svoronos [1904] II.8 no. 35, III pl. II no. 15).

52. See Svoronos (1904) II.91 no. 609, III pl. XIV no. 26. It shows the first two Ptolemaic royal couples together on both sides of the coin. Such a combination is well known from Ptolemaic gold coins, but this is the only example struck in silver.

53. Noted by Mildenberg (1979) 189 n. 32; and applied by Meshorer (1982) 18. Despite these data, Mildenberg reaches the conclusion that the Ptolemaic Yehud coins belong to the days of Ptolemy I. On the Berenice portrait on Magas's coins, see Robinson in *BMC Cyrenaica* pp. cxlix–cliii; and cf. Bagnall (1976) 185 and n. 38.

Cos.[54] These coins were thought by Svoronos to have been issued over a period of half a century, from 308 B.C. onwards.[55] The sequence of the various types and the historical circumstances allow us to be more specific and suggest that one type belongs to the years 308–306 B.C.[56] Attention should also be given to the form of the portrait of Berenice on the Judean coins: she appears alone on the reverse (with her husband on the obverse), while on the coinage of Ptolemy II she is always paired with Ptolemy I. The coins of Magas and Cos show only Berenice, and not on the reverse, but on the obverse. The designer of the Judean coin under discussion did not, in any case, copy or imitate an existing royal coin.

But even if the type bearing Berenice's portrait belongs to the days of Ptolemy II, this does not imply that all the Judean Ptolemaic coins belong to the period of the same ruler. At least one type (Pl. III.12, 13) certainly antedates the Berenice type, as it does not show a dynastic portrait. As for the rest, there is insufficient reason to date them after the Berenice type.[57]

The decisive consideration is the sequence of the coinage. The argument raised above with regard to the dating of the second group of the Hezekiah coins applies also concerning the dating of the Judean Ptolemaic coins, and even more strongly. One cannot imagine renewal of coining in such an exceptional denomination, and in traditional style and palaeo-Hebrew letters, after its being discontinued for at least nineteen years. This is especially true for the time of Ptolemy II, who established the thorough centralization of regime and economy

54. See Svoronos (1904) I pp. πβ′–πε′, IV.30–32; Hill (1923) 209.

55. Svoronos (1904) IV.30–32.

56. See Extended Notes, n. 7 p. 298 below.

57. It has been suggested that the Hebrew spelling יהודה ("Yehudah"), which appears on some of the Yehud Ptolemaic coins (Pl. IV.8, 9, 11, 12), postdates the Aramaic spelling יהד ("Yehud"), which appears on other Yehud coins of the Ptolemaic period, among them the Berenice coins (first Kindler [1974] 73–76, followed by many others). However, as Aramaic continued to be prevalent in Judea alongside Hebrew long after the Persian period, the spellings יהד and יהודה could have been used concurrently under Ptolemy I. This is proved by one of the Persian Yehud coins (the owl type), which carries on the obverse the legend יהודה and on the reverse יהד (in the collection of the Israel Museum). The same can be deduced from the coin in Meshorer (1982) pl. 3 no. 17, which, in the absence of a portrait or a typical Ptolemaic symbol, cannot be attributed to the Ptolemaic period (against Meshorer, pp. 14–15).

that so characterized the Ptolemaic empire for generations to come, and even for the second period of Ptolemy I's reign, not long after the year 295, when Ptolemaic coinage was finally standardized.[58]

Direct evidence for the existence of this sequence may be found in the coin that shows on the reverse the winged lynx, known from the second group of the Hezekiah coins, and on the obverse a Hellenistic portrait, probably of Ptolemy I (Pl. II.11a).[59] If this identification is incorrect and the coin belongs to the Hezekiah series, it then depicts an anonymous man, like two or three others seen in the second group of Hezekiah (Pl. II.8, 8a, 11). An unknown man also appears on what is certainly the earliest of the Ptolemaic Yehud coins (Pl. III.12, 13).[60] The striking of such a portrait in the Ptolemaic period, and not that of Alexander or Ptolemy I, can be explained only by the continuing tradition of the local mint.

SUMMARY

The first group of the Hezekiah coins is to be dated to the end of the Persian period, from about 340 B.C.; and the second group, to the period of Alexander and the Successors. The striking of the latter group seems to have continued until the Ptolemaic occupation of Judea in 302/1, on the eve of the battle of Ipsus. The numismatic material thus indicates that Hezekiah served as governor of Judea in the period between roughly 340 and 302/1 B.C., with some possible interruptions during the short periods of Ptolemaic occupation. Under the Persians he was called *pehah*, but his official title after the Macedonian conquest is not known. The preservation of the old Persian provincial divisions and the retention in office of former oriental governors are well known from Alexander's administrative system. Coins of Johanan the High Priest were struck simultaneously with Hezekiah's first group. The series of the Ptolemaic Yehud coins has to be dated to the reign of Ptolemy I, and it remains remotely possible that one type (Ptolemy I–Berenice) may be attributed to the early days of Ptolemy II.

58. On this standardization see Mørkholm (1991) 67.

59. See p. 258 above.

60. Mildenberg (1979) 188 suggests that the portrait on the Ptolemaic coin is a variation of the face that figures in the first group of the Hezekiah coins (Pl. I). But there is no similarity between the two.

Appendix B
The Dating of Pseudo-Aristeas

In the above discussion we reached the conclusion that Pseudo-Hecataeus's *On the Jews* was not written before the *Letter of Aristeas* (ch. IV.3). The dating of the latter book can thus provide an additional *post quem* date for the composition of *On the Jews*.

Pseudo-Aristeas, who presents himself as a gentile courtier, claims to be recording events in the time of Ptolemy II (283–247) and to have played an active role in them. This has been universally rejected, and the book has been acknowledged as a pseudonymous Jewish work. Its date, however, is still much disputed, with various suggestions ranging from the late third century B.C. to the second half of the first century A.D. The evidence for the various datings has been rejected or responded to in a way that has left room for doubt.[1] There is, though, one passage in the book, within the geographical description of Judea, referring to the Jerusalem citadel (paras. 102–4),

1. See the review of the main suggestions and the excellent evaluation of the pros and cons by Goodman in Schürer et al. (1973–86) III.679–84. Note the penetrating references to the question of unity and the allegorical interpretations (679–80); the connection with the writings of Aristobulus, the Jewish philosopher (680 and n. 281, 683); the biblical associations in the geographical descriptions (681 and n. 282); the Ptolemaic official terminology (683); the Jewish-Egyptian background (683 and n. 289; cf. p. 285 below); and the arguments from the account of the harbors (682 n. 285; see further n. 7 below). As for Aristobulus, it should be added that one would expect this Jewish courtier to have referred to Aristeas, who is presented as a Ptolemaic courtier, in his report about the antiquity of the Greek translations (Eus. *PE* XIII.12.1–2) had he been acquainted with Pseudo-Aristeas.

that has not attracted much attention,[2] but may provide an approximate date for the composition of the book.[3] The conclusion is supported by other references and the Ptolemaic background; and there is no evidence that the passage is a later interpolation.

But before any discussion of this as well as of other relevant passages, some preliminary remarks must be made about the general character of the account of the Holy Land in the *Letter* and its sources of information. It has rightly been pointed out by many scholars that the book tends to idealize the Jewish country, Jerusalem, and the Temple by drawing on biblical stereotypes and associations,[4] rules taken from Hellenistic city building and architecture,[5] and especially on motifs borrowed from Greek and Hellenistic utopian literature.[6] There is no possibility of deciding whether the author had actually visited Jerusalem and the surrounding countryside. The utopian character of the account is no evidence: in describing what he regarded as a holy land and city, Pseudo-Aristeas may have preferred to follow the practice of some Hellenistic authors who idealized their subjects instead of faithfully reporting their experiences and true knowledge, which would certainly have been less exciting. It is therefore imperative to exercise caution in evaluating the geographical information. Only data that do not have biblical or Hellenistic sources of inspiration, and do not by themselves

2. Graetz (1876) 295ff. and Willrich (1924) 90–91 identify the citadel with the Roman *Antonia*, which is certainly absurd in view of its manning by Jews and command by the High Priest (cf. Goodman in Schürer et al. [1973–86] III.682 n. 285). Hadas (1951) 12–13 is inconclusive. His discussion includes some mistakes on decisive points (e.g., the location of the pre-Maccabean citadel) and ignores Jewish sovereignty over the citadel. On the suggestion of Schürer, developed by Goodman, see pp. 275–76 below.

3. Cf. in short Bar-Kochva (1989) 53 n. 83.

4. See Tramontano (1931) 107; Hadas (1951) 64; Tcherikover (1958) 77–79; Bonphil (1972); Bickerman (1976–80) I.133; Goodman in Schürer et al. (1973–86) III.681 and n. 282.

5. See, e.g., Bickerman (1976–80) I.133–34.

6. See Guttman (1928) 42ff.; Hadas (1951) 49–51; Tcherikover (1958) 64–68; Bonphil (1972) 131; Bickerman (1976–80) I.133–34. The latter is, however, mistaken in favorably evaluating the description of the course of the Jordan River (Pseudo-Aristeas 116; see Bickermann 128–29, 131). For its utopian and imaginary character, see Hadas 50, 147. Cf. Bonphil 139–40 on its Jewish parallels.

present an unrealistic picture, can be utilized for determining the date of the book.[7]

1. THE CITADEL AND THE TEMPLE

Now to the passage itself. The author describes the citadel of Jerusalem. The pretext for the account is the visit of Ptolemaic delegates to the city for negotiations on the translation of the Torah and other matters. The following statements are relevant to the discussion (cf. Map 2, p. 111 above):

1. The citadel is situated on the highest place, controlling and overlooking the Temple and its court, so that the sacrificial ritual can be observed from it (paras. 100, 103).

2. It was planned by its founder and serves to defend the Temple (para. 104).

3. This protection is required in case of a revolt (*neoterismos*) or an invasion by a foreign enemy (para. 101).

4. The local garrison consists of five hundred soldiers, all of whom are Jews (paras. 102, 104).

---

7. Thus, for instance, the various attempts at determining the date according to the relationship between the ports and Jerusalem (Pseudo-Aristeas 115) fail to satisfy. The author describes the ports as serving the trade of Jerusalem according to philosophical conceptions of the ideal city-state (see, e.g., Plato, *Leges* 704–5: the influence of these conceptions on Pseudo-Aristeas 107–8, 115 is undeniable; cf. Arist. *Pol.* 1327[a–b]). The account therefore cannot be taken to indicate that the book was written at a time when Judea and the coastal plain were (or belonged to) one political unit. It should be added at this point that the names of the harbors mentioned in Pseudo-Aristeas (Ptolemaïs, Jaffa, Ascalon, and Gaza) can only indicate a dating before the destruction of Gaza by Alexander Jannaeus, and not a much earlier date. These four cities were traditionally known as the most important Palestinian ports, and it is only natural that less famous ports, which may have flourished in certain periods (like Strato's Tower, Dora, Iamnia, and Azotos), were not mentioned (*contra* Rappaport [1970] 38–41). A different approach, leading to the same results, is taken by Goodman: "Verse 115 probably does not refer to political control but only geographical proximity and the passage of trade (which would not be affected by the ports being in gentile hands), in which case it is irrelevant to the dating of the book" (in Schürer et al. [1973–86] III.682 n. 285). See also Hadas (1951) 146: "Aristeas does not necessarily imply that the Jews owned the ports but only that they used them."

5. These Jews are absolutely loyal to their country and religion (paras. 102, 104).

6. The garrison stands under the direct command of the High Priest (para. 103).[8]

7. The delegates of the Ptolemaic king had to receive permission from the High Priest to enter the citadel, and even then gained admission only with much difficulty, being disarmed before entering (paras. 103–4). The purpose was only to "see the sacrifices" from an observation point (para. 103), which obviously could not be allowed for gentiles in the Temple itself.

In contrast to the bulk of the account on Jerusalem and the Holy Land, this passage cannot be dismissed as an imaginary idealization or the like. The author speaks *inter alia* about the role of the citadel as a defense against an internal revolt, which in practice means uprisings against the High Priest involving the Temple. This is certainly anything but an idealization of the holy place and its admired guardian. Notably, the location of the citadel "on the highest place," soaring above the Temple, contradicts a passage in another context according to which the Temple was high above the city on the crest of a mountain "rising to a lofty height" (paras. 83–84). As was observed long ago, the latter account is imaginary and does not accord with the geography of Jerusalem. It was inspired by a combination of elements drawn from Hellenistic utopian literature and city planning,[9] as well as from Isaiah's celebrated vision of the End of Days (2.1).

In the case of the citadel, the author is drawn into another type of description by the need to explain its functions, and thus reveals more than he would wish. The role and location of the citadel, as well as other basic facts in themselves, sound quite realistic and, as we shall see, recall the specific situation in a particular period. The account does

8. The description ὁ προκαθηγούμενος refers according to para. 122 to the High Priest. See Wendland (1900) *ad loc.*; Tramontano (1931) 78–79; Hadas (1951) 141; followed by many others.

9. The location of temples on commanding heights, which is well known from classical archaeology, appears also in utopian literature; see, e.g., Euhemerus *ap.* Diod. VI.1.6 (though it was far from the city: V.42.6). Cf. Plato, *Critias* 112, 113–15; *Leges* 778c–d, 848c–d; Arist. *Pol.* 1331[a]. For the location of Jerusalem in the center of the country by Pseudo-Aristeas (para. 83), cf. Plato, *Leges* 745a.

not contain any biblical associations, and the role and command of the citadel do not recall Hellenistic practice, nor do they echo any Greek or Hellenistic utopia.[10] In view of the traditional Greek *asylia*, one can indeed be sure that the account of a citadel protecting a temple and supervised by a High Priest was not inspired by Hellenistic literature and practice.[11] In the absence of parallels, the author had to resort to reality and drew on his own personal knowledge. It does not require the direct acquaintance of an eyewitness to be able to write down the main features of such an account. They could have been reported in Alexandria by pilgrims returning from Jerusalem.

Taken as reflecting historical reality, it appears quite obvious that the account was not written while Jerusalem was under Hellenistic rulers, and the citadel manned by a foreign garrison. Even if one allows for some idealization in the account, the above conclusion remains valid: an Alexandrian writer who so emphatically stressed his loyalty (and that of the Jews) to the Ptolemaic dynasty would not have described what should have been the stronghold and symbol of Ptolemaic rule in Judea as an independent Jewish citadel unless he was actually recording the situation in his own time.

It has, though, been suggested that the account records a special situation that supposedly prevailed in Judea under the Ptolemies. According to this suggestion, foreign troops were stationed in the Jerusalem citadel only occasionally, and most of the time it was garrisoned by Jews.[12] This solution seems highly unlikely: the confrontation between the Ptolemies and the Jews in 302/1 and in the years of the Syrian wars,[13] the continuing, protracted hostility between the Ptolemies and the Seleucids over the future of Coile Syria, and the agitation of the

10. Cf. the somewhat different phrasing of Goodman in Schürer et al. (1973–86) III.681: "It is reasonable to assume that those details for which no biblical and Egyptian sources, and no apologetic reason for invention can be found, are more likely to derive from contemporary conditions than the author's imagination."

11. Plato, *Leges* 848c–d, does not contradict this assertion: it relates to the security of the citizens and the city, not that of the temples.

12. See Schürer (1901–9) III.611–12; Goodman in Schürer et al. (1973–86) III.681–82.

13. On the year 302/1, see p. 74 above. On the confrontation during the Third Syrian War, M. Stern (1962) 43; the Fourth Syrian War, Jos. *Ant.* XII.130 and perhaps also the trilingual stele from Pithom, I.23 (see Gauthier and Sottas

pro-Seleucid party in the Jewish community—all these do not permit us to believe that the Ptolemies ordinarily entrusted the security of Judea to Jewish hands.[14] The reference to revolt, which would apply in this case to a Jewish anti-Ptolemaic rebellion, renders this suggestion even less acceptable. Furthermore, there is no indication in the passage of Jewish loyalty to the Ptolemaic kingdom, or that the fortress in any way served Ptolemaic interests. Such assertions would be expected even more in a report on a visit by a Ptolemaic delegation. The author stresses instead the dedication of the Jewish troops to their *patris* (para. 102). In addition, the delegation gains access to the fortress with much difficulty, is disarmed, and even then is able only to "see the sacrifices" (para. 103). There is no indication that they were allowed to review the military installations from inside.

It should also be pointed out that the location of the fortress on the "highest place" (para. 100), overlooking the Temple altar (103), and the stipulation that its purpose was to protect the Temple (104) make it difficult to identify the citadel with the *Akra* known from the Ptolemaic and Seleucid periods. The latter was situated a few hundred meters south of the Temple, on a hill considerably lower than the Temple Mount,[15] and its purpose was to control the city, not the Temple. And there was not and could not have been any other fortress in Jerusalem under Hellenistic rule.[16] These data do not in themselves constitute decisive proof, since the author could still have made a mistake in determining the exact location of the citadel, but they certainly do not suggest an early dating.

[1925] 54–56; but cf. the opposing view of Thissen [1966] 19, 60–63); the Fifth Syrian War, *Ant.* XII.131, 133, 135–36; Daniel 11.14.

14. *Ant.* XII.133 does not imply that Ptolemaic troops were only occasionally assigned to the fortress, as argued by Schürer (and Goodman in Schürer et al. [1973–86] 682). They were previously expelled by the Jews in the first stage of the Fifth Syrian War, when Antiochus III invaded Syria (in the year 202/1; see *Ant.* XII.131, 135; Polyb. XVI.22a; on the stages of that war, see Bar-Kochva [1979] 146, 256, and bibliography there).

15. See the detailed discussion in Bar-Kochva (1989) 445–65. The general location of the Seleucid *Akra* on the southeastern hill was agreed upon by Schürer et al. (1973–86) I.154 n. 39 and Goodman therein, III.681, as well as by most philologist-historians.

16. See my arguments in Bar-Kochva (1989) 462–65, in contrast to Goodman in Schürer et al. (1973–86) III.681. The latter is forced to presume that Hyrcanus only restored the Temple citadel (n. 283).

It can, therefore, be said that the status of the citadel and its garrison and command indicate a period of Jewish independence, namely the time of the Hasmonean state. This conclusion is supported by further considerations: the role of the High Priest as supreme military commander, taken together with the references to his authority in civil matters (paras. 81, 122), recalls the appointments bestowed upon the early Hasmoneans since the time of Jonathan;[17] the need to protect the Temple from foreign invasions and internal unrest is understandable for the early Hasmonean rulers, in whose time there was great sensitivity with regard to possible new attacks on the Temple by foreign enemies, and religious sects disputed the ritual practices performed in the Temple and the very right of the Hasmoneans to serve there as High Priests. Given this general dating to the Hasmonean period, the intention to use the citadel to protect the Temple and its location "in the highest place" suggest its identification with the *Baris*, the Hasmonean citadel built north of the Temple in the place of the later *Antonia* (*Ant.* XIII.307, XV.409; *Bell.* V.238–47). The *Baris* did indeed tower over the Temple and also served other purposes connected with the Temple, such as safeguarding the ceremonial garments of the High Priest (*Ant.* XVIII.91).

The construction of the *Baris* can thus provide a *post quem* date for Pseudo-Aristeas. Josephus mentions in the narrative of the Herodian and the Roman period that it was built by John Hyrcanus (*Ant.* XV.403, XVIII.91). If one tries to be more precise and date the construction within Hyrcanus's reign of three decades (135–104 B.C.), one can be sure that it was built only after 129, when Hyrcanus regained his independence after the death of Antiochus VII Sidetes in the eastern provinces. It was not built immediately after 129: I Maccabees, written not long after that year,[18] mentions, in praise of Hyrcanus's achievements, only the rebuilding of the city wall, and not the fortress (16.23). It is true that Josephus's account of the period of John Hyrcanus (*Ant.* XIII.230–300) does not record the building of the fortress, but he does not refer to

17. On the sovereignty of the High Priest as an argument for the dating of the book to the time of the Hasmonean rulers, see M. Stern (1983) 225.

18. On the dating of I Maccabees, see Bar-Kochva (1989) 158–66. The conclusion reached below regarding the dating of Pseudo-Aristeas to the years 118/16–113, which is based on a number of arguments aside from the date of I Maccabees, supports the view that the latter book could not have been composed long after the year 129.

the reconstruction of the wall, either. Josephus devotes only a little coverage to the years 128–113. For the last decade of Hyrcanus's rule, 113–104, he provides much more detail (though the chronology and sequence are distorted).[19] This suggests that the fortress was built before the year 113. In view of the historical circumstances, a date close to the year 125 seems reasonable: the building of the citadel could not have been delayed much longer, since the *Akra*, the former Hellenistic citadel, was demolished by Simeon around the year 140.[20] The period of peace and economic prosperity after the rise of Alexander Zabinas in Syria in 126 (*Ant.* XIII.273) provided the resources and breathing space to build a formidable citadel. The year 125 may thus be taken as a tentative *post quem* date for the composition of Pseudo-Aristeas. This conclusion is supported from another angle: on the basis of the striking similarity between Pseudo-Aristeas 13 and the document at I Maccabees 10.36, it has rightly been suggested that Pseudo-Aristeas was the later of the two.[21] This means that the *Letter* was composed at least some years after 128.

The year 113 also seems to mark a *terminus ante quem* for the composition of Pseudo-Aristeas itself. The general atmosphere of peace and affluence that prevails in its description of the country (paras. 100–120)[22] accords with Josephus's evaluation of the middle years of John Hyrcanus's reign (*Ant.* XIII.273–74). This period came to an end with the invasion of the coastal plain by Antiochus IX Cyzicenus (113) and its reconquest by Hyrcanus (112). This was followed by unremitting wars of expansion pursued by the Hasmonean state beginning in the year 112/11, and the subsequent military interventions of Hellenistic kings in the course of events.

---

19. See p. 292 below on the misplaced document in *Ant.* XIV.249, which refers to the invasion of the coastal plain by Antiochus IX Cyzicenus, and belongs to the year 113/12; p. 131 nn. 28, 29, on the occupation of Idumea and Samaria (*Ant.* XIII.254–58); and p. 136 n. 49 on the events surrounding the siege of Samaria and Scythopolis (*Ant.* XIII.275–83).

20. On the destruction of the *Akra* and its date, see Tsafrir (1975a) 502 and n. 5; Bar-Kochva (1989) 453–54. The source: Jos. *Ant.* XIII.215–17.

21. Momigliano (1930) 164–65, (1932) 161–73. Cf. M. Stern (1965) 104–5, (1983) 225; Murray (1967) 338–40. The reservations of Schürer, Vermes, and Millar (1973–86) I.179 and Goodman therein, III.682 and n. 286, are unjustified: the similarity is too striking to be accidental.

22. This atmosphere has been rightly noticed by Goodman, ibid. III.681.

2. IDUMEA AND SAMARIA

The same conclusion appears from the passage referring to Idumea and Samaria (para. 107). Bickerman, in one of his inspiring articles, drew attention to this passage long ago and used it as evidence for dating the book between the years 145 and 127.[23] He based his analysis on the traditional assumption that Idumea and central Samaria were conquered by John Hyrcanus around the year 128. The recent excavations in Marisa and Mount Gerizim have, however, definitely proved that Idumea and southern Samaria were occupied only in 112/11 or shortly thereafter.[24] In addition, the chronological implications of the passage on the Jerusalem citadel escaped his notice. A modification of Bickerman's chronological analysis of the references to Idumea and Samaria and his arguments is therefore required (cf. Maps 3, 5, pp. 118, 126 above).

Pseudo-Aristeas tries to explain why Jerusalem is not a large city.[25] Following the autarkian ideal, he says that the founders were aware of the advantages of a proper dispersion of the population in the rural, agricultural lands, so as to provide the city with adequate supplies. In this context he describes the terrain and agricultural possibilities of the lands belonging to the city (para. 107):

> For the country is large and good, and some [of its parts], those in the so-called Samareitis [τῶν κατὰ τὴν Σαμαρεῖτιν λεγομένην][26] and those adjacent to the country of the Idumeans [συναπτόντων τῇ τῶν Ἰδουμαίων χώρᾳ], are flat. But other [parts] are mountainous, those ⟨in the center of the country. With regard to them it is necessary⟩[27]

23. Bickerman (1930) 280ff. See also nn. 33 and 55 below.

24. See p. 131 nn. 28, 29 above.

25. For his motive, the inevitable comparison with Alexandria, see p. 110 above.

26. In the codd.: λεγομένων. The obvious emendation λεγομένην has been universally accepted.

27. It has been accepted by all editors and commentators that the text suffers here from a lacuna. Thackeray ([1902] 570) suggested τινῶν δὲ ὀρεινῶν, τῶν ⟨συναπτόντων τῇ τῶν Ἰουδαίων χώρᾳ, χρὴ⟩ πρός.... This restoration does not provide an explanation for the omission in the text, and does not make sense: a statement about the necessity of carefully tilling mountainous lands outside the Jewish land is irrelevant to the context and the obvious purpose of the passage as a whole. They indicate that the mountainous parts of the Jewish land itself are meant. Moreover, it appears from the previous clauses of the

to attend constantly to agriculture and soil, so that in this way they will also bear much fruit.

The author thus calls the Hebron Hills "the country of the Idumeans." In the time of the First Temple the region belonged without interruption to the Judean kingdom and was inhabited by the tribe of Judah. After the evacuation of the Jewish population with the destruction of the Temple, the region was settled by Idumeans. Consequently it was named Idumea from at least the beginning of the Hellenistic period.[28] In 112/11 it was occupied by John Hyrcanus; its inhabitants were converted to Judaism, and the region was integrated into Judea.[29] The official name of the Hebron region under the Hasmoneans is anybody's guess.[30]

Whatever its name after the occupation was, the author uses the phrase "the country of the Idumeans," which is much more expressive than just "Idumea." A Jewish author living in Alexandria would not have used this phrase in the generation immediately after the

---

sentence that the region around Jerusalem (between "its parts" in Samareitis and "those adjacent to the country of the Idumeans") is mountainous (as was also well known to Hellenistic writers in the generation of John Hyrcanus; see p. 109 above). We must therefore accept *exempli gratia* the restoration suggested by Mendelssohn and Wilamowitz (see Wendland [1900] 32, [1900a] 14): τῶν πρὸς ⟨μέσην τὴν χώραν, χρὴ τὰ πρός⟩.... This restoration (without the redundant τά) was rightly preferred in almost all subsequent editions and translations; see, e.g., Andrews (1913) 105; Tramontano (1931) II.113; Meecham (1935) 238; Hadas (1951) 143 (see his translation); Cahana (1956) II.42; Pelletier (1962) 156. Thackeray himself changed his mind: see (1903) 360 n. 2, (1904) 24 n. 2; but his emendation was repeated by Hadas (1951) 142 (in the text) and by Shutt in Charlesworth (1985) II.20 n. z. The suggestions of Mendelssohn (1897) 33 and Meisner (1973) 59, τῶν ⟨τὰ χρὴ⟩ or τῶν ⟨χρὴ⟩, are not acceptable, and were rightly rejected by Wendland (*locc. citt.*): the structure of the clause clearly indicates that the τῶν was followed by a location of the preceding τινῶν δὲ ὀρεινῶν.

28. See M. Stern (1968) 226, and esp. Diod. XIX.95, 98, drawing on Hieronymus of Cardia.

29. *Ant.* XIII.257; on the date, see p. 131 n. 28 above.

30. The only piece of information directly relevant to the Hasmonean kingdom is to be found in *Ant.* XIV.10. However, that statement, which refers to Herod's grandfather, was taken from Nicolaus of Damascus (cf. *Ant.* XIV.9, *Bell.* I.123–24), Herod's court historian. He may well have used terminology from the time of his Idumean Maecenas, when the region naturally acquired a special status. On this status, see M. Stern (1968) 226.

annexation and forced Judaization of the region by John Hyrcanus,[31] when there must still have been considerable sensitivity about the Judaization of the region.[32] An explicit admission that the region was "the country of the Idumeans" would also have caused considerable embarrassment to Egyptian Jews in their confrontations with the Idumean settlers in Egypt.[33] These confrontations produced, some generations earlier, the Idumean version of the notorious ass libel, which was based on, among other things, the ethnographical-religious division between Judea and the Hebron region.[34] Furthermore, if the accepted restoration of the lacuna in the sentence about the mountainous regions is correct (which it almost certainly is),[35] then only the mountainous regions "in the center"—that is, between Jerusalem and the plains "adjacent to the country of the Idumeans" on one side and the plains of "the so-called

31. On the forced character of the Judaization of the Idumeans, see the recent sensible comment of Shatzman (1990) 58 n. 90; Feldman (1993) 325–26 (*pace* Kasher [1986] 46–77, 79–85). On the reference in Strabo XVI.2.34, see my note in *Anti-Semitism and Idealization of Judaism*, chap. VI.6. It is well in line with Posidonius's idealized and fictitious conception of the *origo* of the Jewish people (Strabo XVI.2.35–36), which was by itself inspired by his political and religious ideals.

32. Josephus does indeed refer many times to the converted Idumeans as "the Idumeans" in his account of the Great Revolt against the Romans, and at least half the former Idumean territory still preserved the old name, being a toparchy of Judea proper in the time of the Revolt (*Bell.* III.55; and see M. Stern [1968] 226–29 on the toparchies of Idumea and Engeddi). But the Judaization of the area was by then already an established fact; the Idumeans had proved their loyalty and even extreme zealousness during the Revolt, and there was thus no reason to disguise their ethnic origin. Moreover, it seems quite clear that Josephus wanted to stress their non-Jewish descent and thereby explain their ruthlessness and immoral behavior (e.g., *Bell.* IV.231, 310).

33. Bickerman (1930) 28off. argued that the expression "land of the Idumeans" proves that the book was written before the occupation of Idumea. In a later version of the article ([1976–80] I.131 n. 93) he changed his mind and noted that the reference has no political but rather a purely geographical connotation, and refrained from using it as evidence for his dating (following Tcherikover [1961a] 317 n.8). Regrettably, he was not aware of the propagandist significance of geographical and administrative designations in the newly independent and expanding Jewish state. A similar policy can be observed in modern Israel, especially after the 1967 war ("Judea and Samaria").

34. *Ap.* II.112. On the origin of the story among the Idumean settlers in Egypt, see M. Stern (1974–84) I.98.

35. See n. 27 above.

Samareitis" on the other—are referred to. The Hebron region is thus not counted among the sources of supply for Jerusalem, which means that it did not belong to the Jews. All in all, the passage could not have been written after 112/11, when the region passed into Jewish hands and was integrated into Hasmonean Judea.

Less significant is the exact geographical meaning of the reference to flatlands "adjacent to the country of the Idumeans." These lands may be the valleys of the southern Shephela, the hilly region west of the central mountain range (like the Elah Valley and several smaller ones), adjacent to the Idumean territory. However, it would have taken considerable expertise to be so accurate, and even had the author gone on a pilgrimage to Jerusalem (which is still doubtful),[36] this would not have been enough: after all, not too many modern Israelis have a precise knowledge of the topographical features of the fringe areas of the Judean Hills. It may well have been an "armchair deduction" from the account in I Maccabees of the flight of the Seleucid troops after the battle of Ammaus, on the fringe of the Judean Hills: the Seleucid troops, who camped "near Ammaus, in the land of the plain" (3.40), are said to have fled after the battle to the "plain" (4.14), and then to have been pursued up to the "plains of Idumea, Ashdod, and Jabneh" (4.15). Pseudo-Aristeas evidently utilized and interpreted for his own purposes certain other minor details found in I Maccabees.[37]

The reference to Samaria is a bit more complicated. Part of the fertile flatlands belonging to the Jews is said to be in "the so-called Samareitis." The chronological conclusion from the reference to the "country of the Idumeans" does not allow us to interpret the sentence as referring to the situation after 112/11, when southern Samaria was occupied by John Hyrcanus—and certainly not after the conquest of northern Samaria and the Great Valley in the year 107. The possibility of identifying these plains with the internal valleys of central Samaria or the Jezreel Valley has therefore to be discounted. Bickerman's suggestion that the author had in mind the three toparchies in southern Samaria (Aphairema, Lydda, Ramathaim), attached to Judea in 145 (I Macc. 10.30, 38; 11.34), remains the only possible solution. Bickerman has also pointed out that Lod, one of the toparchies, is indeed flat.[38] As a matter of fact, one would

---

36. See pp. 272, 275.
37. See p. 278 and n. 21 above. Cf. next paragraph.
38. Bickerman (1976–80) I.130–31.

not expect the author to have known this. He may well have believed, on the basis of their mention in two royal documents in I Maccabees, that all three toparchies were (or had) fertile plains. The attachment of the three Samaritan toparchies to Judea by the Seleucid kings is listed in two documents among many other economic concessions and grants (I Macc. 10.38, 11.34), a fact that by itself could have led to the conclusion that they were especially fertile. Moreover, the second document even declares remission of taxes on the "produce of the soil and fruit trees" for the annexed toparchies alone (11.34).[39] As "produce of the soil" in this context is certainly wheat, Pseudo-Aristeas could have deduced that the three toparchies were flat. His thorough reading of the documents need not surprise us, given that he could reshape and integrate a single piece of information from the first document (10.36), elsewhere in the course of his narrative (para. 13).[40]

The passage indicates that the three toparchies were still popularly named "the Samarias" or the like: hence, probably, the expression "in the so-called Samareitis,"[41] and not just "in Samareitis." The phenomenon of the preservation in colloquial usage of a former administrative designation or place name some generations after an official change has taken place is well known in the geographical history of the Holy Land. This was often done out of habit or was meant to call attention to the history of a region or locality. In contrast to what was said above about "the country of the Idumeans," there need not have been any ideological or practical reservation against applying the name "Samaria" in this case: it was, after all, one of the two traditional biblical names of the region (the other being Mount Ephraim), and the area of the three toparchies traditionally belonged to the northern Israelite kingdom and the northern tribes.

It is worth stressing that the absence of any reference to agricultural lands belonging to the Jews on the coastal plain does not necessitate a dating before the occupations of Jaffa and the corridor to the sea by Simeon and several of the coastal cities by John Hyrcanus.[42] The

---

39. In the first document (I Macc. 10.30), the concession refers to the whole territory of Judea, together with the three toparchies.

40. See p. 278 and n. 21 above.

41. On the ending -*itis* for Samaria, cf. Pseudo-Hecataeus *ap.* Jos. *Ap.* II.43; and see p. 114 n. 189 above.

42. For the date of these occupations, see pp. 124–27 above and 292 below.

author does not refer to the Jericho Valley either, which had been included in the boundaries of Judea since the Restoration.[43] This flat land on the eastern side of the Judean Hills was considerably larger than the "corridor," and its fertility and unique flora were celebrated by Hellenistic historians and geographers.[44] It thus appears that for one reason or another connected with the special context and purpose of the account,[45] the author restricted himself to the mountain range (and its internal valleys).

3. FURTHER CONSIDERATIONS

In seeking a *terminus ante quem* it should be added that the description of the High Priest in the *Letter* does not mention any characteristic features or symbols of kingship, and that such an omission excludes the period after the year 104, when the Hasmoneans assumed the throne.[46] Another consideration points to almost the same date: Pseudo-Aristeas describes Gaza as an active and flourishing port serving the commerce of Jerusalem and its vicinity (para. 115). This would not have been written after the siege and destruction of Gaza by Alexander Jannaeus

43. See Ezek. 2.34, Neh. 7.35, I Macc. 9.50; Jos. *Ant.* XIV.91, *Bell.* III.55–56; Plin. *NH* V.70; and esp. E. Stern (1982) 245ff. (also referring to the evidence of the Yehud stamps).

44. See pp. 109–10 above.

45. The purpose of the account being to explain why the polis of Jerusalem was rather small, the answer elaborates on the need to devote manpower to cultivating the surrounding agricultural lands (paras. 107–8) for the benefit of the city (para. 111). The Jewish lands in the mountain range were naturally regarded in Hellenistic eyes as the *chōra* of Jerusalem. The new Hasmonean territories on the coastal plain, however, were for years considered to be the *chōrai* of the old Hellenized cities. Whatever their status under the occupation, the author would have found it difficult to include them in an account of the Jerusalem *chōra*. This still does not explain the absence of the Jericho Valley, unless one assumes that the author was misled by its fame in the Hellenistic world to believe Jericho was a polis. My feeling is that there may also be another reason, which applies equally to the flat areas on both sides of the mountain range: inclusion of these celebrated large and fruitful regions in the account would only have highlighted the question that stands at the center of his account—why Jerusalem was not a large city. The author therefore restricted his account to the mountain range, whose produce could not maintain a very large city.

46. Rightly noted by Goodman in Schürer et al. (1973–86) III.682 n. 286.

in the years 102–101,[47] nor even after 103, when Jannaeus began to harrass the city consistently (*Ant.* XIII.334).

The account of the Holy Land and Jerusalem thus indicates a dating between the years 125 and 113. Internal events in Ptolemaic Egypt in those years may provide a more accurate date. The years 125–113 fall in the reign of Ptolemy VIII Physcon (145–116), Cleopatra II (116), and Cleopatra III (116–101). Ptolemy Physcon (Euergetes II) was the most evil of all the Ptolemies, and his period the darkest in Ptolemaic history. It was marked by the long struggle between Ptolemy Physcon and his sister-wife, Cleopatra II, which was accompanied by frequent civil disturbances, excesses, and atrocities. Ptolemy Physcon became notorious for his monstrous appearance and conduct, and for his brutal and ghastly treatment of the royal house (including his seven-year-old son), as well as massacres of the citizens of Alexandria. The scholars and artists of Alexandria, who were the pride of the dynasty, were expelled from Egypt.[48] What is especially significant: the Jewish high commanders of the army, appointed in the time of the sole rule of his brother, Ptolemy VI Philometor (164/3–146), and the Jewish soldiers who gained special importance in the latter's days,[49] sided with Cleopatra II. Consequently, Ptolemy Physcon relentlessly persecuted the Jews of Alexandria (*Ap.* II.49–56, and possibly III Maccabees). The hostile policy toward the Jews went on, with several interruptions, for more than two decades.[50] Ptolemy Physcon was finally reconciled with Cleopatra II in the year 121,[51] and in the year 118 they jointly issued a comprehensive amnesty decree granting far-reaching concessions and privileges to various sections of the population (*SEG* XII.548).[52] These developments brought relief to the Jews as well. Cleopatra II regained power after the death of Physcon, in 116, but her abrupt death in the same year brought to the throne her daughter Cleopatra III, niece and

---

47. See Extended Notes, n. 3 p. 292.

48. On the days of Ptolemy Physcon, see Extended Notes, n. 8 p. 299.

49. For the background and details, see Tcherikover (1957) 19–21, (1961) 275ff.

50. See Extended Notes, n. 9 p. 300.

51. For the year 121 (and not 124) as the date of the final reconciliation, see Bevan (1927) 314–15; Otto and Bengtson (1938) 103–9; Fraser (1972) II.218 n. 243.

52. The edict: *SEG* XII.548. On this much-discussed *philanthrōpia*, see, e.g., Bevan (1927) 315–19; Rostovtzeff (1940) II.878–81; Lenger (1956) 437ff.

second wife of Ptolemy Physcon. The young queen (if not already
her mother) restored Jewish officers to supreme command of the army.
These officers excercised great influence on her policy.[53]

Now, Pseudo-Aristeas provides an enthusiastic description of Ptolemaic kingship, including its attitude toward intellectuals, and of Ptolemaic-Jewish relations. The author's only reservation is in regard to
the maltreatment of the Jews in the generation preceding the time of
the story. This is so different from the atmosphere during the long
reign of Physcon that it would hardly be expected (even as nostalgia)
from an author writing under that king, certainly not in the turbulent
days before the reconciliation of 121 or the amnesty of 118.[54] It can,
therefore, be suggested that the book was written between the year 116
(or 118 at the earliest) and approximately the year 113, the end of the
period of peace that characterized the middle years of John Hyrcanus's
reign.[55]

53. *Ant.* XIII.285–87, 349–51, 353–54, based on Strabo; and see in detail
pp. 241–44 above.

54. Some scholars, who accepted Bickerman's dating of Pseudo-Aristeas to
the years 145–127, tried to find indications in the book of particular events
in the time of Ptolemy Physcon. See Jellicoe (1965/6) 144–50, (1968) 50;
Meisner (1973) 43; Collins (1983) 83–84. But see the criticism of Goodman
in Schürer et al. (1973–86) III.683 nn. 287, 289. In addition, their analysis
is based on Tcherikover's erroneous reconstruction of the development of
relations between Ptolemy Physcon and the Jews, suggesting that after his
first years Physcon changed his attitude. (See Extended Notes, n. 9 p. 300.)
At the same time, another passage may well be a summary of the situation
of Egyptian Jewry, looking back to the recent years of Physcon: "Residence
abroad brings contempt upon poor men, and upon the rich, disgrace, as though
they were in exile for some wickedness" (para. 249).

55. This conclusion does not contradict the evidence of the Ptolemaic titulature recurring in the book. Bickerman cites two such titles to support his dating
to the years 145–127 ([1976–80] I.127–28). Andreas, one of the messengers
to Jerusalem, is described as ἀρχισωματοφύλαξ ("commander of the bodyguard," para. 12) and τῶν ἀρχισωματοφυλάκων ("[one] of the commanders of
the bodyguard," para. 40). Bickerman's attempt to determine a *post quem* date
based on these titles has rightly been refuted. (See Fraser [1972] II.972–73
n. 122.) However, his claim that they support a dating before the year 125 still
deserves consideration. The two titles disappeared from official usage in 130
and 110, respectively (Bickerman I.128 n. 78; Mooren [1977] 21–23), and in

To close the discussion it behooves us to allude to two arguments *ex silentio* raised in the past against a dating of the book after the Maccabean Revolt. It has been pointed out that there is no reference in the book to the religious persecutions by Antiochus Epiphanes, which marked a watershed in Jewish history, and that the book does not offer any response to the anti-Jewish libels that flourished in the Hellenistic world in the aftermath of the religious persecutions.[56]

To begin with the lack of reference to the persecutions, recalling them would have detracted from the purposes of the book. Despite all that has been imputed to this book, Tcherikover's view that the *Letter* was written for a Jewish and not a gentile audience is most convincing.[57] It was intended first and foremost to legitimize the use of

the late days of Physcon there seems to have been a "generous granting" of the second title. Bickerman argues that since the author strives to represent Andreas as an important court official, the use of the title must have preceded those years. But one does not know whether its "generous granting" continued on after the year 116, under Cleopatra III. The disappearance of the title after the year 110 may indicate that this was not the case. As a matter of fact, a contemporary author who remembered the titles might well have used them to create an impression of antiquity long after they had fallen out of use.

56. See, e.g., Jellicoe (1968) 48–49 (quoting H. Z. Orlinsky); Rappaport (1970) 40–41; Goodman in Schürer et al. (1973–86) III.681; and apparently also Fraser (1972) II.970 n. 121.

57. Tcherikover (1958), and even more decisively in the Hebrew version of the article, (1961a) 316–38. Cf. Cahana (1956) II.6–8. The long and elaborate discussion of Jewish separatism (paras. 128–69), which may look apologetic, was also intended for Jewish readership. The author was aware of the apparent contradiction between his call for adherence to the precepts of the Torah on the one hand, and for the adoption of Greek culture on the other. Jewish dietary laws, which inevitably led to social segregation, could not have been harmonized with certain basic features of Hellenistic culture. The question must have puzzled the moderate reformers in Alexandria. The author's main explanation: the separation was needed in order to protect Jews from being influenced by the pagan and immoral aspects of the surrounding cultures, and thereby to assure their adherence to the enlightened philosophical principles and values of Judaism (paras. 130, 139, 142, 152). A similar complimentary explanation was given about two generations later by Posidonius of Apamea (*ap.* Strabo XVI.2.35). Nevertheless, the author does not totally prohibit social contacts and participation in Greek symposia. They are even recommended in the case of highly educated and talented personalities who are qualified to present the Jewish case, and determined to reject the negative manifestation of Hellenism. However, it must always be guaranteed that only kosher food

the Septuagint in religious services, to encourage the adaptation by the Jews of the enlightened features of Greek culture and its achievements, and to promote their use in interpreting Judaism. At the same time the author advocated adhering to Jewish beliefs and religious practices (paras. 127ff.). Hence, among other things, the laborious rationalization of Jewish dietary laws (paras. 124ff.), which at first sight did not coincide with the "Hellenization" advocated by the author. Now, the confrontation in the time of Antiochus IV started with the attempt of the Jewish Hellenizers to force their way of life on Jerusalem, and was followed by the religious persecutions instigated by the king. A reference to these traumatic events would only have called attention to the dangers inherent in the process of Hellenization and played into the hands of the "stubborn" Jews, who were said to have turned their backs resolutely on Greek culture (para. 123).[58]

The writing of the book for internal purposes also explains why it does not try to refute the anti-Jewish libels. Jews did not look for arguments to be convinced about their falsehood. The three notorious stories, the leper, the ass, and the blood libels, were so absurd that there was no need for their refutation in a book written for Jews. Similarly, Hebrew literature in the Middle Ages did not offer arguments against the blood libel, despite its recurring horrible consequences. As a matter of fact, even those Jewish Hellenistic authors who may also have written for gentiles are silent on this issue, notably Philo, despite his prolific literary output. Only Josephus, in his polemic *Against Apion*, bothered to go into detail and undermine the three libels.

Be that as it may, the three libels were not invented after the religious persecutions. Two of them were known in Egypt already at an early stage of the Hellenistic era,[59] and all of them seem to have been inherited in one way or another from Egyptian traditions of the Persian period.[60] The absence of any reference to the libels in any case does not require dating Pseudo-Aristeas before the time of the Hasmonean state.

---

is served and that certain pagan table ceremonies are avoided (paras. 181–82, 184).

58. On these groups among the Jews of Alexandria, see pp. 171, 176–81 above.

59. See M. Stern (1976) 1111, 1114, 1120.

60. See my detailed discussion in *Anti-Semitism and Idealization of Judaism*, chaps. II.2 and III.5.

Extended Notes

1. HECATAEUS AS A SOURCE OF DIODORUS'S EGYPTIAN ETHNOGRAPHY (P. 15 N. 23)

Burton ([1972] 1–34) lists a fair number of sources from which, she thinks, Diodorus drew the information for his Egyptian ethnography. In addition to the objections of Murray and others, it is worth stressing the following basic point: as has been decisively demonstrated and unanimously accepted, in his historical reports on the Greek, Hellenistic, and Roman world, Diodorus adhered to a single source in describing rather long periods of time, and only rarely inserted information taken from other sources. Having done this with periods and countries for which he had abundant source material, and in which he had much more personal interest, why would he have bothered so much with regard to the partly mythological Egyptian ethnography?

Three points raised by Burton have not yet been answered. (a) That Hecataeus is mentioned only once by Diodorus (I.46.8; see Burton [1972] 7, 9) is not surprising: Diodorus, like other Hellenistic historians, rarely mentions his sources. (b) Burton argues that the reference to the placing of Maron, the follower of Osiris-Dionysus, in charge of viticulture in Thrace (Diod. I.20.2; cf. 18.2) reflects the occupation of Maroneia by the Ptolemies, which took place only after the time of Hecataeus (Burton [1972] 17). This is far-fetched. The parallel reference to Triptolemus, Osiris's second follower, as introducing agriculture in Attica (Diod. I.20.2) surely cannot be connected with any Ptolemaic occupation. Moreover, both traditions are well known from pre-Hellenistic sources. (c) The absence of the Persian period in

Diodorus's historical account of Egypt does not prove that it was not taken from Hecataeus (in contrast to Burton [1972] 32). The omission was caused by the ethnographical character of Hecataeus's book. As we shall see later, in the discussion about the structure of the book, its historical section, like that of other ethnographies, is not a consistent history of Egypt, but rather a collection of stories about the major achievements of prominent kings (especially military expeditions and building projects). The rebellious Egyptian kings of the fourth century did not leave behind impressive monuments or other remarkable achievements.

The question of Diodorus's sources and his adaptation of the material was recently raised again by Sacks (1990). The author tries to prove that Diodorus was not a mindless compiler, as is usually believed, but a historian of some intellectual ability who knew how to write interesting prefaces and introduce comments that express his own attitudes and values (though they are not original). (Cf. Sartori [1984].) These claims, however, do not detract from the accepted view about the main source of Book I, since they refer only to the introductions (*prooimia*) and some general historiographical and political-moral comments of the sort common in Hellenistic literature, and not to the narrative material. At the same time, in a few lines in the epilogue to his book, Sacks ([1990] 206) raises the conjecture that Diodorus, who himself made a tour of Egypt, contributed much information of his own to the Egyptian ethnography. Sacks further argues that Book I of Diodorus often presents Egyptian customs as superior to Greek ones, which would hardly be expected of a Greek "court historian." However, Diodorus drew even the information on his native island in a period not far from his own (Books XXXII–XXXVII) solely from Posidonius of Apamea (apart from a number of general notes). Diodorus's own contribution can be fairly easily traced by simple methods of source criticism (already done by past scholars), and it seems to be rather meager and insignificant. Sacks's second argument does not take into account the didactic and political purposes of the Egyptian ethnography (see pp. 16–18 above). Besides, the cases in which criticism of Greek practices is voiced or implied are not many (e.g., I.74.6–7, 76). The fusion of Greek and Egyptian traditions was, after all, one of the main features of the Ptolemaic kingdom (and court) from its very beginning.

2. STAGES IN THE JEWISH OCCUPATION OF THE COASTAL PLAIN
AT THE TIME OF JOHN HYRCANUS (P. 127 N. 13)

Years 135–132. According to the Roman document in *Ant.* XIII.261, the Jews claimed back Jaffa and Pegae (the later Antipatris) as well as "ports" and "cities" taken from them by Antiochus VII. The document has rightly been dated after the death of Antiochus VII Sidetes in 129 (see M. Stern [1961] 7ff., [1965] 148ff.; and see further below. The dating of the document to the time of the siege of Jerusalem itself by Rajak [1981] falls on several counts; see Bar-Kochva, *Anti-Semitism*, Appendix 2). Only the occupation of Jaffa and Gezer is recorded in the comprehensive account in I Maccabees of the days of Simeon. It appears, therefore, that Pegae and the other "cities" and "ports" were occupied by John Hyrcanus, and before the invasion of Antiochus VII. Josephus provides two different dates for the invasion taken from Strabo and Nicolaus, his two sources for the event (ibid., chap. V.1). According to Strabo, whose account is rather detailed and informative (whereas Nicolaus's is very brief), the invasion took place sometime in the years 132–131 (see the Olympiad date in *Ant.* XIII.236; on the use of this system by Strabo, see Hölscher [1904] 41). In 130, as is universally accepted, Antiochus launched his eastern expedition. If Strabo's chronology is accepted, this allows the first three years of Hyrcanus's reign for conquests on the coastal plain. Antiochus's demand for the payment of the *phoros* for Jaffa "and the other cities outside Judea" (*Ant.* XIII.246) is thus put into context. The suggestion that the document refers to possible tiny ports near Jaffa (Kasher [1990] 118) lacks relevant archaeological support. (The article referred to by Kasher's n. 8 does not mention such ports.)

Years 127–125. *Ant.* XIII.273 indicates a period of expansion "in the time of Alexander Zabinas" (the years 128–123), who is reported to have "made friends" with Hyrcanus (XIII.269). Occupations on the coastal plain before the year 113 can be deduced from the Roman document in *Ant.* XIV.249 (see below). The reconquest and expansion could not have taken place before 127: in 128, Demetrius II tried to invade Egypt (Justin XXXIX.1.2; the date according to the sequence in Eus. *Chron.* I.257–58), which shows that the Seleucids were still in control of the southern coast. After his humiliating retreat, however, the circumstances were ideal for Jewish expansion, and Hyrcanus seems to have seized the opportunity: Alexander Zabinas rose to power in Antioch, and the two contenders to the throne exhausted themselves in an internal war. The Ptolemaic court was concurrently occupied with the *amixia*, the ruthless struggle, between Ptolemy Physcon and his sister-wife, Cleopatra II. It is less likely that the expansion took place after 125: with the appearance of Antiochus VIII Gryphus, who was actively supported by the Ptolemaic court, and the gradual reconciliation in Alexandria between the king and his sister, the situation had considerably changed, and Hyrcanus must have been much more careful. It stands to reason that at that time he also terminated his alliance with Alexander Zabinas. Notably, the days of the sole reign of Antiochus VIII Gryphus (123–113) are described by Josephus as a time of peace for Judea (*Ant.* XIII.273; on the background see Cohen in van't Dack et al. [1989] 15–16). All these considerations point to dating the Jewish delegation to Rome and the *senatus consultum* in *Ant.* XIII.259–66 to the year 128. Whatever the date of the reconquest, after 128 the Jews could well fend for themselves. The document was dated, on the basis of the Roman names, between 128 and 125 (see Stern, *locc. citt.*).

Year 112.   The document in *Ant.* XIV.249, dated to the year 113/12 (see M. Stern [1961] 12–22, [1965] 151ff.), demands the return of the "ports" taken from the Jews by Antiochus IX Cyzicenus in the same year (see Stern, *locc. citt.* on the date of that occupation; his arguments have recently been supported by the Cyzicenus coins of the years 113/12 and 112/11 found in Marisa and Mount Gerizim respectively— see p. 131 nn. 28, 29). A few "ports" were thus in Jewish hands by the time of Cyzicenus's invasion. The region must have returned to complete Jewish control after the withdrawal of Cyzicenus from the country, shortly before Hyrcanus returned to embark on the campaigns against the Idumeans and the Samaritans (112/11). A campaign against these cities after 112/11 is less likely also because, unlike the time of the first conquests (135–132), the events in the years 112/11–107 are recorded by Josephus in relatively great detail. Although he draws on two sources, Josephus refers only to campaigns against Samaria and Scythopolis.

3. THE DATE OF THE DESTRUCTION OF GAZA BY
ALEXANDER JANNAEUS (P. 127 N. 15 AND P. 285 N. 47)

The destruction of Gaza (*Ant.* XIII.364) has been dated by scholars to the year 96 (e.g., Schürer [1901–9] I.279; M. Stern [1981] 40 n. 88) on the basis of the subsequent statement that Antiochus VIII Gryphus was murdered "at about the same time" (XIII.365). The murder is known to have taken place in the year 96 (Schürer [1901–9] I.176–77; Bellinger [1949] 72; Schürer et al. [1973–86] I.134). However, Marcus ([1943] 408 n. a) rightly argued that the phrase "at about the same time," often used by Josephus, plays an obvious literary role and is sometimes incorrect (see also D. R. Schwartz [1982], esp. 252–54). Thus the destruction of Gaza need not necessarily be linked to the date of the murder of Antiochus VIII Gryphus. According to another reference (XIII.358) it occurred close in time to the withdrawals of Cleopatra III to Egypt and Ptolemy Lathyrus to Cyprus. Marcus therefore suggested dating the destruction of Gaza to the year 100 (repeated by Fuks [1982] 136; Kasher [1990] 145). This dating is still not accurate enough, and more data must to be taken into account.

Josephus combined two sources: according to one passage (*Ant.* XIII.352, 356–57 = *Bell.* I.87) taken from Nicolaus (see Hölscher [1904] 15–16), the first expedition to Trans-Jordan (the occupation of Gadara and Amathos) was followed by the campaign against the southern coastal cities and Gaza (for Gaza, see the parallel in *Bell.*). According to the second (*Ant.* XIII.358–64), drawing on Strabo (Hölscher, *loc. cit.*), the siege of Gaza is explicitly linked to the returns of Cleopatra III to Egypt and Ptolemy Lathyrus from Gaza to Cyprus (XIII.358). The linkage clearly seems to have been indicated in the original and not to have been an addition by Josephus (see the reference to Lathyrus in XIII.359). The exact date of these events is not known, but an approximate chronology can be constructed. According to an inscription from the Memphis Serapeum, an attack by Ptolemy Lathyrus was expected at Pelusium on 20 February 102 (see van't Dack [1981] 309–10; Clarysse in van't Dack et al. [1989] 83–84; cf. Otto and Bengtson [1938] 186–87), and Cleopatra died in Egypt in October 101 (Samuel [1967] 152). The statement in *Ant.* XIII.352 that Lathyrus stayed in Gaza in the winter after retreating from Egypt is obviously mistaken and must refer to the period preceding the abortive invasion.

The numismatic material is also instructive: the latest known autonomous coins of Gaza before its revival by Pompey are dated in the year 210 of the Seleucid era, i.e., 103/2 B.C. (*BMC Palestine*, p. LXX). As the siege lasted a year (*Ant.* XIII.364), its beginning must be dated between March and October 102 (102 is suggested by Clarysse and van't Dack, in van't Dack et al. [1989] 109, referring only to Lathyrus's movements). Gaza was thus destroyed sometime between March and October 101. These data also indicate that Nicolaus's sequence for Jannaeus's campaign is wrong, and the siege of Gaza preceded the ten-month siege of Gadara. Nicolaus's failure to preserve the proper sequence of events in this case is not exceptional. Cf., e.g., *Ant.* XIII.213–19, 254–57, 275–79 (see Bar-Kochva [1989] 452–54; and p. 125 n. 8, p. 131 n. 29 above). The siege of Gadara could thus have taken place only at a later stage, concurrently with the expedition to Moabitis and Gaulanitis.

4. THE HASMONEAN RULERS AND THE HELLENISTIC CITIES (P. 128 N. 21)

The impassioned and apologetic arguments of Kasher ([1990] 122–23, 160–69, 172–73, and *passim*) against the information provided by Josephus about the harsh treatment of the Hellenistic cities do not stand up to criticism. Apart from the obvious contradictions in the argumentation (see, e.g., pp. 123, 128–29, 157, as compared with pp. 165–66 and the justification of the Hasmonean mistreatment of the local population on p. 119), he ignores the explicit and relatively detailed information of Syncellus about the total massacre by Jannaeus (I.558), which together with the list of cities was not taken from Josephus or Nicolaus (see p. 125 n. 11 above), as well as information in the Scroll of Fasting, a reliable early Pharisaic document (despite the reference on Kasher's p. 128). Similarly, he does not take notice of the recent excavations in the cities of Marisa, Mount Gerizim, and Shechem, which show total destruction of their large public and residental areas in 112/11, from which they did not recover (see p. 131 nn. 28, 29). The findings at these three sites, being the only ones in which the Hellenistic strata were thoroughly and properly excavated, are indicative of at least a few other places listed by Josephus. I would add that Kasher's argument ([1990] 162–63) from the use of the verb συνθέω (*Bell.* I.166) is quite odd, to say the least, and the same applies to the justification for the destruction of Pella (pp. 156–59).

At the same time the argument of Shatzman ([1992] 54–63) against Kasher, that the information of Josephus about the treatment of the gentile population by the Hasmonean rulers was taken from Jewish sources, must be rejected. There can be little doubt that the excellent analysis of the sources by Hölscher (1904), which showed that the information was taken from Nicolaus and Strabo, is still basically valid. However, the exact determination of the sources of certain passages in Josephus refutes the recurring arguments of Kasher that the accounts of Hasmonean brutality toward the gentile population were taken from anti-Jewish sources "permeated with Gentile animosity toward the Jews." As a matter of fact, at least two of the most relevant passages in Josephus, recounting the destruction of Pella and Gaza, were drawn from Strabo (*Ant.* XIII.395–97, 358–64; cf. XIII.240, on Hyrcanus I), who also left us the most enthusiastic report on ancient Judaism written by a gentile (XVI.2.35–36).

Surely not all the cities suffered the same amount of destruction, especially not ports and strategic sites, which could be useful for the Jewish state and settlers. This still does not mean that the local population was spared the fate of other cities. It certainly does not make the accounts of the treatment of the cities by the Hasmonean rulers into "anti-Hasmonean propaganda" or "narrow, one-sided," as argued by Kasher. And how could this characterization apply to the reports in I Maccabees about the massacres in Azotos (10.84, 11.4) and in Trans-Jordan (5.5, 28, 50–51) and the statement celebrating the banishment of the population of Beth Shean (Scythopolis) and "its valley" in the Scroll of Fasting (15–16 Sivan)? Characteristically enough, Kasher, who discredits the information about the maltreatment of the Hellenistic cities by the Hasmoneans, does not deny the accounts of the destruction of temples and cults and even tries to find more evidence for such operations, enthusiastically speaking of all-out "purification" of the Holy Land (e.g., Kasher [1990] 123, 131, 150–51, 163–64; cf. Efron in Kasher, pp. 318–41: the zealously enthusiastic language is even more conspicuous in the Hebrew original of that book).

5. THE BEGINNING OF THE FIRST SECTION IN HECATAEUS'S
EGYPTIAN ETHNOGRAPHY (P. 195 N. 51)

This section begins in Diodorus I.10 according to Diodorus himself
(9.6, "We shall begin our history with Egypt"). However, a number of
scholars since Reinhardt have argued that chaps. 7 and 8, which describe
the cosmogony and zoogony of mankind, also originated in Hecataeus's
Egyptian ethnography, and some even say that they headed it. See
Norden (1913) 379ff.; Reinhardt (1921) 495–98; Vlastos (1946) 51–60;
Gigon (1961) 771–76; Cole (1967) 16, 174–95; Murray (1970) 169–70.
This opinion has been contested on several counts: see Dahlmann (1928)
23ff.; Jacoby (1943) 39, 85–86; Spoerri (1959) 164–211, (1961) 63ff.;
Pfligersdorffer (1959) 143–44; Nock (1962) 50–51; Burton (1972) 15–
16, 47–51; Sacks (1990) 56–60. Without entering into detail, it should
be made clear that even if the zoogony in Diodorus I.7.4–8 had its origin,
in one way or another, in Hecataeus, the latter's Egyptian ethnography
opened with the account abbreviated by Diodorus in chap. 10, and not
that of chaps. 7 and 8. There is an evident difference between the
zoogony in chaps. 7 and 8 and that of chap. 10: the first explicitly
describes the creation of life and societies, languages, and nations in
different parts of the inhabited world (8.4), and even the hardships
that the first human beings experienced in the cold winters (8.7), while
chap. 10 states that life and human society originated in Egypt alone.
There is no room for assuming that Hecataeus wrote a general preface
on the creation of life in more than one country and supplemented
it with a local Egyptian version on its sole origin in that land. In
line with his intention of glorifying the Egyptian past, it was only
natural for Hecataeus to present Egypt as the cradle of human life
and civilization. This also appears from the great elaboration at the
end of the *origo* section on the creation of nations by migration from
Egypt (chaps. 28–29). Among them are included even the Athenians,
who regarded themselves as autochthonous (see Isocrates, *Paneg.* 23ff.;
Plato, *Menex.* 245d; Cicero, *Flac.* 62; Justin II.6.1ff.).

At the same time it seems that Diodorus's explanation of the genesis
of life in I.7.4–8 indeed originates with Hecataeus but was taken out
of its local Egyptian context and adapted by Diodorus to the whole
inhabited world, as one would expect of a general preface to a comprehensive historical "library." Scholars have already noted that in his
general preface Diodorus demonstrates more original thinking than in

the later parts of his work. This is understandable for a preface that he actually wrote last, when he was able to recall and properly to adapt ideas and opinions from the various sources he had used for writing his universal history. See Kunz (1935) 101; Palm (1955) 140; Murray (1970) 170; Sacks (1990) 10–11. Cf., e.g., Diodorus's explanation of the development of material culture as a whole (I.8.9), which is also found in his Indian ethnography (II.38.2), drawing on Megasthenes.

As for the cosmogony in Diodorus I.7.1–3, its attribution to Hecataeus faces a stumbling block that has so far not been removed. The absence of any trace of atomistic theory, which would be expected of a "Democritean" scholar like Hecataeus (see p. 9 above), cannot be explained by suggesting that Hecataeus had adopted the Egyptian point of view. This cannot be the case in an idealizing work. Diodorus I.42.1, which has been quoted as evidence, is in fact an interpolation, not written by Diodorus. I tend therefore to accept the view that Diodorus took his cosmogony from another source. For Hecataeus's dependence on Democritus of Abdera, see, e.g., Reinhardt (1921) 492ff.; Diels (1922) pp. xi ff.

6. THE POSITION OF THE HIGH PRIEST IN THE PERIOD OF THE SUCCESSORS (P. 256 N. 8)

Tcherikover ([1961] 58–59) quotes Hecataeus's statement that the Jews never had a king and that ἡ τοῦ πλήθους προστασία ("the leadership of the multitude") was in the hands of the High Priest (Diod. XL.3.5). Tcherikover interprets *prostasia*, according to one of the secondary meanings of *prostatēs* in the Hellenistic period, as referring to the representative of the nation to the ruling empire, and thinks that the statement reflects the political arrangements in Hecataeus's day. However, there is no reason *not* to understand the word in its primary meaning in Greek (and Hellenistic) literature: leadership of the people. The use of *plēthos* ("multitude") in the phrase (instead of, for instance, "Jews") somewhat weakens Tcherikover's point. For its sources in classical Greek political terminology, see p. 34 n. 81 above.

Significantly enough, according to Hecataeus, the authority of the High Priest included performing sacrifices, judging major cases, supervising the observance of the divine laws, and delivering God's precepts to the nation (Diod. XL.3.4–6). There is no reference to secular duties typical of a governor, such as those related to economic and military matters. The omission does not seem to be accidental; Moses, on the other hand, who is not described as High Priest, leads the nation to war (XL.3.7). In any event, Hecataeus's excursus does not preclude the possibility that under the Successors the office of governor was held by a Jew who was not the High Priest, and was not actually the leader of the nation, as had previously been the case. Of the various Jewish governors in the Persian period (see p. 87 and n. 103), only Sheshbazzar, Zerubabel, and Nehemiah were the leading figures of the community—the first two, owing to their descent; the third, to his personality. Hecataeus does not offer more indications about the governorship of his time, because the *pehah* was, after all, the representative of the foreign rule, and he (like his Jewish Egyptian informants) is interested in describing Jewish traditional leadership.

7. THE SEQUENCE AND DATING OF THE BERENICE COINS FROM COS (P. 269 N. 56)

The chronology of the Coan coins of the fourth and third centuries that bear female portraits has not so far been clarified. In view of the link between the various types, the number of eponymic magistrates, the relations of Cos with the empires, and events on the island, the following sequence for the various types may be suggested:

1. Obverse, a bearded Heracles (actually Mausolus; see Hill [1923] 208); reverse, a female with curly hair and a veil at the back of the head (*BMC Caria*, pl. XXX no. 11, pl. XLV no. 5; Hill [1901] pl. XVII no. 703). The woman should be identified with Artemisia (Hill [1923] 208–9), and the coins should be dated to the period of Hecatomnid control in Cos, which lasted, in one way or another, until the conquests of Alexander. (On the duration of Hecatomnid rule, see Sherwin-White [1978] 75–77; S. Hornblower [1982] 133–35.) For numismatic evidence for a dating shortly before 330, see Paton and Hicks (1891) 303, 306 (no. 15b).

2. Obverse, the same as in type no. 1; reverse, a portrait of a female in an Egyptian style, with straight hair over the forehead and a veil falling straight down (*BMC Caria*, pl. XXX no. 10 = Hill [1923] pl. IX no. 3; Svoronos [1904] vol. III pl. XVIII nos. 23–25). The woman has been identified with Berenice (Svoronos [1904] IV.30–32; Hill [1923] 209). The identity of the obverse with the Artemisia coins requires the dating of this type as close as possible to the latter. The only event

that could have introduced Berenice's portrait onto Coan coins of the fourth century was her stay in Cos in 308 and the birth there of her son, later Ptolemy II. This would not have occurred after 306, when the island passed over to the realm of Antigonus and remained loyal to the Antigonids even after the battle of Ipsus, up to 286 or 280, when it returned to the Ptolemaic sphere of influence. (On the relations of Cos with the Hellenistic empires, see Sherwin-White [1978] 82–108.) The specimens of the two variations of this type have indeed just two eponymic *monarchoi*, which indicates a short period of production. (On the *monarchoi*, the Coan magistrates, see Sherwin-White [1978] 187–99.)

3. Obverse, the same as in types 1 and 2; reverse, a female whose hair is entirely covered by a veil running diagonally to the back of the neck (*BMC Caria*, pl. XXX no. 12). The direction of the veil suggests that the coiffure hidden by the veil is similar to that of Berenice in the Magas coins (*BMC Cyrenaica*, pl. XXIX nos. 11–18, pl. XXX no. 11; Svoronos [1904] vol. III pl. III nos. 40–45). The single (unclear) name of the magistrate on specimens of this type suggests a short period of production, probably concurrently with type no. 2.

4. Obverse, a female similar to that on the reverse of type no. 3; reverse, a crab, the traditional emblem of the island (*BMC Caria*, pl. XXX nos. 13–15; Svoronos [1904] vol. III pl. XVIII nos. 24, 25). As the legends include the names of about a dozen eponymic magistrates, this type should be dated to a long period. They could only be from 286 or 280, in the days of Ptolemy II. These coins are certainly connected with the celebration of Cos in Ptolemy II's day as his birthplace, which is well known from contemporary Alexandrian literature.

8. THE RULE AND PERSONALITY OF PTOLEMY PHYSCON (P. 285 N. 48)

For the turbulent times of Ptolemy Physcon, see the reconstruction of events by Otto and Bengtson (1938) 23–112; and the summaries of Bevan (1927) 306–25; Mitford (1959); Fraser (1972) I.121–23 (with several important chronological contributions); Will (1967) II.356–60.

The sources: Polybius XXXIV.14.6–8; Diodorus XXXIII.6–6a, 12–13, 20, 22–23; XXXIV/XXXV.14.20; Pompeius Trogus, *Prol.* XXXVIII; Livy, *Per.* LIX; Justin XXXVIII.8; Athenaeus IV.184, XII.549d–550a; Valerius Maximus IX.2.5. The sources are unanimous with regard to the monstrous appearance and personality of Ptolemy Physcon. This has been accepted by almost all modern historians. Mahaffy's attempted rehabilitation of Ptolemy Physcon ([1895] 383, 388; *id.* [1898] 204–5; cf. Tarn [1939] 323; Tarn and Griffith [1952] 35–36) was rightly rejected by Bevan ([1927] 318–24). Another approach is advocated by Rostovtzeff ([1940] II.872–73). He does not deny the historicity of the reports about Physcon's crimes, but tries to explain them as a reaction to the enormous pressures of that generation and disregards Physcon's degenerate features: "The fact that he succeeded in maintaining his power for about thirty years and the methods by which he did this show that he was a clever politician, resourceful, courageous, and energetic, though utterly devoid of scruple and moral sense, and unusually cruel and cynical" (ibid.). However, the special circumstances and conflicting interests in Egypt in the second half of the second century B.C. may have enabled the survival of a degenerate ruler for many years, which is not unparalleled in history. Rostovtzeff's monumental work was written before the forties of our century.

The accounts about Physcon are plentiful and unequivocal, and given their variety and sources of information, they can be accepted as trustworthy (except for some sensational motifs in Justin's account; see, e.g., Macurdy [1932] 156): Polybius visited Alexandria in the early days of Physcon's reign (XXXIV.14.1; see Walbank [1957–79] I.5 n. 10) and seems to have witnessed the bloody events in the city (14.6–8). Diodorus's account was taken from Posidonius of Apamea, who drew on an account of the visit to Alexandria by his teacher Panaetius (Athen. XII.549d–e; the present reading, "Posidonius," is certainly wrong) when describing Physcon's physical degeneracy (ibid. e–f). Athenaeus IV.184 (on the banishment of the intellectuals) quotes the contemporary Menecles of Barca or Andron of Alexandria (see *FGrH* IIIA, pp. 222–23). And finally: Justin's *epitomē* of Pompeius Trogus goes back to Timagenes of Alexandria, who must have been well informed about occurrences in his native city two generations earlier.

9. THE PERSECUTION OF THE JEWS BY PTOLEMY PHYSCON (P. 237 N. 16 AND P. 285 N. 50)

Tcherikover ([1957] 21–23, [1961] 281–82; followed by Kasher [1985] 8–10) conjectures that the persecutions recorded by Josephus lasted just one year, and that the relations between the king and the Jews became normal after Physcon married Cleopatra II in 144. The only real argument is the discovery of two synagogue dedications to Ptolemy Physcon and the two reigning queens (*CIJ* II nos. 1441–42). Fraser rightly responded that the dedications need not necessarily reflect admiration for the contemporary king, but rather "the general attitude of the Jews to the Crown" ([1972] II.215 n. 232, and see I.282–84 on this practice in synagogues of Ptolemaic Egypt). Moreover, they may well have been the Jewish substitute for the ruler worship demanded by Physcon, and need not reflect good will on the part of the community. (For this meaning of synagogue dedications of Ptolemaic kings, see Bevan [1927] 26; cf. Fraser [1972] I.226.) Be that as it may, the dedications could have been made after the final reconciliation in the year 121 or the generous amnesty in 118 (see p. 285 and nn. 51, 52 above).

More significant is the first epistle to the Jews of Egypt in II Maccabees, calling for the celebration of Channuka (1.1–10a). The authenticity of the document was decisively proven by Bickerman ([1933] 233–54, and there also on its two components), and has been widely accepted. It is dated to the year 188 of the Seleucid era (verse 9: end of 124 B.C.; see Bickerman [1933] 144–45) and clearly indicates that the Jews in Egypt were then in great trouble (vv. 5–6, esp. verse 6; cf. Bickerman [1933] 155–56; Tcherikover [1957] 24 n. 58 cannot be accepted: the verse clearly refers to a specific situation). Furthermore, the reference is followed by a fragment of an earlier document (vv. 7–8), dated to the year 169 S.E. (verse 7: 143/2 B.C.), which was integrated into the epistle. It is only natural to assume that the fragment was misplaced because the original document from which it was taken mentioned a similar situation to that referred to in vv. 5–6. The purpose of both epistles was therefore to encourage (or comfort) the Jews of Egypt in their plight by recalling the rescue of the Jews and Judaism from the persecutions of Antiochus Epiphanes. This means that in 143/2, two years after the great confrontation between the Jewish soldiers and Ptolemy Physcon, there was a new outburst against the Jews. The information about events in Egypt in 144–142 supports this assumption: the first reconciliation of Ptolemy with Cleopatra II, early in 144 (for the date, see Otto and Bengtson [1938] 28), marks only a lull in the internal war. As is stated by a number of sources, the struggle was renewed with the rape of Cleopatra III, the daughter of the queen, dated in late 144 or early 143 (see Otto and Bengtson [1938] 30), which was followed by the marriage of Cleopatra III and Physcon sometime between February and

September 142 (the date in Otto [1934] 12 n. 4). The first event had preceded the epistle of 143/2.

We can conclude that in addition to the persecutions of the year 145/4, there is evidence that the Jews in Egypt suffered greatly in the year 124 and probably also in the year 143/2. Indeed, Tcherikover's hypothesis raises a considerable difficulty: the struggle between Physcon and Cleopatra II, as has been said, did not end in 145/4. It continued to seesaw inconclusively for a generation. There was a dramatic turn of events in 131 in Cleopatra's favor when Physcon fled from Alexandria, to which he was to return only in 127/6. We know that the intellectuals who had supported Cleopatra II at the beginning of her campaign continued to lend her assistance during the long years of the struggle. They were consistently opposed by the Egyptian populace and chance mercenaries who supported Physcon. The Jews of Alexandria identified from the outset with the enlightened Greek community. Why should they suddenly have changed their mind, abandoned their benefactor, Cleopatra II, and joined Physcon and the Egyptian populace which for centuries had manifested toward them nothing but hostility? In view of all these considerations and data, there is no justification for the suggestion that a substantial and durable change in the basic policies and sympathies of Ptolemy and the Jews took place after 145/4. For a cautious reconstruction of the relationship between Physcon and the Jews, see M. Stern (1985) 93–95, (1991) 112–13.

Whatever the case may be, even were Physcon to have changed his attitude toward the Jews for any length of time during the 30's of the second century, this would not affect the issue of the dating of the *Letter of Aristeas:* the geographical information in the *Letter* points to about 125 as the first possible date for its composition. From the reconquest of Alexandria in 127/6 and up until 118, the political situation in Egypt and the situation of the Jews differed little from that which had prevailed at the beginning of Physcon's reign. This appears from the accounts of the acts of cruelty he perpetrated during the reconquest of Egypt in 127/6, from the rebellions throughout Egypt in the years 124–121, and especially from the explicit testimony of II Maccabees concerning the suffering of the Jews in 124.

Chronological Table

Events in Judea and Egypt
mentioned in the discussion

I. 538–333 B.C.: PERSIAN RULE IN JUDEA

538	Cyrus's declaration
537(?)	First *aliyah*: governorship of Sheshbazzar
521(?)	Second *aliyah*: governorship of Zerubabel
458	*Aliyah* of Ezra
444–425(?)	Nehemiah governor of Judea
348	Rebellion of Tennes
ca. 340	Hezekiah becomes governor of Judea
336	Death of Johanan the High Priest
	Accession of Darius III and Alexander

II. 333–142 B.C.: HELLENISTIC RULE IN JUDEA

1. 332–301   Alexander and the Diadochs

332–323	Alexander
323–320	Laomedon's governorship
320	Ptolemy and Nicanor invade the country
320–316	Ptolemy's rule in Syria and Phoenicia
316–312	Antigonus Monophthalmus occupies the region
312	Battle of Gaza: Ptolemy defeats Demetrius Poliorcetes
	Few months of Ptolemaic occupation
312–302	Second period of Antigonus's rule in Syria and Phoenicia

302/1	Ptolemy invades Coele Syria
	Occupation of Jerusalem and devastation of the city; Hezekiah deposed from governorship of Judea; deportation of many Jews (and Hezekiah) to Egypt
301	Battle of Ipsus: new division of the Macedonian Empire

2. 302/1–200 Ptolemaic Rule

283	Accession of Ptolemy II Philadelphus
277	Magas's revolt in Cyrenaica
247	Death of Ptolemy II
217	Battle of Raphia
200	Battle of Panium

3. 200–142 Seleucid Rule

168	Beginning of religious persecutions by Antiochus Epiphanes
166–160	The Jewish Revolt: Judas Maccabaeus
164	Death of Antiochus Epiphanes; purification of the Temple
164–163	Military operations of Judas Maccabaeus against the gentile neighbors: destruction of a temple and altars in Azotos and Karnayim
160	Death of Judas Maccabaeus
160/59	Building of a network of fortresses by Bacchides
160–143	Leadership of Jonathan
152	Alexander Balas rises to power in Antioch
	Alexander Balas appoints Jonathan as High Priest and grants additional rights
152/1	Demetrius I recognizes the annexation to Judea of three districts from Samaria
148/7	Destruction of the Hellenistic temple in Azotos by Jonathan
145	Further confirmation of the annexation of the three districts by Demetrius II

145/4 First confrontation between Jewish Egyptian soldiers and Ptolemy Physcon

143 Death of Jonathan

III. 143/2–63 B.C.: THE HASMONEAN STATE

1. 143/2–135 Simeon's Rule in Independent Judea

143/2 Occupation of Jaffa
142/1 Demetrius II recognizes Jewish independence
Occupation and purification of Gazara
Siege and occupation of the Jerusalem *Akra*
140 (Sept.) Public ceremony in the Temple: Simeon praised for settling Jews in the "corridor" and fortifying the country
140 Demolition of the Jerusalem *Akra*
139–129 Antiochus VII Sidetes
139 Antiochus Sidetes demands the return of Jewish occupations in the "corridor" and on the coast

2. 135–104 John Hyrcanus (Hyrcanus I)

135–132 Jewish occupations in the coastal plain
132 Invasion of Judea by Antiochus Sidetes; siege of Jerusalem; surrender of the Jews
131–127/6 Ptolemy Physcon in Cyprus
129 Death of Antiochus VII Sidetes during expedition to the East
Building of fortresses by John Hyrcanus
Demetrius II tries to invade Egypt
128–123 Alexander Zabinas in Syria
127–125 Jewish occupations in the coastal plain
125 Building of the Hasmonean fortress in Jerusalem (*Baris*) and other fortresses
124 New anti-Jewish outbursts by Ptolemy Physcon
123–113 Sole rule of Antiochus VIII Gryphus
121 Final reconciliation between Ptolemy Physcon and Cleopatra II
118 General amnesty declared in Egypt

116–96	Struggle for the Seleucid throne between Antiochus Gryphus and Antiochus Cyzicenus
116	Death of Ptolemy Physcon; sole rule of Cleopatra II; her death; accession of Cleopatra III
113	Antiochus IX Cyzicenus invades the coastal plain
112–111	Hyrcanus regains control of the coastal plain
	Occupation of Idumea and its annexation
	Occupation of Shechem and destruction of the Samaritan temple on Mount Gerizim
108–107	Siege of Samaria
	Controversy in the Ptolemaic court over the Samaritan question
	Antiochus Cyzicenus and Ptolemy Lathyrus invade Judea
	Occupation of Scythopolis; banishment of its inhabitants; destruction of Samaria
	Jewish occupations south of Mount Carmel and in the Great Valley and Lower Galilee
	Ptolemy Lathyrus banished to Cyprus
3. 104/3	Judas Aristobulus (Aristobulus I)
	Occupation of Upper Galilee
4. 103–76	Alexander Jannaeus
103	Alexander Jannaeus besieges Ptolemaïs
	Confrontation between Jannaeus and Ptolemy Lathyrus
(Sept.)	Cleopatra occupies Ptolemaïs
102	Jewish lobby in action: Ananias and Helkias, Jewish Ptolemaic chiefs of staff, save Alexander Jannaeus (and Jewish independence)
102–100	Jannaeus's occupations in the coastal plain and Phoenicia: destruction of Hellenistic cities and cult centers
102 (20 Feb.)	Attack by Ptolemy Lathyrus expected at Pelusium
102/1	Siege and destruction of Gaza by Alexander Jannaeus
101 (Oct.)	Cleopatra III dies in Egypt

	96	Murder of Antiochus VIII Gryphus
		Ptolemy Lathyrus sole king in Alexandria
	96–93	Jannaeus's first round of campaigns in Trans-Jordan
	93–87	Internal upheaval in Judea
	86–76	Jannaeus's second round of occupations in Trans-Jordan
5.	76–67	Rule of Salome Alexandra
6.	67–63	Aristobulus II and Hyrcanus II
	63	Pompey in Syria, the Jewish delegation, and the Roman invasion

Plates

All coins are of silver.

Legends are in palaeo-Hebrew script.

Reproductions are taken from Reifenberg (1940) pl. I; Mildenberg (1979) pls. 21, 22; Meshorer (1982) I pls. 2 and 3 and p. 184; Sternberg (1991) nos. 194, 196; and from the collection of the Kadman Numismatic Museum, Tel Aviv.

PLATE I: THE HEZEKIAH COINS, FIRST GROUP

1. ↑; hemiobol; 0.23 g; 7.5 mm. Meshorer pl. 2 no. 10.

    Obverse: Head facing (age unclear), surrounded by border of connected dots. No legend. *Reverse*: Owl standing to right, head facing. On the left, reading outwards and up, יחזקיה (*yḥzqyh*, "Hezekiah"). On the right, reading outwards and down, הפחה (*hpḥh*, "the governor"). Note the sign ◿ at the end of the legend, below on right.

2. ↘; hemiobol; 0.20 g. Meshorer pl. 2 no. 10a.

    Obverse: As on no. 1. *Reverse*: As on no. 1, but legend in different positions: on the right, reading outwards and down, יחזקיה (*yḥzqyh*). On the left, reading outwards and up, הפחה (*hpḥh*).

3. ↓; hemiobol; 0.21 g; 7.5 mm. Reifenberg pl. I no. 2. Found in the Beth Zur excavations (1931).

    Obverse: Blank. *Reverse*: As on no. 2.

4. ↓; hemiobol; 0.21 g; 7 mm. Meshorer pl. 2 no. 10b.

    Obverse: As on no. 1, but portrait slightly different. *Reverse*: As on no. 1, but owl and legend of barbaric style and in larger letters. Position of legend as on no. 2.

5. ↓; tartemorion; 0.14 g; 7 mm. Meshorer pl. 3 no. 11a.

    Obverse: Head facing. Cable border. No legend. *Reverse*: Owl standing to right, head facing. Legend retrograde and of crude style; on the right, reading outwards and up, יחזקיו (*yḥzqyw*). On left, reading outwards and up, הפחה (*hpḥh*).

6. Hemiobol; 6.5 mm. Meshorer pl. 3 no. 11b.

    Obverse: Head facing. Border of connected dots. No legend. *Reverse*: Owl standing to left (!), head facing. Legend almost illegible.

7. ↗; obol; 0.51 g; 7 mm. Meshorer pl. 2 no. 11.

    Obverse: Head facing. Cable border. No legend. *Reverse*: Owl standing to right, head facing. Legend: on right, reading down and outwards, יוחנ[ן] (*ywḥn[n]*, "Johanan"). On left, reading up and outwards, הכהן (*hkhn*, "the priest").

1

2

3

4

5

6

7

PLATE II: THE HEZEKIAH COINS, SECOND GROUP

8. Hemiobol; 0.23 g; 6–7.5 mm. Sternberg no. 194.

    Obverse: Male head to left, of Hellenistic style. No legend.
    Reverse: Forepart of a winged lynx to left. Legend below wing
    from right to left: יחזקיה (*yḥzqyh*).

8a. ↗ ; hemiobol; 0.25 g; 6.5–8 mm. Meshorer pl. 3 no. 12.

    Obverse: Male head to left, of Hellenistic style, differing from
    that of no. 8. On this specimen the obverse has been struck
    twice by mistake, first with the ordinary obverse die and then
    with an obverse die in which a coin struck earlier had remained
    stuck, yielding its reverse impression (part of the lynx's wing
    and legend in incuse mirror impression). *Reverse*: Same as
    no. 8, with slight variations in the script.

9. → ; tartemorion; 0.28 g; 7–7.2 mm. Mildenberg no. 20.

    Obverse:Hellenistic male head to the left, neck and chin stretched.
    No legend. *Reverse*: Winged lynx as on no. 8, but legend in
    semicircle: חזקיה (*ḥzqyh*).

10. Tartemorion; 0.18 g; 6.2–7.2 mm. Kadman Museum, Tel Aviv.
     K-404.86.

    Obverse: Blank. *Reverse*: Winged lynx to left, without legend.

11. Tartemorion; 0.23 g; 6 mm. Sternberg no. 196.

    Obverse: Male head to right, of Hellenistic style. *Reverse*: Winged
    lynx to left; legend off center, probably as on nos. 8 and 9.

11a. ← ; hemiobol; 0.23 g; 7 mm. Meshorer pl. 3 no. 13.

    Obverse: Male head to right, of Hellenistic style. No legend. The
    image is of an older man than on nos. 8 and 9, probably that of
    Ptolemy I (see the discussion, p. 258). If the identification is
    correct, this coin does not belong to the Hezekiah group, but
    should be regarded as one of the first Ptolemaic Yehud coins.
    Reverse: Winged lynx to left and traces of a legend.

8

8a

9

10

11

11a

PLATE III: THE PTOLEMAIC YEHUD COINS

12. ← ; tartemorion; 0.12 g; 6–8 mm. Meshorer pl. 3 no. 14.

Obverse: Young male head to left. No legend. Reverse: Eagle with wings spread standing on thunderbolt to left. Legend: from left below, reading outwards: יהד (yhd, "Yehud").

13. → ; hemiobol; 0.22 g; 7.5 mm. Meshorer pl. 3 no. 14a; Mildenberg no. 22.

Obverse: Head to left, similar to no. 12. No legend. Reverse: Eagle standing to left with wings spread. Legend: from left below, reading outwards: יהד (yhd).

14. ↑ ; triobol; 1.75 g; 11–11.5 mm. Meshorer p. 184 no. 1

Obverse: Head of Ptolemy I to right, diademed. No legend. Reverse: Eagle with wings spread standing to left on thunderbolt. Legend: from left below, reading outwards: יהדה (yhdh, "Yehudah"). In field, between the eagle and the legend: BA, most probably standing for ΒΑΣΙΛΕΩΣ.

15. ↑ ; triobol; 1.55 g; 10.5–13 mm. Meshorer p. 184 no. 2.

Obverse: Head of Ptolemy I to right, diademed; of cruder style than no. 14. No legend. Reverse: Eagle with wings spread standing to left on thunderbolt. Legend: from left below, reading outwards: יהדה (yhdh).

16. ↑ ; tartemorion; 0.18 g; 7.5 mm. Meshorer pl. 3 no. 16.

Obverse: Head of Ptolemy I to right. No legend. Reverse: Eagle with wings spread standing to left on thunderbolt. Legend: from left below, reading outwards: יהדה (yhdh).

17. ↖ ; tartemorion; 0.18 g; 6.5 mm. Mildenberg no. 25.

Obverse: Head of Ptolemy I to right, diademed. No legend. Reverse: Similar to no. 16.

18. ↘ ; tartemorion; 0.19 g; 7 mm. Meshorer pl. 3 no. 16b.

Obverse: Similar to no. 17. Reverse: Similar to no. 17.

18a. ↑ ; tartemorion; 0.17 g; 7 mm. Mildenberg no. 24.

Obverse: Head of Ptolemy I to right, diademed. No legend. Reverse: Similar to nos. 16–18.

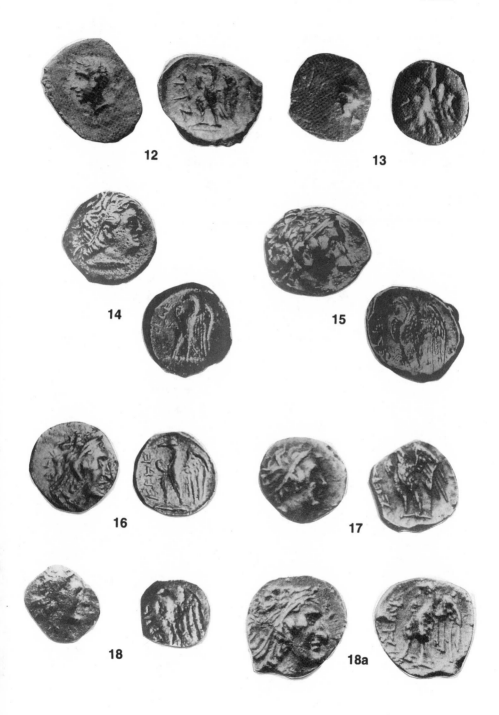

12

13

14

15

16

17

18

18a

PLATE IV: BERENICE ON THE PTOLEMAIC YEHUD COINS

19. ↖ ; tartemorion; 0.19 g; 7 mm. Mildenberg no. 26.

 Obverse: Head of Ptolemy I to right, diademed.   No legend.
 Reverse: Head of Berenice to right, hair in parallel curls combed
 up at neck. Legend from right above, reading outwards: יהד
 (*yhd*).

20. ↑ ; tartemorion; 0.16 g; 5 mm. Meshorer pl. 3 no. 15.

 Obverse: Same as no. 19.   *Reverse*: Head of Berenice to right.
 Legend as in no. 19.

21. ↑ ; tartemorion; 0.15 g; 6 mm. Meshorer pl. 3 no. 15a.

 Same as nos. 19 and 20, but of cruder style.

19

20

21

Abbreviations

BMC	*British Museum Catalogue (Coins)*. London, 1873–.
BT	Babylonian Talmud.
CIJ	J. B. Frey, *Corpus Inscriptionum Judaicarum*. Rome, 1936–52.
CPJ	V. A. Tcherikover, A. Fuks, and M. Stern, *Corpus Papyrorum Judaicarum*. Cambridge, Mass., 1957–64.
EG	R. Herscher, *Epistolographi Graeci*. Paris, 1873.
FGrH	F. Jacoby, *Die Fragmente der griechischen Historiker*. Berlin, 1923–.
FHG	C. Müller and T. Müller, *Fragmenta Historicorum Graecorum*. Paris, 1847–70.
GGM	C. Müller, *Geographici Graeci Minores*. Paris, 1855–61.
LCL	The Loeb Classical Library. Cambridge, Mass.
OGIS	W. Dittenberger, *Orientis Graeci Inscriptiones Selectae*. Leipzig, 1903–5.
PG	*Patrologia Graeca*. [J.-P. Migne, ed., *Patrologiae Cursus Completus*, Series Graeca (Paris, 1857–66)]
P. Tebt.	B. P. Grenfell, A. S. Hunt, J. G. Smyly, and E. J. Goodspeed, *Tebtunis Papyri*. Berkeley, 1902–38.
PT	Palestinian Talmud.
RE	A. Pauly, G. Wissowa, and W. Kroll, *Real-Encyclopädie der classischen Altertumswissenschaft*. Stuttgart, 1893–.
SEG	*Supplementum Epigraphicum Graecum*. Leiden, 1923–.
SIG[3]	W. Dittenberger, *Sylloge Inscriptionum Graecarum*. 3d ed. Leipzig, 1913–24. [= *Syll.*[3]]
SNG	*Sylloge Nummorum Graecorum*. Copenhagen, 1931–.
SVF	H. von Arnim, *Stoicorum Veterum Fragmenta*. Leipzig, 1909–25.

References

Aalders, G. J. D.
 1975 *Political Thought in Hellenistic Times.* Amsterdam.

Abel, A. L.
 1968 "The Myth of Jewish Slavery in Ptolemaic Egypt." *Revue des Études Juives* 127: 253–58.

Abel, F. M.
 1933–38 *Géographie de la Palestine.* 2 vols. Paris.
 1949 *Les livres des Maccabées.* Paris.
 1951 *Histoire de la Palestine.* Paris.

Abrahams, I.
 1902 "Recent Criticism of the Letter of Aristeas." *Jewish Quarterly Review* 14: 321–42.

 1927 *Campaigns in Palestine from Alexander the Great.* London.

Ackroyd, P.
 1984 "The Jewish Community in Palestine in the Persian Period." In *The Cambridge History of Judaism* I: 130–61. Cambridge.

Adler, E. N., and M. Seligsohn
 1902–3 "Une nouvelle chronique samaritaine." *Revue des Études Juives* 44: 188–222; 45: 70–98; 46: 123–46.

Aharoni, Y.
 1962 *Excavations at Ramat Rahel.* Vol. I, *Seasons 1959 and 1960.* Rome.

Albeck, H.
 1959 *Introduction to the Mishna.* Jerusalem. [In Hebrew]

Alberro, C. A.
 1976 "The Alexandrian Jews during the Ptolemaic Period." Dissertation, Michigan State University.

Albright, W. F.
 1934 "Light on the Jewish State in Persian Times." *Bulletin of the American Schools of Oriental Research* 53: 20–22.

1957 "The Seal Impression from Jericho and the Treasures of the Second Temple." *Bulletin of the American Schools of Oriental Research* 148: 28–30.

Alexandre, M.

1967 "Le culture profane chez Philo." In R. Arnandez et al., eds., *Philo dAlexandrie*, 105–30. Paris.

Alon, G.

1957 *Studies in Jewish History.* Tel Aviv. [In Hebrew; published in English as G. Alon, *Jews, Judaism and the Classical World* (Jerusalem 1977)]

Alt, A.

1953–59 *Kleine Schriften zur Geschichte des Volkes Israel.* 3 vols. Munich.

Altheim, F., and R. Stiehl

1970 *Geschichte Mittelasiens im Altertum.* Berlin.

Aly, W.

1957 *Strabon von Amasia.* Bonn.

ʿAmir, Y.

1973 "Philo of Alexandria." In M. Stern, ed., *The Diaspora in the Hellenistic-Roman World, 238–64.* Jerusalem. [In Hebrew]

1980 "Philo's Version of the Pilgrimage to Jerusalem." In A. Oppenheimer, U. Rappaport, and M. Stern, eds., *Jerusalem in the Second Temple Period: Abraham Schalit Memorial Volume,* 154–64. Jerusalem. [In Hebrew]

Andrews, A. T.

1913 "The Letter of Aristeas." In R. H. Charles, ed., *The Apocrypha and Pseudepigrapha of the Old Testament in English* II: 83–122. Oxford.

Annas, J.

1980 "Truth and Knowledge." In M. Schofield, M. Burnyeat, and J. Barnes, eds., *Doubt and Dogmatism,* 84–104. Oxford.

Annas, J., and J. Barnes.

1985 *The Modes of Scepticism.* Cambridge.

Attridge, H. W.

1984 "Historiography." In M. E. Stone, ed., *Jewish Writings of the Second Temple Period,* Compendia Rerum Iudaicarum ad Novum Testamentum II.2: 157–85. Assen.

1986 "Jewish Historiography." In R. A. Kraft and G. W. E. Nickelsburg, eds., *Early Judaism and Its Modern Interpreters,* 311–44. Philadelphia.

Attridge, H. W., and R. A. Oden

1981 *Philo of Byblos: The Phoenician History.* Washington, D.C.

Avigad, N.

1957 "A New Class of Yehud Stamps." *Israel Exploration Journal* 7: 146–53.

1976   *Bullae and Seals from a Post-Exilic Judean Archive*. Jerusalem.
1984   *Discovering Jerusalem*. Oxford.

Avi-Yonah, M.

1954   "The Walls of Nehemiah: A Minimalist View." *Israel Exploration Journal* 4: 239–48.
1956   "Archeology and Topography of Jerusalem in the Time of the Second Temple." In M. Avi-Yonah, ed., *Sepher Yerushalayim* ["The Book of Jerusalem"], 305–19. [In Hebrew]
1966   *The Holy Land from the Persian to the Arab Conquest*. Grand Rapids.
1971   "Syria." In A. H. M. Jones, ed., *The Cities of the Eastern Roman Provinces*, 2d ed., 226–94, 446–69. Oxford.

Babbit, F. C.

1936   *Plutarch: Moralia*. Vol. V. Cambridge, Mass. [LCL]

Babelon, E.

1893   *Catalogue des monnaies grecques des Perses achéménides*. Paris.

Bagnall, R. S.

1976   *The Administration of the Ptolemaic Possessions outside Egypt*. Leiden.

Baillet, M., J. T. Milik, and R. de Vaux

1962   *Les 'petites grottes' de Qumran*. Vol. III of *Discoveries in the Judaean Desert*. Oxford.

Barag, D. P.

1966   "The Effects of the Tennes Rebellion on Palestine." *Bulletin of the American Schools of Oriental Research* 183: 6–12.
1985   "Some Notes on a Silver Coin of Johanan the High Priest." *The Biblical Archaeologist* 48: 166–68.
1986/7   "A Silver Coin of Yohanan the High Priest and the Coinage of Judea in the Fourth Century B.C." *Israel Numismatic Journal* 9: 4–21.

Barkay, G.

1992/3   "The Marisa Hoard of Seleucid Tetradrachms Minted in Ascalon." *Israel Numismatic Journal* 12: 21–26.

Bar-Kochva, B.

1976   "Gamla in Gaulanitis." *Zeitschrift des deutschen Palästina-Vereins* 92: 54–71.
1977   "Manpower, Economics and Internal Strife in the Hasmonean State." In H. van Effenterre, ed., *Armées et fiscalité dans le monde antique*, Centre National de la Recherche Scientifique, Colloques Nationaux, no. 936: 166–96. Paris.
1979   *The Seleucid Army: Organization and Tactics in the Great Campaigns*. 2d ed. Cambridge.

1989   *Judas Maccabaeus: The Jewish Struggle against the Seleucids.* Cambridge.

           Anti-Semitism and Idealization of Judaism: Hellenistic Intellectuals on Jews before the Roman Occupation of Judea (333– 63 B.C.) [Forthcoming]

Baumgarten, A. I.
1981   *The Phoenician History of Philo of Byblos.* Leiden.

Baumgartner, W.
1950   "Herodots babylonische und assyrische Nachrichten." *Archív Orientální* [Quarterly Journal of African, Asian, and Latin American Studies, Prague] 18: 69–106.

Bekker, I.
1853–54   *Diodori Bibliotheca Historica.* 4 vols. Leipzig.

Bell, H. I.
1948   "Philanthropia in the Papyri of the Roman Period." In *Hommages à Joseph Bidez et à Franz Cumont,* Collection Latomus 2: 31–37. Brussels.

Bellinger, A. R.
1949   "The End of the Seleucids." *Transactions of the Connecticut Academy of Arts and Sciences* 38: 51–102.

1963   *Essays on the Coinage of Alexander the Great.* New York.

Bengtson, H.
1964   *Die Strategie in der hellenistischen Zeit.* 2d ed. 3 vols. Munich.

Bentzen, A.
1952   *Daniel.* Tübingen.

Benzinger, I.
1961   *Die Bücher der Chronik.* Tübingen.

Bernays, J.
1861   *Chronik des Sulpicius Severus.* Berlin. [Reprinted in J. Bernays, *Gesammelte Abhandlungen* II (Berlin 1885) 200–281]

Bernays, U.
1905   *Studien zu Dionysius Periegetes.* Heidelberg.

Bernfield, I.
1930   "Hekatäus von Abdera." *Encyclopaedia Judaica* 7: 1135–36. Berlin.

Berve, H.
1926   *Das Alexanderreich auf prosopographischer Grundlage.* 2 vols. Munich.

Betylon, J. W.
1982   *The Coinage and Mints of Phoenicia: The Pre-Alexandrine Period.* Chico.

1986   "The Provincial Government of Persian Period Judea and the Yehud Coins." *Journal of Biblical Literature* 105: 633–42.

Bevan, E. R.

1927   *The House of Ptolemy: A History of Egypt under the Ptolemaic Dynasty.* London.

1927a   "Hellenistic Judaism." In E. R. Bevan and C. Singer, eds., *The Legacy of Israel,* 29–67. London.

Beyer, G.

1933   "Die Stadtgebiete von Diospolis und Nikopolis im 4. Jahrh. n.Chr. und ihre Grenznachbarn." *Zeitschrift des deutschen Palästina-Vereins* 55: 216–53.

Bickerman, E.

1930   "Zur Datierung des Pseudo-Aristeas." *Zeitschrift für die neutestamentliche Wissenschaft* 29: 280–96. [= Bickerman (1976–80) I.123–36]

1933   "Eine jüdische Festschrift vom Jahre 124 v.Chr." *Zeitschrift für die neutestamentliche Wissenschaft* 32: 233–54. [= Bickerman (1976–80) II. 136–58]

1938   *Institutions des Séleucides.* Paris.

1967   *Four Strange Books of the Bible.* New York.

1976–80 *Studies in Jewish and Christian History.* 3 vols. Leiden.

1983   "The Seleucid Period." In *The Cambridge History of Iran* III.1: 3–20. Cambridge.

1988   *The Jews in the Greek Age.* Cambridge, Mass.

Bidez, J., and F. Cumont

1938   *Les mages hellénisés.* 2 vols. Paris.

Bieber, M.

1964   *Alexander the Great in Greek and Roman Art.* Chicago.

Billows, R. A.

1990   *Antigonos the One-Eyed.* Berkeley and Los Angeles.

Blass, F., and A. Debrunner

1967   *A Greek Grammar of the New Testament.* Ed. R. W. Funk. Chicago.

Bloch, H.

1879   *Die Quellen des Flavius Josephus in seiner Archäologie.* Leipzig.

Blum, R.

1991   *Kallimachos: The Alexandrian Library and the Origins of Bibliography.* Madison.

Bolton, J. D. P.

1962   *Aristeas of Proconnesus.* Oxford.

Bonphil, R.

1972   "On Judea and Jerusalem in the Letter of Aristeas." *Beth Mikra* 17: 131–41. [In Hebrew]

Borgen, P.

1981   *Bread from Heaven.* Leiden.

1984   "Philo of Alexandria." In M. E. Stone, ed., *Jewish Writings of the Second Temple Period*, Compendia Rerum Iudaicarum ad Novum Testamentum II.2: 233–82. Assen.

Bouché-Leclercq, A.
1879–82   *Histoire de la divination dans l'antiquité.* 4 vols. Paris.

Bousset, W., and H. Gressmann
1926   *Die Religion des Judentums im späthellenistischen Zeitalter.* Tübingen.

Bowersock, G. W.
1983   *Roman Arabia.* Cambridge, Mass.

Bowman, A. K.
1986   *Egypt after the Pharaohs.* Oxford.

Boyce, M.
1984   "The Persian Religion in the Achaemenid Period." In *The Cambridge History of Judaism* I: 279–307. Cambridge.

Boysen, C.
1898   *Flavii Josephi Opera ex Versione Latina Antiqua.* Part VI, *De Iudaeorum Vetustates sive Contra Apionem.* Corpus Scriptorum Ecclesiasticorum Latinorum 37. Vienna.

Breloer, B.
1933   "Megasthenes (etwa 300 v.Chr.) über die indische Gesellschaft." *Zeitschrift für Semitistik und verwandte Gebiete* 88: 130–64.

Bresciani, E.
1985   "The Persian Occupation of Egypt." In *The Cambridge History of Iran* II: 502–28. Cambridge.

Broshi, M.
1975   "La population de l'ancienne Jérusalem." *Revue Biblique* 82: 5–14.
1977   "The Population of Ancient Jerusalem." In M. Broshi, ed., *Between Hermon and Sinai: Memorial to Amnon*, 65–74. Jerusalem. [In Hebrew]
1982   "The Credibility of Josephus." In U. Rappaport, ed., *Josephus Flavius, Historian of Eretz Israel in the Hellenistic-Roman Period*, 21–29. Jerusalem. [In Hebrew]

Broshi, M., and R. Gophna
1984   "The Settlement and Population of Eretz Israel in the Early Bronze Age I–II." *Eretz Israel* 17: 147–57. [In Hebrew]
1984a   "Palestine in the Middle Bronze II: Its Settlements and Population." *Cathedra* 31: 3–26. [In Hebrew]

Brown, T. S.
1955   "The Reliability of Megasthenes." *American Journal of Philology* 76: 18–33.

Brox, N.
1977   *Pseudepigraphie in der heidenischen und jüdisch-christlichen Antike.* Darmstadt.

Brugsch, H.
1871   "Ein Dekret Ptolemaios des Sohnes Lagi, des Satrapen." *Zeitschrift für ägyptische Sprache und Altertumskunde* 9: 1–13, 56–61.

Brunner, H.
1977   "Vogelschau in Ägypten." *Göttinger Miszellen* 25: 45–46.

Buchberger, H.
1986   "Vogel." In W. Helck and W. Westendorf, eds., *Lexikon der Ägyptologie,* 1046–51. Wiesbaden.

Büchler, A.
1895   *Die Priester und der Cultus.* Vienna.
1898   "La relation de Josèphe concernant Alexandre le Grand." *Revue des Études Juives* 36: 1–26.
1899   *Die Tobiaden und die Oniaden im II Makkabäerbuche und in der verwandten jüdisch-hellenistischen Literatur.* Vienna.

Bull, R. J.
1975   "An Archaeological Context for Understanding John 4.20." *The Biblical Archaeologist* 38: 54–59.

Bull, R. J., and E. F. Campbell
1968   "The Sixth Campaign at Balâtah (Shechem)." *Bulletin of the American Schools of Oriental Research* 190: 4–19.

Bull, R. J., and G. E. Wright
1965   "Newly Discovered Temples on Mt. Gerizim in Jordan." *Harvard Theological Review* 58: 234–37.

Burnyeat, M. F., ed.
1984   *The Skeptical Tradition.* Berkeley and Los Angeles.

Burstein, S.
1978   *The Babyloniaca of Berossus.* Malibu.
1989   *Agatharcides of Cnidus on the Erythraean Sea.* London.

Burton, A.
1972   *Diodorus Siculus, Book I: A Commentary.* Leiden.

Bury, R. G.
1933–49   *Sextus Empiricus.* 4 vols. Cambridge, Mass. [LCL]

Busolt, G.
1890   "Quellenkritische Beiträge zur Geschichte der römischen Revolutionszeit." *Jahrbücher für klassische Philologie* 141: 321–49.

Buttrey, T. V.
1982   "Pharaonic Imitations of Athenian Tetradrachms." *Transactions of the Ninth International Congress of Numismatics, Bern, 1979:* 137–40. Bern.

Cahana, A.
1956   The Apocrypha and Pseudepigrapha. 2d ed. Tel Aviv. [In Hebrew]

Campbell, F. F.
1979   "Jewish Shrines of the Hellenistic and Persian Period." In F. M. Cross, ed., Symposia Celebrating the Seventy-fifth Anniversary of the Founding of the American Schools of Oriental Research (1900–1975), 157–67. Cambridge, Mass.

Cataudella, Q.
1933   "Jos. c. Apion I.189." Rivista di Filologia Classica 61: 75–76.

Chadwick, H.
1953   Origenes: Contra Celsum. Cambridge.

Charlesworth, J. H.
1976   The Pseudepigrapha and Modern Research. Missoula.
1985   The Old Testament Pseudepigrapha. 2 vols. New York.

Cherniss, H., and W. C. Helmbold
1957   Plutarch: Moralia. Vol. XII. Cambridge, Mass. [LCL]

Coggins, R. J.
1975   The Samaritans and the Jews: The Origins of the Samaritans Reconsidered. Oxford.

Cohen, G.
1978   The Seleucid Colonies: Studies in Founding, Administration and Organization. Wiesbaden.

Cohen, S. J. D.
1982/3   "Alexander the Great and Jaddus the High Priest according to Josephus." Association for Jewish Studies Review 78: 41–68.

Cole, T.
1967   Democritus and the Sources of Greek Anthropology. Hartford.

Collins, J. J.
1974   The Sibylline Oracles of Egyptian Judaism. Missoula.
1983   Between Athens and Jerusalem: Jewish Identity in the Hellenistic Diaspora. New York.
1984   Daniel, with an Introduction to Apocalyptic Literature. Grand Rapids.

Colson, F. H.
1916–17   "Philo on Education." Journal of Theological Studies 18: 151–62.

Conzelmann, H.
1981   Heiden-Juden-Christen: Auseinandersetzungen in der Literatur der hellenistisch-römischen Zeit. Tübingen.

Couissin, P.
1929   "L'origine et l'évolution de l'EΠOXH." Revue des Études Grecques 42: 373–97.

Cowley, A. E.
1923   Aramaic Papyri of the Fifth Century B.C. Oxford.

Crawford, D. J.
1971   *Kerkeosiris: An Egyptian Village in the Ptolemaic Period.* Cambridge.

Creuzer, F.
1806   *Historicorum Graecorum Antiquissimorum Fragmenta.* Heidelberg.

Cross, F. M.
1963   "The Discovering of the Samaria Papyri." *The Biblical Archaeologist* 26: 110–21.
1974   "Discoveries in Wadi ad-Dâliyeh." *Annual of the American Schools of Oriental Research* 41: 57–59.
1975   "A Reconstruction of the Judean Restoration." *Journal of Biblical Literature* 94: 1–18.
1983   "Shomron and Jerusalem." In H. Tadmor, ed., *The Restoration: The Persian Period,* 81–94. Jerusalem. [In Hebrew]

Crowfoot, J. W.
1942   *Samaria.* Vol. I, *The Buildings.* London.

Crown, A. D.
1985   "The Samaritan Diaspora." In A. D. Crown, ed., *The Samaritans,* 195–217. Tübingen.

Cumont, F.
1960   *Astrology and Religion among the Greeks and Romans.* New York.

van't Dack, E.
1981   "Le conflit judéo-syro-égyptien de 103/102 av. J.-C." *Proceedings of the Sixteenth International Congress of Papyrology,* 303–12. Chico.

van't Dack, E., W. Clarysse, G. Cohen, J. Quaegebeur, and J. K. Winnicki
1989   *The Judean-Syrian-Egyptian Conflict of 103–101 B.C.: A Multilingual Dossier concerning a "War of Scepters."* Collectanea Hellenistica 1. Brussels.

Dahlmann, J. H.
1928   *De Philosophorum Graecorum Sententiis ad Loquellae Originem Pertinentibus.* Weida.

Dahlquist, A.
1962   *Megasthenes and Indian Religion.* Stockholm.

Dähne, A. F.
1834   *Geschichtliche Darstellung der jüdisch-alexandrinischen Religionsphilosophie.* 2 vols. Halle.

Dalbert, P.
1954   *Die Theologie der hellenistisch-jüdischen Missionsliteratur unter Ausschluss von Philo und Josephus.* Hamburg.

Dal Pra, M.
1975   *Lo scetticismo greco.* 2d ed. Rome.

Dandamaev, M. A.
1975 "La politique religieuse des Achéménides." In *Monumentum H. S. Nyberg* I [*Acta Iranica* 14]: 193–200. Leiden.

Dandamaev, M. A., and V. G. Lukonin
1989 *The Culture and Social Institutions of Ancient Iran.* Cambridge.

Daniel, S.
1966 *Recherches sur le vocabulaire du culte dans la Septante.* Paris.

Dar, S.
1991 "The Geographical Region of the Hasmonean Iturean Encounter." *Cathedra* 59: 3–11. [In Hebrew]

Davies, M. D.
1982 *The Territorial Dimension of Judaism.* Berkeley and Los Angeles.

Davis, N., and C. M. Kraay
1973 *The Hellenistic Kingdoms: Portrait Coins and History.* London.

Decleva-Caizzi, F.
1981 *Pirrone: Testimonianze.* Naples.

Deissman-Merten, M.
1984 "Zur Socialgeschichte des Kindes in antiken Griechenland." In J. Martin and A. Nitschke, eds., *Zur Sozialgeschichte der Kindheit,* 267–316. Freiburg.

Delcor, M.
1971 *Le livre de Daniel.* Paris.

Delling, G.
1981 "Alexander der Grosse als Bekenner des jüdischen Gottesglaubens." *Journal of the Study of Judaism in the Persian, Hellenistic and Roman Periods* 12: 1–51.

Denis, A. M.
1970 *Introduction aux pseudépigraphes grecs d'Ancien Testament.* Leiden.

1970a *Fragmenta Pseudepigraphorum Quae Supersunt Graeca una cum Historicorum et Auctorum Judaeorum Hellenistarum Fragmentis.* Leiden.

Denniston, J. D.
1954 *The Greek Particles.* 2d ed. Oxford.

Derret, J. D. M.
1975 "Megasthenes." In *Der kleine Pauly* III: 1150–54. Munich.

von Destinon, J.
1882 *Die Quellen des Flavius Josephus in der Jüdischer Archäologie, Bücher XII–XVIII = Jüdischer Krieg, Buch I.* Kiel.

Diamond, F. H.
1974 "Hecataeus of Abdera: A New Historical Approach." Dissertation, University of California, Los Angeles.

1980   "Hecataeus of Abdera and the Mosaic Constitution." In S. M. Burstein and L. A. Okin, eds., *Essays in Ancient History and Historiography in Honor of Truesdell S. Brown*, 77–95. Lawrence.

Diels, H.

1922   *Die Fragmente der Vorsokratiker, auf Griechisch und Deutsch: Nachträge, zusammengestellt für die Besitzer der dritten Auflage.* Berlin.

Diels, H., and W. Kranz

1935   *Die Fragmente der Vorsokratiker.* 5th ed. Berlin.

Dihle, A.

1961   "Zur hellenistischen Ethnographie." In *Grecs et barbares.* Entretiens sur l'Antiquité Classique 8: 207–39. Geneva.

Dindorf, L.

1828–31   *Diodori Bibliotheca Historica.* 5 vols. Leipzig.

Dodds, E. R.

1951   *The Greeks and the Irrational.* Berkeley and Los Angeles.

Doran, R.

1983   "2 Maccabees 6:2 and the Samaritan Question." *Harvard Theological Review* 76: 481–82.

1985   "Pseudo-Hecataeus." In J. H. Charlesworth, ed., *The Old Testament Pseudepigrapha* II: 905–19. New York.

Dornseiff, F.

1938   "Antikes zum Alten Testament." *Zeitschrift für die alttestamentliche Wissenschaft* 56: 64–85.

1939   *Echtheitsfragen antik-griechischer Literatur: Rettungen des Theognis, Phokylides, Hekataios, Choirilos.* Berlin.

Drews, R.

1962   "Diodorus and His Sources." *American Journal of Philology* 83: 383–92.

1973   *Greek Accounts of Eastern History.* Washington, D.C.

Droysen, J. G.

1877–78   *Geschichte des Hellenismus.* 3 vols. Gotha.

Drüner, H.

1896   *Untersuchungen über Josephus.* Marburg.

Egger, R.

1986   *Josephus Flavius und die Samaritaner.* Göttingen.

Eichorn, J. G.

1793   *Allgemeine Bibliothek der biblischen Literatur.* Vol. V. Leipzig.

Eisenman, R. H., and R. Wise

1992   *The Dead Sea Scrolls Uncovered: The First Complete Translation and Interpretation of Fifty Key Documents Withheld for over Thirty-five Years.* Rockport.

Engers, M.

1923   "De Hecataei Abderitae Fragmentis." *Mnemosyne* 51: 229–41.

Epstein, J. N.
    1957   *Introduction to Tannaitic Literature.* Jerusalem. [In Hebrew]
Eshel, E.
    1989   "How I Found a Fourth-Century-B.C. Papyrus Scroll." *Biblical Archaeology Review* 15: 44–53.
Eshel, E., H. Eshel, and A. Yardeni
    1990/1   "A Scroll from Qumran Which Includes Part of Psalm 154 and a Prayer for King Jonathan and His Kingdom." *Tarbiz* 60: 295–313.
Ewald, H.
    1876–86 *The History of Israel.* 3d ed. London.
Falconer, W. A.
    1923   *Cicero: De Senectute, De Amicitia, De Divinatione.* Cambridge, Mass. *[LCL]*
Feist, S.
    1931   "Ein Zeitgenosse Alexanders des Grossen über die Juden." *Menorah* 19: 468–70.
Feldman, L. H.
    1958/9   "Philo-Semitism among Ancient Intellectuals." *Tradition* 1: 27–39.
    1960   "The Orthodoxy of Jews in Hellenistic Egypt." *Jewish Social Studies* 22: 215–37.
    1984   *Josephus and Modern Scholarship (1937–1980).* New York.
    1989   "Josephus's Portrait of Joshua." *Harvard Theological Review* 82: 351–76.
    1990   "Origen's *Contra Celsum* and Josephus' *Contra Apionem.*" *Vigiliae Christianae* 4: 105–35.
    1993   *Jew and Gentile in the Ancient World.* Princeton.
Ferguson, J.
    1975   *Utopias of the Classical World.* London.
Février, J.
    1924   *La date, la composition et les sources de la lettre d'Aristée.* Paris.
Finley, M. I.
    1985   *Ancient History: Evidence and Models.* New York.
Flacelière, R.
    1961   *Devins et oracles grecs.* Paris.
Flusser, D.
    1991/2   "Some Notes about the Prayer for King Jonathan." *Tarbiz* 61: 297–300.
Foerster, G.
    1981   "The Conquests of John Hyrcanus I in Moab and the Identification of Samaga." *Eretz Israel* 15: 353–56. [In Hebrew]
Fontenrose, J.
    1978   *The Delphic Oracle.* Berkeley and Los Angeles.

Forderer, M.
1955   "Der Schild des Achilleus und der Lobgesang im Feuerofen."
            Studium Generale 8: 294–301.
Fornara, C. W.
1983   *The Nature of History in Ancient Greece and Rome.* Berkeley
            and Los Angeles.
Fraser, P. M.
1972   *Ptolemaic Alexandria.* 3 vols. Oxford.
Freudenthal, I.
1875   *Alexander Polyhistor und die von ihm erhaltenen Reste jüd-
            ischer und samaritanischer Geschichtswerke.* Breslau.
Friedländer, M.
1903   *Geschichte der jüdischen Apologetik als Vorgeschichte des
            Christentums.* Zurich.
Fuks, G.
1979/80   "Tel Anafa: A Proposed Identification." *Scripta Classica Israe-
            lica* 5: 178–84.
1982   "On the Reliability of a Reference in Josephus." In U. Rap-
            paport, ed., *Josephus Flavius: Historian of Eretz Israel in the
            Hellenistic-Roman Period,* 131–38. Jerusalem. [In Hebrew]
1983   *Scythopolis: A Greek City in Eretz Israel.* Jerusalem. [In
            Hebrew]
Funk, R. W.
1970   "Beth Zur." In B. Mazar, ed., *Encyclopaedia of Archaeological
            Excavations in the Holy Land* I: 60–63. Jerusalem. [In Hebrew]
Gabba, E.
1989   "The Growth of Anti-Judaism; or, The Greek Attitude towards
            the Jews." In *The Cambridge History of Judaism* II: 614–56.
            Cambridge.
Gafni, J.
1984   "The Status of Eretz Israel in Reality and in the Jewish Con-
            sciousness following the Bar-Kokhva Uprising." In A. Oppen-
            heimer and U. Rappaport, eds., *The Bar-Kokhva Revolt: New
            Studies,* 224–33. Jerusalem. [In Hebrew]
1990   "Expressions and Types of 'Local Patriotism' among the Jews
            of Sassanian Babylonia." In S. Shaked, ed., *Irano-Judaica* II:
            63–71. Jerusalem.
Gager, J. G.
1969   "Pseudo-Hecataeus Again." *Zeitschrift für die neutestament-
            liche Wissenschaft* 60: 130–39.
1972   *Moses in Greco-Roman Paganism.* Nashville.
1983   *The Origins of Anti-Semitism.* New York.

Gal, Z.
1990   Lower Galilee: Historical Geography in the Biblical Period. Tel Aviv. [In Hebrew; published in English as Lower Galilee during the Iron Age (Winona Lake 1992)]

Galling, K.
1964   Studien zur Geschichte Israels im persischen Zeit. Tübingen.

Gärtner, E.
1912   Komposition und Wortwahl des Buches der Weisheit. Berlin.

Gaster, M.
1905   The Samaritans: Their History, Doctrines and Literature. London.

Gauger, J. D.
1982   "Zitate in der jüdischen Apologetik und die Authentizität der Hekataios' Passagen bei Flavius Josephus und im Ps.-Aristeas' Brief." Journal of the Study of Judaism in the Persian, Hellenistic and Roman Periods 13: 6–46.

Gauthier, H., and H. Sottas
1925   Un décret trilingue en l'honneur de Ptolémée IV. Cairo.

Geffcken, J.
1905   "Die altchristliche Apologetik." Neue Jahrbücher für das klassische Altertum 15: 627–66.
1907   Zwei griechische Apologeten. Leipzig.

Geiger, J.
1984   "The History of Judas Maccabaeus: One Aspect of Hellenistic Historiography." Zion 49: 1–8. [In Hebrew]
1985/8   "Form and Content in Jewish-Hellenistic Historiography." Scripta Classica Israelica 8–9: 120–29.

Gelzer, H.
1885   Sextus Julius Africanus und die byzantinische Chronographie. 3 vols. Leipzig.

Gera, D.
1987   "Ptolemy Son of Thraseas and the Fifth Syrian War." Ancient Society 18: 63–73.

Giannantoni, G.
1981   "Pirrone, la scuola scettica e il sistema della 'successione.' " In G. Giannantoni, ed., Lo scettismo antico: 13–34. Rome.

Gigon, O.
1961   Review of Späthellenistische Berichte über Welt, Kultur und Götter, by W. Spoerri. Gnomon 33: 771–76.

Ginsberg, H. L.
1989   "The Book of Daniel." In The Cambridge History of Judaism II: 504–23. Cambridge.

Ginsburg, M. S.
1934   "Sparta and Judea." Classical Philology 29: 117–22.

Glucker, J.
1978   *Antiochus and the Late Academy*. Göttingen.
Goedicke, H.
1984   "Comments on the Satrap Stela." *Bulletin of the Egyptological Seminar* 6: 33–54.
Golden, M.
1990   *Children and Childhood in Classical Athens*. Baltimore.
Goldstein, J. A.
1976   *I Maccabees: A New Translation, with Introduction and Commentary*. New York.
1983   *II Maccabees: A New Translation, with Introduction and Commentary*. New York.
Goodenough, E. R.
1935   *By Light, Light*. New Haven.
1953–68   *Jewish Symbols in the Greco-Roman Period*. 13 vols. New Haven.
Gooding, D.
1963   "Aristeas and the Septuagint Origins." *Vetus Testamentum* 13: 357–79.
Grabbe, L. L.
1987   "Josephus and the Reconstruction of the Judean Restoration." *Journal of Biblical Literature* 106: 231–46.
Graetz, H.
1876   "Die Abfassungszeit des Pseudo-Aristeas." *Monatschrift für Geschichte und Wissenschaft des Judentums* 25: 289–308, 337–49.
1888   *Geschichte der Juden*. 4th ed. Vol. III. Leipzig.
Graham, A. J.
1964   *Colony and Mother City*. Manchester.
1982   "The Colonial Expansion of Greece." In *The Cambridge Ancient History*, 2d ed., III.3: 83–159. Cambridge.
Grainger, J. D.
1991   *Hellenistic Phoenicia*. Oxford.
Griffith, G. T.
1935   *The Mercenaries of the Hellenistic World*. Cambridge.
Griffiths, J. G.
1976   Review of *Diodorus Siculus, Book I*, by A. Burton. *Classical Review* 26: 122–23.
Grintz, Y. M.
1957   *The Book of Judith*. Jerusalem. [In Hebrew]
1969   *Chapters in the History of the Second Temple*. Jerusalem. [In Hebrew]

Gruenwald, I.

1986   "Polemical Attitudes toward the Septuagint." In M. Gil and
        M. A. Friedman, eds., *Teʿuda: Studies in Judaica* IV: 65–78. Tel
        Aviv. [In Hebrew]

von Gutschmid, A.

1893   *Kleine Schriften.* 4 vols. Leipzig.

Guttman, J.

1928   "The Origin and Main Purpose of the 'Letter of Aristeas.' "
        Ha-Goren 10: 42–59. [In Hebrew]

1940   "Alexander of Macedon in Eretz Israel." *Tarbiz* 11: 271–94. [In
        Hebrew]

1958–63 *The Beginnings of Jewish Hellenistic Literature.* 2 vols. Jeru-
        salem. [In Hebrew]

Hadas, M.

1951   *Aristeas to Philocrates (The Letter of Aristeas).* New York.

1959   *Hellenistic Culture: Fusion and Diffusion.* New York.

Haefeli, L.

1922   *Geschichte der Landschaft Samaria von 722 vor Chr. bis 67
        nach Chr.* Münster.

Hägg, T.

1975   *Photios als Vermittler antiker Literatur.* Stockholm.

Halliday, W. R.

1913   *Greek Divination.* London.

Hammer, B.

1976   *The Book of Daniel.* Cambridge.

Harmon, H. M.

1925   *Lucian.* Vol. IV. Cambridge, Mass. *[LCL]*

Harrington, S. J., and J. Strugnell

1993   "Qumran Cave 4 Texts: A New Publication." *Journal of Biblical
        Literature* 112/13: 491–99.

Harris, H.

1976   *Greek Athletics and the Jews.* Cardiff.

Hart, G. D.

1973   "The Diagnosis of Disease from Ancient Coins." *Archaeology*
        26: 123–27.

Hartman, L. F., and A. A. Di Lella

1978   *The Book of Daniel.* New York.

Hartog, F.

1988   *The Mirror of Herodotus: The Representation of the Other in
        the Writing of History.* Berkeley and Los Angeles.

Head, B. V.   *Historia Numorum.* London.

Hegermann, H.

1989   "The Diaspora in the Hellenistic Age." In *The Cambridge
        History of Judaism* II: 115–67. Cambridge.

Heidel, W. A.
1935 "Hecataeus and the Egyptian Priests in Herodotus Book II." *Memoirs of the American Academy of Arts and Sciences* 18.2: 53–134.

Heinemann, I.
1948/9 "The Relationship between the Jewish People and the Holy Land in Hellenistic Jewish Literature." *Zion* 13/14: 1–9. [In Hebrew]

Helck, W.
1956 *Untersuchungen zu Manetho und den ägyptischen Königslisten.* Berlin.

Hengel, M.
1971 "Anonymität, Pseudepigraphie und 'literarische Fälschung' in der jüdisch-hellenistischen Literatur." In K. von Fritz, ed., *Pseudepigrapha* I, Entretiens sur l'Antiquité Classique 18: 231–329. Geneva.

1973 *Judentum und Hellenismus.* 2d ed. Tübingen.
1976 *Juden, Griechen und Barbaren.* Stuttgart.
1984 *Rabbinische Legende und frühpharisäische Geschichte: Simeon Ben Schetach und die achtzig Hexen von Askalon.* Sitzungsberichte der Heidelberger Akademie der Wissenschaften, Phil.-hist. Klasse, 1984.4. Heidelberg.
1989 "The Political and Social History of Palestine from Alexander to Antiochus III (333–187 B.C.E.)." In *The Cambridge History of Judaism* II: 35–78. Cambridge.

Henry, P.
1935 *Recherches sur la Préparation Évangélique d'Eusèbe et l'édition perdue des œuvres de Plotin.* Paris.

Herbert, S. C.
1979 "Tel Anafa 1978: Preliminary Report." *Bulletin of the American Schools of Oriental Research* 234: 67–84.

Herrmann, L.
1966 "La lettre d'Aristée à Philocrate et l'empereur Titus." *Latomus* 25: 58–78.

Herscher, R.
1853 "Michaelis Pselli ΠΕΡΙ ΩΜΟΠΛΑΤΟΣΚΟΠΙΑΣ ΚΑΙ ΟΙΩΝΟΣΚΟΠΙΑΣ ex Codice Vindobonensi." *Philologus* 8: 168–70.

Heuss, A.
1937 *Stadt und Herrscher des Hellenismus.* Berlin.

Hicks, R. D.
1925 *Diogenes Laertius.* 2 vols. Cambridge, Mass. [LCL]

Hildesheimer, H.
1885 *Beiträge zur Geographie Palästinas.* Berlin.

Hill, C. F.

1901 *Descriptive Catalogue of Ancient Greek Coins Belonging to John Ward.* London.

1923 "Some Coins of Southern Asia Minor." In *Anatolian Studies Presented to Sir William Mitchell Ramsay,* 207–24. Manchester.

Hoepfner, W.

1990 "Von Alexandria über Pergamon nach Nikopolis: Städtebau und Stadtbilder hellenisticher Zeit." In *Akten des XIII. Internationalen Kongress für klassische Archäologie, Berlin 1988,* 275–85. Berlin.

Hoffmann, C.

1988 *Juden und Judentum im Werk deutscher Althistoriker des 19. und 20. Jahrhunderts.* Leiden.

Holladay, C. R.

1983 *Fragments from Hellenistic Jewish Authors.* Vol. I, *Historians.* Atlanta.

1989 *Fragments from Hellenistic Jewish Authors.* Vol. II, *Poets.* Atlanta.

Holleaux, M.

1938–57 *Études d'épigraphie et d'histoire grecques.* 5 vols. Paris.

Holliday, W. R.

1911 *Greek Divination.* London.

Hölscher, G.

1903 *Palästina in der persischen und hellenistischen Zeit.* Berlin.

1904 *Die Quellen des Josephus für die Zeit vom Exil bis zum jüdischen Kriege.* Leipzig.

1940 *Die Hohenpriesterliste bei Josephus und die evangelische Chronologie.* Sitzungsberichte der Heidelberger Akademie der Wissenschaften, Phil.-hist. Klasse, 1939/40, Abh. 3. Heidelberg.

Holtzmann, O.

1913 *Middot.* Berlin.

Hornblower, J.

1981 *Hieronymus of Cardia.* Oxford.

Hornblower, S.

1982 *Mausolus.* Oxford.

Howard, G.

1971 "The Letter of Aristeas and Diaspora Judaism." *Journal of Theological Studies* 22: 336–48.

Ihnken, T.

1978 *Die Inschriften von Magnesia am Sipylos.* Bonn.

Jacobson, H.

1983 *The Exagoge of Ezkiel.* Cambridge.

Jacoby, J.
1909   "Über die Entwicklung der griechischen Historiographie und den Plan einer neuen Sammlung der griechischen Historiker-fragmente." *Klio* 9: 80–123.

1943   *Die Fragmente der griechischen Historiker.* Vol. IIIA. Leiden.
Jaeger, W.
1938   *Diokles von Karystos: Die griechische Medizin und die Schule des Aristoteles.* Berlin.

1938a   "Greeks and Jews: The First Greek Records of Jewish Religion and Civilization." *Journal of Religion* 18: 127–43.
Japhet, S.
1977   *The Ideology of the Book of Chronicles and Its Place in Biblical Thought.* Jerusalem. [In Hebrew]
Jellicoe, S.
1965/6   "The Occasion and Purpose of the Letter of Aristeas: A Re-examination." *New Testament Studies* 12: 144–50.

1968   *The Septuagint and Modern Study.* Oxford.
Jeremias, J.
1934   "Hesekieltempel und Serubbabeltempel." *Zeitschrift für die alttestamentliche Wissenschaft* 52: 109–12.

Jeselsohn, D.
1974   "A New Coin Type with Hebrew Inscription." *Israel Exploration Journal* 24: 77–78.

Jevons, F. B.
1896   "Indo-European Modes of Orientation." *Classical Review* 22: 22–24.

Jones, A. H. M.
1940   *The Greek City from Alexander to Justinian.* Oxford.
1968   *The Septuagint and Modern Study.* Oxford.
1971   *The Cities of the Eastern Roman Provinces.* 2d ed. Oxford.
Kahrstedt, U.
1926   *Syrische Territorien in hellenistischer Zeit.* Berlin.
Kallai, Z.
1960   *The Northern Boundaries of Judah: From the Settlement of the Tribes until the Beginning of the Hasmonean Period.* Jerusalem. [In Hebrew]

1983   "Yehud and the Boundaries of the Jewish Settlement under the Persian Rule." In H. Tadmor, ed., *The Restoration: The Persian Period,* 72–80. Jerusalem. [In Hebrew]

Kalota, N. S.
1978   *India as Described by Megasthenes.* Delhi.
Kamal, A. B.
1905   *Stèles ptolémaïques et romaines.* 2 vols. Cairo.

Kanael, B.
1955   "Notes on Alexander Jannaeus' Campaigns in the Coastal Region." *Tarbiz* 24: 9–15. [In Hebrew]
Kaplony-Heckel, U.
1985   "Das Dekret des spätern Königs Ptolemaios I Soter zugunsten der Götter von Butto (Satrapenstele), 311 v. Chr." In O. Kaiser, ed., *Texte aus der Umwelt des alten Testaments* III: 613–19. Gütersloh.
Kappler, W.
1967   *Maccabaeorum Liber I.* Göttingen.
Karttunen, K.
1986   "Graeco-Indica: A Survey of Recent Work." *Arctos* 20: 73–86.
Kasher, A.
1975   "Some Suggestions and Comments concerning Alexander of Macedon's Campaigns in Palestine." *Beth Mikra* 20: 187–209. [In Hebrew]
1978   "The First Jewish Military Units in Ptolemaic Egypt." *Journal of the Study of Judaism in the Persian, Hellenistic and Roman Periods* 9: 58–60.
1979   "Jerusalem as a 'Metropolis' in Philo's National Consciousness." *Cathedra* 11: 45–56. [In Hebrew]
1985   *The Jews in Hellenistic and Roman Egypt.* Tübingen.
1986   *Jews, Idumaeans and Ancient Arabs.* Tübingen.
1987   "Synagogues in Ptolemaic and Roman Egypt as Community Centers." In A. Kasher, A. Oppenheimer, and U. Rappaport, eds., *Synagogues in Antiquity.* Jerusalem. [In Hebrew]
1990   *Jews and Hellenistic Cities in Eretz Israel.* Tübingen.
Kaufmann, I.
1937–56   *History of the Israelite Religion.* 4 vols. Jerusalem. [In Hebrew]
Kenney, E. J.
1982   "Books and Readers in the Roman World." In E. J. Kenney and W. V. Clausen, eds., *The Cambridge History of Classical Literature*, vol. II, *Latin Literature*, 3–33. Cambridge.
Kent, R.
1953   *Old Persian: Grammar, Texts, Lexicon.* 2d ed. New Haven.
Kenyon, F. G., and C. H. Roberts
1970   "Books, Greek and Latin." In *The Oxford Classical Dictionary*, 2d ed., 172–75. Oxford.
Kienitz, F. K.
1953   *Die politische Geschichte Ägyptens vom 7. bis zum 4. Jahrhundert vor der Zeitwende.* Berlin.
Kindler, A.
1974   "Silver Coins Bearing the Name of Judea from the Early Hellenistic Period." *Israel Exploration Journal* 24: 73–76.

1978 "A Ptolemaic Coin Hoard from Tel Michal." *Tel Aviv* 5: 159–69.

Kippenberg, H. G.

1978 *Religion und Klassenbildung im antiken Judäa: Eine religions-soziologische Studie zum Verhältnis von Tradition und gesell-schaftlicher Entwicklung*. Göttingen.

Klausner, J.

1950 *The History of the Second Temple*. 5 vols. Tel Aviv. [In Hebrew]

Klein, S.

1939 *The Land of Judea*. Tel Aviv. [In Hebrew]

Kloner, A.

1991 "Marisa 1989." *Archaeological Newsletter* 103: 31–33. [In Hebrew]

1991a "Maresha." *Qadmoniot* 24: 70–85. [In Hebrew]

Knox, W. L.

1940 "A Note on Philo's Use of the Old Testament." *Journal of Theological Studies* 41: 30–34.

Koch, K.

1980 *Das Buch Daniel*. Darmstadt.

Kochman, M.

1982 "Yehud Medinta in the Light of the Coinage of Yehud." *Cathedra* 24: 3–30. [In Hebrew]

Koenen, L.

1970 "Kleopatra III als Priesterin des Alexanderkultes." *Zeitschrift für Papyrologie und Epigraphik* 5: 61–84.

Koller, H.

1955 "Enkyklios Paideia." *Glotta* 34: 174–89.

Kornemann, E.

1901 "Zur Geschichte der antiken Herrscherkulte." *Klio* 1: 51–146.

Kraay, C. M.

1970 *Greek Coins*. New York.

Kraeling, E. G.

1953 *The Brooklyn Museum Aramaic Papyri: New Documents of the Fifth Century B.C. from the Jewish Colony at Elephantine*. New Haven.

Krauss, S.

1922 *Synagogale Altertümer*. Berlin.

Kuhl, C.

1930 *Die drei Männer in Feuer: Daniel Kapital 3 und seine Zusätze*. Giessen.

Kuhrt, A.

1987 "Berossus' *Babyloniaka* and Seleucid Rule in Babylonia." In A. Kuhrt and S. Sherwin-White, eds., *Hellenism in the East*, 32–56. Berkeley and Los Angeles.

Kunz, M.
1935   "Zur Beurteilung der Prooemien in Diodors historischer Bibliothek." Dissertation, Zurich.
Lambert, C.
1933   "Egypto-Arabian, Phoenician and Other Coins of the Fourth Century B.C. Found in Palestine." *Quarterly of the Department of Antiquities of Palestine* 2: 1–10.
Launey, M.
1949–50   *Recherches sur les armées hellénistiques.* 2 vols. Paris.
Lebram, J.
1974   "Perspektiven der gegenwärtigen Danielforschung." *Journal of the Study of Judaism in the Persian, Hellenistic and Roman Periods* 5: 1–33.

1974a   "Der Idealstaat der Juden." In O. Betz, K. Haacker, and M. Hengel, eds., *Josephus-Studien: Untersuchungen zu Josephus, dem antiken Judentum und dem Neuen Testament, O. Michel zum 70. Geburtstag gewidmet,* 233–53. Göttingen.
Lenger, M. T.
1956   "Décret d'amnistie de Ptolémée Évergète II et lettre aux forces armées de Chypre." *Bulletin de Correspondance Hellénique* 80: 437–61.
Leopoldi, H.
1892   "De Agatharcide Cnidio." Dissertation, Rostock.
Leschhorn, W.
1984   *Gründer der Staat: Studien zu einem politisch-religiösen Phänomen der griechischen Geschichte.* Stuttgart.
Lesquier, J.
1911   *Les institutions militaires de l'Égypte sous les Lagides.* Paris.
Leuze, O.
1935   *Die Satrapieneinteilung in Syrien und im Zweistromlande von 520 bis 320.* Halle.
Lewy, Hans
1932   "Hekataios von Abdera Περὶ Ἰουδαίων." *Zeitschrift für die neutestamentliche Wissenschaft* 31: 117–32.
1942/3   "Tacitus on Jewish Antiquities and Customs." *Zion* 8: 1–34, 61–84. [In Hebrew]
1960   *Studies in Jewish Hellenism.* Jerusalem. [In Hebrew; as J. H. Levy]
Lieberman, S.
1962   *Hellenism in Jewish Palestine.* 2d ed. New York.
Lightfoot, J. B.
1899   *The Apostolic Fathers.* 2 vols. London.
Lloyd, A. B.
1974   Review of *Diodorus Siculus, Book I,* by A. Burton. *Journal of Egyptian Archaeology* 60: 287–96.

1975–78   *Herodotus, Book II.* 3 vols. Leiden.

1990   "Herodotus on Egyptians and Libyans." In O. Reverdin, ed., *Hérodote et les peuples non-grecs*, Entretiens sur l'Antiquité Classique 35: 215–54. Geneva.

Long, A. A.

1974   *Hellenistic Philosophy.* London.

1978   "Timon of Phlius: Pyrrhonist and Satirist." *Proceedings of the Cambridge Philological Society*, n. s., 24: 68–91.

Long, A. A., and D. N. Sedley

1987   *The Hellenistic Philosophers.* Cambridge.

Mackenzie, S. L.

1984   *The Chronicler's Use of the Deuteronomistic History.* Atlanta.

Macurdy, G. H.

1932   *Hellenistic Queens: A Study in Woman-Power in Macedonia, Seleucid Syria and Ptolemaic Egypt.* Baltimore.

Magen, I.

1986   "A Fortified Town of the Hellenistic Period on Mount Gerizim." *Qadmoniot* 19: 91–101. [In Hebrew]

1989   "The History and Archaeology of Shechem (Neapolis) in the First through Fourth Centuries A.D." Dissertation, Hebrew University of Jerusalem. [In Hebrew]

1990   "Mount Gerizim: A Temple City." *Qadmoniot* 23: 70–96. [In Hebrew]

1992   "Mount Gerizim: A Hellenistic Temple City." In Z. H. Erlich and Y. Eshel, eds., *Judea and Samaria*, 37–60. Jerusalem. [In Hebrew]

Mahaffy, J. R.

1895   *The Empire of the Ptolemies.* London.

1898   *A History of Egypt under the Ptolemaic Dynasty.* London.

Majumdar, R. C.

1958   "The Indika of Megasthenes." *Journal of the American Oriental Society* 78: 273–76.

1960   "The Indika of Megasthenes." *Journal of the American Oriental Society* 80: 248–50.

1960a   *Megasthenes and Arrian.* Calcutta.

Malamat, A.

1953   "The Historical Background of the Assassination of Ammon, King of Judah." *Israel Exploration Journal* 3: 26–29.

Malherbe, A. J.

1977   *The Cynic Epistles.* Missoula.

Malitz, J.

1983   *Die Historien des Poseidonios.* Munich.

Malkin, I.

1987   *Religion and Colonization in Ancient Greece.* Leiden.

1987a   The State in Ancient Greece and the Oracle of Delphi." In
         J. Gafni and G. Motzkin, eds., *Priesthood and Monarchy*, 31–49.
         Jerusalem. [In Hebrew]

Marcus, R.
1937   "Alexander the Great and the Jews." In R. Marcus, ed., *Josephus*
        VI: 512–26. Cambridge, Mass. *[LCL]*
1938   "An Outline of Philo's System of Education." In I. Silberschlag
        and J. Twersky, eds., *Touroff Festschrift*, 223–31. Boston.
1943   *Josephus*. Vol. VII. Cambridge, Mass. *[LCL]*

Marrou, H. I.
1937   *Saint Augustin et la fin de la culture antique*. Paris.
1956   *A History of Education in Antiquity*. New York.

McCrindle, J. W.
1877   *Ancient India as Described by Megasthenes and Arrian*. Cal-
        cutta.

McDougall, J. I.
1983   *Lexicon in Diodorum Siculum*. Hildesheim.

Meecham, H. G.
1935   *The Letter of Aristeas*. Manchester.

Meisner, N.
1970   *Untersuchungen zum Aristeasbrief*. Berlin.
1973   "Aristeasbrief." In W. G. Kümmel, ed., *Jüdische Schriften aus
        hellenistisch-römischer Zeit* II.1: 35–85. Gütersloh.

Meizler, B.
1945   "Geva and Harosheth ha-Goyiim." *Bulletin of the Israel Ex-
        ploration Society* 11: 35–41. [In Hebrew]

Mélèze-Modrzejewski, J.
1989   "The Image of the Jew in Greek Thinking." In A. Kasher, G.
        Fuks, and U. Rappaport, eds., *Greece and Rome in Eretz Israel*,
        3–14. Jerusalem. [In Hebrew]

Mendels, D.
1983   "Hecataeus of Abdera and a Jewish 'Patrios Politeia' of the Per-
        sian Period (Diod. 40.3)." *Zeitschrift für die alttestamentliche
        Wissenschaft* 95: 96–110.
1988   "'Creative History' in the Hellenistic Near East in the Third
        and Second Century BCE: The Jewish Case." *Journal for the
        Study of the Pseudepigrapha* 2: 13–20.
1990   "The Polemical Character of Manetho." *Studia Hellenistica*
        30: 91–110.

Mendelson, A.
1982   *Secular Education in Philo of Alexandria*. Cincinnati.

Mendelssohn, L.
1897   *Aristeae Quae Fertur ad Philocratem Epistulae Initium*. Ed. M.
        Krachenimnikov. Dorpat.

Meshel, Z.
1978   "The Fortresses Controlling Jericho and Their Identification." In E. Netzer, Z. Meshel, and M. Rozen–Ayalon, *Jericho*, 35–57. Jerusalem. [In Hebrew]

Meshorer, Y.
1982   *Ancient Jewish Coinage*. Vol. I. New York.
1989   "The Mint of Azotos and Ascalon at the End of the Persian Period." *Eretz Israel* 20: 287–91. [In Hebrew]

Meshorer, Y., and S. Qedar
1991   *The Coinage of Samaria in the Fourth Century B.C.E.* Jerusalem.

Meyer, E.
1921   *Ursprung und Anfänge des Christentums*. Vol. II. Stuttgart.
1928   "Gottesstaat, Militärherrschaft und Ständewesen in Ägypten." *Sitzungsberichte der preussischen Akademie der Wissenschaften, Phil.-hist. Klasse*, 28: 495–532.

Meyers, C. L., and E. M. Meyers
1987   *Haggai and Zechariah 1–8*. The Anchor Bible, no. 25B. New York.

Mildenberg, L.
1979   "Yehud: A Preliminary Study of the Provincial Coinage of Judea." In O. Mørkholm and N. Waggoner, eds., *Greek Numismatics and Archaeology: Essays in Honor of M. Thompson*, 183–96. Wetteren.
1988   "Über das Kleingeld in der persischen Provinz Judäa." In H. Weipert, ed., *Palästina in vorhellenistischer Zeit*, 721–28. Munich.

Millar, F.
1979   "The Background to the Maccabean Revolution: Reflections on Martin Hengel's 'Judaism and Hellenism.'" *Journal of Jewish Studies* 24: 1–21.

Milne, J. G.
1928   "Egyptian Nationalism under Greek and Roman Rule." *Journal of Egyptian Archaeology* 14: 226–34.

Minns, E. H.
1915   "Parchments of the Parthian Period from Avroman in Kurdistan." *Journal of Hellenic Studies* 35: 22–65.

Mitford, T. B.
1959   "Helinos, Governor of Cyprus." *Journal of Hellenic Studies* 79: 94–131.

Mitteis, L.
1915   "Zwei griechische Rechtsurkunden aus Kurdistan." *Zeitschrift der Savigny-Stiftung für Rechtsgeschichte, Römanistische Abteilung*, 36: 425–29.

Momigliano, A.

1930   *Prime linee di storia della tradizione maccabaica.* Rome.

1932   "Per la data e la caratteristica della lettera di Aristea." *Aegyptus* 12: 161–72.

1934   "Josephus as a Source for the History of Judaea." In *The Cambridge Ancient History* X: 884–87. Cambridge.

1975   *Alien Wisdom.* Cambridge.

1980   "The Date of the First Book of the Maccabees." In A. Momigliano, *Sesto contributo alla storia degli studi classici e del mondo antico* II: 361–66. Rome.

Montgomery, J. A.

1907   *The Samaritans: The Earliest Jewish Sect—Their History, Theology and Literature.* Philadelphia.

Moore, J. F.

1927   "Simon the Righteous." In *Jewish Studies in Memory of Israel Abrahams,* 348–64. New York.

Mooren, L.

1975   *The Aulic Titulature in Ptolemaic Egypt.* Brussels.

1977   *La hiérarchie de cour ptolémaïque.* Louvain.

Mor, M.

1989   "Samarian History: The Persian, Hellenistic and Hasmonaean Periods." In A. D. Crown, ed., *The Samaritans,* 1–18. Tübingen.

Mørkolm, O.

1966   *Antiochus IV of Syria.* Copenhagen.

Mørkholm, O., P. Grierson, and U. Westerman

1991   *Early Hellenistic Coinage from the Accession of Alexander to the Peace of Apamea.* Cambridge.

Mortley, R.

1978   "L'historiographie profane et les Pères." In P. Benoit, N. Philonenko, and C. Vogel, eds., *Paganisme, judaïsme, christianisme: Influences et affrontements dans le monde antique—Mélanges offerts à Marcel Simon,* 315–27. Paris.

Moser, G.

1914   "Untersuchungen über die Politik Ptolemaios' I. in Griechenland (323–285)." Dissertation, Leipzig.

Mosis, R.

1973   *Untersuchungen zur Theologie des chronistischen Geschichtswerk.* Freiburg.

Mras, K.

1944   "Ein Vorwort zu neuen Eusebius-Ausgabe." *Rheinisches Museum für Philologie* 92: 217–36.

1954–56 *Eusebius' Werke: Die Praeparatio Evangelica.* 8 vols. Berlin.

Müller, J. G.

1877   *Des Flavius Josephus Schrift gegen den Apion.* Basel.

Müller, K. E.
 1972–80 *Geschichte der antiken Ethnographie und ethnologischen Theoriebildung.* 2 vols. Wiesbaden.

Murray, O.
 1967 "Aristeas and Ptolemaic Kingship." *Journal of Theological Studies* 18: 337–71.
 1970 "Hecataeus of Abdera and Pharaonic Kingship." *Journal of Egyptian Archaeology* 56: 141–71.
 1972 "Herodotus and Hellenistic Culture." *Classical Quarterly* 22: 200–213.
 1973 "The Date of Hecataeus' Work on Egypt." *Journal of Egyptian Archaeology* 59: 163–68.
 1975 Review of *Diodorus Siculus, Book I,* by A. Burton. *Journal of Hellenic Studies* 95: 214–15.

Naʿaman, N.
 1989 "Population Changes in Palestine following Assyrian Deportations." *Cathedra* 54: 43–62. [In Hebrew]

Newell, E. T.
 1916 *The Dated Alexander Coinage of Sidon and Acre.* Oxford.
 1927 *The Coinage of Demetrius Poliorketes.* London.
 1938 *The Coinage of the Eastern Seleucid Mints.* New York.

Nickelsburg, G. W. E.
 1981 *Jewish Literature between the Bible and the Mishnah: A Historical and Literary Introduction.* Philadelphia.
 1984 "Stories of Biblical and Early Post-Biblical Times." In M. Stone, ed., *Jewish Writings of the Second Temple Period,* Compendia Rerum Iudaicarum ad Novum Testamentum II.2: 33–88. Assen.

Niese, B.
 1888 *Flavii Josephi Opera.* Vol. V. Berlin.

Nilsson, M. P.
 1940 *The Greek Popular Religion.* New York.
 1961 *Geschichte der griechischen Religion.* 2d ed. 2 vols. Munich.

Nock, A. D.
 1959 "Posidonius." *Journal of Roman Studies* 49: 1–15.
 1962 "Sources of Diodorus." *Classical Review* 12: 50–51.
 1972 *Essays on Religion and the Ancient World.* 2 vols. Oxford.

Norden, E.
 1913 *Agnostos Theos.* Leipzig.
 1922 *Die germanische Urgeschichte in Tacitus' Germania.* 2d ed. Stuttgart.
 1923 "Tacitus und Josephus." *Neue Jahrbücher für das klassische Altertum* 31: 637–80.

North, R.

1974   "Does Archeology Prove Chronicles Sources?" In *Old Testament Studies in Honor of J. M. Myers*, 375–401. Philadelphia.

Oden, R. A.

1978   "Philo of Byblos and Hellenistic Historiography." *Palestine Exploration Quarterly* 110: 115–26.

Oldfather, C. H.

1933   *Diodorus of Sicily*. Vol. I. Cambridge, Mass. *[LCL]*

Olmstead, A. T.

1936   "Intertestamental Studies." *Journal of the American Oriental Society* 56: 242–57.

1948   *History of the Persian Empire*. Chicago.

Oppenheim, A. L.

1984   "The Babylonian Evidence of Achaemenian Rule in Mesopotamia." In *The Cambridge History of Iran* II: 529–87. Cambridge.

Oppenheimer, A.

1977   *The 'Am ha-Aretz*. Leiden.

Oren, E. D., and U. Rappaport

1984   "The Necropolis of Maresha–Beth Govrin." *Israel Exploration Journal* 34: 114–53.

Otto, W.

1934   *Zur Geschichte der Zeit des 6. Ptolemäers*. Munich.

Otto, W., and H. Bengtson

1938   *Zur Geschichte des Niederganges des Ptolemäerreiches: Ein Beitrag zur Regierungszeit des 8. und des 9. Ptolemäers*. Munich.

Palm, J.

1955   *Über Sprache und Stil des Diodoros von Sizilien*. Lund.

Parke, H. W.

1967   *Greek Oracles*. London.

Parke, H. W., and D. E. W. Wormell

1956   *A History of the Delphic Oracle*. Oxford.

Paton, W. R., and E. L. Hicks

1891   *The Inscriptions of Cos*. Oxford.

Pearson, L.

1939   *Early Ionian Historians*. Oxford.

Pease, A. S.

1963   *M. Tulii Ciceronis: De Divinatione*. 2d ed. Darmstadt. [Originally published in *Illinois Studies in Language and Literature* 6 (1920): 161–500; 8 (1923): 153–474]

Pelletier, A.

1962   *La lettre d'Aristée à Philocrate*. Paris.

Peremans, W.
1967   "Diodore de Sicile et Agatharcide de Cnide." *Historia* 16: 432–55.

Peterson, H.
1958   "Real and Alleged Literary Projects of Josephus." *American Journal of Philology* 79: 259–74.

Pfeffer, F.
1975   *Studien zur Mantik in der Philosophie der Antike*. Berlin.

Pfligersdorffer, G.
1959   "Studien zu Poseidonius." *Sitzungsberichte der österreichischen Akademie der Wissenschaft in Wien, Phil.-hist. Klasse*, 232.5: 100–146. Vienna.

Plant, R.
1979   *Greek Coin Types and Their Identification*. London.

Plicher, E. J.
1921   "A Philistine Coin from Lachish." *Palestine Exploration Quarterly* 53: 134–41.

Plöger, O.
1955   "Die makkabäischen Burgen." *Zeitschrift des deutschen Palästina-Vereins* 71: 141–72.

Pollard, J.
1977   *Birds in Greek Life and Myth*. London.

Poole, R. S.
1873   *British Museum Coins: Italy*. London.
1882   *British Museum Coins: The Ptolemies, Kings of Egypt*. London.

Popp, H.
1958   *Die Einwirkung von Vorzeichen, Opfern und Festen auf die Kriegführung der Griechen im 5. und 4. Jahrhundert v.Chr.* Erlangen.

Porten, B.
1968   *Archives from Elephantine*. Berkeley and Los Angeles.
1979   "Aramaic Papyri and Parchments: A New Look." *The Biblical Archaeologist* 42: 74–104.
1984   "The Jews in Egypt." In *The Cambridge History of Judaism* I: 372–400. Cambridge.

Posner, G.
1936   *La première domination perse en Égypte: Recueil d'inscriptions hiéroglyphiques*. Cairo.

Préaux, C.
1939   *L'économie royale des Lagides*. Brussels.
1978   *Le monde hellénistique*. 2 vols. Paris.

Preisigke, F.
1924   *Wörterbuch der griechischen Papyrusurkunden*. Heidelberg.

Pritchett, W. K.
1974–91   *The Greek State at War*. 5 vols. Berkeley and Los Angeles.

Pucci Ben Zeev, M.

1993   "The Reliability of Josephus Flavius: The Case of Hecataeus' and Manetho's Accounts of Jews and Judaism—Fifteen Years of Contemporary Research." *Journal for the Study of Judaism in the Persian, Hellenistic and Roman Periods* 24: 215–35.

Qimron, E.

1991/2 "Concerning the Blessing over King Jonathan." *Tarbiẓ* 61: 565–67.

Radin, M.

1915   *The Jews among the Greeks and Romans.* Philadelphia.

Rahmani, L. Y.

1971   "Silver Coins of the Fourth Century B.C. from Tel Gamma." *Israel Exploration Journal* 21: 158–60.

Rajak, T.

1973   "Justus of Tiberias." *Classical Quarterly* 67: 345–68.

1981   "Roman Intervention in a Seleucid Siege of Jerusalem?" *Greek, Roman and Byzantine Studies* 22: 65–81.

1987   "Josephus and Justus of Tiberias." In L. H. Feldman and G. H. Hata, eds., *Josephus, Judaism and Christianity*, 81–94. Detroit.

Rappaport, R.

1965   "Jewish Religious Propaganda and Proselytism in the Period of the Second Commonwealth." Dissertation, Hebrew University of Jerusalem. [In Hebrew]

1970   "The Dating of the Letter of Aristeas." In B. Oded and U. Rappaport, eds., *Studies in the History of the Jewish People and the Land of Israel: Memorial to Z. Avineri* I: 37–50. Haifa. [In Hebrew]

1981   "The First Judean Coinage." *Journal of Jewish Studies* 32: 1–17.

1984   "Numismatics." In *The Cambridge History of Judaism* I: 25–59. Cambridge.

1990   "The Samaritans in the Hellenistic Period." *Zion* 55: 373–96. [In Hebrew]

1993   "Galilee between the Hasmonean Revolt and the Roman Conquest." In A. Oppenheimer and J. Gafni, eds., *Jews and Judaism in the Second Temple, Mishna and Talmud Periods: Festschrift S. Safrai*, 16–30. Jerusalem. [In Hebrew]

Reese, J. M.

1970   *Hellenistic Influence on the Book of Wisdom and Its Consequences.* Rome.

Reicke, B.

1969   *The New Testament.* London.

Reifenberg, A.

1940   *The Ancient Jewish Coins.* Jerusalem. [In Hebrew]

Reinach, T.
1895   *Textes d'auteurs grecs et romains relatifs au Juifs et judaïsme.* Paris.
1930   *Flavius Josèphe: Contre Apion.* Paris. [Budé]
Reinhardt, K.
1921   "Hekataios von Abdera und Demokrit." *Hermes* 47: 492–513.
1928   *Poseidonius über Ursprung und Entartung.* Heidelberg.
Reitzenstein, R.
1901   *Zwei religionsgeschichtliche Fragen nach ungedruckten griechischen Texten der strassburger Bibliothek.* Strassburg.
Reynolds, L. D., and N. G. Wilson
1974   *Scribes and Scholars.* 2d ed. Oxford.
Rice, E. E.
1983   *The Grand Procession of Ptolemy Philadelphus.* Oxford.
de Rijk, L. M.
1965   "Enkylios Paideia: A Study of Its Original Meaning." *Vivarium* 3: 79–85.
Robert, L.
1963   "Samothrace 2.1: Fraser, the Inscriptions on Stone." *Gnomon* 35: 50–79.
Robin, L.
1944   *Pyrrhon et le scepticisme grec.* Paris.
Robinson, E. S. G.
1948   "Greek Coins Acquired by the British Museum 1938–48." *Numismatic Chronicle,* 6th ser., 8: 43–59.
Rofé, A.
1986   "Promise and Desertion: Eretz Israel and the Beginning of the Second Commonwealth." *Cathedra* 41: 3–10. [In Hebrew]
Rohde, E.
1876   *Der griechische Roman und seine Vorläufer.* Kiel.
Rolfe, J. C.
1940   *Ammianus Marcellinus.* 3 vols. Cambridge, Mass. *[LCL]*
Roll, I., and E. Ayalon
1989   *Apollonia and Southern Sharon.* Tel Aviv. [In Hebrew]
Rostovtzeff, M.
1940   *The Social and Economic History of the Hellenistic World.* 3 vols. Oxford.
Rouse, W. H. D.
1902   *The Greek Votive Offerings.* Cambridge.
Sacks, K. S.
1990   *Diodorus Siculus and the First Century.* Princeton.
Safrai, S.
1981   *Die Wallfahrt im Zeitalter des zweiten Tempels.* Neukirchen.

Safrai, Z.
1981 "The Description of Palestine in the 'Geography' of Claudius Ptolemaeus." *The Annual of Bar-Ilan University, Studies in Judaica* 18–19: 270–86.

Samuel, A. E.
1967 *Ptolemaic Chronology.* Munich.

Sandmel, S.
1979 *Philo of Alexandria.* New York.

Sartori, M.
1984 "Storia, utopia e mito nei primi libri della Bibliotheca Historicà di Diodoro Siculo." *Athenaeum* 62: 492–536.

Scaliger, J.
1598 *De Emendatione Temporum.* 3d ed. Frankfurt.
1628 *Epistulae Omnes.* Frankfurt.
1629 *De Emendatione Temporum.* 4th ed. Cologne.

Schäfer, P.
1977 "The Hellenistic and Maccabaean Periods." In J. H. Hayes and J. M. Miller, eds., *Israelite and Judaean History,* 539–604. London.

Schalit, A.
1949 "A Chapter in the History of the Parties Conflict in Jerusalem in the Fifth and the Beginning of the Fourth Century." In M. Schwabe and I. Guttman, eds., *Commentationes Iudaico-Hellenisticae: In Memoriam Iohannis Lewy,* 252–72. Jerusalem. [In Hebrew]
1960 "The Letter of Antiochus III to Zeuxis Regarding the Establishment of Jewish Military Colonies in Phrygia and Lydia." *Jewish Quarterly Review* 50: 289–318.
1967/8 "Die Eroberung des Alexander Jannaeus in Moab." *Theokratia* 1: 3–50.
1968 *Namenwörterbuch zu Flavius Josephus.* Leiden.
1969 *König Herodes.* Berlin.

Schaller, B.
1963 "Hekataios von Abdera über die Juden: Zur Frage der Echtheit und die Datierung." *Zeitschrift für die neutestamentliche Wissenschaft* 54: 15–31.

Schlatter, A.
1893 *Zur Topographie und Geschichte Palästinas.* Stuttgart.
1925 *Geschichte Israels von Alexander dem Grossen bis Hadrian.* 3d ed. Stuttgart.

Schmid, P. B.
1947   *Studien zu griechischen Ktisissagen.* Freiburg, Switzerland.

Schmid, W., and O. Stählin
1920   *Geschichte der griechischen Literatur.* 6th ed. Munich.

Schmidt, F.
1924   *Die Pinakes des Kallimachos.* Kiel.

Schnabel, P.
1923   *Berossos und die babylonisch-hellenistische Literatur.* Berlin.

Schnee, H.
1952–55 *Die Hoffinanz und der moderne Staat.* 3 vols. Berlin.

Schneider, G. J.
1880   *De Diodori Fontibus.* Berlin.

Schofield, M., M. Burnyeat, and J. Barnes
1980   *Doubt and Dogmatism.* Oxford.

Scholfield, A. F.
1958–59 *Aelian: On the Characteristics of Animals.* 3 vols. Cambridge, Mass. *[LCL]*

Schott, A.
1930   "Die inschriftlichen Quellen zur Geschichte Eannas." In J. Jordan, ed., *Vorläufiger Bericht über Ausgrabungen in Uruk-Warka* I: 45–67. Berlin.

Schreckenberg, H.
1972   *Die Flavius-Josephus-Tradition in Antike und Mittelalter.* Leiden.

1977   *Rezeptionsgeschichtliche und textkritische Untersuchungen zu Flavius Josephus.* Leiden.

Schubart, W.
1921   *Das Buch bei den Griechen und Römern.* 2d ed. Berlin.

Schubert, W.
1937   "Das hellenistische Königsideal nach Inschriften und Papyri." *Archiv für Papyrusforschung* 12: 1–26.

Schürer, E.
1901–9 *Geschichte des jüdischen Volkes in Zeitalter Jesu Christi.* 4th ed. Leipzig.

Schürer, E., G. Vermes, and F. Millar, eds.
1973–86 *The History of the Jewish People in the Age of Jesus Christ.* 3 vols. Edinburgh. [Vol. III also ed. M. Goodman]

Schwanbeck, E. A.
1846   *Megasthenis Indica.* Bonn.

Schwartz, D. R.
1982   "KATA TOYTON TON KAIPON: Josephus' Source on Agrippa II." *The Jewish Quarterly Review* 72: 241–68.

1984   "Philo's Priestly Descent." In F. E. Greenspahn, E. Hilgert, and B. L. Mack, eds., *Nourished with Peace: Studies in Hellenistic Judaism in Memory of Samuel Sandmel,* 155–71. Chico.

1990   "On Some Papyri and Josephus' Sources and Chronology for the Persian Period." *Journal for the Study of Judaism* 21: 175–99.

Schwartz, E.
1885   "Hekataeos von Teos." *Rheinisches Museum für Philologie* 40: 223–62.

Schwartz, M.
1985   "The Religion of Achaemenian Iran." In *The Cambridge History of Iran* II: 664–97. Cambridge.

Schwartz, S.
1990   "Georgius Syncellus's Account of Ancient Jewish History." In *Proceedings of the Tenth World Congress of Jewish Studies,* division B, vol. II: 1–8. Jerusalem.

Sedley, D.
1983   "The Motivation of Greek Skepticism." In M. F. Burnyeat, ed., *The Skeptical Tradition,* 9–30. Berkeley and Los Angeles.

Seeligmann, I. L.
1948   *The Septuagint Version of Isaiah.* Leiden.
Seibert, J.
1981   *Alexander der Grosse.* Darmstadt.
1983   *Das Zeitalter der Diadochen.* Darmstadt.
Sellers, O. R.
1933   *The Citadel of Beth Zur.* Philadelphia.
Sethe, K.
1904   *Hieroglyphische Urkunden der griechisch-römischen Zeit.* Vol. I. Leipzig.

Sethna, K. D.
1960   "Rejoinder to R. C. Majumdar." *Journal of the American Oriental Society* 80: 243–48.

Sevenster, J. N.
1975   *The Roots of Pagan Anti-Semitism in the Ancient World.* Leiden.

Seyrig, H.
1971   "Le monnayage de Hiérapolis de Syrie à l'époque d'Alexandre." *Revue Numismatique,* 6th ser., 13: 11–21.

Shatzman, I.
1990   *The Armies of the Hasmonaeans and Herod.* Tübingen.
1992   "The Hasmonaeans in Greco-Roman Historiography." *Zion* 57: 5–64. [In Hebrew]

Sherwin-White, S.
1978   *Ancient Cos.* Göttingen.

Shroyer, M. J.
1936   "Alexandrian Jewish Literalists." *Journal of Biblical Literature* 55: 261–84.

Sinclair, T. A.
1951   *A History of Greek Political Thought*. London.

Sint, J. A.
1960   *Pseudonymität in Altertum: Ihre Formen und ihre Gründe*. Innsbruck.

Sirinelli, J., and E. de Places
1974   *Eusèbe de Césarée: La Préparation Évangélique*. Paris.

Skeat, T. C.
1954   *The Reigns of the Ptolemies*. London.

Smallwood, E. M.
1970   *Philonis Alexandrini Legatio ad Gaium*. Leiden.

Smith, M.
1971   *Palestinian Parties and Politics That Shaped the Old Testament*. New York.

Smith, S.
1924   *Babylonian Historical Texts Relating to the Capture and Downfall of Babylon*. London.

Spaer, A.
1977   "Some More Yehud Coins." *Israel Exploration Journal* 27: 200–203.
1979   "The Coin of Jeroboam." *Israel Exploration Journal* 29: 218.
1986/7   "Jaddua the High Priest?" *Israel Numismatic Journal* 9: 1–3.

Speyer, W.
1971   *Die literarische Fälschung im heidnischen und christlichen Altertum*. Munich.

Spoerri, W.
1959   *Späthellenistische Berichte über Welt, Kultur und Götter: Untersuchungen zu Diodorus von Sizilien*. Basel.
1961   "Zu Diodorus von Sizilien." *Museum Helveticum* 18: 63–82.
1979   "Hekataios (4)." In *Der kleine Pauly* II: 980–82. Munich.

Stein, E.
1929   *Die allegorische Exegese des Philo aus Alexandria*. Giessen.
[as M. Stein]
1934   "Pseudo-Hecataeus: The Date and Purpose of His Book on the Jews." *Zion* 6: 1–11. [In Hebrew; reprinted in M. Stein, *The Relationship between Jewish, Greek and Roman Cultures* (Tel Aviv 1970) 82–92]
1937   *Philo of Alexandria*. Warsaw. [In Hebrew]
1938   *Religion and Science*. Krakow. [In Hebrew]

Sterling, G. E.
1992   *Historiography and Self-Definition: Josephus, Luke-Acts and Apologetic Historiography*. Leiden.

Stern, E.
1982   *Material Culture of the Land of the Bible in the Persian Period, 338–332 B.C.* Warminster.

Stern, M.
1961   "The Relations between Judaea and Rome during the Rule of John Hyrcanus." *Zion* 26: 1–22. [In Hebrew]

1962   "Notes on the Story of Joseph the Tobiad." *Tarbiz* 32: 35–47. [In Hebrew]

1965   *The Documents on the History of the Hasmonaean Revolt.* Tel Aviv. [In Hebrew]

1968   "The Description of Eretz Israel by Pliny the Elder and the Administrative Division of Judea at the End of the Second Temple Period." *Tarbiz* 37: 215–29.

1973   "Hecataeus of Abdera and Theophrastus on Jews and Egyptians." *Journal of Egyptian Archaeology* 59: 159–63.

1974–84   *Greek and Latin Authors on Jews and Judaism.* 3 vols. Jerusalem.

1976   "The Jews in Greek and Latin Literature." In S. Safrai and M. Stern, eds., *The Jewish People in the First Century: Historical Geography, Political History, Social, Cultural and Religious Life and Institutions,* Compendia Rerum Iudaicarum ad Novum Testamentum, I.2: 1101–59. Assen.

1981   "Judaea in the Days of Alexander Jannaeus." In L. I. Levine, ed., *The Jerusalem Cathedra* I: 22–47. Jerusalem.

1983   "The Jewish-Hellenistic Literature." In M. Stern, ed., *The Diaspora in the Hellenistic-Roman Period,* 208–37. Jerusalem. [In Hebrew]

1985   "The Relations between the Hasmonean Kingdom and Ptolemaic Egypt in View of the International Situation during the Second and First Centuries B.C.E." *Zion* 50: 81–106. [In Hebrew]

1991   *Studies in Jewish History: The Second Temple Period.* Jerusalem. [In Hebrew]

1993   "Timagenes of Alexandria as a Source for the History of the Hasmonean Monarchy." In A. Oppenheimer, J. Gafni, and M. Stern, eds., *Jews and Judaism in the Second Temple, Mishna and Talmud Periods: Festschrift S. Safrai,* 3–15. Jerusalem. [In Hebrew]

Stern, S.
1950   *The Court Jew.* Philadelphia.

Sternberg, F.
1991   *Antike Münzen,* Auction Catalogue No. 25, November 1991. Zurich.

Stough, C. L.
1969   *Greek Skepticism.* Berkeley and Los Angeles.

Sukenik, E. L.
1934   "Paralipomena Palaestinensia." *Journal of the Palestine Oriental Society* 14: 178–84.
1935   "More of the Oldest Coins of Judea." *Journal of the Palestine Oriental Society* 15: 341–43. [In Hebrew]

Susemihl, F.
1891   *Geschichte der griechischen Literatur in der Alexandrinerzeit.* 2 vols. Leipzig.

Svoronos, J. N.
1904   Τὰ νομίσματα τοῦ κράτους τῶν Πτολεμαίων. 4 vols. Athens.

Tadmor, H.
1973   "On the History of Samaria in the Biblical Period." In *Eretz Shomron: The Thirtieth Archaeological Convention of the Israel Exploration Society (September 1972)*, 67–74. Jerusalem. [In Hebrew]

Talmon, S.
1973   "Biblical Tradition on the Early History of the Samaritans." In *Eretz Shomron: The Thirtieth Archaeological Convention of the Israel Exploration Society (September 1972)*, 19–33. Jerusalem. [In Hebrew]

Tarn, W. W.
1939   Review of *Zur Geschichte des Niederganges des Ptolemäerreiches*, by W. Otto and H. Bengtson. *Journal of Hellenic Studies* 59: 323–24.

Tarn, W. W., and G. T. Griffith
1952   *Hellenistic Civilisation.* 3d ed. London.

Tcherikover, V.
1927   *Die hellenistischen Städtegründungen von Alexander dem Grossen bis auf die Römerzeit.* Leipzig.
1937   "Palestine under the Ptolemies." *Mizraim* 4/5: 9–90.
1957   *Corpus Papyrorum Judaicarum.* Vol. I. Cambridge, Mass.
1957a   "Jewish Apologetic Literature Reconsidered." In *Symbolae R. Taubenschlag Dedicatae* III, Eos (Commentarii Societatis Philologae Polonorum) 48.3: 169–93. Warsaw.
1958   "The Ideology of the Letter of Aristeas." *Harvard Theological Review* 51: 59–85.
1961   *Hellenistic Civilization and the Jews.* 2d ed. Philadelphia.
1961a   *The Jews in the Greco-Roman World.* Jerusalem. [In Hebrew]
1963   *The Jews in Egypt in the Hellenistic-Roman Age in Light of the Papyri.* Jerusalem. [In Hebrew]

Thackeray, H. St. J.
1902   "The Letter of Aristeas." In H. B. Swete, ed., *An Introduction to the Old Testament in Greek*, 531–606. Cambridge.

1903   "Translation of the Letter of Aristeas." *Jewish Quarterly Review* 15: 337–91.

1904   *The Letter of Aristeas.* London.

1909   *A Grammar of the Old Testament in Greek according to the Septuagint.* Cambridge.

1918   *The Letter of Aristeas, Translated, with an Appendix of Ancient Evidence on the Origin of the Septuagint.* London.

1926   *Josephus.* Vol. I. Cambridge, Mass. *[LCL]*

Thissen, H. J.

1966   *Studien zum Raphiadekret.* Meisenheim.

Thompson, M., and A. R. Bellinger

1955   "The Hoard of Alexander Drachms." *Yale Classical Studies* 14: 3–45.

Timmer, B. C. J.

1930   *Megasthenes en de indische maatschappij.* Amsterdam.

Torrey, C. C.

1954   *The Chronicler's History of Israel.* New Haven.

Tracy, S.

1928   "III Maccabees and Pseudo-Aristeas." *Yale Classical Studies* 1: 241–52.

Tramontano, R.

1931   *La lettera di Aristea a Filocrate.* Naples.

Treadgold, W. T.

1980   *The Nature of the Bibliotheca of Photius.* Washington, D.C.

von Treitschke, H.

1879   "Herr Graetz und seine Judentum." *Preussische Jahrbücher* 44: 661–70. [15 October 1879]

Trichel, J.

1974   "Étude pétrographique de la roche constituante la statue de Darius découverte à Suse en décembre 1972." *Cahiers de la Délégation Archéologique Française en Iran* 4: 57–59.

Troiani, L.

1977   *Commento storico al "Contro Apione" di Giuseppe.* Pisa.

Trüdinger, K.

1918   *Studien zur Geschichte der griechisch-römischen Ethnographie.* Basel.

Tsafrir, Y.

1975   "The Desert Fortresses in the Time of the Second Temple." *Qadmoniot* 8: 41–53. [In Hebrew]

1975a   "The Location of the Seleucid Akra in Jerusalem." *Revue Biblique* 82: 501–52.

1983   "The Circumference of Jerusalem and the Course of Its Wall." In H. Tadmor, ed., *The Restoration: The Persian Period,* 66–72. Tel Aviv. [In Hebrew]

Turner, E. G.
1968   *Greek Papyri*. Oxford.
1971   *Greek Manuscripts of the Ancient World*. Oxford.
Uebel, F.
1968   *Die Kleruchen Ägyptens unter den ersten sechs Ptolemäern.*
        Berlin.
Uffenheimer, B.
1961   *The Visions of Zechariah*. Jerusalem. [In Hebrew]
Veltri, G.
1992   *Eine Tora für den König Talmai*. Tübingen.
Vincent, H.
1908   "Jerusalem d'après la Lettre d'Aristée." *Revue Biblique* 17:
        520–32.
1909   "Jerusalem d'après la Lettre d'Aristée." *Revue Biblique* 18:
        555–75.
1949   "Les épigraphes judéo-araméennes post-exiliques." *Revue Bib-
        lique* 56: 274–94.
Vinogradov, J.
1981   *Olbia: Geschichte einer altgriechischen Stadt am Schwarzen
        Meer.* Konstanzer Althistorische Vorträge und Forschungen,
        ed. W. Schuller, Heft 1. Constance.
Virgilio, B.
1972   "I termini di colonizzazione in Erodoto e nella tradizione
        preerodotea." *Atti della Accademia delle Scienze di Torino,
        Classe di Scienze Morali, Storiche et Filologiche*, 106: 345–406.
Vlastos, G.
1946   "On the Pre-history of Diodorus." *American Journal of Philol-
        ogy* 67: 51–60.
Wacholder, B. Z.
1963   " 'Pseudo-Eupolemos': Two Greek Fragments on the Life of
        Abraham." *Hebrew Union College Annual* 34: 83–113.
1971   "Hecataeus of Abdera." In *Encyclopaedia Judaica* VIII: 236–37.
        Jerusalem.
1974   *Eupolemus: A Study of Judaeo-Greek Literature*. Cincinnati.
Wachsmuth, K.
1860   *Die Ansichten der Stoiker über Mantik und Dämonen*. Leipzig.
1871   "Ein Dekret des ägyptischen Satrapen Ptolemaios I." *Rhein-
        isches Museum für Philologie* 26: 463–72.
1895   *Einleitung in das Studium der alten Geschichte*. Leipzig.
Waddel, W. G.
1940   *Manetho*. Cambridge, Mass. *[LCL]*
Walbank, F. W.
1957–79 *A Historical Commentary on Polybius*. 3 vols. Oxford.
Walker, J.
1941   *Catalogue of the Arab-Sassanian Coins*. London.

1956   *A Catalogue of the Arab-Byzantine and Post-Reform Umaiyad Coins.* London.

Walter, N.

1964   *Der Thoraausleger Aristobulos: Untersuchungen zu seinen Fragmenten und zu pseudepigraphischen Resten der jüdisch-hellenistischen Literatur.* Berlin.

1965   "Zu Pseudo-Eupolemus." *Klio* 43/45: 282–90.

1967–68   *Untersuchungen zu den Fragmenten der jüdisch-hellenistischen Historiker.* Halle.

1976   *Historische und legendarische Erzahlungen: Fragmente jüdisch-hellenistischer Historiker.* Band 1, Lieferung 2 of W. G. Kümmel, ed., *Jüdische Schriften aus hellenistisch-römischer Zeit.* Gütersloh.

1989   "Jewish Greek Literature of the Greek Period." In *The Cambridge History of Judaism* II: 385–408. Cambridge.

Walton, F. R.

1955   "The Messenger of God in Hecataeus of Abdera." *Harvard Theological Review* 48: 255–57.

1967   *Diodorus of Sicily.* Vol. XII. Cambridge, Mass. [LCL]

Wardy, D.

1979   "Jewish Religion in Pagan Literature during the Late Republic and Early Empire." In H. Temporini and W. Haase, eds., *Aufstieg und Niedergang der römischen Welt* 19.1: 592–644. Berlin.

Weinberg, S. S.

1971   "Tel Anafa: The Hellenistic Town." *Israel Exploration Journal* 21: 86–109.

Weinfeld, M.

1964   "The Universal Tendention and Separatism in the Time of the Jewish Restoration." *Tarbiẓ* 33: 228–42. [In Hebrew]

Weische, A.

1961   *Cicero und die neue Akademie: Untersuchungen zur Entstehung und Geschichte des antiken Skeptizismus.* Aschendorff.

Welles, C. B.

1934   *Royal Correspondence in the Hellenistic Period.* New Haven.

1949   "The Ptolemaic Administration in Egypt." *Journal of Juristic Papyrology* 3: 39–44.

Wellhausen, J.

1905   *Prolegomena zur Geschichte Israels.* 6th ed. Berlin.

Welten, P.

1973   *Geschichte und Geschichtsdarstellung in den Chronikbüchern.* Neukirchen.

Wendland, P.
1900   "H. Willrich, *Judaica*: Forschungen zur hellenistisch-jüdischen Geschichte und Literatur." *Berliner philologische Wochenschrift* 39: 1197–1204.
1900a   "Der Brief des Aristeas." In E. Kautzsch, ed., *Die Apokryphen und Pseudepigraphen des Alten Testaments* II: 1–31. Tübingen.
1912   *Die hellenistisch-römische Kultur in ihren Beziehungen zu Judentum und Christentum: Die urchristlichen Literaturformen.* Tübingen.

Wendland, P., and L. Mendelssohn
1900   *Aristeae ad Philocratem Epistula.* Leipzig.

Werner, R.
1971   "Probleme der Rechtsbeziehungen zwischen Metropolis und Apoikie." *Chiron* 1: 19–73.

Whittaker, M.
1984   *Jews and Christians: Greco-Roman Views.* Cambridge.

Widengren, G.
1977   "The Persian Period." In J. H. Hayes and J. M. Miller, eds., *Israelite and Judaean History*, 489–538. Philadelphia.

von Wilamowitz-Moellendorff, U.
1881   *Antigonos von Karystos.* Berlin.
1931   *Der Glaube der Hellenen.* Berlin.

Will, E.
1967   *Histoire politique du monde hellénistique.* 2 vols. Nancy.

Will, E., and C. Orrieux
1986   *Ioudaismos-Hellenismos: Essai sur le judaisme judéen à l'époque hellénistique.* Nancy.

Williamson, H. G. M.
1977   *Israel in the Book of Chronicles.* Cambridge.
1977a   "The Historical Value of Josephus' *Jewish Antiquities* XI.297–301." *Journal of Theological Studies* 28: 49–66.

Willrich, H.
1895   *Juden und Griechen vor der makkabäischen Erhebung.* Göttingen.
1900   *Judaica: Forschungen zur hellenistisch-jüdischen Geschichte und Literatur.* Göttingen.
1924   *Urkundenfälschung in der hellenistisch-jüdischen Literatur.* Göttingen.

Winnicki, J. K.
1981   "Griechisch-demotische Soldatenkorrespondenz aus Pathyris (Gebelen)." In *Proceedings of the Sixteenth International Congress of Papyrology*, 547–52. Chico.
1989   "Militäroperationen von Ptolemaios I. und Seleukos I. in Syrien in den Jahren 312–311 v.Chr." *Ancient Society* 20: 55–92.

1991   "Militäroperationen von Ptolemaios I. und Seleukos I. in Syrien in den Jahren 312–311 v.Chr." *Ancient Society* 22: 147–201.

Winston, D.

1979   *The Wisdom of Solomon.* New York.

Wolfson, H. A.

1948   *Philo: Foundations of Religious Philosophy in Judaism, Christianity and Islam.* 2d ed. Cambridge, Mass.

Wright, G. E.

1965   *Shechem: The Biography of a Biblical City.* New York.

Yadin, Y.

1965   *Masada: First Season of Excavations, 1963–64.* [*Israel Exploration Journal* 15: 1–120; in Hebrew.]

1977   *The Temple Scroll.* 3 vols. Jerusalem.

Yankelevitch, R.

1980   "The Concept of Galut in Jewish Thought of the Ancient Period." In *Proceedings of the Tenth World Congress of Jewish Studies,* division C, vol. I: 69–76. Jerusalem.

Zambrini, A.

1982   "Gli Ἰνδιϰά di Megasthene." *Annali della Scuola Normale Superiori de Pisa, Classe di Lettere e Filosofia* 12: 71–149.

1985   "Gli Ἰνδιϰά di Megasthene." *Annali della Scuola Normale Superiori de Pisa, Classe di Lettere e Filosofia* 15: 781–853.

Zeitlin, S.

1925   "Simon the Just and Kenesset ha-Gedolah." *Ner Maʿaravi* 2: 137–42. [In Hebrew]

1950   *The First Book of the Maccabees.* New York.

Zimmermann, F.

1912   *Die ägyptische Religion nach der Darstellung der Kirchenschriftsteller und die ägyptischen Denkmäler.* Paderborn.

Zipser, M.

1871   *Des Flavius Josephus Werk "Über das hohe Alter des jüdischen Volkes gegen Apion."* Vienna.

Zornius, P.

1730   *Hecataei Abderitae Philosophi et Historici His Mille Adhinc Annis Longe Celeberrimi Eclogae sive Fragmenta Integri Olim Libri de Historia et Antiquitatibus Sacris Veterum Ebraeorum Graece et Latine cum Notis Iosephi Scaligeri et Commentario Perpetuo Petri Zornii.* Altona.

Zuntz, G.

1958   "Zum Aristeas-Text." *Philologus* 102: 240–46.

1959   "Aristeas Studies." *Journal of Semitic Studies* 4: 21–36, 109–26.

Index of Names and Subjects

Aaron, 214
Abraham, 190, 213
Acre, 72, 258n14, 262. *See also*
    Ptolemaïs
Adida, 123
Adora, 131, 133
Aesop, 155
Agatharcides of Cnidus, 14, 73
    ethnography of, 205–7
    on Jews' treatment by Ptolemy I,
        74–75, 76, 77–78n73
Agrippa I, 84, 112n182, 165
Agrippa II, 84
Akra. See under Jerusalem
Alcimus, 88n107
Alexander (brother of Philo), 175
Alexander (the Great), 69n52
    annexes Samaria to Judea (ac-
        cording to Pseudo-Heca-
        taeus), 52, 53, 114, 116–21,
        134–35, 227, 229, 247
    coins of, 258n14, 261
    death of, 46, 47
    in India, 202, 203
    Jews in army of, 48, 49, 50, 51,
        229
    settles Jews in Alexandria, 114,
        115n194, 246
Alexander Balas, 118, 243
Alexander Jannaeus, 136, 160, 177
    conquests of, 103n152, 125, 127,
        128, 138–39
    destroys pagan cults, 130, 132–
        33
    as leader of all Jews, 236

saved from Ptolemaic occupation
    by Egyptian Jews, 242–43,
    252
Alexander Polyhistor, 54–55,
    103n156, 186, 189, 190
Alexander Zabinas, 278, 291, 292
Alexandria
    compared with Jerusalem, 110
    Jewish community of, 171–80,
        227
    Jews settled in by Alexander,
        114, 115n194, 296
    Library, 183
    persecution of Jews in, 285–86
    Pseudo-Hecataeus's familiarity
        with, 146, 147
Amathos, 138n54
Ammaus, 282
Ammonitis, 137, 138
Ananias, 241, 242, 243, 244
Andreas, 286–87n55
Andron of Alexandria, 300
Anthedon, 127, 132
Antigonus Monophthalmus, 82,
    225, 257, 299
Antigonus of Carystus, 59n18
Antiochus III, 220n99
Antiochus IV Epiphanes, 129
    death of, 138n56
    defiles Temple, 161, 164
    persecutes Jews, 81, 90, 92, 93,
        122, 241, 301
Antiochus VII Sidetes, 19,
    112n182, 127, 215, 277, 291
Antiochus VIII Gryphus, 131, 292,

Antiochus VIII Gryphus (continued) 293
Antiochus IX Cyzicenus, 127, 131, 136, 242, 278, 292
Antiochus XII Dionysius, 139n58
Antipatris, 291
anti-Semitism, 1, 5, 39n98, 215, 295; three libels, 281, 288
Antonius Julius, 110
Aphairema, 108, 116, 282
Apollo, 60–61
Apollodorus of Cyzicus, 9
Apollonia, 125, 130
Apollonius Molon, 189
Arados, 262
Arethusa, 259n17
Argives, 209
Aristeas the Exegete, 189–90
Aristeas of Proconnesus, 199n59
Aristobulus (philosopher), 148, 155, 159, 173
Aristobulus I, 130, 132
Aristobulus II, 165n101
Aristocles, 59n18
Aristotle, 97
Ark of the Covenant, 167
Artaphanus, 100n146, 159, 190
Artaxerxes I, 265
Artaxerxes II, 265
Artaxerxes III, 144
Artemidorus of Ephesus, 67n48, 206
Artemisia, 298
Ascalon, 125, 127, 130, 133, 262, 273n7
Ascanius, 8n5
Asia Minor, 267
Ayalon Valley, 108
Azotos (Ashdod), 273n7, 282, 295
  coins of, 262
  conquered by John Hyrcanus, 125, 130
  pagan altars and temples destroyed, 129

Babylon, 262
Babylonia, 13, 16, 267
  Jews deported to, 48, 49, 55, 87, 96, 101, 143–44
Bacchides, 106, 123
Bagoses (Bagoas), 92, 93
Barag, Dan, 263–64
Beer Sheva, 133
Bel, temple of, 48, 49
Belus, 209
Ben Sira, 177–78
Berenice I, 268–69, 298, 299
Berossus the Babylonian, 158, 191, 192
Beth Basi, 123
Beth El, 108
Beth Zur, 106, 108, 123
Bickerman, E., 279, 281n33, 282, 286–87n55
Brunner, H., 70n53
Bucolopolis, 104n158
Burkert, W., 65n41, 68n50
Burton, A., 289
Byblos, 262

Cadmus, 19, 29, 209
Calanus, 96
Callimachus, 183
Callixenus, 166n107
Canaan, 32, 41, 100, 180, 220, 221, 222, 225
Carneades, 64, 69
Cassiodorus, 45
Castor, 46, 47, 185n11
Channuka, 301
Charon of Lampsacus, 10
Cicero, 63–64
Cilicia, 260, 262
Cimon, 259n17
circumcision, 23, 24, 210, 246
Clearchus, 54n2, 96, 97, 182
Cleopatra II, 285, 292, 300, 301–2
Cleopatra III, 139, 287n55, 293, 301
  Jewish army commanders of,

136, 241–43, 285–86
Colchi, 209, 210
Cos, 269, 298–99
Crocodilopolis, 104n158
Cross, F. M., 82
Ctesias, 192, 199
Cyprus, 15, 242, 267
Cyrenaica, 267, 268

Damascus, 213
Damocritus the Tactician, 189, 191
Danaus, 19, 29, 209, 210
Daniel, 92, 93–95
Daphne (Antioch), 241
Darius I, 265
David, City of, 110–13
David, King, 164
Dead Sea, 216
Demetrius (chronographer), 155,
    191
Demetrius I, 77, 117, 118
Demetrius I or II, 214
Demetrius II, 291
Demetrius III, 138n56
Democritus, 9, 16
Deuteronomy, 222
Diodorus
    abbreviates Hecataeus, 15, 197,
        209, 210–11
    criticized by Photius, 18–19, 21
    lacks originality, 194–95
    use of Agatharcides, 205–7
    use of Hecataeus, 24, 194–99,
        207–11, 189–90, 296
    use of Megasthenes, 200–205
Diogenes of Sinope, 62n31, 64, 155
Dionysus, 201, 202
divination and omens. *See also*
    Mosollamus story
    Cicero on, 63–64
    disciplina auguralis, 66–67
    Egyptian, 59–60, 69–70n53
    Greek, 58, 61, 62–64, 65, 66–69
    Hecataeus on, 58–60
    in Hellenistic period, 65n41

Jewish disdain for, 2
    Lucian on, 69n52
    Pliny on, 63n33
    Porphyry on, 63n33
    Xenophon on, 62
Dok, 123
Dora, 104n158, 127, 132, 273n7
Dositheus, 178, 241

Egypt. *See also* Alexandria; *names
    of individual rulers*
    divination in, 59–60, 69–70n53
    ethnographies of, 13, 193–97,
        209
    influence of, 16
    Jews deported to, 74, 79, 144
    Jews expelled from, 28–29
    Jews migrate to, 48, 49, 78–79,
        81, 225–26, 228, 234–35,
        237–38, 239–40, 244–45
    Jews persecuted in, 301
    religion of, 98–99
Elah Valley, 282
Eleazer the Martyr, 90
Eleutheros River, 104n158
Engeddi, 281n32
epitomē, 24, 56, 157
Esdralon (Jezreel) Valley, 132, 282
Esther, 92, 93, 238
Esther Scroll, 178, 238
Ethiopia, 206–7
ethnography. *See also* geography;
    history; *nomina; origo*
    Greek, 10–11
    Hecataeus's contributions to,
        9–10, 13–14
    Hellenistic, 11–13, 23
    structure of, 191–219, 250
    utopian, 12–13
Euhemerus, 12, 13n17, 154, 173,
    274n9
Eupolemus, 144, 155, 160
Exodus, 32, 100, 190, 215, 225, 234
    Hezekiah story as antithesis to,
        227, 229

Exodus *(continued)*
  mentioned by Hecataeus, 32, 41
  not mentioned by Pseudo-
    Hecataeus, 220, 230, 232,
    234
Ezra, 90, 238

founder *(ktistēs)*, 26, 31

Gadara, 138, 294
Galaditis, 138, 139
Galilee, 103n152, 108, 109, 119,
  132
Gauger, J. D., 115n194, 185n11
Gaulanitis, 138n56, 139, 294
Gaza
  battle of, and destruction of by
    Ptolemy, 46, 47, 55, 72, 74,
    77, 78, 79, 107, 185n11, 229
  coins of, 262
  destruction of by Alexander Jan-
    naeus, 127, 132–33, 273n7,
    284–85, 292–94
  geography, 229, 231
  in Greek ethnographies, 10, 12,
    22, 217, 218
  in Pseudo-Hecataeus, 250
  in Tacitus, 215, 216
Gezer, 106, 123, 125, 129, 291
Glucker, John, 8–9n5
Goodman, M., 271n1
Great Revolt, 103n152, 109, 110,
  114n189, 127, 217
  Idumea at time of, 281n32
  size of Jerusalem at time of, 112
Greek. *See also* ethnography
  education, 148–59, 178–79, 180
  influence on Hezekiah coins, 261
Guttman, Joshua, 35–36n90

Hasmonean period. *See also*
  names of specific rulers
  conquest during, 124–28, 137
  construction of fortresses during,
    123–24, 277–78

Diaspora Jews during, 236–37
tithe practices, 159–60
violence against foreign religions, 97, 128–34, 135, 294–
  95
Hebron Hills. *See* Idumea
Hecataeus of Abdera. *See also*
  under Diodorus; Moses;
  nomina; origo
  ascription of *On Abraham* to,
    2–3, 54
  ascription of *On the Jews* to,
    1–6, 248
  attitude toward Jews, 39–40
  attitude toward divination and
    omens, 58–60, 69
  attitude toward paganism, 98–99
  on High Priests, 20, 26, 27, 29,
    33–34, 36n92, 42
  influenced by Herodotus, 194
  on Jerusalem and the Temple,
    27, 57
  Josephus on, 46, 47
  life, 7–9
  On the Egyptians, 2, 9n9, 13–
    18, 22, 24, 28, 29n65, 37, 38,
    189, 194
    audience of, 16–17
    beginning of, 295–96
    dating of, 15, 55
    errors in, 26
    Jewish excursus in appendix of
      the *origo* section, 3, 15–16,
      18–20, 22–37, 39–43, 207–11,
      297–98
  On the Hyperboreans, 3, 9, 39,
    60–61, 189, 198–99, 199n59
  purpose of using his name on
    On the Jews, 248
  structure of ethnographies, 9–10,
    13–18, 194–99, 202–3
Hecataeus of Miletus, 10, 192–93
Hecatomnids, 298
Heliopolis, 69n52
Helkias, 241, 242–43, 244

Hellanicus of Lesbos, 10
Hellenistic Judaism, 148
  allegorists, 172–76, 247
  conservatives, 176–80
  literature of, 153
  religious divisions in, 169–80
  syncretists, 170–71
Hellenistic literature. *See also*
    ethnography
  book titles, 187–88
Heracles, 201, 202, 298
Hermippus, 184
Herod, 84
Herod Agrippa. *See* Agrippa I;
    Agrippa II
Herodotus, 11, 193–94, 199
Herennius Philo, 1, 184–85, 191.
    See also Philo of Biblos
Hesiod, 9
Hezekiah, King, 164
Hezekiah coins, 85–86, 255–66
Hezekiah story
  absence of Greek philosophical
    terms in, 150–51
  analyzed, 221–28
  as antithesis to Exodus, 227, 229
  influenced by Hecataeus, 153
  and Josephus, 82, 83, 84, 226
  modeled after Moses tradition,
    227–28
  not written by Hecataeus, 80, 88
  omissions from, 238
  role in *On the Jews*, 220, 229–
    30, 232–48, 251
  as substitute for *origo*, 250
  text of, 46, 47
  understood by Josephus, 226
  unknown to Pseudo-Aristeas,
    78–79, 80, 139
  unreliability of, 71–72, 79–81,
    88–89
Hezekiah the Governor, 86–88, 90,
    244, 251, 264, 265
Hieronymus of Cardia, 72–73, 74,
    77, 109, 183

Hierapolis, 69n52
High Priests. *See also* Hezekiah
    story; *individual high priests
    by name*
  in command of citadel of Jeru-
    salem, 274
  Hecataeus on, 20, 26, 27, 29,
    33–34, 36n92, 42
  non-migration of, 81–82
  records of, in Persian and Hel-
    lenistic periods, 70–71, 82–84
  replacement of, 233n3
  Samaritan, 89n108
  selection of, in Roman period,
    84–85, 88n107
history
  in Greek ethnographies, 10, 12,
    22, 219
  in Tacitus, 216–17
Homer, 9, 16
Hyperboreans, 9, 60–61, 99, 198–
    99
Hyrcania, 87, 144

Iaddous (Jaddua), 82, 83
Iamnia (Jabneh), 125, 130, 127n17,
    273n7, 282
Idumea, 108, 131, 137, 138n53,
    279–82, 292
India, 199, 200–201, 202, 203–4
infanticide, 153
Ipsus, 74, 77, 78, 79, 270, 299
Isaiah (Greek translation), 236
Israel, 213
Iturea, 132

Jacoby, Felix, 14, 208, 210, 211
Jaeger, Werner, 26n52, 30
Jaffa, 123, 129–30, 273n7
  destroyed by Ptolemy, 72
  occupation and expulsion of
    population by Simeon, 125,
    128, 283, 291
Jason (High Priest), 88n107
Jason of Cyrene, 149, 155, 159, 168

Jeremiah, 90
Jericho, 108, 216
Jericho Valley, 108, 109, 214, 284
Jerusalem. *See also* Temple
  Akra, 106, 123, 125n8, 129, 276, 278
  Antonia, 277
  citadel, 273–78
  compared with Alexandria, 110
  countryside around, 279–80
  founding of, 19, 30
  Hecataeus on, 27
  Josephus on, 110, 112
  map, 111
  population, 112–13
  Pseudo-Aristeas on, 110, 233, 273–80
  Pseudo-Hecataeus on, 48, 49, 50, 51, 146
  Ptolemy's capture of, 74–75, 76–77
  size, 110
  Strabo on, 109. *See also* Temple
Jesus, 90
Jews. *See also* anti-Semitism; Exodus; Great Revolt; Hasmonean period; Hellenistic Judaism; High Priests; Jerusalem; Judea; Moses; Pentateuch; Septuagint; Torah; Temple; *and see under* Alexandria; Babylonia; Egypt
  in army of Alexander, 48, 49, 50, 51, 246
  destroy pagan cults and temples, 97, 100, 128–34, 246
  emigrate to Phoenicia, 101, 104–5
  ethnographies on, 189–91, 207–17
  expelled from Egypt, 28–29
  God of, 34–35, 34–35n84
  hostile toward strangers, 20, 23, 29, 99
  idealized in Hellenistic

  ethnography, 54
  persecuted by Persians, 91–97
  in royal service, 96, 136, 238–39, 241–44, 251–52, 285–86
Job, 179, 190
Johanan, 82–83, 87, 93, 259n17, 263–65
John Hyrcanus, 160, 215
  conquests of, 108, 116, 125, 127, 128, 135, 138, 242, 279, 280, 283, 291–92
  constructs *Baris*, 277–78
  destroys pagan cults, 130–32
Jonathan, 123, 137
  annexes southern Samaria, 116, 117, 134
  appointed High Priest, 118–19n204
  destroys pagan temples, 129, 243–44
Jordan Valley, 242
Joseph, 190, 213
Joseph and Asenath, 159
Josephus
  on agricultural qualities of Jewish territory, 109
  on violence against pagan cult, 100
  Contra Apionem, 44, 89n108, 183, 184, 288
  on Hecataeus, 46, 47
  on Hezekiah story, 226
  on Jerusalem, 110, 112
  list of High Priests, 70–71, 82–84
  on Moses, 100
  on *On the Jews*, 1, 182–83
  selection of passages from *On the Jews*, 186, 221, 239
  use of Megasthenes, 201–2n67
Joshua, 33, 128, 151n40
Judah, tribe of, 280
Judas Maccabaeus, 90, 129
Judea
  characteristics of, 109–10

fortresses in, 48, 49, 105–7, 123–24
overpopulated, 28, 49, 101, 127, 244
size, 108

Kalanoi, 96
Karnak, Demotic inscription (year 103), 136n50
Kasher, A., 294–95
katoikēsis, 221, 222, 223, 225, 227, 234
Kaufmann, I., 93
Klein, S., 106n167, 112n185
Kosher food, 246, 287n57
ktisis (foundation story), 22, 30, 31, 32, 208. See also *origo*
On the Jews not, 230–31

Larissa, 259n17
Lebanon Valley, 132
Leontopolis, 90, 147, 166, 177, 241, 247
Levites, 159
Lewy, Hans
advocates authenticity of *On the Jews*, 4, 152, 185–86n13
on Hecataeus quote in Pseudo-Aristeas, 140–41
on Hezekiah story, 150, 221–22
on Mosollamus story, 64, 155
on Pseudo-Hecataeus on Temple, 154
Lod, 282. *See also* Lydda
Lycurgus, 16
Lydda, 18, 116, 124n7, 282

Maccabean Revolt, 104n159, 117, 287
Maccabees, I, 277n18
Maccabees, II, 159, 169, 176, 177, 178, 285, 301–2
Maccabees, IV, 149, 159
Magas, 268, 269, 299
Mallus, 72

Manetho, 100, 158, 192
Marcus, R., 293
Marisa, 131, 133, 279, 292, 294
Marriage and burial customs, 23, 23n45
Mazdi, 257–58, 260
Medeba, 138
Megasthenes, 54n2, 199–205
Menecles of Barca, 300
Menelaus (High Priest), 88n107
Meshorer, Y., 256, 266
Middot, 163
Mildenberg, L., 258
Millar, F., 88n107, 225
Mishna, 85, 167n107
misoxenia, 35, 39, 99
Moabitis, 137, 138, 294
Mordecai, 238
Moses, 164
in gentile ethnographies, 191
Hecataeus on, 18, 19–20, 21, 22, 23, 26, 27n56, 29, 30–31, 32, 33, 41, 42, 298
as "High Priest," 90
in Jewish ethnographies, 190
Josephus on, 100
omitted by Pseudo-Hecataeus, 57, 230, 232, 234, 246
Pompeius Trogus on, 213–14
Strabo on, 212, 213
tradition, as basis for Hezekiah story, 227–28
Mosollamus story, 2, 57–58
grammar of, 156–57
inspiration for, 69n52
as Jewish fabrication, 71
not written by Greek, 61–62, 64, 65–66, 68, 150, 151–52, 155
text of, 50–53
Mount Carmel, 103–4
Mount Ephraim, 283
Mount Gerizim, 83n87, 292
destroyed by John Hyrcanus, 116, 131, 133, 138n53, 279, 294

Mount Gerizim (continued)
  Ptolemy sends captives from to
    Egypt, 75
Mount Shomron, 114n189
Murray, Oswyn, 15
Musaeus, 16

Nearchus, 199, 203
Nebuchadnezzar, 201, 202
Nehemiah, 112n185, 238, 298
Nicanor, 76
Nicarchus, 189, 191
Nicolaus, 293, 294
Niese, B., 44
nomina (customs)
  in Agatharcides, 206–7
  in Hecataeus, 22–23, 24, 25, 30,
    31, 32, 40–41, 195, 196, 197,
    198, 208, 209, 210, 211, 213
  in Hellenistic ethnographies,
    218, 219, 250
  in Herodotus, 10
  in Megasthenes, 201, 203–5
  in Pseudo-Hecataeus, 229, 231,
    250
  in Tacitus, 215–16
Numenius, 184

Obedas I, 138n56
On Abraham, 2–3, 141, 185, 188
Onias (army commander of Ptolemy VI), 241
Onias (army leader of Cleopatra II), 241
Onias III (High Priest), 82, 241
Onias IV, 90–91, 166, 177, 241,
  243, 244
Ophel, 110
Origen, 184–85
origo or origo-archaeologia
  in Agatharcides, 206, 207
  in Hecataeus, 22, 23, 24, 25, 31,
    40–41, 195, 196, 198–99,
    203, 209, 210, 211
  in Hellenistic ethnographies, 12,

217–18, 219
  in Herodotus, 10
  lacking in Pseudo-Hecataeus,
    220, 229, 230, 250
  in Megasthenes, 200–202, 204,
    205
  in Pompeius Trogus, 213, 214
  in Strabo-Posidonius, 212, 213
  in Tacitus, 215
Orpheus, 16

paideia, 33
Palimbothra, 200
Pallas Athene, 261
Panaetius, 64, 69, 300
Paneion, in Alexandria, 146n23
Panium (in Coile Syria), 81n81
Paralia, 104n159
Passover, 235
  Second, 245
patrios politeia, 21
Pegae, 291
peḥah (governor), 86–87, 257–58
Pella (in Trans-Jordan), 133, 295
Pelusium, 104n158
Pentateuch, 160, 179, 222. See also
    Septuagint; Torah
  fabrications in, 79
  Hecataeus quotes from, 27
  idealization of Holy Land in, 108
  influence of Hellenism on, 173
  not referred to by Pseudo-
    Hecataeus, 161, 222, 223
  purity of priests demanded by,
    145
  used by conservative Hellenistic
    Jews, 176
Peraea, 109, 137, 138
Persian period. See also individual
    rulers by name
  coinage, 267
  extent of Judea in, 108
  High Priest in, 86
  Jews in royal service in, 95
  name "Phoenicia" in, 103

treatment of Jews in, 91, 92, 94, 101
Persian Wars, 67
Pharisees, 176, 177
Philadelphia, 137n52
Philo Judaeus, 162, 179
    compared with Pseudo-Hecataeus, 149, 159, 169
    on Egyptian Jews, 176
    as Hellenistic Jew, 148, 173–74, 175
    on Jerusalem and Temple, 147, 160
    on Jewish residence abroad, 245–46
Philo of Byblos (Herennius Philo), 1, 3, 54, 58, 61, 103n56, 189
Phoenicia, 267
    coins of, 260, 262
    defined, 103–4
    Jewish emigration to, 48, 49, 101, 104–5
    map, 102
    subjugated by Ptolemy I, 72–73
phoros (tribute), 119–20, 134, 291
Photius, 18–21, 78n73, 205, 207, 213, 244, 250
Plato, 16, 184
politeia, 153, 222, 223, 225, 228, 234
Pompeius Trogus, 109, 213–15
Pompey, 21, 23, 24, 217, 294
Posidonius (unknown), 67n48
Posidonius of Apamea, 109, 212, 213, 290, 300
priests. *See also* High Priests
    receive greater lots, 28, 35, 42
    receive tithes, 159, 160
Protagoras, 16
Proverbs, 179
Psammeticus, King, 39, 60
Psellus, Michael, 67n48, 68n49
Pseudo-Aristeas, 155
    absence of Hezekiah story in, 78–79, 80, 139

audience of, 287–88
borrowing from Hecataeus by, 140–41
compared with Pseudo-Hecataeus, 142, 149, 152, 179, 181, 233, 234
dating of, 139, 271, 277, 278, 284–86
on Egyptian Jews, 169, 174
on Greek religion, 152
as Hellenistic Jew, 148
Hezekiah story unknown to, 78–79, 80, 139
idealization of holy land and Jerusalem by, 272
on Jerusalem, 110, 272–80
on Temple, 160, 168
on treatment of Jews, 74, 76, 78–79, 80
Pseudo-Eupolemus, 190
Pseudo-Hecataeus, *On the Jews*. *See also* Hezekiah story; Mosollamus story; *under* Temple
    audience, 246–48
    authenticity advocated, 3–5, 54–58, 152, 185–86n13
    authenticity challenged, 3–4, 54–56, 57, 58, 249
    author, 55, 57, 143, 145–47, 249–50
        Greek education of, 148–59
        Jewish education, 159–68
        knowledge of Temple, 57, 145, 147, 150, 154, 159, 160–68, 250
        not Hellenistic Jew, 181
        religious-cultural position of, 169, 180
    compared with Pseudo-Aristeas, 142, 149, 152, 179, 181, 233, 234
    contents summarized, 1–2
    dating of, *terminus ante quem*, 137–39, 243, 249

Pseudo-Hecataeus, *On the Jews*
(continued)
dating, *terminus post quem*,
122–39, 243, 249
Exodus not mentioned, 220, 230,
232, 234
importance, 6
issues in evaluating, 56
on Jerusalem, 48, 49, 50, 51, 146
length, 186–87
mistakes, 145
Moses not mentioned, 57, 230,
232, 234, 246
nomina, 229, 231, 250
not *ktisis*, 230–31
origo lacking, 220, 229, 230, 250
Pentateuch not mentioned, 161,
222, 223
structure, 250
title, 188–89
tone, 2
Ptolemaic period. *See also individuals by name*
Jerusalem in, 275–76
Samaria in, 116
Ptolemaïs, 103n152, 136n50,
273n7. *See also* Acre
Ptolemy I, 8, 38, 185n11, 220
coinage at time of, 266–67
on coins, 258, 263, 269, 270
deports Jews, 55, 74, 228, 244,
250–51
philanthrōpia of, 46, 47, 73–74,
152, 232, 251
as successor of pharaohs, 16
treatment of Jews, 74–78, 79, 80,
225–26, 248
treatment of occupied lands, 72–
74
Ptolemy II, 115n192, 166, 268,
269, 271, 299
Ptolemy IV, 38–39, 247
Ptolemy VI, 166, 241, 243, 285
Ptolemy VIII, 237, 241, 292
persecution of Jews, 247, 285,

286, 301–2
personality of, 285, 299–300
Ptolemy X, 139
Ptolemy Lathyrus, 241, 293
invasion of Judea, 136, 242–43,
244, 249
persecution of Jews, 139
Pyrrho, 9, 59
Pythagoras, 184

Qumran Scrolls, 162

Ramathaim, 108, 116, 282
Raphia, 38–39, 127, 132
Rappaport, U., 256
Roman-Jewish War, 217
Rostovtzeff, M., 299–300

Sabbath, 91, 92, 214, 246
Sacks, K. S., 290
sacrifice, 20, 23, 32
Sadducees, 176
Salamis (Cyprus), 15
Samaga, 138
Samareitis, 114n189, 116n198, 283,
283n41
Samaria (city), 72, 133
Samaria (region), 262
agricultural qualities of, 109
annexation to Judea by Alexander, 52, 53, 114, 116–21,
134–35, 220n99, 227, 229,
247
annexation of southern, to
Judea, 282–83
coins of, 257
conquest of by John Hyrcanus,
108, 131–32, 134, 135, 279,
292
map of southern, 118
name of, 114n189
Ptolemy I in, 72, 75
referred to in Pseudo-Aristeas,
282–83
Samos, 99

Sandracottus (Candragupta), 199, 202

Scaliger, Josef, 3–4

Schoinometrēsis Syriae, 111n182

Schwartz, Eduard, 14

Scopas, 81n81

Scroll of Fasting, 294

Scythians, 193–94

Scythopolis, 128, 132, 134, 292, 295

Seleucid period, 13, 81, 105
  conquests by Jews in, 129, 130–31
  fortresses in Judea in, 106
  Samaria in, 116. *See also individual rulers by name*

Septuagint
  efforts to legitimize, 142, 172, 233, 287–88
  influence of language of, 167, 168
  on Jewish migration to Egypt, 234–36
  not used by Pseudo-Hecataeus, 142n76, 180
  rejection of by conservative Jews, 176, 178
  used by allegorists, 172
  used by author of Wisdom of Solomon, 179

Shatzman, I., 123, 294–95

Shechem, 116, 131n29, 133, 190n27, 294

Shephela, 123, 124n7
  southern, 282

Sheshbazzar, 298

Sibylline Oracles, 180, 248

Sidon, 72, 81, 103, 105, 262

Simeon, 278
  conquests of, 125, 128, 283
  destroys foreign cults, 129–30
  fortifies Judea, 123, 124

Sinai, 104n158

Socrates, 62

Solomon, 161, 162

Solon, 16

Sophocles, 3, 185

Sparta, 35, 36

Stoics, 63, 173, 179

Strabo, 109, 212–13, 218

Stratonice, 75n68

Strato's Tower, 104n158, 125, 127, 130, 132, 273n7

Svoronos, J. N., 269

Syncellus, 125

Syria, 228
  Ptolemy's conquest of, 46, 47, 71, 72, 76–77, 225, 243

Syrian wars, 81n81, 275

Tacitus, 215–17

Tarichea, 109

Tarsus, 260

Tcherikover, V., 287, 297, 300, 301

Tel Anafa, 133

Telegonus, 67n48

Temple (Jerusalem)
  altars, 161–63, 167–68
  Baris protecting, 277
  citadel overlooking, 273–78
  First, destruction of, 143, 144
  golden lamp, 163
  golden table, 166–67
  Hecataeus on, 27, 57
  location, 113, 153–54
  Mount, 110, 123, 147, 276
  Pseudo-Aristeas on, 142n76
  Pseudo-Hecataeus on, 113, 142n76, 145, 147, 150, 154, 159, 160–68, 247, 250
  purification rituals in, 144–45
  Tabernacle, 161
  votive offerings, 164–66

Tennes, 87, 144

thaumasia, 10, 204, 207

Theodorus, 138n54, 190

Theodotus, 190, 190n27

Theophrastus, 54n2

theologoumena, 195

therapeutai, 171

Timagenes of Alexandria, 300
Timochares, 109, 110, 112n182
Timon, 59n18
Titus, 215, 216
Tobias, 137, 238
toparchy, 118, 124n7
Torah, 27, 28, 144, 175, 221–22,
    225
  prohibits returning to Egypt,
    251. *See also* Pentateuch
Trans-Jordan, 114n189, 129, 137,
    139, 295
Tyre, 103, 105, 258n14, 262

Vespasian, 109

Wacholder, B. Z., 115n192
Wadi Dâliyeh caves, 117, 260n18
Willrich, Hugo, 4, 56, 90,

105n162, 246
Wisdom of Solomon, 149, 159,
    169, 176, 178

xenēlasia, 35
Xenophanes, 98
Xerxes, 214

Yaddua, 86n99, 265
Yehud, 255, 257, 260, 261, 262
  coins of Ptolemaic period, 266–
    70
Yom Kippur, 171, 233n3, 242

Zadok, 84, 87, 89
Zeno of Citium, 98
Zeno papyri, 104n158
Zerubabel, 298
Zorn, Peter, 4

Index of Greek Terms
in Transcription

apanthrōpia, 32, 39, 42, 99
aphorologētos, 114, 134, 134n42
apoikia, 19, 30, 208, 211, 224n111,
    227n119, 228, 232, 245, 246
archē, 242n28
aroura, 108
asylia, 275

basileia, 146n23
bios, 197
bōmos, 167

chōra, 103, 134, 147, 284n45

despotēs, 226
diadochē, 83
dianoia, 91
diaphora, 221
diphthera, 221, 223nn108–109

ekthesis, 153
enkōmia, 151
enkratēs, 238n18
ephēbeion, 175
epikephalaia, 195
epistēmōn, 150
epitomē, 24, 56, 157, 213
ēthos, 224n112
eusebeia, 31, 150

grammatikos, 8, 157

homoiographon, 224
hyparchos, 257
hysēla, 167

katoikēsis, 153, 221, 222, 223, 225,
    227, 234
katoikia, 13, 30, 38n94, 208, 211,
    227n117
klēros, 20
klērouchia, 37, 38, 38n94
koinē, 153, 156
ktisis, 22, 26, 30, 31, 32, 208, 230,
    231n123
ktistēs, 30

logoi, 192, 193, 195n44

machimoi, 37, 38
mantis, 57, 64
meridarchēs, 243
mētropolis, 245, 246
misoxenia, 32, 39, 42, 99
monarchoi, 298, 299

neōs, 167
neoterismos, 273
nomima, 10, 22, 23, 25, 30, 31, 32,
    40, 41, 193, 195, 196, 197,
    203, 204n70, 205, 206, 208,
    209, 211, 212, 213, 218, 219,
    229, 250

oikistēs, 26
oiōnos, 66
origo or origo-archaeologia, 10,
    12, 22, 23, 24, 25, 31, 40–41,
    195, 196, 198–99, 200–202,
    203, 204, 205, 206, 207, 209,
    210, 211, 212, 213, 214,

origo (continued)
    215, 217–18, 219, 220, 229,
      230, 250
ornis, 66, 152

paideia, 33
paradoxa, 18
paradoxon, 98
patria, 245
patris, 276
philanthrōpia, 71, 73, 74n65, 89,
    152, 232, 251, 285
philanthrōpon, 153n46
philotimia, 226
phoros, 119, 120, 134, 134n42
phronimos, 150
pinakes, 183n3
plēthos, 20, 297
politeia, 153, 221, 222, 223, 225,
    228, 234, 237

pragmata, 237
prooimia, 290
prostasia, 20, 34, 297
prostatēs, 297

sophos, 150
sōter, 73, 78n73
stasis, 244
stratēgos, 243
symmigēs, 186
syngraphē, 223, 224n110
synēthēs, 224n112

thaumasia, 207
theologoumena, 195
thysiastērion, 167, 168
timē, 224, 225

xenēlasia, 20, 35

Index Locorum

GREEK, HELLENISTIC, AND ROMAN AUTHORS

Aelian
  De Natura Animalium
    I.48: 67n48
    V.34: 63n33
    VII.9: 66
    X.14: 66
    X.36: 63n33
    XI.1: 22n40, 61, 99, 99n142,
      198
    XII.4: 66
    XII.5: 98n137
    XIII.18: 200
    XVI.41: 204

Aeschylus
  SCT 26: 66n43
  SGT 24: 67n48
  Agam. 112: 66n43
  PV 487ff.: 67n48

Aesop (ed. Hausrath)
  no. 170: 62n31, 64

Ammianus Marcellinus
  XV.9–12: 217
  XXI.1.9: 62n33

Antiphon
  II.3.3: 223n109

Apollonius Rhodius, scholia to
  FGrH IIIA, 264 F 10, line 4:
  198, 198nn56,57

Appian
  Syriakē
    50 (252): 75

    52 (264): 76

Aristophanes
  Birds 719: 66n43

Aristotle
  Athen. Pol.
    2.2: 34n81
    20.4: 34n81
    21.1: 34n81
    21.8: 34n81
  De Caelo
    $278^{b}9$–24: 34n84
    $293^{b}32$–$294^{a}1$: 34n84
    $297^{a}8$: 34n84
  De Mundo (Ps. Arist.)
    $391^{b}19$–$392^{a}5$: 34n84
    $399^{a}1$–6: 34n84
  Phys.
    $203^{b}10$: 34n84
  Ethica Eudemia
    $1220^{b}38$ff.: 150
  Ethica Nicomachea
    $1095^{a}19$: 34n82
    $1095^{b}22$: 34n82
    $1102^{a}22$: 34n82
    $1114^{b}10$ff.: 150
  Hist. Anim.
    $IX.615^{b}2$: 61n30
  Politica
    $1265^{b}35$ff.: 36n92
    1266^{b}: 35n86
    $1267^{a}40$: 34n82

Aristotle, Politica (continued)
1269^{a}35: 35
1270^{a}18ff.: 35n86
1273^{a}34: 35
1297^{b}9: 34n82
1320^{b}7: 34n82
1326^{a-b}: 146n20
1326^{b}4ff.: 36n92
1327^{a-b}: 273n7
1331^a: 146n20, 274n9
1355^{b}20ff.: 36n92

Arrian
Anab.
II.26.4–27: 66n46
Indica
V.4–8: 202
V.9–13: 201
VII–IX.8: 201
VII.1–3: 200
VIII.6: 202
VIII.15.1–2: 204
VIII.15.8–12: 204
IX.8: 202
IX.10–12: 202
X: 200
XIII: 204
XIII–XV: 204
XV.5–7: 204n71
XVII.6: 200
XVII.6–7: 203
XVII.17: 203

Athenaeus
Deipnosophistae: 205
IV.153d: 205
IV.184: 299, 300
V.196: 166n107
V.199b–c: 166n107
XII.549d–e: 300
XII.549d–550a: 299
XII.549e–f: 300
XV.616: 78n73

Callimachus
Hymn V.123–24: 67n48

Cicero
De Divinatione
I.5: 58
I.12: 64
I.47: 96n131
I.74: 65n42
I.84: 58
I.85: 64n36
I.86: 58
I.87: 65n42
I.109: 67n48
I.118: 63
I.118–19: 63n33
I.120–21: 67n48
I.127: 67n48
II.9: 63n35, 65n39
II.16: 63n35
II.18–21: 63n35
II.30: 63n35
II.36: 63n35
II.35–39: 63n33
II.53: 63n35
II.56: 64n36
II.56–57: 63n35
II.72: 63n35, 76n45
II.76: 63n35, 76n45
II.80: 63n35, 64n36, 68n49
II.82: 68n49
II.82–83: 63n35
De Natura Deorum
I.36: 98n137
De Oratore
III.15.57: 151n40
Pro Flacco
62: 296
Rep.
V: 151n38
VI: 151n38
Tusc.
V.77: 96n131

Curtius Rufus
IV.6.12: 66n46
IV.8.9–11: 117
VIII.9.32: 96n131

Damastes
  FHG
    II.64.1: 189n22

Diodorus Siculus
  I: 14, 290
  I.7.1–3: 297
  I.7.4–8: 296
  I.8.4: 296
  I.8.7: 296
  I.8.9: 297
  I.9.6: 295
  I.10: 195, 296
  I.10ff.: 14
  I.10–29: 195
  I.11: 195
  I.11.2: 98
  I.11.4: 98
  I.11.5–6: 98
  I.12: 195
  I.12.9: 98, 99, 196n52
  I.13: 195
  I.13ff.: 13, 16
  I.13.1ff.: 98
  I.14–20: 196
  I.15.3–5: 98, 196n52
  I.18.2: 289
  I.20.2: 289
  I.21.1: 17n30
  I.21.9–10: 196n52
  I.21–27: 196
  I.23.2: 60
  I.23.5: 59
  I.24.2: 60
  I.24.5: 60
  I.25.2–3: 60
  I.25.3: 59, 60
  I.25.7: 59
  I.26.1: 17n30
  I.26.6–7: 98
  I.27.1: 24n47
  I.27.1–2: 16
  I.28: 296
  I.28–29: 13, 16, 22, 195, 208
  I.28.1: 208–9, 211

  I.28.2: 23, 29n66, 209, 210, 211
  I.28.3: 24, 209, 210
  I.28.4: 24n47
  I.28.4–29.5: 209
  I.29: 18n32, 296
  I.29.5: 209
  I.29.6: 195
  I.30–31: 195
  I.30–31.8: 15, 196
  I.30–41: 196
  I.30.1: 15
  I.30.4: 18
  I.31.9: 196
  I.32–41: 14, 195, 196
  I.39.5: 203
  I.39.5–42.2: 203
  I.40.1–41.5: 203
  I.41.10: 195, 197
  I.42.1: 297
  I.42.1–2: 195, 203
  I.42.2–68: 195, 197
  I.43–44: 203
  I.43.6: 17n30
  I.44.4–5: 197
  I.45.2–4: 98
  I.46.8: 289
  I.47: 96n131
  I.49.5: 98
  I.53.8: 59
  I.55.5: 210
  I.56.2: 98
  I.65.5–7: 59, 60
  I.66.10: 59, 60
  I.67.8–11: 39
  I.67.10–11: 18
  I.69–98: 195, 197
  I.69.1–2: 195
  I.69.2: 18, 197
  I.69.3–4: 16
  I.69.4: 18, 39
  I.69.5–6: 16
  I.69.6: 197
  I.69.7: 13, 17n30, 60
  I.70–71: 16
  I.70–72: 197

Diodorus Siculus *(continued)*
I.70.9: 59
I.70.11: 144n8
I.71.5: 197
I.72.2–3: 35
I.72.6: 197
I.73–74: 197
I.73.4: 16, 59, 60
I.73.7–9: 18n32, 24n48, 37n93
I.73.9: 33
I.74.6–7: 18n32, 290
I.75ff.: 16
I.75–80.2: 197
I.76: 18n32, 290
I.77.7: 153n54
I.80.3: 153n53
I.80.3–81: 197
I.80.6: 37n93
I.81.4–6: 59, 60
I.82: 197
I.83–90: 197
I.83.1: 98n137
I.83.6–8: 17n28
I.83.8: 59n21, 98n138
I.83.9: 99n138
I.84.4: 198
I.86ff.: 14
I.86.2: 17n30
I.86–90: 16
I.87.6–9: 70n53
I.87.7–9: 59, 66
I.87.9: 262n26
I.88.5: 18, 39
I.89.4: 98, 198
I.90.2–3: 98
I.90.2–4: 98
I.91–93: 197
I.94–95: 197
I.94.2: 24n48, 26
I.95.6: 24
I.96ff.: 16
I.96.2: 17n30
I.96–98: 197
I.98.3–4: 59, 60
I.98.5: 59

II.1–2: 195
II.4: 196
II.9.3: 146n21
II.35–37: 200
II.35–42: 200
II.35.4: 200
II.36.1: 200
II.36.2: 205n71
II.36.3: 202n67
II.36.4: 200
II.36.6–7: 200
II.37.3: 200
II.38–39: 200, 201n65, 203
II.38.2: 297
II.39: 201
II.39.1: 202n69
II.47: 198
II.47.1–2: 198
II.47.2: 99, 99nn141,142
II.47.2–3: 198
II.47.2–6: 198
II.47.4: 39
II.47.4–6: 198
II.47.5: 99n141
II.47.6: 61, 99, 198n56
II.48.9: 109
II.98.5–9: 99
III.2–7: 206
III.2–10: 205
III.2.1: 206
III.2.2–3: 206
III.2.4–3.1: 206
III.3.1–5.4: 206
III.5–7: 206
III.5.1–9.4: 206
III.6.3–4: 207
III.8: 206
III.9: 206
III.9.1–2: 207
III.10: 207
III.10.6: 207n77
III.11–12: 205
III.38.1: 207
V.42.4–46.7: 199
V.42.5: 198

V.42.6: 154n58, 274n9
V.42.6–44: 154n58
V.42.6–44.5: 154
V.47.4: 199n59
VI.1.6: 154, 154n58, 274n9
VI.1.6–10: 154n58
XVI.41.1: 104n160
XVII.50–51: 69n52
XVII.107: 96n131
XVIII.14.1: 73
XVIII.28.5–6: 73
XVIII.43: 76
XIX.55.6: 73
XIX.56.1: 73
XIX.58.1: 257
XIX.79.1–3: 72
XIX.79.4–6: 72
XIX.79.6: 72
XIX.80.4: 38, 69n53
XIX.85.3: 73
XIX.85.5: 72, 77
XIX.86.3: 73
XIX.93.4–6: 225
XIX.93.7: 72, 73n61, 76–77
XIX.95.2: 257
XIX.98: 109
XX.3: 66n46
XX.100.3: 78n73
XX.113: 77
XX.113.1–2: 72
XXXII–XXXVII: 290
XXXIII.6–6a: 299
XXXIII.12–13: 299
XXXIII.20: 299
XXXIII.22–23: 299
XXXIV–XXXVI.1–2: 29n67
XXXIV–XXXV.1.1–3: 23
XXXIV–XXXV.1.1–4: 24
XXXIV–XXXV.1.1–5: 19
XXXIV–XXXV.1.5: 134n42
XXXIV–XXXV.14.20: 299
XL: 18
XL.1a: 21
XL.2.2: 21n39, 24
XL.3.1: 21, 23n43, 30, 208, 210

XL.3.1–2: 22, 211
XL.3.1–3: 31, 208, 227
XL.3.1–8: 3, 18, 208
XL.3.2: 26, 28n65, 29, 32, 40, 210
XL.3.2–3: 22
XL.3.3: 22, 26, 27, 28n65, 30, 31, 34, 151, 153, 211, 228
XL.3.3–8: 208
XL.3.4: 3, 22, 23, 26, 27, 29, 32, 33, 34, 35, 39, 99, 141, 230
XL.3.4–5: 22, 27, 29
XL.3.4–6: 31
XL.3.5: 26–27, 28, 33, 34, 151, 297
XL.3.5–6: 22, 26, 27, 85
XL.3.6: 27, 29, 31, 33, 141
XL.3.6–7: 22
XL.3.7: 27, 28, 31, 33, 35, 55, 298
XL.3.7–8: 22
XL.3.8: 3, 22, 23, 24, 27, 31, 32, 35, 37, 153
XL.4–6: 297

Diogenes (Pseudo)
   EG, Diog. 38: 62n31, 64n38, 155n62

Diogenes Laertius
   IX.61: 9n5
   IX.62: 8n5
   IX.63: 8n5
   IX.64: 59n18
   IX.69: 8, 59
   IX.69–70: 8n5
   IX.115–16: 9n5

Dionysius of Halicarnassus
   Antiquitates Romanae
   I.12.1: 33n77
   I.13.3: 33n77
   I.22.2: 33n77
   II.7.1: 31
   II.7.4: 31n73
   II.15.1–3: 31n74

Dionysius of Halicarnassus
(*continued*)
De Comp. Verb.
IV.30: 74n65
Dionysius Periegetes
GGM II.160: 103–4n156
Euripides
Bacch. 347: 67n48
Phoen. 839: 66n43
Hellanicus
FHG
1.57: 189n22
1.92: 189n22
1.93: 189n22
Herodotus
I.131: 35n85
II.2: 193n43
II.2–4: 193
II.2–43: 193n43
II.2–182: 192
II.4.3: 193n43
II.5–34: 193
II.35–98: 193
II.37–76: 193
II.65.2: 98n137
II.99–182: 193
II.104: 209
II.151ff.: 60
III.5.91: 103n154
III.102–5: 204n71
IV.5–15: 194, 194n44
IV.5–82: 192
IV.11.4: 33n77
IV.13.1: 199n59
IV.16–58: 194
IV.32–36: 194
IV.36–45: 194
IV.59–63: 194
IV.59–82: 194
IV.99–101: 194
VII.89: 103n154
Hesiod
Erg.
8.28: 66n43

Hesychius of Miletus
FHG IV.174: 59n18
Homer
Iliad
VIII.247: 66
IX.443: 151n40
Odyssey
II.181: 66
Iamblichus
Pyth.
97–98: 144n8
Isocrates
Busiris
5.10: 98n137
Nic.
15: 74n65
Panegyricus
23ff.: 296
Justin
II.6.1ff.: 296
XVI.2.45: 109
XXXVI.1.12: 29n67
XXXVI.2.1–14: 213
XXXVI.2.1–3.8: 213
XXXVI.2.14–15: 214
XXXVI.3.1: 109
XXXVI.3.1–7: 214
XXXVIII.8: 299
XXXIX.1.2: 291
XL.2.4: 215
Juvenal
XV.1–13: 98n137
Livy
Periochae
LIX: 299
Lucian
De Syria Dea
36–37: 69n52
De Or. Dial.
16.1(244): 65n39
Macrobius
Saturnalia
I.23.13: 69n52

Megasthenes
  FGH II.397–439: 199n61
  FGH III.C.715: 199n61
Mela
  III.65: 96n131
Melampus
  Peri Palmōn Mantikē: 67n48
Onasander
  X.24: 65n41
  X.26: 65n42
Pausanias
  I.8.6: 78n73
  IX.16.1: 67n48
Pindar, scholia to
  FGrH IIIA, 264 F 9: 198
Plato
  Critias
    112: 274n9
    113–15: 274n9
    116c: 146n20
  Euthyphro
    11e: 150
  Leges 36
    704b–c: 33n77
    704–5: 273n7
    737d–e: 146n20
    740d: 146n20
    741b: 35n86
    741d: 39n62
    745a: 146n20, 274n9
    745b–d: 34
    759a–b: 34
    778c–d: 146n20, 274n9
    848c–d: 146n20, 274n9,
      275n11
    928c–930: 36n92
    947a–b: 34
  Menexenus
    245d: 296
  Phaedo
    84b: 61n30
  Respublica 36
    375–90: 33n79

Pliny
  Naturalis Historia
    pref. 24–25: 187
    II.21: 98n137
    IV.94: 198
    V.62–63: 110n181
    V.69: 104n161
    V.70: 109, 284n43
    VIII.14.1: 204
    X.33: 63n33
    XIII.72: 187
Plutarch
  Aemilius Paulus
    19.4: 65n41
  Alex.
    69: 96n131
  Cicero
    17.5: 65n39
  De Iside et Osiride
    353A–B: 144n8
    354D: 40, 98
    379E ff.: 98n137
    380F: 98n137
  De Pythiae Oraculis
    407c: 65n39
  Dion
    24: 62n33
  Lycurgus
    9.5: 65n39
  Quaestiones Conviviales
    IV.4.3.1: 198
  Sollert. Anim.
    975A–B: 62n33
  Them.
    12: 65n42, 68n49
Polyaenus
  IV.20: 65n41
Polybius
  II.61: 238n18
  III.60.11: 238n18
  III.95.7: 238n18
  IV.22.5: 238n18
  V.11.6: 74n65
  V.24.9: 65n41

Polybius *(continued)*
V.71.11: 114n189, 116
VI.56.6–12: 65n41
IX.19.1: 65n41
XVI.22a: 276n14
XVI.39: 114n189, 116
XXIII.10.17: 65n41
XXXIII.17.2: 65n41
XXXIV.14.1: 300
XXXIV.14.6–8: 299, 300
XXXVI.17.5–11: 38

Pompeius Trogus
Historiae Philippicae: 213
Prologi
I: 214
XXXVI: 215
XXXVIII: 299
XXXIX: 215

Porphyry
De Abstinentia
II.26: 40n99, 54n2, 98n137
III.5.3: 63n33
III.16: 98n137
IV.9: 59n21, 70n53
IV.9–10: 98n137

Pseudo-Scylax
GGM I.79: 103n154

Ptolemaios (Claudius)
Geogr. V.14.3: 104n161

Seneca
NQ
II.32.3–4: 62n33, 63n34
II.32.3ff.: 62n33
II.32.5: 66n5

Sextus Empiricus
Pyrrhoniae Hypoptyposeis
I.17: 59n18
III.219: 98n137

Sophocles
OT 52: 66n43
Ant. 953: 67n48

Strabo
VII.3.6: 198

XV.1.6–7: 202
XV.1.15: 204
XV.1.36: 200
XV.1.37: 204
XV.1.42–45: 204
XV.1.44: 204n71
XV.1.44–45: 204
XV.1.49: 204n70
XV.1.50–52: 204n70
XV.1.53–55: 203
XV.1.55: 204n70
XV.1.56: 204
XV.1.58: 204
XV.1.58–60: 204
XV.1.58.1: 204
XV.1.59.1: 204
XV.1.68: 96n131
XVI.2.21: 103nn154,156, 104n158
XVI.2.27: 104n158
XVI.2.28: 104n158, 104n161, 127
XVI.2.33: 104n158
XVI.2.34: 137, 212, 281n31
XVI.2.34–39: 212
XVI.2.35: 287n57
XVI.2.35–36: 212, 281n31, 295
XVI.2.35–37: 100n147
XVI.2.36: 98n137, 109, 212, 213
XVI.2.36–39: 54
XVI.2.37: 213
XVI.2.39: 213
XVI.2.40: 109, 213
XVI.2.41: 109
XVI.2.41–45: 212
XVI.43: 212n88
XVII.1.8: 110n181

Tacitus
Agricola
10: 218n98
11: 215
11b–12: 218n98
13ff.: 217

Germania: 217
  1: 218n98
  5: 218n98
  5.1ff.: 215
Historiae: 5
  V.2: 215
  V.2–10: 215
  V.3: 215
  V.3.1: 29n67, 216
  V.4: 215
  V.4–5: 215
  V.5: 165, 215, 216,
    216n95
  V.5.1: 216
  V.6: 109
  V.6–8: 216
  V.6.1: 110
  V.8: 216
  V.8–10, 216
  V.8.2: 217
  V.8.2–3: 217
  V.8.3: 217
  V.9–10: 217
  V.11–12: 216
  V.13.3: 113n186

Valerius Maximus
  IX.2.5: 299

Xenophanes
  Diels-Kranz (1935)
    21 (11) B 23: 35n85
Xenophon
  Ages.
    III.5: 151n38
    IV.1: 151n38
    V.5: 151n38
    VI.4: 151n38
    VIII.1,4: 151n38
    XI: 151n38
  Anab.
    I.9: 151n38
    II.26.4–27: 65n42, 67n48,
      68n49
    VI.1.23: 65n42
    VI.5.2: 65n42
  Cyr.
    I.3.10–11: 151n38
    I.3.16–18: 151n38
    I.4.18–24: 151n38
    I.5.6–7: 151n38
    I.6.1: 62n33
    I.6.1–6: 151n38
  Hipp.
    IX.8–9: 62n33
  Memorabilia
    I.1.3–4: 62

JEWISH HELLENISTIC AUTHORS

Josephus
  Antiquitates Judaicae
    I.158–59: 188
    I.256: 151n38
    III.49: 151n40
    III.159: 163n95
    III.199: 163n95
    III.279: 144n9
    IV.198: 149
    IV.200: 150n35
    IV.207: 100
    IV.224: 235n9
    IV.327–31: 151n38

    V.118: 151n40
    VII.390–91: 151n38
    X.227: 201
    XI: 84
    XI.297: 82, 92, 93
    XI.297–302: 264
    XI.298: 34n80
    XI.298–99: 93
    XI.301: 92, 93
    XI.302–3: 82
    XI.302–4: 264
    XI.302–46: 116
    XI.302–47: 83n87

Josephus *(continued)*

XI.304: 264n36
XI.304–5: 264n36
XI.313–46: 135
XI.318: 220n99
XI.338: 120
XI.347: 82
XII: 84
XII.3: 73, 78n73
XII.3–9: 226
XII.4: 75, 76
XII.6: 75n67, 76n69
XII.7: 75, 115n192
XII.8: 115n192, 220n99
XII.9: 84, 115n192, 226
XII.10: 136
XII.12–118: 115n192
XII.130: 275n13
XII.131: 276n13, 276n14
XII.133: 116, 276n13, 276n14
XII.135: 276n14
XII.135–36: 276n13
XII.147: 220n99
XII.150: 220n99
XII.154: 116
XII.157: 34n80
XII.237–38: 34n80
XIII.65: 243
XIII.66: 166
XIII.74: 136
XIII.76: 138n56
XIII.213–19: 294
XIII.215–17: 278n20
XIII.230–300: 277
XIII.236: 291
XIII.240: 295
XIII.246: 291
XIII.247: 134n42
XIII.254–57: 294
XIII.254–58: 131, 131n29, 278n19
XIII.255: 138
XIII.255–56: 116
XIII.257: 280n29

XIII.257–58: 131
XIII.259–66: 292
XIII.261: 291
XIII.264: 116
XIII.269: 291
XIII.273: 278, 291, 292
XIII.273–74: 236, 278
XIII.275–77: 136n49
XIII.275–79: 294
XIII.275–83: 116, 278n19
XIII.277–79: 242
XIII.277b: 136n49
XIII.278: 131n27, 136, 242
XIII.278–80: 136n49
XIII.281: 132
XIII.284–87: 241
XIII.285–87: 241, 286n53
XIII.286: 242
XIII.307: 277
XIII.318–19: 132
XIII.322–23: 132n32
XIII.324: 125n9, 132
XIII.324–25: 104n161
XIII.326: 127
XIII.331–47: 242
XIII.334: 285
XIII.335: 127, 132
XIII.337–38: 132n32
XIII.344: 132n32
XIII.348ff.: 136
XIII.348–49: 242
XIII.349–51: 286n53
XIII.350: 103n156
XIII.351: 243
XIII.351–55: 242–43
XIII.352: 293
XIII.353–54: 136, 286n53
XIII.355: 243
XIII.356: 138, 138n54
XIII.356–57: 293
XIII.357–64: 127, 132
XIII.358: 293
XIII.358–64: 293, 295
XIII.359: 293
XIII.364: 133, 293, 294

XIII.365: 138n56, 293
XIII.374: 138, 138n54
XIII.376–79: 138n56
XIII.382: 138
XIII.391: 139n58
XIII.393–94: 139
XIII.395: 125, 132
XIII.395–96: 103n156
XIII.395–97: 133, 138n55, 295
XIII.397: 133
XIV.9: 280n30
XIV.10: 280n30
XIV.34–35: 165n100
XIV.74–76: 133
XIV.76: 132, 133
XIV.87–88: 133
XIV.88: 131
XIV.91: 284n43
XIV.202: 120
XIV.206: 120
XIV.249: 278n19, 291, 292
XV.394–95: 165
XV.403: 277
XV.409: 277
XVIII.91: 277
XIX.294: 165
XX: 83
XX.227ff.: 83
XX.234: 83
XX.261: 83, 88
Bellum Judaicum
    I.50: 125n8
    I.61: 127
    I.64–66: 136n49
    I.66: 104n161
    I.76: 132
    I.86–87: 138
    I.87: 127, 132, 293
    I.89: 138, 138n54
    I.104–5: 139
    I.123–24: 280n30
    I.159: 112n182
    I.166: 294
    II.37: 114n189

II.48: 114n189
II.487: 147n30, 227
III.35–40: 103n152
III.35–58: 109
III.35: 104n161
III.41–43: 109
III.44–47: 109
III.48–50: 109
III.51–58: 109
III.55: 281n32
III.55–56: 284n43
IV.231: 281n32
IV.310: 281n32
IV.456–75: 109
V.210–12: 165
V.215: 162n92
V.215–21: 167
V.216: 166
V.225: 161, 161n92
V.229: 144n9
V.238–47: 277
V.567: 112n186
VI.420: 112–13n186
VII.428: 166
Contra Apionem: 44, 89n108, 183, 184, 288
    I.2: 140
    I.2–5: 1
    I.22: 115n194, 220
    I.31–36: 83
    I.42: 142
    I.43: 134
    I.57–59: 186
    I.73: 158n73
    I.138: 237n18
    I.144: 201
    I.161ff.: 182
    I.175: 115n194, 220
    I.179: 40n99, 54n2, 96
    I.183: 1, 7n1, 115, 182, 186, 188, 225
    I.183–204: 1, 115n194
    I.183–205: 46–52, 53
    I.184: 55, 185n11
    I.184–85: 185n11

Josephus, *Contra Apionem*
  (*continued*)
  I.185: 1, 115n194, 220,
    229n121
  I.186: 2, 55, 81, 152, 157,
    186, 221n102, 225, 227,
    229n121, 237
  I.186–87: 221
  I.186–89: 1, 71, 221
  I.187: 2, 79, 107, 150, 157,
    160, 221n102, 225,
    227, 265
  I.187–89: 71, 82, 88
  I.188: 54, 55, 149, 159, 160,
    220, 221, 221n102,
    230
  I.189: 2, 7n1, 153,
    185nn11,13, 221n102,
    221–23
  I.190: 91, 100
  I.190–93: 2
  I.190–94: 220
  I.191: 2, 91, 229, 247
  I.192: 92n115, 168n110, 229
  I.193: 2, 97, 99, 128, 167,
    246
  I.194: 55, 101, 113, 115n195,
    124, 128, 137, 143, 144,
    228, 229, 244
  I.194–95: 107
  I.194–97: 2
  I.194–99: 105
  I.195: 2, 108, 142n76, 145
  I.195–99: 57
  I.195–200: 220
  I.196: 153, 154n58, 167n109
  I.196–97: 2, 107
  I.197: 105, 110, 112, 123,
    142n76, 146, 153
  I.197–99: 155
  I.197–204: 44–45
  I.198: 113, 142n76, 145, 146,
    154, 161, 162, 163, 167
  I.198–99: 2, 107, 247
  I.199: 2, 90, 144, 154, 159,

    163, 168n110, 247
  I.200: 61, 70, 157
  I.200–204: 2
  I.201: 2, 7n1, 57, 70, 150,
    156, 157, 185n13
  I.201–2: 220
  I.201–4: 2, 57, 155, 187, 246
  I.202–4: 157
  I.202–4a: 45, 157
  I.203: 57
  I.203–4: 157
  I.204: 57–58, 62, 156
  I.205: 1, 71, 100, 157, 182,
    186, 188
  I.205–11: 73, 74
  I.206–8: 76n69
  I.208–9: 76n69
  I.209–10: 75
  I.210: 76, 77n73
  I.213–14: 73, 74
  I.214: 183
  I.229: 29n67
  I.239–40: 29n67
  I.248–50: 29n67
  I.254: 98n137
  I.258: 65n39
  I.269–70: 100
  I.304–9: 29n67
  II.12: 114
  II.35: 147n30, 227, 247
  II.42: 147n30, 247
  II.43: 1, 2, 52, 53, 113–14,
    115n192, 135, 137, 186,
    220, 227, 229, 239, 247
  II.44: 239
  II.44–47: 115n192
  II.46: 115n192
  II.48: 165n101
  II.49: 241
  II.49–56: 285
  II.51–52: 241
  II.52: 239
  II.52–113: 45
  II.56: 239
  II.64: 239

II.68: 239
II.112: 281n34
II.116: 104n161
II.177: 237n18
II.237–46: 100
III.1: 57
III.8: 57
Vita: 103n152
6: 83
31: 104n161

Philo Judaeus
De Decalogo
52: 173n125
76–80: 98n137
De Congressu
133: 173n125
De Vita Contemplativa
3–9: 173n125
8–9: 98n137
De Ebrietate
177: 174n130
De Fuga et Inventione
184ff.: 34
De Mutatione Nominum
61: 64n36
De Providentia
II.22: 147n25
II.24: 147n25
II.58: 174n130
Hypothetica: 175
In Flaccum
45–46: 228n119, 245
46: 227
Legatio ad Gaium
132: 171
134: 172n120
200–202: 169n112

281: 228n119, 245
Leg. Alleg.
I.48–52: 164n97
De Migr. Abrahami:
92–93: 174n122
Quod Omnis Probus Sit
26: 174n130
141: 174n130
Quest. et Solut. in Genesim
II.79: 64n36
De Specialibus Legibus
I.13: 173n125
I.53: 100n146
I.60: 152n43
I.60–63: 152n43
I.62: 69
I.69: 147n25
I.74: 161n84, 164n97
I.98: 144n9
I.274: 161, 162n93
I.275: 150
I.285: 163n96
I.287: 150
II.62: 171, 175
IV.158: 235n9
De Vita Mosis
I.23: 98n137
I.232: 245
II.31: 174n129
II.37–40: 172
II.106: 168n111
II.161–62: 98n137
II.169: 98n137
II.205: 100n146
II.270: 98n137
Quaest. Exod.
II.52: 161n84

EARLY CHRISTIAN AND BYZANTINE AUTHORS

Clement
Stromateis
I.15: 40n99, 54n2, 201n67,
205

I.23: 190n26
I.154.2–3: 190n26
II.130.4: 9
V.14.113: 2

Eusebius
Chronica
  I.257–58: 291
Praeparatio Evangelica
  I.10: 188
  VIII.6.6–7: 174
  VIII.7.12–13: 175
  VIII.14.58: 174n130
  IX.4.2–9: 44–45
  IX.9: 182n1
  IX.17: 190
  IX.18: 190n26
  IX.19.1: 189n24
  IX.22: 190n26
  IX.23: 190
  IX.25: 190
  IX.25.1–4: 190n26, 190n31
  IX.27.4: 100n146
  IX.27.7–8: 241n27
  IX.27.9: 98n137, 100n146
  IX.27.10: 100n146
  IX.27.12: 98n137, 100n146
  IX.35: 109, 110
  IX.35.1: 109n77, 112n182
  IX.36.1: 111n182
  XIII.12.1–2: 271n1
  XIV.14: 59n18
  XIV.18.14: 59n18
  XIV.18.26: 59n18

Hieronymus
Commentarii in Danielem
  XI.14: 81n81
  XI.15: 81–82n81
De Viris Illustribus
  11: 147n27
Origen
Contra Celsum
  I.14: 188
  I.15: 1, 58, 184, 188, 220
  III.18: 98n137
  III.19: 98n137
  IV.88: 62n33
Photius
Bibliotheca
  213: 78n73
  244.379a–380a: 19
  244.380a–381a: 19–21
Suda
  s.v. Ἑκαταῖος: 9
Stephanes Byz.
  s.v. Γάζα: 103n156
  s.v. Ἰόπη: 103n156
Syncellus, Georgias
  (ed. Dindorff)
  I.548: 125
  I.558: 132, 133, 294
  I.558–59: 138, 139
  I.559: 103n152

OLD TESTAMENT

Exodus: 32
  1.7: 27
  1.11: 27
  14.13: 235n10
  20.4: 86n99
  20.5: 86n99
  20.25: 150, 161
  25.38–39: 163
  27.1: 161
  27.20: 163n95
  28.13: 164n99
  28.14: 165n102

  29–30.21: 145n12
  30.1–10: 162
  30.7–8: 163n95
  36.23: 164n99
  See also next entry

Exodus (Septuagint)
  28.13: 164n99
  28.14: 164n99
  28.25: 164n99
  36.16: 164n99
  36.18: 164n99

36.23: 164n99
36.26: 164n99
See also preceding entry

Leviticus
6.9: 163n96
6.12: 163n96
6.13: 163n96
6–10: 145n12
10.8–11: 144
13–16: 145n12
21–22.16: 145n12
24.2–3: 163n95
25.25–34: 27n55
26.46: 27n54
27.1–8: 164
27.16–24: 164
27.28: 164
27.34: 27n54

Numbers
18.21: 159
18.24: 159
21.8–9: 164
26.34: 27n55
36.13: 27n54

Deuteronomy: 222
12.2–3: 128
16.21: 163
17.8–12: 27, 27n58
17.16: 234, 240
27.5–6: 150, 161
28.68: 235
28.69: 27n54
32.44: 27n54

I Samuel
3.3: 163n95
21.9: 164

I Kings
6.22: 162n92
7.14: 167n107
21.3–4: 27n55

II Kings
11.10: 164
18.4: 164

I Chronicles
9.13: 160

II Chronicles
2.13: 167n107
4.1: 161
4.19: 162n92
17.8–9: 27n58
19.5–10: 27n58

Ezra
2.36–38: 160
6.3: 113n187

Nehemiah
5.15: 266
6.15: 266n43
7.35: 284n43
8.1–8: 27
8.6: 27
10.33: 266n43
11.10–14: 160
11.34–36: 124n7
12.3: 112n185
12.12: 112n185
12.18: 112n185
12.20: 112n185
12.22: 82, 84n90
13.7–13: 87n102

Esther
3.8: 93

Isaiah: 236
1.26: 246
2.1: 274
5.1–5: 165n102
10.24: 235
11.16: 236n13
43.2: 95

Isaiah (Septuagint)
11.16: 236n13

Jeremiah
2.21: 165n102
29.4–7: 235
42.15–22: 235

Ezekiel
2.34: 284n43

Ezekiel (continued)
  17.5–8: 165n102
  40.5: 113n187
  40.47: 113n187
  41.13–14: 113n187
  43.13–17: 161
  44.21: 144n9
  45.2: 113n187

Zechariah
  6.9–15: 164
  6.11: 165n100
  6.13: 87n102
  6.14: 165n100

Malachi
  2.7: 27–28

Psalms
  48: 154
  66.10–12: 95
  80.9–12: 165n102

Daniel: 94
  1–6: 93
  3: 93
  6: 95
  6.6–8: 95
  6.15–16: 95
  7–12: 93
  11.14: 276n13

APOCRYPHA, PSEUDEPIGRAPHA, AND DEAD SEA SCROLLS

Judith
  4.4: 114n189

Wisdom of Solomon: 149, 159,
  169, 176, 178
  1–3: 179
  2: 179
  2.12: 179
  6.10: 179
  7.17: 179
  7.17–20: 179
  9.8: 168n111
  11.15: 98n137
  12.3ff.: 180
  13.1–9: 179
  13.14: 98n137
  14: 179
  14.15: 179
  15.18–19: 98n137
  16.5–6: 165n104

Sirach
  50.1: 264n34

I Maccabees: 277n18
  1.21: 162n93
  1.21–22: 164
  1.22: 167n107
  3.10: 114n189

  3.40: 282
  4.14: 282
  4.15: 282
  4.47: 161
  4.49: 162n92, 167n107
  4.57: 164
  4.59–60: 113
  5.5: 295
  5.28: 295
  5.43–44: 129
  5.50–51: 295
  5.68: 129
  9.50: 284n43
  9.50–52: 106, 123
  9.62ff.: 123
  10.3–6: 119n204
  10.7–14: 118n204
  10.12: 123
  10.18–20: 118n204
  10.25–45: 119nn204,205
  10.29: 134n42
  10.30: 114n189, 117–18,
  119n204, 282, 283n39
  10.33: 134n42
  10.36: 278, 283
  10.38: 116, 117, 119n204, 282,
  283

10.50: 104n159
10.51–65: 243
10.84: 129, 295
11.1–6: 244
11.4: 129, 295
11.28: 114n189, 134, 134n42
11.30–37: 119n205, 134n42
11.34: 114n189, 116, 119n204, 282, 283
11.41: 123
11.57: 137
12.38: 123
13.11: 123, 129
13.15: 134n42
13.31–16.22: 125n8
13.33: 123
13.38: 123
13.47–48: 129
13.48: 123
13.50: 129
13.53: 123
14.7: 129
14.16: 123
14.33: 123
14.34: 123
14.36–37: 123
15.7: 123
15.35: 130
15.38: 104n159
15.40: 125n8
16.8–10: 125n8
16.23: 277
22.29–37: 92

II Maccabees: 302
1.1–10a: 301
1.5–6: 301
1.6: 301
1.7: 301
1.7–8: 301
1.9: 301
1.10–2.18: 236n14
1.19–20: 143–44
1.19–22: 163n96
2.17: 236n14

2.18: 236
2.19: 168n111
4.7ff.: 34n80
4.8: 134n42
13.24: 104n159
14.12: 116
15.1: 114n189

III Maccabees: 159, 169, 176, 177, 178, 285
3.18: 153
6.3: 245

Pseudo-Aristeas
12: 74, 286n55
12–14: 240
13: 228, 278, 283
22–23: 74
23: 76
30: 172
31: 39n98, 54, 80, 140
35: 85, 144
36: 228
36–37: 74
40: 286n55
41: 85
50: 161n84
51–72: 166
58–60: 167n107
81: 277
83: 142n76, 274n9
83–84: 274
83–120: 229
84: 142n76
100: 273, 276
100–120: 278
101: 273
102: 273, 274, 276
102–4: 106, 271
103: 273, 274, 276
104: 273, 274, 276
105: 110, 142n76
107: 108, 110, 114n189, 142n76, 279–80
107–8: 273n7, 284n45
108–9: 110

Pseudo-Aristeas *(continued)*
   111:   284n45
   112:   108, 142n76
   113:   142n76
   115:   273n7, 284
   116:   272n6
   121–22:   174n131
   122:   151n38, 274n9, 277
   123:   288
   124ff.:   288
   127ff.:   288
   128–69:   287n57
   130:   287n57
   131:   230n122
   131–44:   230n122
   135–37:   173n125
   138:   98n137
   139:   181, 230n122, 287n57
   142:   287n57
   144:   230n122
   152:   287n57

154–62:   230n122
155:   230n122
158:   230n122
158–60:   174n128
159:   230n122
162:   230n122
170:   230n122
181–82:   288n57
182–84:   174n131
184:   288n57
208:   153
212–27:   151n38
249:   237, 286n54
265:   74n65, 153
271:   153
Temple Scroll
   col. VIII: 162n93
   col. IX, line 11:   163
Third Sibylline Book: 180, 248
   75:   98n137
   79:   98n137

NEW TESTAMENT

Luke
   21.5:   165

RABBINIC LITERATURE

Scroll of Fasting
   15–16 Sivan: 132, 295

Mishna
   Avoth
      1.3:   82
   Ma'aser Sheni
      5.15:   85n95
   Sota
      9.10:   85n95
   Shqalim
      6.1:   85n95
   Yoma
      1.1:   233n3

Hagiga
   3.8:   163
Menaḥot
   11.5:   166
'Arachin
   5.1:   165n103
Tamid
   1.1:   145
   3.9:   163n95
   6.1:   163n95
Middot
   1.2:   145
   1.9:   145
   2.2:   147n24

3.1: 161, 162n88
3.4: 150, 161
3.8: 164, 165, 165n102
4.6: 147n26
5.4: 83n88
Yadayim
4.1: 85n95
Tosefta
Hagiga
2.9: 83n88
'Arachin
3.1: 165n103
Palestinian Talmud
Succa
5.1 (55a): 171n120
5.1 (55b): 234n9
Babylonian Talmud
Sabbat
39a–b: 163n95
Yoma

39b: 163n95
79a: 135n44
Succa
51b: 171n120, 234n9
Megillah
9a: 172n121
Gittin
57a: 127n18
Sanhedrin
93.1: 94n122
Midrash
Sifri, Numbers
116: 83n88
Lament, Rabba
2.2: 127n18
Maimonides
Temidim
II.1: 163n96
Mishne Tora, Judges, Kings
V.7–8: 234n9

INSCRIPTIONS AND PAPYRI

CIJ
II nos. 1441–42: 300
CPJ
I.22: 114n190
I.28: 114n190
I.128: 114n90
II.1441–42: 300
Elephantine papyri: 51nf, 228
Cowley (1923) 30–32: 87n102
From the Memphis Serapeum:
293
OGIS
I.229 lines 100, 104: 120n210
Pithom stele
I.23: 275n13

P. Tebt
I. no. 5, line 93: 120n209

Ptolemaic "satrap stele"
5: 73n61
5–6: 73
6: 73n61

SEG
VIII.33: 132
XII.548: 285

SIG^3
1167: 67
I.no. 344, line 70: 120n209

Zeno papyri: 104n158

COINS

BMC Arabia, Mesopotamia,
    Persia
  189 no. 49:   268n51
  190 no. 54:   268n51
BMC Caria
  pl. XXX No. 10:   298
  pl. XXX no. 11:   298
  pl. XXX no. 12:   299
  pl. XXX nos. 13–15:   299
  pl. XLV no. 5:   298
BMC Cyrenaica
  pl. XXIX nos. 11–18:   299
  pl. XXX no. 11:   299
BMC Palestine
  p. LXX: 293
Hill (1901)
  pl. XVII no. 703:   298
Hill (1923)
  pl. IX no. 3:   298
Kadman Museum
  no. K-26989:   258n16
  no. K-30791:   268n51
  no. K-40486:   312
Kindler (1974)
  pl. II no. a: 258n14, 260n18
Meshorer (1982)
  pl. 2 no. 10:   310
  pl. 2 no. 10a: 310
  pl. 2 no. 10b: 310
  pl. 3 no. 12:   312
  pl. 3 no. 14:   314
  pl. 3 no. 14a: 314
  pl. 3 no. 15:   316
  pl. 3 no. 15a: 316

pl. 3 no. 16:   314
pl. 3 no. 16b: 314
pl. 3 no. 17:   269n57
p. 184 no. 1:   314
p. 184 no. 2:   314

Meshorer and Qedar (1991)
  nos. 71–153:   259n17

Mildenberg (1979)
  pl. 22 no. 20:   312
  pl. 22 no. 23:   258n14
  pl. 22 no. 24:   258n16, 314
  pl. 22 no. 25:   314
  pl. 22 no. 26:   316
  pl. 24 no. 22:   314

Newell (1916)
  13 no. 28:   268n51
  41 no. 8:   268n51

Paton and Hicks (1891)
  306 (no. 15b):   298

Plant (1979)
  nos. 1299–1308:   260n18

Sternberg (1979)
  pl. 21 no. 194:   312
  pl. 22 no. 196:   312

Svoronos (1904)
  II.8 no. 35:   268n51
  II.91 no. 609:   268n52
  III pl. II no. 15:   268n51
  III pl. III nos. 40–45:   299
  III pl. XIV no. 26:   268n52
  III pl. XVIII nos. 23–25:   298
  III pl. XVIII no. 24:   299
  III pl. XVIII no. 25:   299

Compositor:	Theodora S. MacKay
Text:	10.5/13.5 Aldus
Display:	Aldus
Greek Font:	Ibycus by Silvio Levy
Printer:	Thomson-Shore, Inc.
Binder:	Thomson-Shore, Inc.